Women, Power, and Property

Quotas for women in government have swept the globe. Yet we know little about their capacity to upend entrenched social, political, and economic hierarchies. *Women, Power, and Property* explores this question within the context of India, the world's largest democracy. Brulé employs a research design that maximizes causal inference alongside extensive field research to explain the relationship between political representation, backlash, and economic empowerment. Her findings show that women in government – gatekeepers – catalyze access to fundamental economic rights to property. Women in politics have the power to support constituent rights at critical junctures, such as marriage negotiations, when they can strike integrative solutions to intrahousehold bargaining. Yet there is a paradox: quotas are essential for enforcement of rights, but they generate backlash against women who gain rights without bargaining leverage. In this groundbreaking study, Brulé shows how well-designed quotas can operate as a crucial tool to foster equality and benefit the women they are meant to empower.

RACHEL E. BRULÉ is Assistant Professor of Global Development Policy at Boston University. She specializes in comparative politics, the political economy of development, gender, South Asia, representation, inequality, and migration.

Cambridge Studies in Gender and Politics

Cambridge Studies in Gender and Politics addresses theoretical, empirical, and normative issues at the intersection of politics and gender. Books in this series adopt incisive and comprehensive approaches to key research themes concerning the construction and impact of sex and gender, as well as their political and social consequences.

General Editors

Karen Beckwith, *Case Western Reserve University* (Lead)
Lisa Baldez, *Dartmouth College*
Christina Wolbrecht, *University of Notre Dame*

Editorial Advisory Board

Nancy Burns, *University of Michigan*
Matthew Evangelista, *Cornell University*
Nancy Hirschmann, *University of Pennsylvania*
Sarah Song, *University of California, Berkeley*
Ann Towns, *University of Gothenburg*
Aili Mari Tripp, *University of Wisconsin–Madison*
Georgina Waylen, *University of Manchester*

Books in the Series

J. Kevin Corder and Christina Wolbrecht, *Counting Women's Ballots*
Mala Htun, *Inclusion without Representation in Latin America*
Mala Htun and S. Laurel Weldon, *The Logics of Gender Justice*
Aili Mari Tripp, *Women and Power in Postconflict Africa*
Kristin N. Wylie, *Party Institutionalization and Women's Representation in Democratic Brazil*

Women, Power, and Property

The Paradox of Gender Equality Laws in India

RACHEL E. BRULÉ
Boston University

CAMBRIDGE
UNIVERSITY PRESS

CAMBRIDGE
UNIVERSITY PRESS

University Printing House, Cambridge CB2 8BS, United Kingdom

One Liberty Plaza, 20th Floor, New York, NY 10006, USA

477 Williamstown Road, Port Melbourne, VIC 3207, Australia

314–321, 3rd Floor, Plot 3, Splendor Forum, Jasola District Centre, New Delhi – 110025, India

79 Anson Road, #06–04/06, Singapore 079906

Cambridge University Press is part of the University of Cambridge.

It furthers the University's mission by disseminating knowledge in the pursuit of education, learning, and research at the highest international levels of excellence.

www.cambridge.org
Information on this title: www.cambridge.org/9781108835824
DOI: 10.1017/9781108869287

First published 2020

A catalogue record for this publication is available from the British Library.

Library of Congress Cataloging-in-Publication Data
Names: Brulé, Rachel E, 1980– author.
Title: Women, power, and property : the paradox of gender equality laws in India / Rachel E Brulé, Boston University.
Description: New York, NY : Cambridge University Press, 2020. | Series: Cambridge studies in gender and politics | Includes bibliographical references and index.
Identifiers: LCCN 2019056217 (print) | LCCN 2019056218 (ebook) | ISBN 9781108835824 (hardback) | ISBN 9781108798846 (paperback) | ISBN 9781108869287 (epub)
Subjects: LCSH: Women's rights–India. | Women–India–Social conditions. | Women–India–Economic conditions. | Representative government and representation–India. | Democracy–India. | Equality–India.
Classification: LCC HQ1236.5.I4 B78 2020 (print) | LCC HQ1236.5.I4 (ebook) | DDC 305.40954–dc23
LC record available at https://lccn.loc.gov/2019056217
LC ebook record available at https://lccn.loc.gov/2019056218

ISBN 978-1-108-83582-4 Hardback

To Michael Harsch and the late John Brulé for boundless support, and Delphine for waiting.

Contents

Figures

Tables

Acknowledgments

This book could not have been written without the enormous encouragement, not to mention wisdom and deep support of extraordinary beings. The list is long because the journey from this project's first consideration to penultimate publication spans a decade. Indeed, the name *"bh'ains"* (water buffalo) Machilipatnam's court records room staff gave me – given my willingness to remove surprisingly large objects (a steel typewriter from the colonial era) and stand poring over disputes for incomparably long hours to learn about land – encapsulates my lumbering, happy path.

I am grateful to the scholars who mentored me from the earliest stages of this project, first and foremost my dissertation chair at Stanford, Beatriz Magaloni. Saumitra Jha also provided immense insights and support. Jonathan Bendor steadfastly pushed my theory development forward, helping me hone my focus on problems of great complexity. Jim Fearon provided patient guidance throughout the design, data collection, and its early interpretation. Alberto Diaz-Cayeros, Avner Greif, Steve Haber, Josh Ober, Barry Weingast, and the late Douglass North kindly offered great inspiration and critical questions throughout.

I was lucky enough to make New York University my first professional home after Stanford University. There, David Stasavage generously convened the book workshop that catalyzed this book's structure, when he, Anjali Bohlken, Thad Dunning, Frances Rosenbluth, Cyrus Samii, and Shanker Satyanath provided a first of many rounds of invaluable, reflective advice. In addition, Neal Beck, Dana Burde, Kanchan Chandra, and Josh Tucker have been enormously supportive of this work and erudite guides throughout the publication process, as have Amy Catalinac, Una Chaudhuri, Becky Morton, Peter Rosendorff, Melissa Schwartzberg, Alastair Smith, Arthur Spirling, and Kate Stimpson at many points throughout this project's development. The manuscript evolved from its first, early state thanks to the book workshop's participants and attentive care by Jim Alt, Swethaa Ballakrishnen, Rikhil Bhavnani, Thomas Blom-Hansen, Maria Carreri, Pat Egan, Nick Haas, Kimuli Kasara, Dorothy Kronick, Gabi Kruks-Wisner, Bethany Lacina, Akshay Mangla, Pamela Mensch, Cristian Pop-Eleches, Bhumi Purohit, Arturas Rozenas, and Surili Sheth who provided multiple, close reads of this manuscript. I have been honored to collaborate with thinkers I admire deeply, each of whom have helped this project advance: Sonia Bhalotra, Simon Chauchard, Sarah Khan, Nikhar Gaikwad, Jenn Larson, Norbert Monti, Solédad Prillaman, Sanchari Roy, and Aliz Tóth.

At NYU Abu Dhabi, this manuscript grew immensely thanks to the encouragement of Fatma Abdulla, the late Hilary Ballon, Al Bloom, Carol Brandt, Hervé Crès, Fabio Piano, Ron Robin, and Bryan Waterman. I continue to value insights from May Al-Dabbagh, Bob Allen, David Blakeslee, Aurelie Dariel, Morgan Hardy, Nikos Nikiforakis, Christopher Paik, Leonid Peisakhin, Melina Platas, Rahul Sagar, and Peter van der Windt. To the extent my attempts to reside in multiple worlds at once were successful, this is in no small measure thanks to Hans-Joachim Giessmann, who gave me a sunlit perch at the Berghof Foundation in Berlin to write up my fieldwork and the opportunity to translate scholarship on women's empowerment into practice and Macartan Humphreys, who warmly welcomed me into his Research Unit on Institutions and Political Inequality at the Wissenschaftszentrum Berlin fur Sozialforschung (WZB) where he and his extraordinary research community, including Alex Scacco, Bernd Beber, and Clara Bicalho Maia Correia, shared not only their intellectual home but also illuminating advice as I revised this manuscript.

I would be remiss to ignore the wealth of advice I received at invited lectures, in particular those at Columbia University, with invaluable feedback from Sheri Berman, Allison Carnegie, Jon Elster, Timothy Frye, John Huber, Isabela Mares, John Marshall, and Carlo Prato; the Heidelberg Research Group on Development Economics Conference, especially from Jean-Phillipe Platteau and Philip Keefer; Georgetown University, from Matthew Carnes, Desha Girod, Diana Kapiszewski, and Charles King; the London School of Economics, Department of International Development, from Teddy Brett, Jean-Paul Faguet, Ken Shadlen, and Mahvish Shami; the Massachusetts Institute of Technology, from Vipin Narang, Rich Nielsen, Danny Hidalgo, and Chappell Lawson; the School of Oriental and African Studies, from Matthew Nelson and Rochana Bajpai; the University of California at Berkeley, from Leo Arriola, Jennifer Bussell, Pradeep Chibber, and Cecilia Mo; the Center for the Advanced Study of India at the University of Pennsylvania, from Devesh Kapur, Bilal Baloch, Rithika Kumar, and Dawn Teele; the Modern South Asia Workshop at Yale University, from Jennifer Bussell and Tanika Sarkar; and everyone at the Conference for the Empirical Study of Gender hosted by Amanda Clayton at Vanderbilt University with Tiffany Barnes and Diana Z. O'Brien; the LIA-SPINPER-UC Berkeley Conference on Political Representation, hosted by Gilles Verniers at Ashoka University, with Christophe Jaffrelot, Jennifer Bussell, and

Thad Dunning; and the School of Advanced International Studies – Carnegie Endowment for Peace's South Asia Political Economy Workshop organized by Devesh Kapur and Milan Vaishnav. I am immensely thankful for the confidence and guidance of editors at Cambridge University Press, Robert Dreesen and Sara Doskow; the immense commitment to collaborative improvement by my independent editor, Jody Hauber; and constructive critique by anonymous reviewers for Cambridge University Press and the *Journal of Politics*.

The final stages of this project have been particularly joyful because they are completed in the presence of my new community at Boston University's Pardee School of Global Studies and Global Development Policy Center.

The project grew out of an intensive year of research assistance helping implement, and later design, field experiments for economists Esther Duflo, Abhijit Banerjee, and Sendhil Mullainathan at MIT's JPAL. I learned from them as well as the network of journalists, activists, and fierce Indian women and men with whom I was privileged to engage. Each person – often with insight, determination and wit – frequently redrew the boundaries of public and private agency in what were mainly conservative, muscularly patriarchal communities. This gave me a road map into an intimate domain: the reciprocal familial relationships where people navigate social and economic obligations and recognize – or bury – political voices and priorities.

The first, halting work to realize this research agenda occurred within my doctoral work. I heartily thank Bina Agarwal, Lisa Blaydes, Peter Burgess, Klaus Deininger, Jean Drèze, Jennifer Green, Justin Grimmer, Paul Gowder, Danielle Harlan, Ruth Kricheli, David Laitin, Sangeeta Mediratta, Nitya Rao, Francesca Refsum Jensenius, Rob Reich, Amanda Robinson, Sharika Thiranagama, Ashutosh Varshney, and Jeremy Weinstein for great direction and encouragement throughout my early, winding research path. With their guidance, and particularly strong encouragement from Saumitra Jha, I found my way to the World Bank, where Biju Rao, and later Klaus Deininger and Aparajita Goyal opened many doors by kindly sharing their ongoing research and collaboratively brainstorming about how to advance studies of property rights reforms' impact. Thanks to these initial conversations, I learned about the incredible work begun by the Hyderabad-based Society for the Elimination of Rural Poverty (SERP). In particular, Jamuna Paruchuri, who was their Director of Advocacy when I arrived, and her "right-hand woman," Aruna, were powerhouses. Their abundant support for this project was a reflection of their deep commitments to not just women's empowerment but also to collaboratively rebuilding a more egalitarian, mutually supportive society. Jamuna modeled this vision throughout. Whenever we met, Jamuna's first question would be: "Where do you need to go next?" Jamuna initially built and managed all-female groups *(Mahiya Samakhya)* for SERP as vehicles for state-funded, locally distributed microfinance institutions. However, she quickly ensured they also operated as broader fulcrums of support for women to navigate economic, social, and political challenges through collective organization, and

XX					*Acknowledgments*

she warmly welcomed me to join them and engage on the strategies they employed throughout successes and failures.

This project's wide scope is thanks to the generous institutional support of Jamuna, Aruna, and SERP; the National Council of Applied Economic Research, in particular Hari Nagarajan, who encouraged me to apply for a pre-doctoral fellowship and supported my research once my application was accepted; and Andy Foster, for giving me permission to extend his and Mark Rosenzweig's groundbreaking research using the panel survey they built over many decades: the Rural Economic and Demographic Survey. Anupam Chatterjee, Vaibhav Chamoli, Niharika Chaube, D Gopi, Santosh Srivastava, and Chenchula Sudanagunta helped create the backbone of my early research design strategy, with illuminating conversations, support fielding of surveys, and insightful translation of the results. Ankita Banerjea, Clarissa Lehne, Norbert Monti, Mastish Taddese Terefe, and Aliz Tóth provided major research support instrumental to this manuscript. This project would not have been possible without inspired support by Jai Pal Singh and Kailash Chandra Pradhan to navigate NCAER's bureaucracy and data. Thanks to Chandelle Arambula and Eliana Vasquez at Stanford; Diana Barnes and Stephanie Nica at NYU NY; and Dora Morgan-Coakle, Katherine Stevens, Audrey Longo, Deirdre Tabak, Flora Alipio, Janet Kelly, Julie McGuire, and Diana Pangan at NYU AD, bureaucratic institutions became spaces of human connection and empowerment.

My research was supported financially by a Doctoral Dissertation Fellowship from the National Council of Applied Economic Research (India) and the International Development Research Center (Canada), the Truman Scholarship, and Graduate Summer Research Grants through Stanford's Center for the Study of South Asia. In addition, some of the arguments and data were previously published at the *Journal of Politics*: Rachel E. Brulé. 2020. "Reform, Representation, and Resistance: The Politics of Property Rights Enforcement." 82(4). https://doi.org/10.1086/708645.

Throughout this project, the empathy and infinitely positive energy of my dear friends and family have been the steady current which sustains me. Words are a poor substitute for gratitude but hopefully the spirit is clear. Each of my work's strengths is thanks to theirs. In Abu Dhabi, I would like to thank my friends May Al-Dabbagh, Mona Hammami, Villy Kotini, Parissa Khadem and Dan Lincoln, Beth Dickinson and Mario Chacon, Melina Platas and Angelo Izama, Mohan and Fiona Kidd, Amélie Mouton and Pedro Monaville, Maria Grigoryeva and Blaine Robbins, Zeynep Ozgen and Eric Hamilton, Saba Brelvi and John O'Brien, Christina Zenker and Jeff Jensen, and Matty Silverstein and Bertie Wertman. In New York City, I would like to thank the following people: David Baharvar Ramsey; Julia, Cody, and Jane Jarcho; and Justin Ryan. At Stanford, I would like to thank the following people: Patricia Carbajales, Danielle Harlan, Paul Gowder, Vivek Srinivasan, and Rajesh Veeraraghavan. My surrogate family in India: Gudu and Gordip Sodhi in Yamunanagar, Haryana; Dipti Jain (Goel) and her parents, Tanya and Vikas Miglani, Sneha Prakash, Richa and Daniel Naujoks, and Katrin and Stefan Bannach in Delhi; Jennifer Green in Lucknow; Mussa Azami in Varanasi; Renu in Udaipur; Jamuna in Hyderabad; and Aruna and her family in Vijayawada. In California, I would like to thank the following people: Len, Vivian, and Debbie Lehmann; Virginia and Brad Ferguson; Liz, Erik, and Sebastian Vance; and Amanda Bensel. I would also like to thank my Truman partners in travel and reflection: Tomas Carbonell, Samidh Chakrabarti, Jini Kim, Dan Pastor, Rena Patel, Megan Wells Jamieson, and Heidi Williams. Thanks also to my dear study mates from Oxford: Megan Bradley, Kate Desormeau, Minh-Chau Le, Anna Sheftel, Meredith Williams, Shani Winterstein, and their families and my soul mates from Mount Holyoke College and childhood: Marielle Amrhein, Christiana Axelsen, Indika Senanayake, and Emily, Mark, and Becky Meckler. Most importantly, my family: Mary, the late Arnold, Steve, Mary Ellen, Carolyn and Matt Woiler; Jane Marks; Alice Frank; Jan and Steve Meuse, Herta and Wolfgang Harsch; Susanne, Jorg, Julian, and Adrian Weisheit; Rina, Jeff, and Millie Johnson; Jim, Jill, Dolores, the late John and Sally, Mark, Francine, Alyssa, and Corey Brulé; Lili Estorion who lovingly enables me to be a mother, scholar, and writer; and of course my joyful partner in all things academic and otherwise, Micha, and our daughter, Delphine, for her patience, confidence, and whole-hearted, wise curiosity throughout.

I

Introduction

> When the *devas* [male gods] are unable to cope with the corruption, they have to send Durga [goddess of creation and destruction]. [We humans will have to do the same in politics.] *Stri hi shakti ahe* [Women are the embodiment of power].
> —Indirabai, deputy *Sarpaunch*, Vitner, Maharashtra[1]

> It is important to remember that there are more elected women in India than in the rest of the world put together.
> —Mani Shankar Aiyar, 2014[2]

We are living a time of great reckoning. Optimism about our collective ability to challenge enduring forms of inequality – particularly around gender – abounds. As of 2015, women possess equal political rights to those of men in every country except for the Vatican.[3] In 2020, female heads of state across the world, from Germany and Iceland to New Zealand and Taiwan, distinguished themselves by their effective responses to the coronavirus pandemic.[4] And yet, the awkward fact persists that women's rather modest demands for an equal place behind the podium, in the board room, or at the regular community meeting around the village bodhi tree still lead to booming cries of alarm. In Mary Beard's words, women, "even when they are not silenced, still have to pay a very high price for being heard."[5]

How close are we to achieving gender equality? As of November 2018, women comprise half or more of the popularly elected parliament in only 3 of the world's 195 countries, and less than a quarter of all elected representatives to national parliaments.[6] At best, the "rising tide" of gender equality that Inglehart and Norris (2003) optimistically associate with economic and

---

[1] Sathaye (1998, 105–6).
[2] Personal interview with Mani Shankar Aiyar, First Union Minister of Panchayat Raj, on January 27, 2014, in his Delhi Office.
[3] George (2019).   [4] Leta Hong Fincher (2020).   [5] Beard (2017, 8).   [6] UN Women (2019).

political development appears to be "uneven and stalled," as England (2010) documents.

In the 2016 US presidential elections, Strolovitch, Wong, and Proctor (2017) argue that concerns about losing traditional entitlements propelled a majority of white women and men to cast their votes against the first strong female contender, Hillary Clinton, in favor of a white, male candidate who boasted of sexual assault. This electoral outcome evinces a broad hostility that is growing as women become increasingly vocal about the problem of intimidation – from workplace harassment to violent sexual assault – they confront on the path to achieving greater equality. Steven Bannon, US President Trump's former chief strategist, exemplified this viewpoint when he characterized #MeToo and related global activism as an "anti-patriarchy movement [that] is going to undo 10,000 years of recorded history."[7] This echoes responses to an earlier time, 1992, the "Year of the Woman" when the number of women elected to the US House of Representatives jumped from 28 to 42. Shortly thereafter, Susan Faludi documented how American "women's political awakening provoked instant political reprisal."[8]

Women's global struggle for gender equality is indicative of an even broader problem: dominance – where interlinked social, economic, and political systems of power constrain low-status groups. This concerns not only women. Racial minorities (most clearly, those whose ancestors endured slavery, such as African Americans and Afro-Brazilians), those with disadvantages formalized through hierarchies of religion and class (such as members of Scheduled Castes [SCs] in India), and individuals whose participation in larger systems of labor migration pushes them into positions of near-permanent marginality (including migrants from Central and South America to the United States, South and South East Asia to the Gulf countries, and from rural to urban centers within China and India) also confront this challenge. Thus, the larger contribution of this book is to advance the debate on how low-status groups can successfully challenge what appear to be highly stable systems of dominance in the attempt to bring about more egalitarian orders.

I argue that one favored innovation bears great promise: quotas that open political representation – and the agency associated with such power – to low-status groups, including women. Indeed, quotas for women in government are sweeping the world as a revolutionary tool to leapfrog over constraints to female political inclusion. Such reforms are often considered a silver bullet because they offer a "fast track" to greater gender equality that may otherwise take generations to achieve.[9]

We have learned that quotas affect change in one clear arena: female representation increases the investment citizens are willing to make in their society. Worldwide, the introduction of quotas for women in parliaments and political parties over the past two decades has doubled the average share of

---

7 Higgins (2018).   8 Faludi (2006, xi).   9 Dahlerup and Freidenvall (2005).

female parliamentarians, resulting in a sharp jump in one major investment: public health expenditures.[10] This suggests that descriptive representation does lead to substantive representation: "presence" changes policy (Pitkin, 1967; Phillips, 1995). Across 102 developing countries, comparing those where female representatives occupied a "critical mass" (at least 20 percent of parliament) to countries without such representatives, representation correlates with higher rates of early childhood immunizations (10–12 percentage points), higher infant survival rates (by 0.7 percentage points), and higher child survival rates (by 1 percentage point).[11] These patterns are often invoked as support for a broader policy agenda that frames women's empowerment as a vital economic issue.[12]

Yet we still know very little about another important dimension of female political representation: its ability to fundamentally change the interconnected systems of power premised on gender inequality. This is in part because neither quotas nor broader battles for female political representation have been fought for and won on the grounds that they will trigger social revolution.

What we do know, as Duflo (2012) points out, is that mandating more elected seats for women does have a revolutionary consequence: fewer opportunities for men. But we have not yet taken stock of how quotas alter the calculation of advantage outside politics.[13] Ultimately, when can quotas enable representatives and their constituents to upend hierarchies in favor of the women they are meant to empower?

This book seeks to answer that question. My theory explains the connection between political representation and economic power. Specifically, I explore how quotas expanding women's ability to gain the most influential elected role in local government give rise to a fundamental reordering of power. Once in office, female leaders revolutionize how women occupy the public sphere, create *new* spaces for women's benefit, and repurpose the private sphere. I consider how this matters for women's entitlements to a crucial economic resource: land inheritance.

Women at the helm of government – replacing traditionally male gatekeepers – catalyze the claiming and enforcement of female rights to land inheritance. This results in a paradox, where women's successful empowerment energizes many forms of resistance, particularly in the short-term.[14] Most striking is women's ability to transform conflict over traditional rights into consensus over new distributions of resources when three factors align for an individual: access to female political representation, substantial economic

---

[10] Clayton and Zetterberg (2018).　[11] Swiss, Fallon, and Burgos (2012).

[12] Coleman (2013). Yunus (2007), the World Bank's Gender Action Plan, and the UN Millennium Development Goals also identify gender equality as instrumental to achieve economic development.

[13] Exceptional work includes Krook (2016) and Mansbridge and Shames (2008).

[14] Mansbridge and Shames (2008, 632) theorize one form of resistance – backlash – as "reaction with coercive power to loss of power as capacity."

rights, and social bargaining power. My field research pinpoints and my large-scale data analysis confirms a key window of opportunity for women to secure their rights: marriage negotiations – when multiple valuable resources are distributed. Where female gatekeepers can support young women to claim rights at this critical juncture, they are able to move from conflict to mutually beneficial cooperation, striking integrative solutions to intra household bargaining. This harnessing of political power in the service of inclusion thus holds the potential to produce lasting reform with long-term acceptance.

I focus on the right of women to inherit property because of its radical power around the globe. Land inheritance provides the firmest guarantee of economic stability in much of the world. Where women have land rights, evidence shows they exert greater authority in the household, are less likely to experience domestic violence, have healthier children, and farm agricultural land more effectively, yielding greater output for their entire household.[15] In other words, where women inherit land, this creates opportunities for everyone to benefit.

However, women face particular barriers to procuring and safeguarding property ownership.[16] They enjoy equal access to landownership in just 42 percent of the world's countries.[17] They constitute less than roughly 5 to 20 percent of the world's agricultural landholders.[18] Women face major constraints in negotiating these rights, as "patriarchal tradition and ancient social beliefs threaten women's land rights" in more than half of all countries.[19] In particular, the World Bank cites bureaucratic reluctance to enforce women's land rights as the crux of the problem.[20]

And yet it is precisely in the domain of rights enforcement that I find a source of hope. My empirical focus is a particularly hard case for gender equality: India, the world's largest democracy. Despite constitutionally mandated gender equality since its establishment as a Democratic Republic in 1950, India is rated the worst place to be a woman of all G20 countries, lagging behind even Saudi Arabia.[21] Gender disparity affects life at all levels, from conception to old age.[22] In India, three-quarters of women derive their income from agriculture, but own less than 13 percent of the land.[23] In addition, civil servants charged with enforcing property rights often have a direct interest in denying women's entitlements to land.[24] I chose to study India because it provides the most formidable crucible of a democratic state's ability to achieve gender equality.

---

[15] For example, see Udry (1996); Panda and Agarwal (2005); Allendorf (2007).

[16] See the Kevane and Gray (1999) in addition to Deere and Leon (2003); Rao (2005a); Ayuko and Chopra (2008); and World Bank (2012).

[17] World Economic Forum (2018, vii).

[18] Allendorf (2007); World Bank (2009). See also Landesa (2002).

[19] Villa (2017).   [20] World Bank (2009, 150).   [21] Thomson Reuters Foundation (2018).

[22] In particular, see Raj, Balaiah, and Silverman (2009); Bhalotra and Cochrane (2010); Pathak and Raj (2013); Trivedi and Timmons (2013); Bhalotra et al. (2018).

[23] Oxfam India (2018).

[24] Sanjoy Patnaik, India Country Director, Landesa (2014); c.f. Rosenberg (2016).

1.1 RECKONING WITH POWER

My field research highlights the promise and perils of one major push to alter the status quo of male political power in India: electoral quotas for female heads of local government *(Pradhans)*. The story of one woman whom quotas brought to power in the southern state of Andhra Pradesh (AP) illustrates a broader pattern across rural India.

Now a *Pradhan,* Padmawathi began navigating local challenges to her autonomy long before quotas were legislated. Initially, she stepped outside her home to organize neighborhood women who were co-members of the most socially denigrated group, SCs, formerly known as "untouchables." She convinced a growing number of SC women to congregate in the evenings and map out a plan to collectively access capital for small financial initiatives. Even in this nascent activism, Padmawathi was already exhibiting a political strategy many female *Pradhans* employ to cut through resistance – collective mobilization, especially of female constituents. As one journalist observing female *Pradhans'* work in the state of Maharashtra, in western India, explained:

Instead of dealing with opponents individually they adopt a collective approach. For this purpose the forum of Gram Sabha *meetings [convened by the* Pradhan, *open to all constituents] proved to be useful. Women ensured large participation in these public meetings and took decisions related to all government schemes and public works through this open forum. As [a] large number of women began participating in* Gram Sabha *meetings, their views and opinions got reflected in the decision-making processes. Gradually the resistance by the opponents declined.*[25]

For Padmawathi, resistance to her crossing traditional boundaries was quick and fierce. Her husband regularly threw open the door to their house, grabbed her long, plaited hair and dragged her inside, railing loudly at the shame she was bringing upon their family. Padmawathi persisted. Later, when she mobilized increasingly larger groups of women to demand state resources from local officials, they spat at her. Members of private firms threw garbage in her path. Padmawathi's experience reflects evidence collected by UN Women and the Center for Social Research in 2014, which found that 48 percent of the female politicians and campaigners they surveyed faced some form of physical assault. According to Asha Kotwal: *The backlash begins from the moment [any woman] steps into politics.*[26] This threat is omnipresent, with the result that "over 60 percent of women do not participate in politics due to fear of violence" (Majumdar, 2014).

It took more than a decade for Padmawathi to jump from informal organization to electoral politics. India's 1993 mandate creating quotas for female representatives as heads of elected local governments paved her path. When her village was required to apply quotas, she ran and was elected as its *Pradhan.* Proudly holding court to a number of local bureaucrats and female

[25] Birvaykar and Yadav (2011, 4). [26] Majumdar (2014).

citizens when I visited her government office, she was ready with photographs of the goods and services she had helped secure for her village: additional wells for drinking water, paved roads, proper homes with thatched roofs, and an electricity grid that now covers the entire village. This stood in stark contrast to male-run *Panchayats* I visited, where the meeting space was occupied exclusively by men, whose discussions of public works were rarely grounded in precise, well-documented specifics.

Indeed, Padmawathi is part of a select cohort of female elected leaders who have facilitated a major redistribution of resources: the transfer of more than 650 acres of land to women following disputes they mediated.[27] Young women in her village are now less likely to enter into child marriages, preferring to compete for scholarships granting them access to higher education and long-term independence. Padmawathi's advocacy of women's land rights and the autonomy that accompanies independent access to material wealth has influenced marriage timing, choice of spouse, and the resource transfers women receive.

Her political power is clear to any observer. The male bureaucrats and *Gram Panchayat* officials in her locality often choose to stand or occupy more remote seats to reserve the chairs closest to Padmawathi's desk for her female constituents. However, even deference has its limits. Padmawathi has an iron-clad rule to ensure that women, rather than disinterested or even oppositional bureaucrats, retain control of their property rights: *"All documents must be kept in the village, otherwise [women] couldn't leave to marry or simply move to another village"* confident that their property and marriage rights would be secure.[28]

Unlike her male peers, Padmawathi does not consider female concerns to be private, family matters. Instead, she feels privileged to be a proactive advocate for women, particularly those raised in the village she heads. Her assistance is especially valuable to young women beginning married life with husbands and their families in distant villages. Women who have come of age since Padmawathi's election enjoy a much more supportive environment in which to claim their inheritance rights and negotiate marriages than women in villages without a female *Pradhan*.

What does this support mean in practice? At the school Padmawathi helps support, a young woman of about 15 came forward:

About a year ago, I was enjoying coming to school, but my parents forced me to leave, to marry a man I didn't know. I was so scared. I wasn't ready to leave my home and friends and school, to be a wife. But my parents pressured me, saying I had to do this, that this was the only way they could afford to care for me. We are poor and this man agreed to marry me for very little [monetary] dowry, so this was important to

---

[27] Personal interview with Jamuna Paruchuri, then–Director of Advocacy for the Hyderabad-based Society for the Elimination of Rural Poverty, on January 21, 2014.

[28] Personal interview with Padmawathi in her Panchayat Office on January 18, 2016, at Kanchikacherla Mandal Headquarters, Krishna District, AP.

my parents. But I didn't want to go. So I ran away and came back to this school, to my teacher and Padmawathi for help. They took my problems seriously. Padmawathi brought me into her home while she negotiated with my parents and the other family. She got the other family to return the dowry my parents had given them in preparation for the wedding. She also told my parents she would pay for my education until I could support myself. I want to become a teacher, and she is making sure I continue in school until this point. Padmawathi made my parents promise not to marry me off before I complete school and offered to take care of me if they were not ready to take me back home. She made them see how much better things will be for me and for them if they wait until I complete my education. Then I can choose a better life and marriage. Finally, after many months of arguing, they agreed. Now they are proud of me for staying in school. I am certain I will become a teacher thanks to Padmawathi's support.[29]

When this young woman returns to negotiate her future marriage, Padmawathi will be ready to ensure she gets her fair share of inheritance as land titled in her name rather than monetary dowry. *Pradhans* are indeed formally tasked with preventing dowry, which has been prohibited since 1961. However, dowry persists. Another woman explains its entrenchment. "It is a hidden thing, secretive. How can we talk about it? Is it like a purchase deed in the *taluka* [local revenue department] office? It's done in the houses without an open word. Then how can we prevent it?"[30] Thus, public, political support for women as they make decisions around marriage represents a major break from the status quo.

The story of an older woman, whom I will call S., typifies that of many women who married into Padmawathi's village *prior* to her ascension as *Pradhan*. S. was married at age 11, nearly a decade before Padmawathi's election and seven years before she could marry legally. She left home without anything to secure her well-being except her married family's goodwill. By the time S. reached 18, she was a widow with two daughters. Her situation became dire:

My mother-in-law said: "You have only daughters, you should not stay with us, you should get out." They no longer gave me food. Treating me in such a manner was the same as throwing me out. "If you had a boy child,' they said, 'your family would grow [and we would accept you as our daughter-in-law], but you could not [produce] a boy and add to our family."[31]

When this occurred, gender-equalizing land inheritance reform had been in place for nearly two decades. However, female inheritance rights were rarely, if ever, enforced by the local male hierarchy. Around this time, Padmawathi

29 Personal interview with Y. W. and her classmates, January 18, 2016, in a public school at Kanchikacherla Mandal Headquarters, Krishna District, AP.
30 Joshi (1998, 45).
31 Personal interview with S., January 18, 2016, in a public school at Kanchikacherla Mandal Headquarters, Krishna District, AP.

was elected *Pradhan*. But, given that S. began her marriage as a child without a female *Pradhan's* negotiating power and assistance, S. was unable to demand the resources at marriage that would have secured her later welfare. When her natal family refused to take S. back, she turned to Padmawathi and the growing network of women whose public engagement the female *Pradhan* enabled. Padmawathi's support was vital. She helped S. join a women's microfinance (or Self Help) group (SHG) and facilitated broader monetary assistance from all SHGs in the village so that S. could secure an income independent of her family, avoid starvation, and educate her daughters. However, familial ostracism against S. by her marital and natal families was too severe to enable Padmawathi to negotiate inheritance or other forms of familial support.

These two contrasting cases illustrate the potential of female local electoral representatives to catalyze change for a subset of women: those who enter marriage negotiations under their guidance. For these women, female elected leaders can maximize their agency to strike mutually beneficial bargains with family members. This fits with theoretical work by Doepke and Tertilt (2009), who argue that men are most inclined to support more expansive notions of women's rights as a means to improve the scope of future opportunities for their daughters. In contrast, women who finalize marriage arrangements before a female *Pradhan* (like Padmawathi) is elected are at the mercy of their marital and natal families. Resistance is strongest against women who have already accepted dowry, and thus relinquished the highest valued asset they could have employed in bargaining.

This is not simply a local phenomenon. Evidence from across India supports the conclusion that, as women become more present and adept at negotiating power in public and private domains, official capacity to hear and respond to their demands has greatly enlarged. For example, a female-led *Panchayat* in Metikheda, Maharashtra, *"simply by taking up issues other* Panchayats *ignore has also had a ripple effect within the village"* on women's economic empowerment.[32]

Stories of female-run *Panchayats* being able to widen their role beyond narrow, official definitions extend from my field research in South India, to the preceding case from Maharashtra in West India, to the East, in West Bengal – where such *Panchayats* "have been involved in dowry, literacy and health campaigns, and have lobbied for equal land rights for women" – to the North, in Rajasthan, where their interventions have resolved intrahousehold disputes.[33] Throughout, women's agency fractures, then reconstructs, the gendered division between public and private spheres that remains common practice across much of rural India. For another female *Pradhan*:

Husbands who would never talk gently, now talk a little gently, with concern. "Where do you have to go today, do you have a meeting today?" Women are more content now.

[32] Bishakha, cited in Datta (1998c, 87).   [33] Datta (1998b, 126–7).

Because the women have come out. Now [the Pradhan] *has taken these women out.... How long will the women remain under your pressure?... Now they cannot be denied their rights. Now they cannot be told "No."*[34]

The broader implication from my two years of fieldwork is that gender equality requires more than reforming legal rights. Progress is contingent on the long-term work of building formal and informal pathways for women to negotiate across multiple domains – property inheritance, monetary dowry, and responsibilities for familial care. This becomes possible when political institutions such as quotas enable female representatives to help negotiate these rights and obligations at critical junctures.

1.2 ARGUMENT IN BRIEF

I build a theory linking women's political representation to their economic agency, specifically their ability to inherit land on a par with men. In India, this requires all members of the community – including the elected political officials who run the local state, the bureaucrats who draw it into its current form, and members of extended families, peers, and local social authorities who acknowledge and reinforce the identity of their daughters, sisters, wives, and mothers – to rewrite long-standing social agreements about property rights and power.

I argue that simply "reserving" the highest elected position in a given village government for a woman can set in motion seismic waves that unsettle this entire system. In India, traditionally, men have used local political power to safeguard the status quo. When women occupy these positions of authority, they observe the state from a different vantage point and organize it to solve the challenges their unique perspective throws into light. In this new terrain, the state-led reforms mandating equal land inheritance rights for women create a particularly meaningful lever for female citizens to make claims upon and through the state.[35] Women's negotiation of substantial property rights overturns and reassembles the system of power in potentially productive ways. Unsurprisingly, the possibility for such sweeping change sets in motion varied forms of resistance. Sometimes, this is the end of the story. But not always.

What is most surprising is the evidence I uncover of many women's ability to navigate and redirect challenges to their new authority. My research identifies an important focal point for coordination that enables women to assert their

---

34 Interview with Satyabhama "Nani" Lawand, female *Pradhan* of Bitargaon, Maharashtra, by Sharmila Joshi (1998, 61–2).

35 See the Kruks-Wisner (2018) theory of claim making for a powerful exposition of the process through which citizens make a much broader set of claims for rights and recognition upon the local state, and Brulé and Gaikwad (Forthcoming) on how lineage norms alter gendered claim making.

rights: bargaining around marriage choices.[36] When women approach this transformational social event with a powerful female interlocutor – that is, a female head of local government who can advocate for their equal economic rights – they are able to revise prior systems of power. I call this a "gate-keeper theory" whereby female political representation – placing women in traditionally male positions of power as "gatekeepers" – facilitates alignment of the local state machinery with enforcement of women's claims for economic rights.

I examine how changes in female representation create a new enforcement mechanism. This affects a broader ecosystem of social norms, each of which can advance or constrain women's agency. Norms about property inheritance are frequently intertwined with institutions that dictate social obligation in other domains – familial organization and care – and confer social worth based on the fulfillment of such duties.[37] In India, responsibilities are critical in one particular area: parental care in old age. Sons remain at home after marriage to support parents in exchange for property inheritance. In contrast, there are no traditional imperatives for adult, married daughters to offer such care. Upon marriage, daughters sever ties with their parents and enter new marital homes and lineages. Additionally, the payment of dowry to these marital families marks the final obligation of parents to their female offspring.[38] Accordingly, I consider how the timing of individual exposure to female representation – in relation to other institutions and economic reforms – affects three related behaviors: the distribution of inheritance across sons and daughters, who cares for parents in old age, and whether parents are willing to proactively abort daughters to ensure their own care in old age.

In each of these domains, I dig into the process through which individuals renegotiate traditional obligations and entitlements, including inheritance and dowry. I investigate the conditions under which women can most advantageously leverage female gatekeepers to strike "integrative bargains" where families coordinate around new, more egalitarian distributions.[39] Given the importance of social relationships, I study how women's agency shifts before and after critical junctures when women have substantive power to negotiate their position and resources within the family.

Specifically, I suggest that beneficiaries of property rights reform fall into two categories: women who enter and exit marriage negotiations *before reform*,

[36] Thomas Schelling (1960) explains that when multiple equilibria are possible, social norms enable coordination around a "focal point," that is, a single course of behavior.

[37] For applications of the relationship between levels of economic development and the distribution of economic opportunities and social responsibilities across geographic regions, see Folbre (1994); Lundberg and Pollak (1996, 2001); Braunstein and Folbre (2001); Pollak (2003); Iversen and Rosenbluth (2006, 2008); Alesina, Giuliano, and Nunn (2013).

[38] Botticini and Siow (2003).

[39] See Stasavage (2011) for evidence of enforcement institutions' varied impact in an alternate context: the influence of mercantile elites in structuring political institutions to monitor public credit and enforce debt repayment in medieval and early modern European states.

versus women who enter marriage negotiations *at or after the time of reform.*
When women exit marriage negotiations *before property rights reform,* I
predict they will have limited ability to negotiate trade-offs. This is because,
absent substantial legal rights to inherit property, women widely accept their
traditional "share" of inheritance: monetary dowries given at marriage, whose
illegality has not stemmed their use. Once a dowry is paid, it is assumed a
woman has received her portion of inheritance, and it becomes improbable if
not impossible to ask for more because to do so would violate a strong social
norm. Parents and brothers are likely to resist providing such women property
rights. In anticipation of changes triggered by enforcement, sons widely resist
by reducing their future obligations – refusing to care for aging parents. This
has a grim influence on attitudes toward subsequent generations: both women
and men, as parents, become more willing to selectively abort daughters. Thus,
we observe a paradoxical outcome: the political institutions that ensure the
enforcement of women's property rights – reservations for female heads of local
government – may unintentionally contribute the most to mobilizing backlash
against women.

In contrast, I find that women who enter marriage negotiations *at or after
the time of property rights reform* and who can turn to female representatives
for support are less likely to accept dowry. This is because these women, who
have something of familial value to trade, can take advantage of the deferred
entitlement of property inheritance. In these cases, female representatives can
help the brides negotiate rights and also intercede with parents to gain their
acceptance and approval. Indeed, my empirical results show that women who
strike mutually beneficial agreements with parents and brothers enjoy an
increase in overall welfare. Their value as daughters and sisters is amplified.
Amongst the younger generations, I anticipate that, over time, initial resistance
will gradually be transformed into actual support for women. Parents will have
increasing reason to regard daughters as future contributors to the welfare
of their natal families. Thus, increasing women's property inheritance will
hopefully lead to a decrease in the willingness of parents to carry out female
infanticide as a means to ensure sons remain supportive in their old age.

This study contributes to resolving the debate over whether and when
legislating rights is sufficient to alter patterns of exclusion. One set of optimistic
scholars in political economy and law contends that legal reform is sufficient
to engender positive social change.[40] This focus on narrow, technocratic policy
reform as the central driver of behavioral change is widespread amongst
development economists and practitioners. For example, in *Poor Economics,*
Abhijit Banerjee and Esther Duflo argue that many "failures [of development]
have less to do with some grand conspiracy of the elites to maintain their hold
on the economy and more to do with some avoidable flaw in the detailed design
of policies ... it is possible to improve governance and policy without changing

[40] Particularly, Posner (2000) and Schelling (1960).

the existing social and political structures."[41] In a more extreme vein, the Asian Development Bank's Gender Team argues that appropriate policies will fundamentally change social institutions. "Land is one of the last bastions of patriarchal privilege. This hegemony cannot be shattered without radical policy and legislative reforms."[42] The strongest proponents of legal change argue that legislation alone can uniformly improve women's land inheritance.[43] However, these theories ignore the difficulty of enforcing reform within the web of contravening social norms.[44] As Galanter (1981, 2–3) explains, the state is never the only provider of "justice." Most claims around the world are adjudicated "in the shadow of the law," outside the state, where the influence of social norms is undeniable (Dixit, 2007). In India, changes in property inheritance rights can directly affect willingness to care for aging parents and parental investments in children.

A second, less starry-eyed set of optimists, grounded within international relations, stresses the importance of global conventions for influencing domestic policy and behavior. Finnemore and Sikkink's (1998) theory of international "norm cascades" contends that accepted international standards around issues of international concern and consensus such as human rights often filter from global leaders to domestic audiences. Once a "critical mass of states" has adopted such norms, imitation by other states leads to growing internalization of these standards. The result is that new norms become "the standard of appropriateness" across states.[45] The specific norm of gender equality, Simmons (2009) argues, spread with the signing of the UN Convention for the Elimination of Discrimination Against Women (CEDAW). She presents evidence that CEDAW ratification improves state support of women's equality and autonomy.[46] While "norm cascade" theory can be helpful in explaining the passage of national legislation, it cannot account for the impact of such legislation. This is particularly true in the case of land reform in India, where widespread evidence documenting the ineffectiveness of property reform alone[47] exists alongside the country's weak commitment to international conventions around gender equal distribution of land rights.[48]

---

[41] Banerjee and Duflo (2012, 270–1).

[42] Jalal (2015).

[43] For example, Deininger, Goyal, and Nagarajan (2013) and Field (2007).

[44] See Agarwal (1994); Mackie (1996); Udry (1996); Platteau (2000a); Roy and Tisdell (2002); Fafchamps and Quisumbing (2007); Ambrus, Field, and Torero (2010); and Bhalotra, Brule, and Roy (2018).

[45] Finnemore and Sikkink (1998, 895).

[46] The UN General Assembly adopted CEDAW in 1979. Simmons identifies CEDAW as "the most comprehensive treaty on women's rights in history" (Simmons, 2009, 52).

[47] Besley and Burgess (2002); Ban and Rao (2008).

[48] Although India signed CEDAW in 1980 and completed ratification in 1993, the government added codicils negating the state's responsibility for gender equality around fundamental issues including land inheritance.

In contrast, skeptics argue that legal reform alone is insufficient to change behavior, highlighting the role of political institutions – either international or domestic – in driving effective reform.[49] My argument builds upon this work. In particular, I help bridge theories that focus on the importance of political institutions with those of behavioral economists and legal sociologists on the importance of social norms.[50] My contribution helps unpack the ways in which popular opinion, which holds that enforcement of reform is difficult and uneven, can generate a map of when we should expect resistance that blocks the intended benefits of property rights reforms. The nature of this resistance is rarely studied directly or in depth. I show that where support from political institutions is present, egalitarian property rights are more likely to be enforced. This, in turn mobilizes backlash when enforcement is costly to those most directly impacted. However, transformation of this resistance into support is possible when reform's intended beneficiaries can strike integrative bargains with those whose stake in the status quo is highest.

1.3 RESEARCH DESIGN

In India, much debate has focused on one institutional shift to increase descriptive representation: quotas that change the identity of elected local government heads. Since 1993, a three-tiered system of local governance with quotas or "reservations" for women as heads *(Pradhans)* of local government councils *(Gram Panchayats)* has been mandated. This replaced traditional, male-run councils that relied on appointments with electoral representation.[51] The new system is supported by fiscal resources, regular elections, and quotas for women and members of SCs and Tribes (STs). My focus is the *Gram Panchayat,* the most decentralized and local of the three tiers. In any given election, at least one-third of these elected positions are "reserved" exclusively for female candidates.

I exploit the exogenous (independent) application of these electoral quotas for women in India to identify the impact of female representation on enforcement of landmark reforms granting Hindu women equal rights to inherit property. These reforms, amendments to the Hindu Succession Act of 1956 (hereafter the HSAA or "reforms"), were enacted state-by-state, beginning in 1976 and culminating in a national legislative mandate in 2005. They equalized the rights upon birth of roughly 400 million daughters to inherit a share of joint family property (Agarwal, 1994; Agnes, 2000). They are significant because the majority of land in rural India remains owned by families, and pre-reform, sons

---

49 North and Weingast (1989); Chandra (2004); Acemoglu et al. (2008); Nooruddin (2011); Dasgupta, Gawande, and Kapur (2016); Page and Pande (2018).
50 In addition to Simon (1982) and Rubinstein (1998), recent work ties Galanter's path-breaking analysis of law and social change in India (Galanter, 1978a, 1984), with research on the unintended consequences of global competition for gender equality, such as Ballakrishnen (2019).
51 See Datta (1998a) for careful reporting on a handful of exceptional cases.

were the only children entitled by birth to inherit independent shares in jointly
owned property (Desai, 2010).[52]

I analyze the 2006 round of the Rural Economic and Demographic Survey
(REDS) collected by the National Council of Applied Economic Research
(NCAER), leveraging information on individual land inheritance, household
composition, and state capacity.[53] This rich database allowed me to quantify
the impact of reform across time and space for 8,500 households in 17 Indian
states. In addition, I built the most comprehensive summary of the state-level
selection mechanisms for reservations applied by relevant states.[54] As a result,
we know more about how reservations enact change across India than ever
before.

I include extensive qualitative data collected during two years of field
research. This incorporates interviews with agriculturalists, land revenue
bureaucrats, lawyers, politicians, police, and local activists. Most interviews
were conducted in rural districts across the erstwhile state of AP (see
Figure 5.2's map), now divided into Telangana and AP. I also interviewed
similar figures in Delhi and in villages extending north along the Yamuna
River, nearly to Chandigarh, and in the urban centers of Hyderabad, Pune, and
Varanasi. These interviews deepened my understanding of the political motives
for reform and the machinery that drives its local impact, informing my theory
and empirical investigation.

Finally, I draw upon archival resources from state and national legislatures,
district courts, land revenue bureaus and state and local newspapers. These
help illuminate political debates, legal action, and the encouraging or inhibiting
of women's land inheritance by local bureaucrats and activists. This evidence
forms the basis of my historical investigation into the origins of the progressive
laws I study (quotas mandating female political representation and property
inheritance reforms), and my theory of representation's impact on the effectiveness of women's economic rights.

[52] Roy (2015) calculates 84 of household property to be ancestral using REDS's 1999 round; Sircar
and Pal (2014) estimate 73 percent of plots households own or access are inherited. The 1956
Hindu Succession Act granted daughters the right to inherit a share of their father's land, while
sons retained their independent share of the coparcenary in addition to a share of their father's
land. HSA Amendments substantially increased the salience and size of women's inheritance.
The HSAA grants daughters equal rights to inherit fathers' ancestral property if three major
conditions are met: (i) Fathers die after the time their state legislated gender-equalizing reform;
(ii) without a will (intestate); and (iii) without partition of the ancestral land prior to their death
(Agarwal, 1994; Desai, 2010; Roy, 2015). Wills are extremely rare; Deininger et al. (2013)
estimate that at least 65 percent of Indians die without writing a will, with more intestate deaths
in rural India. Partition is also difficult, as it requires consensus about the timing and substance
of ancestral property's distribution amongst all coparceners.

[53] I am indebted to Andy Foster along with Hari Nagarajan and the rest of the extraordinary
academics and staff at the National Council for Applied Economic Research for access to this
extensive panel data. For more details on the data, please see Chapter 5, in particular Table 5.2.

[54] Prior studies have not verified reservations' random allocation beyond Rajasthan and West
Bengal.

The combination of survey data, interviews, and historical documents paints a vivid picture of how local political and social institutions shape outcomes. This applies to the intended domain of land inheritance and the unintended domains of dowry provision, sex selection, and the perceived obligation of children to care for their aging parents. The premise for this work – that politics are intimately intertwined with social organization – builds upon seminal feminist theory, most concisely articulated by Carol Hanisch's 1969 essay: "The Personal Is Political," with global application by Kandiyoti (1988) and recent extensions by Khan (2017), Prillaman (2017) and Brulé (2020). My theory and analysis are also firmly grounded in three strands of economics: microeconomics, on cooperation in firms (Cyert and March, 1963) and households (Becker, 1981), behavioral economics on bounded rationality (Simon, 1982; Rubinstein, 1998; Bendor, 2010; Kahneman, 2011; Mullainathan and Shafir, 2013), and economic anthropology on the importance of bargaining power (Ensminger, 1996; Hoodfar, 1997). My field research suggests female *Pradhans* can use the bargaining skills they hone within the household to effect larger change, in property rights institutions, political organization, and (social) ideologies. Kamalbai, the first *Pradhan* of an all-women's *Gram Panchayat* linked these domains as an explicit political qualification: "If I can run the house, why not a *Panchayat?*"[55]

1.4 CONTEMPORARY INDIA AS THE SITE OF EMPIRICAL STUDY

Solving the question of dominance has been central to the Indian state since its birth. Designing India's political institutions upon Independence, policy makers acknowledged the challenge of aligning inegalitarian social practices with egalitarian democratic principles. In the words of the Indian Constitution's main architect, Ambedkar:

> *On the 26th January 1950 [when India's Constitution became effective] we are going to enter a life of contradictions. In politics we will have equality and in social and economic life we will have inequality. In politics we will be recognizing the principle of one man, one vote, one value. In our social and economic life we shall, by reason of our social and economic structure, continue to deny the principle of one man, one value. How long shall we ... live this life of contradictions?*[56]

These remarks illustrate that while equality has been essential to India's political identity, it has been difficult to realize in practice. Yet the principle of equality has lent legitimacy both to citizens' demand for rights and state actions to enforce them.

Land inheritance is possibly the most radical domain of state intervention in this regard. As one legislator commented upon the first attempt by India's independent central state to grant women inheritance rights equal to those of

---

55 Interviewed by Shedde (1998, 2).   56 Kohli and Singh (2013, 212).

men: *I do not think there has been any bill so radical and so revolutionary which is trying to change the very foundations of Hindu society.*[57]

I focus on the inheritance reforms mentioned previously – amendments to India's Hindu Succession Act of 1956 (HSA) – as they created gender-equal property rights for the roughly 90 percent of India's population subject to Hindu law. These rights were enacted at different times by the various Indian states. Four states initially amended the HSA: AP (1986), Tamil Nadu (TN) (1989), and Karnataka and Maharashtra (1994). Kerala carried out what is commonly conceived of as a similar reform when it abolished the Joint Hindu Family in 1976. In addition, in 2005, a national mandate specifically equalized the inheritance rights of all daughters subject to Hindu law. These monumental reforms have fundamentally altered the foundational right of all citizens to claim substantial ancestral property in India.

However, in India, local bureaucratic and political power to enforce property inheritance reforms rests with an almost exclusively male elite that does not see enforcement as its mission. In particular, the nearly all-male cadre of the local land revenue bureaucrats responsible for ensuring land inheritance distribution interacts "almost entirely with men, whether at their offices or at the villages."[58] Officials familiar with reforms are often reluctant to facilitate women's inheritance for fear of "causing discord within the village or trouble within the family" unless the entire family unanimously requests those rights.[59] Although local political officials can bring pressure to enforce reform, they rarely do so. For example, a study of 44 heads of local government in three Central and South Indian states found agreement by the mainly male heads they interviewed that "women who stake claim on their land share would be treated badly in the village and ... *Gram Panchayats* [the elected village governments they head] may not be able to protect these women."[60] Yet this is not the final story. According to the BJP legislator Sri Indrasena Reddy,

When the Select Committee traveled several areas, it saw positive attitude towards this Bill, and at other places, some negative attitudes. The young women felt that this Bill is quite the right thing, but older women felt that this Bill is not quite right as it leads to some unnecessary disputes and might take away the love in the family.[61]

Thus, despite resistance by men, along with women from older generations, there is great potential for change amongst the younger generation of women,

[57] B. V. Keskar, constituent assembly member from Uttar Pradesh, *Constituent Assembly of India (Legislative) Debates*, Vol. V(1), 1948, 3647, c.f. in Kishwar (1994, 2146).

[58] Sircar and Pal (2014, 15).

[59] Personal interview with Land Revenue Officials (Tehsildars) in Telangana State, March 25, 2010.

[60] Sircar and Pal (2014, 16).   [61] Andhra Pradesh, State Legislative Assembly (1985, 428).

who, from the earliest moments of legislative consultations aimed at designing property inheritance reforms, have supported a different path.

1.5 BOOK ORGANIZATION

In this book, I set out to develop and test a theory about the relationship between women's political representation and their economic power. In Chapter 2, I utilize analysis of electoral behavior and negotiations of political authority and rights garnered from my field research to develop my "gatekeeper theory" of how women's representation impacts enforcement of their economic rights and subsequent welfare. I include individual narratives to explain the scope and significance of my theory. I do so by painting a picture of traditional expectations about what constitutes "appropriate" behavior for women and men as property owners, parents, and children. I also investigate how social norms and their enforcement and contestation are evolving in light of changes in political representation and the expected versus realized distribution of ancestral wealth. This chapter's theory explains the hypotheses I test in later chapters, which investigate the impact of gender-equalizing reform on individuals and families.

In Chapter 3, I provide an historical political overview of traditional norms governing the intrahousehold distribution of power. I then explore the unintended consequences of multiple attempts during British Colonial rule to legislate gender-equalizing social reforms. Where relevant, I include insights from my field research about the continuity of familial expectations around what it means to be a "good" Hindu son or daughter. I also highlight how norms and their enforcement evolved during Pre-Colonial and Colonial India as well as in the transition to independence. In Chapter 4, I bring to light the strategic political origins of gender-equalizing land inheritance reforms despite opposition on many fronts, using legislative debates translated to English for the first time in combination with analysis of historical behavior and motivations. This foreshadowed both the potential support for and resistance to contemporary reforms.

In Chapters 5 to 7, I evaluate the causal influence of political representation on economic reform across multiple terrains. Chapter 5 evaluates the impact of property inheritance reform on women's receipt of land inheritance and monetary dowry, as well as women and men's political participation and willingness to violently enforce marriage norms. In Chapter 6, I consider the unintended consequences that property inheritance reforms can have on care of aging parents, which I argue can help explain resistance to such gender-equalizing reforms. Chapter 7 explores whether reform alters the widespread practice of sex selection.

In Chapter 8, I conclude by discussing the implications of my theory's ability to predict how female representation affects the enforcement of economic reforms. I also seek to answer the larger question of whether people are tangibly better off as a result. I reflect on my theory's ability to travel across contemporary states as well as its predictions for the broader evolution of equality at the intersection of state policy and social action. As Machiavelli opined: "If laws are to be observed, there is need of good customs," and, I would add, political institutions.[62]

---

[62] See Machiavelli (1957).

2

A Theory of Political Representation and Economic Agency

Yahan to lugai adami ki sampati maani jaave hai vo keesa sampati mein adhikar maange? Literally: "Here [in Haryana], a woman is considered the property of a man. Where does the question of her claiming *her share in the property* arise?"
—Sumitra Devi[1]

How do women access social, economic, and political power in settings where multiple, interlinked systems prevent female influence and agency? More fundamentally: How does a low-status group challenge and destabilize what prior to that point appeared to be a highly stable, inegalitarian system? I consider a hard case: contemporary, rural India where the political, economic, and social subsystems that each subordinate women reinforce each other and the cultural system supplies consistent norms and life meanings. In this context, I argue that constitutional reforms raising women's political voice and power enable female representatives to catalyze change. We see this clearly where economic reforms present an opportunity for women to translate political voice into entitlements to inherit the most precious resource and primary repository of wealth in contemporary India: land.

In this chapter, I construct a theory linking women's political representation to their economic agency, specifically their ability to inherit land on a par with men. In India, this is a revolutionary concept that requires everyone, from elected government officials to bureaucrats to family members to change deeply held, entrenched opinions and behaviors, backed by strong social norms about property rights, politics, and the role of females in the family and in the broader society. I argue that the simple act of mandating that women hold the

---

[1] Interview of Sumitra Devi in the rural Haryanavi village of Meham and translation by Chowdhry (2012, 46); emphasis added.

highest elected position in their village government can generate a cascade of effects that runs through this entire system. In India, traditionally, men have used this political position to act as guardians and enforcers of the status quo. When women occupy these seats of authority, they start to see and use the state differently. In this case, mandating equal land inheritance rights for women creates a fertile ground for reworking distribution of resources that then reverberates throughout multiple, interconnected domains. Unsurprisingly, the potential for such sweeping change sets in motion varied forms of resistance. This results in paradoxical politics: women's successful empowerment is closely tailed by backlash. What is extraordinary is that women are able to navigate and redirect challenges to their new authority. My research pinpoints a key widow of opportunity for women to assert their rights: marriage negotiations. Women who enter this point of social reckoning and recombination with powerful female interlocutors – that is, female heads of local government who can advocate for their equal economic rights – are able to transform prior systems of power.

Throughout this chapter's theory building, I delve into personal accounts drawn from field research – interviews that further spell out the contemporary, interconnected dynamics of political space and intimate, interpersonal terrain in the face of Indian women's changing legal, social, and political opportunities. Subsequent chapters test these hypotheses.

2.1 GENDER-EQUALIZING ECONOMIC REFORM

I consider the potential social impact of landmark reforms that granted Hindu women equal rights to inherit ancestral property. These reforms, amendments to the Hindu Succession Act of 1956 (hereafter the HSAA or "reforms"), were enacted state by state, beginning in 1976 and culminating in a national legislative mandate in 2005. They equalized the rights upon birth of roughly 400 million daughters to inherit a share of joint family property (Agarwal, 1994; Agnes, 2000).

These reforms are significant because inherited rights to property are a major stock of social, economic, and political power, which, given their concentration, also sustains and magnifies inequality. Today, the majority of land in rural India remains jointly owned, and prior to reform, sons were the only children entitled by birth to inherit independent shares in such property (Desai, 2010).[2]

Reforms equalized the rights of daughters and sons *upon birth*, conditional on their father's death postreform. Notably, two other rarely utilized conditions define eligibility across all HSA Amendments: the absence of a will, and partition of the ancestral land prior to paternal death (Agarwal, 1994; Desai,

---

[2] The 1956 Hindu Succession Act granted daughters the right to inherit a share of their father's land, while sons retained their independent share of the *coparcenary* in addition to a share of their father's land. HSA Amendments substantially increased the salience and size of women's inheritance.

2010; Roy, 2015).[3] Wills are extremely rare; Deininger et al. (2013) estimate that at least 65 percent of Indians die without writing a will, with more intestate deaths in rural India.[4] Partition is also limited by its difficulty, as it requires inheritors' consensus about ancestral property's distribution.

By attempting to alter foundational norms about the distribution of wealth and responsibility, these reforms lay the groundwork for a social revolution. According to the land and gender scholar Prem Chowdhry, redefining women's inheritance rights alters a crucial building block in a much-larger system of norms used to construct both the family and the village-level community. She explains:

> *The Hindu Succession Act [and its Amendments] . . . introduced fundamental and radical changes in the law, breaking from the past. The land of the village is taken to belong to the male descendants of ancestors who originally settled and worked on it, the male agnatic descendants, as members of localized clan[s] alone are considered to have reversionary rights in the estate. . . .*
> *The only ideal and "izzatwala" (honorable) pattern of inheritance is acknowledged to be by males from males. This means basically that daughters and sisters who are potential introducers of fresh blood and new descent lines through their husbands are to be kept from exercising their inheritance rights. With the result that the most virulent objection to the breach of caste/community taboos in marriage comes from the powerful landowning classes of the village.[5]*

Chowdhry's account highlights property inheritance norms as central to the structure and exercise of power within the family, village, and larger communities of caste and religion. Taken at face value, this affirms inheritance rights as the embodiment of power in multiple social domains.

Indeed, analysis of Colonial India by Parashar Kulkarni (2017) finds that cultural elites – *Brahmans* – perceived the process of codifying Hindu land inheritance rights for one particularly vulnerable set of women – widows – as so threatening to their power that they developed an alternative social institution to preclude women's inheritance: *sati* or widow immolations. Considering cases of widow burning from 1815–21, Kulkarni finds that districts with Hindu

---

3 Early versions of the amendments also required daughters to be unmarried at the time of reform. However, national reform equalized all daughters' rights regardless of marriage status at reform.
4 The combination of low levels of literacy, the expense of drafting formal, legal documents with lawyers' assistance, and the general taboo against wives' discussion of their husbands' deaths present a strong barrier to widespread writing of formal wills for all but the most lucrative plots of land (Personal focus group interviews with agriculturalists in Rangapuram, Konchikarcherla Mandal, Krishna District, April 16, 2010). One VRO in a particularly wealthy village claims to have seen a significant increase in the registration of legally binding oral wills over the past decade, following rising land prices (Personal interview, March 25, 2010, Khammam, Andhra Pradesh [AP]). Roy (2015) presents complementary evidence that patriarchs exclude daughters from inheritance through premortem land transfers. Also see Sircar and Pal (2014, 13) on use of "No-Objections Certificates."
5 Chowdhry (1997, 1025).

law that was more favorable to women's inheritance rights (Dayabhaga) were significantly more likely to practice *sati* after formalizing these rights than districts with less favorable law (Mitakshara). This evidence supports my assumption that the specter of female inheritance rights – even for a limited, socially stigmatized subset of the population – represents a radical enough break with the male-dominated Hindu socio-economic world to justify the systematic murder of women by social elites (*Brahman* males).

Jumping ahead to the present day, work provides a mixed assessment of property rights reforms' effectiveness in contemporary India: while Deininger et al. (2013) find supportive evidence, Roy (2015) shows that reform failed to increase the likelihood of property inheritance by women. This suggests that the impact of reform is at best heterogeneous, with reasons for its variance poorly understood.

Overall, what these chronicles of reform tell us is that any change made by legislation at the national level percolates downward into daily life, disrupting and disturbing the equilibrium at the local, intimate level of the household. These changes around colonial legislation of land are a forerunner of later responses to equalization of Hindu women's land inheritance rights in contemporary, independent India. They also make clear that the politics of negotiating resources cannot simply be relegated to national legislatures or even local political fora because they pervade the very intimate fabric of the household.

In this chapter, I develop a theory about how legal change affects relationships and resources across multiple spheres of life, through a crucial mediator: political institutions. With this in mind, we turn to consider contemporary political dynamics.

2.2 HOW QUOTAS CHANGE STREET-LEVEL BUREAUCRACY IN INDIA

In 1993, the 73rd and 74th amendments to the Indian Constitution were adopted. These mandated a three-tiered local governance system of *Panchayats* with regular elections and quotas, known as "reservations," for members of systematically underrepresented groups: women and members of communities combating deep social stigma: Scheduled Castes and Tribes (SCs and STs). I focus on the most decentralized and local of the three tiers, the *Gram Panchayat*, or elected village council. The constitutional amendments mandated that not less than one-third of elected positions for *Gram Panchayat* heads (*Pradhans*) be women.[6]

---

[6] Titles vary across India, including *adhyakhsa*, *Sarpanch*, or president in South India. Council-based rule is an ancient concept, but an effective *Panchayat* system did not exist prior to India's constitutional amendments (Ghatak and Ghatak, 2002). The impact of these amendments on SCs and STs is the focus of a growing body of research including: (Pande, 2003; Besley et al., 2004; Bardhan et al., 2005; Besley, Pande, and Rao, 2005; Bardhan and Mookherjee, 2010; Chin and Prakash, 2011; Dunning and Nilekani, 2013; Jensenius, 2015).

Reservations represented a significant break with past practices of local governance (Chattopadhyay and Duflo, 2004b; Beaman et al., 2009; Bhavnani, 2009). They replaced traditional, appointed local councils of elders, which were male run, with elected local governments supported by fiscal resources, regular elections, and quotas for traditionally excluded groups. These amendments and their resulting changes occurred independent of state-level gender-equalizing land inheritance reforms, and took place over a decade prior to national property rights reforms of 2005.[7]

Political strategy motivated this radical shift in the local state's organization. The Ashoka Mehta Committee report that created the template for these constitutional amendments explicitly blamed bureaucracy for the failure of earlier, piecemeal attempts at decentralization because the two centers of authority competed for power.[8] To redistribute power away from bureaucrats – local Indian Administrative Service (IAS) officers – the Ashoka Mehta Committee proposed giving *Panchayats* the power to tax citizens, to run schools, and the institutional infrastructure necessary to identify and solve fundamental problems of local governance and development.[9]

Political targeting of the bureaucracy as a source of "unproductive" competition for new entrants attempting to assert control over established political machines – such as Rajiv Gandhi and P. V. Narasimha Rao, the main proponents of decentralization and reservations[10] – is unsurprising, given bureaucracy often plays a central role in formalizing and protecting political power. While bureaucratic officials have historically constituted the most effective local arm of the state – due to their comparatively well-informed and well-resourced administrative capacity and the political authority that followed – these officials are conservative by design (Singer, 2007). Such conservatism derives not only from the nature of bureaucracy – as a means of ensuring consistent responses to dynamic systems – but also from the nature of local power. In particular, officials tasked with regulating local land rights are likely to spend a great deal of time working with large landholders who are typically the most conservative members of a village. Given that effective work requires building

---

7 Prior to these amendments, state-established *panchayats* were largely ineffective and operated as secondary to traditional *panchayats* run by local, male political elites (Banerjee, Gertler, and Ghatak, 2002; Chattopadhyay and Duflo, 2004b). In addition, Anderson and Genicot (2015) find no relationship between the timing of each state's legislation of gender-equalizing economic reforms and its implementation of reservations for women.

8 Committee et al. (1978) *Report of the Committee on Panchayati Raj Institutions*, New Delhi: Government of India, Ministry of Agriculture and Irrigation, Department of Rural Development, c.f. Singer (2007, 101). Chapter 4 further details the political agenda motivating local-level women's reservations.

9 See Singer (2007, 101–2). This analysis is thanks to insightful questions from Akshay Mangla and Gabrielle Kruks-Wisner, whose forthcoming analysis on the microdynamics of policing in contemporary India provides nuanced analysis of how the dynamics of power affect enforcement in this related component of the local state.

10 Bohlken (2015).

rapport, efficient local bureaucrats will likely be able to empathize with large landholders, quite possibly adopting their world view in the course of extended, mutually beneficial relationships (within and across villages). As a result, the disinterest amongst bureaucrats in challenging the status quo is rational as well as disheartening.

In India, the land revenue bureaucracy is also a repository of social power invested in maintaining the status quo. We see this, in part, because material incentives encourage bureaucrats to uphold existing social entitlements to land. In particular, tax collection is easiest where rights to land registered on the books align with who pays taxes. In most states, the bureaucrat charged with formalizing inherited property rights is the village revenue official (hereafter VRO). He (or rarely she) must announce the provisional legal list of inheritance transactions and receive a written endorsement from the village's adult electors over which the *Pradhan* presides (the *Gram Sabha*) prior to initiating land inheritance transfers.[11] According to one property lawyer, VROs are biased against women across all their land-related duties because they "are only looking at putting down the name of the head of the family, who will pay the taxes."[12]

Contrary to contemporary bureaucratic interests, state-level amendments to the Hindu Succession Act require the VRO to transfer (mutate) equal shares of ancestral land to all eligible family members – male and female – known as coparceners. Transfers of formal land titles are initiated upon a surviving family member's request. By law, the VRO must publish this request to solicit objections from the other coparceners (Andhra Pradesh 1993). Absent valid objections, the VRO is mandated to register all coparceners as joint owners of ancestral land. In the case of oral wills, known as *sada beinama* (white paper), the VRO determines inheritance, should the distribution be contested.

Absent reservations, the nearly always male VROs typically argue that claiming rights is women's responsibility alone, and male *Pradhans* concur, adding they cannot guarantee protection for those women who do so (Sircar and Pal, 2014, 16). The former head of the AP-based Society for Elimination of Rural Poverty, B. Rajsekhar, explains that when male *Pradhans* are in office: *"Women have only a subordinate status" and no voice to demand officials' help securing property rights.*[13]

Indeed, VRO reluctance to *formally* enforce inheritance reform is rampant: out of 1,192 individuals – predominantly women – I interviewed across AP, not

---

[11] This example is drawn from Sircar and Pal (2014, 18). The VRO's title varies: *karnam, lekpal, munsiff, Panchayat secretary, patwari, village assistant, village land revenue officer,* or *watandar* are also used, dependent on region and pre-independence land revenue bureaucracy system. These individuals are responsible for enacting land transfers and enforcing their distribution in line with legislation. More broadly, VROs are responsible for maintaining, monitoring, and transferring records of land titles and land cultivation, and for collecting relevant taxes (Baden-Powell, 1882; Government of India, 2008).

[12] Personal interview on January 7, 2017, at AV College, Hyderabad, AP.

[13] Personal interview with B. Rajsekhar, IAS, then CEO, SERP, Government of Andhra Pradesh, India, on March 22, 2010, SERP Office, Hyderabad, AP.

a single female reported receiving ancestral land using a VRO-initiated land transfer. As daughters usually move to a distant village upon their marriage, they are thus easy to ignore at the time of land transfers.[14] Officials familiar with women's rights are unwilling to formalize their inheritance for fear of "causing discord within the village or trouble within the family," unless the entire family unanimously requests it.[15] My interviews in north India and methodical review of revenue records from nearly half a century in rural AP confirm the trends that I find in contemporary AP: the VRO overwhelmingly sides with status quo beneficiaries throughout the process of claiming land rights, both in the past and present.

This consistent, sustained bureaucratic resistance is striking, given that all the women that I have studied had at least limited rights to inherit their father's land.[16] The local land revenue bureaucracy's limited responsiveness to recognizing women's property rights presents a major barrier to women who wish to claim even minimal rights.

2.3 GETTING THEIR HANDS DIRTY: WOMEN IN POLITICS DERACINATE PRIVILEGE

Why should a women rather than a man sitting at the highest local elected office make a difference?

Mandatory female inclusion created an important entry point for women into politics. This follows the aim of descriptive political representation, or what Phillips (1995) calls the "politics of presence," as a means to improve substantive representation, that is making policy more responsive to the interests of chronically underrepresented groups.[17] Such intervention was necessary because, despite great numbers of women's active participation in the movement for Indian independence, "it was easier to get arrested for supporting democracy (during the freedom struggle) than it is to get elected to the democratic institutions that Indian nationalists were fighting to obtain."[18] Although "institutional/male" sources are frequently deemed responsible for women's reservations, women's engagement in politics as pivotal electoral constituencies was central to the calculations of chief ministers who provided early versions of women's reservations, as well as to national legislation.[19] Chapter 4 provides more details on political strategy motivating the national mandate.

[14] Personal interview with Ex-Deputy Collector, Khammam, March 24, 2010, confirmed across interviews.

[15] Personal interview with VROs on March 25, 2010, AP.

[16] See Appendix Figure 9.4 and accompanying note on rights prior to gender-equalizing reform.

[17] Pitkin (1967).

[18] Noted by Chowdhary et al. (1997), cited from Buch (2010, 10).

[19] I refer to the chief ministers of AP and Karnataka as early proponents of reservations. On national reservations, I rely on detailed analysis by Bohlken (2015) of the complementary mandate for members of SCs and STs – as a part of the broader process by which the national *Panchayati Raj* amendments proposed by Rajiv Gandhi and implemented under P. V. Narasimha Rao evolved, and work by John (2008), Nair (2008a), Singer (2007), and Sen (2002).

The elected position I focus on – reservations for women as heads of local government (*Pradhans*) – is a crucial one. I call *Pradhans* political gatekeepers because in India, they are the most influential local politician in a village. *Pradhans* preside over the *Gram Panchayat*, and oversee implementation of public works, social justice projects, and land allocation. Indeed, "[T]he *Sarpaunch (Pradhan)* shoulders the workload in almost all villages. This is partly due to the structure of *Panchayat Raj*, which gives only the *Sarpaunch* – and the *Gram Sevak* (Secretary) – power over *Panchayat* funds. . . . The *Sarpaunch* is inevitably the most vocal member at meetings, and the only member with some knowledge of *Panchayat Raj* mechanisms. . . . In some villages, the *Sarpaunch* is effectively the *Panchayat*" (Datta, 1998b, 122).

Large-scale survey work identifies the *Pradhan* as the person most likely to be approached for assistance, regardless of the service being requested.[20] *Pradhans* are key allies for individuals attempting to register crimes with the police; to acquire voting rights in a locality by ensuring one's name is listed in the locality's voter rolls; and most crucially for this study, to secure formal land inheritance rights. *Pradhans*' ability to influence legal rights' enforcement is also well documented.[21] Reservations are crucial because they determine who controls the enforcement of all legislation in the local context. Given this authority, reservations are game changing.

In my interviews, I heard the oft-repeated refrain that once female *Pradhans* enter office they alter how politics work, changing expectations about who can approach the *Pradhan* and how they will be treated. This counters the widespread narrative that women in office are typically mere proxies for their husbands, such that the "Pradhan Patti" or "Sarpaunch Patti" (husband of the elected official) wields the real power. In the words of Dr. Daggubati Purandeswari, a female member of parliament from AP:

> *When the 73rd and 74th Amendments were passed, people did [initially] have* Pradhan Pattis *(husbands), such that women were only figureheads for their husbands. . . . Now the* patnis *(wives) themselves are running the show. The Amendments have given women the confidence that they can assert themselves.*[22]

In fact, many female *Pradhans* consider themselves personally responsible for increasing women's engagement with the state. In the words of one such woman:

> *We only get to know about what happens in neighbouring villages. . . . We also keep a watch on what is happening in the world, which village is going what way, where*

---

[20] On *Pradhans*' centrality for citizens' assistance: Kruks-Wisner (2011); Bussell (2019). On the broader context of participation in the *Gram Panchayat* and the assembly of all adults it convenes, the *Gram Sabha*'s importance for accessing rights, see: Ban, Jha, and Rao (2012).

[21] Brass (1997); Srinivasan (2014). Notably, Chauchard (2014) and Jensenius (2017) also identify relevant nonmaterial benefits individuals achieve when they are descriptively represented by *Pradhans* of the same caste or ethnicity.

[22] Personal interview with Dr. Daggubati Purandeswari, MP from Visakhapatnam, AP, on January 24, 2014 at her residence in Hyderabad, AP.

people are happy. [As Pradhan, I try to make other women understand something of what I know because] it is our job to make them understand. If there is a small child going towards dirt it is our job to pick it up. Slowly, I have brought the women out. It's my duty to explain and to tell them to improve. I have made them move ahead, little by little. My authority was such, no one ever said anything to me. So I took them out slowly, made them move about, to the office, to meetings, to attend, to discuss. (Joshi, 1998, 44)

These efforts fundamentally change how women see the state. As Joseph explains, "*Women feel much more confident to approach a lady President [Pradhan] with their problems – which would never have been presented otherwise*" (Joseph, 2001).

Female constituents of *Panchayats* headed by women agree:

[T]he most obvious benefit of women being in the Panchayat *has been that women are no longer completely housebound. It has suddenly become legitimate for women to move out of the house because of the [female-run]* Panchayat, *as the members may say, for instance, "we would like the women to be present at so-and-so place at this hour" and since it is on work, no one can prevent them from being there.* (Sathaye, 1998, 107)

Most fundamentally, female *Pradhans* are simultaneously changing how women conceive of their rights, just as they open space for women to raise their political voice about economic and social concerns that the state might never have heard otherwise. According to Jamuna Paruchuri, then a member of the National Rural Development Mission:

Earlier, [male] Sarpaunches (Pradhans) were opposed to women's organizations, and any form of women's organizing. Now, because women Pradhans are in power, they go sit with women in their sangha (groups). [Where female Pradhans are in power] lands are now being given in women's names, and gender issues are now being taken up.[23]

2.3.1 Women's Political Rules of Engagement

Yet, why do we observe female *Pradhans* acting any differently than men? Given the importance of electoral politics in bringing women to power, can we learn anything from the way women compete in and win campaigns, relative to men?

I examine female electoral competitiveness relative to that of men in two ways. First, I ask: How competitive are female – as opposed to male – incumbents? This tells us how voters respond to the candidates about whom they know the most: incumbents. Second, how successful are female (reserved) candidates at mobilizing voter turnout by women and men, relative to male (nonreserved) candidates? The Rural Economic and Demographic Survey (REDS) collected by the National Council of Applied Economic Research (NCAER) 2006–9 enables these tests by mapping the competitiveness of female and male political candidates across the first three rounds of *Gram Panchayat* (Village Council) elections with reservations for female heads.

[23] Personal interview on January 21, 2014 in Hyderabad, AP, India.

TABLE 2.1. *Probability Incumbent Is Reelected*

Panchayat Election	All Incumbents			Female Incumbent			Male Incumbent		
	Obs	Mean	Std. Dev.	Obs	Mean	Std. Dev.	Obs	Mean	Std. Dev.
Second	233	0.034	0.182	51	0.020	0.140	182	0.038	0.193
Third	233	0.028	0.159	72	0.042	0.201	161	0.019	0.136

Note: The sample includes all villages where information is available on identity of the *Pradhan* and can be traced across consecutive elections. "Second" refers to the winner of the first round of *Panchayat* elections being reelected in the second round of *Panchayat* elections. "Third" refers to the winner of the second round of *Panchayat* elections being reelected in the third round of *Panchayat* elections.
Source: REDS 2006/9, NCAER.

First, are women – elected almost exclusively through reservations – competitive in subsequent elections? One major concern about quotas is that they may give the candidates they seek to empower a transitory political advantage that may act as a crutch – enabling minority candidates to win elections only when quotas exist, absent "real" competition – rather than a lever enabling long-term political autonomy. If so, the women who gain office through reservations may lack both the interest and ability to compete in elections outside the "cover" of quotas.[24] Bhavnani (2009) finds evidence that once reservations are withdrawn, female incumbents who initially won their seat with reservations are five times more likely to be reelected than female non-incumbents in metropolitan Mumbai, Maharashtra. Yet thus far, we know little about how female incumbents fare *relative to males*.

Given the limited advantage incumbents typically experience in India – where they are more likely to lose than win subsequent elections – female incumbents should face particularly severe constraints to reelection.[25] Indeed, the structure of female reservations – which are generally redrawn for each new electoral cycle – presents a particular disadvantage to reelection of female candidates, nearly all of whom first win elections within reserved constituencies. Thus, incumbency advantage should set a high bar for assessing the efficacy of female elected leaders. If voters are willing to elect women at rates equal to or greater than that of men, this provides strong evidence that women are indeed *at least as effective as men, if not more so.*

What we learn from Table 2.1 is that the skeptics of women's reservations were initially correct. For the first elections with female incumbents – round two

[24] If women are indeed weaker candidates, we might still see quotas cause a change in state provision of resources and citizen trust if descriptive representation motivates constituents to apply sustained pressure on "their" representatives that is strong enough to force even uncompetitive candidates to support petitioners. However, voters should still be less likely to reelect an ineffective female representative conditional on the presence of more effective alternative candidates.

[25] Uppal (2009).

of *Gram Panchayat* elections – female candidates were nearly half as likely to be reelected relative to their male counterparts (with 2 vs. 3.8 percent reelection rates, respectively). However, incumbents in the next batch of female candidates reverse these trends. In the third *Gram Panchayat* elections, female incumbents are reelected at more than twice the rate of men (at 4.2 vs. 1.9 percent, respectively). This suggests that with longer national exposure to the system of reservations and the opportunities it entails, women competing as incumbents are able not only to meet but to exceed male heads of local government in demonstrating effectiveness to voters such that they merit reelection. Of course, the strength of inference is limited by the number of local elections available for analysis to date.[26]

Second, do female candidates in reserved constituencies mobilize voter turnout at different levels than men? Optimists predict that female candidates are more adept than men at raising turnout by women. Pessimists frequently express concerns that voters will collectively be less likely to vote when constituencies are reserved for female candidates only. Appendix Table 9.1 examines adult voter participation in each electoral round using Ordinary Least Squares (OLS) regressions so that we can control for the year of each *Gram Panchayat* election (Column 2), as well as the state in which the election occurs (Column 3), and compare results for the full sample of states versus a subsample that excludes those who were either extremely late in applying reservations, or whose criteria for "randomly" selecting constituencies for elections may induce bias (Column 4).[27]

Looking at the impact of reservations for women for each round of *Gram Panchayat* elections, Appendix Table 9.1 indicates limited distinctions between voter responses to female candidates competing in reserved constituencies and the majority-male candidates in nonreserved constituencies. Across elections, the consistent pattern is women's lower levels of voting relative to men, by 1–3 percentage points.[28] Yet, this difference is not statistically significant after excluding states that used non-random mechanisms to select localities for reservations or were late to implement them.[29] In line with optimists, female *Pradhans* do appear to significantly boost voting by women in their constituencies by 3 percentage points in the first round of *Gram Panchayat* elections, eliminating the gender gap in voting.[30] However, this relationship loses statistical significance once we focus on predicting variation within states.[31]

---

[26] *Lok Dhaba* provides excellent state-level data on candidates. See Jensenius and Verniers (2017) for details. Their data is available at: http://lokdhaba.ashoka.edu.in/LokDhaba-Shiny/.

[27] These criteria are explained in the Appendix Table 9.1 note, with more nuance in Chapter 5 analysis.

[28] Appendix Table 9.1, Columns 1–3 in Panels A, B, and C, and Column 4, Panel C.

[29] Appendix Table 9.1, Column 4 in Panels A and B.

[30] Appendix Table 9.1, Panel A, Columns 1–2, significant at the 90 percent confidence interval.

[31] Including fixed effects for states, Appendix Table 9.1, Panel A, Columns 3–4.

Most notably, as Figure 2.1 illustrates, we do see a significant divergence in voter turnout for the subset of women with experience leading *Gram Panchayats*. For villages with two consecutive reservations for female heads, constituents are significantly more likely to vote than they are in villages without reservations, by 4–20 percentage points.[32] Here, there is limited evidence that reservations may also erase the gender gap – not by depressing voting by men, but rather by increasing voting by everyone, with women voters turning out to vote at even higher rates for female candidates.[33] Again, the caveat applies that this analysis is merely suggestive given the limited subsample of villages that experience two consecutive reservations in the first three rounds of *Gram Panchayat* elections.[34]

This final set of analyses suggests that once female heads of local government accrue experience – alongside their constituents' acclimation to female leaders – *women are more effective than men at mobilizing all constituents to vote.* To the extent this finding holds across subsequent local elections, it suggests that women are not just more effective at supporting the galvanizing of this fundamental source of political engagement – voting – by female constituents; they are better at encouraging voting by everyone, including men.

Overall, this investigation of the electoral incentives female candidates (under quotas) face in comparison to male candidates (outside of quotas) suggests that women are at least as responsive to electoral incentives as are men, if not more so. Experience – measured as at least one term as elected head of the local government – enables women to pull ahead of men in terms of incumbency advantage and effectiveness at mobilizing voter turnout (Tables 2.1 and 9.2).

Thus, not only do women respond to electoral incentives, they are also better at harnessing experience to prove their political acumen (flipping men's initial incumbency advantage to their favor) and increase turnout. Altogether, this provides initial evidence that electoral incentives matter. Indeed, women elected through reservations spur increased turnout by women and men, suggesting that once in office they have incentives to invest in meaningful changes not only for women but for *all constituents.*

---

[32] Table 9.2, Panel A, Columns 1–4; Panel B, Columns 1–2.

[33] Table 9.2, Panel A, Columns 1–2.

[34] Out of 233 villages for which NCAER provides data on *Gram Panchayat Pradhan* reservations, 61 are reserved for female candidates in the second electoral round, of which 10 villages were also reserved for female *Pradhans* in the first round of elections. These include two in Karnataka, one in Rajasthan, and seven in Uttar Pradesh. In comparison, 130 villages were neither reserved for female *Pradhan* candidates in the first nor in the second elections. For the third round of elections, 71 villages were reserved for female *Pradhan* candidates, of which 14 had also been reserved in the second round of elections. These include five villages in Karnataka, one in Maharashtra, one in Madhya Pradesh, two in Uttar Pradesh, two in Chhattisgarh, and three in Tamil Nadu. In comparison, 115 villages were neither reserved for female candidates in the second nor third rounds of elections. Given the small numbers of villages with two consecutive reservations, it is likely prudent to focus analysis on the specifications that do not include fixed effects for state of residence.

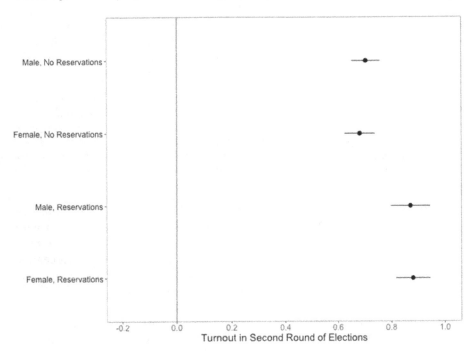

FIGURE 2.1. Impact of Two Consecutive Reservations on Voter Turnout, Second *Panchayat* Elections, Predicted Values

Source: NCAER Rural Economic and Demographic Survey, 2006/9. The sample includes all individuals for whom there are records of voting in *Gram Panchayat* elections in constituencies with information on reservations. Each point on the graph represents the predicted values of turnout for individuals belonging to the given group. "Reservation" refers to whether the *Pradhan* seat was reserved for a female candidate in the first and second rounds of elections. Predictions are based on OLS regression analysis with fixed effects for the year of elections, with standard errors clustered at the village level (9.2, Panel A, Column 2). Lines represent 95 percent confidence intervals.

2.4 GATEKEEPER THEORY OF ECONOMIC RIGHTS' ENFORCEMENT

How do women put this political acumen to work once they enter elected office? I propose that political representation creates revolutionary changes in women's relationship to the local political and bureaucratic arms of the state. Where quotas for female gatekeepers exist, they catalyze a virtuous cycle of women's political inclusion: more women participate both formally and informally, engaging the state as a partner in enforcing rights as it becomes more accessible and responsive.

How exactly do female gatekeepers effectively apply this new political power? Let me return to the three strategies that I introduced in the prior section: they revolutionize how women occupy the public sphere, create *new* public spaces for women's benefit, and repurpose private spaces. The head of AP's State Women's Commission, Dr. Tripurana, explains that female *Pradhans* explicitly encourage new strategies of political action, including:

Women have gotten confidence because they [act] as a group, not just one – so on behalf of the group they [demand resources, including to] go to the bank and register for loans. This gives women political confidence too. After 1993 [the Constitutional Amendment requiring reservations], there was a lot of change in villages. Before, just men sat in Panchayat meetings, but now women participate, speak up. Because of the 1993 Amendment, now there is a political shift in leadership [which makes political space women's collective space].[35]

Historically, Indian women have been unwilling to engage the state due to the absence of a positive template for successful female negotiations with public servants, including land revenue bureaucrats (VROs) and *Pradhans*. When women do approach state spaces – particularly, those for enforcement of rights – such as the local *Panchayat*, court *zilla adalat or kachari* or police station *(thana)* alone, they are at best ignored or dismissed and at worst assaulted.[36] The very structure of local state institutions – such as the district courts I visited from Haryana and Uttar Pradesh in north India to AP in south India – indicates an explicit disregard for women by the lack not only of women's presence as authorities to even the minimal facilities needed to support them, for example by neglecting to reserve even a single toilet for women's use (as opposed to many such facilities for men). In contrast, where women are female *Pradhans,* they are better able to provide a safe, explicitly public space in which women can present their demands for rights' enforcement.

For women outside of elected office, seeing a female representative at the helm of local government explicitly changes their calculation of what it means to engage the state. According to Gangaben Solanki, a Bombay-based *Dalit* activist: *"If women are elected, then women can go to them and ask for help without feeling afraid. Suppose there is a dispute. The woman feels hesitant coming before a group of men [to arbitrate marital and family disputes] ... she cannot speak freely."*[37]

Another female *Pradhan,* Muthukanni, elected to head Madhavakurichi Panchayat in Tirunelveli District of Tamil Nadu personifies the change women leaders can enact once in office (Rao, 2018b). Her popularity amongst women gave her a strong electoral victory – winning the votes of six out of seven hamlets thanks in part to her 17 years of active participation in a state microfinance program, *Pudhu Vaazhuvu*. Once in office, she faced the double disadvantage of her gender and her caste (she is a member of the *dalit* community, formerly

[35] Personal interview on January 21, 2014 in Hyderabad, AP, India.   [36] Majumdar (2014).
[37] Shah and Gandhi (1991, 19) *The Quota Question*. Mumbai: Akshara, c.f. Datta (1998b, 120). Datta (ibid) notes: "Although Gangaben is talking in the context of *Caste Panchayats* ... her point holds for *Gram Panchayats*."

known as untouchables). As of her first day as the *Pradhan,* men from the dominant, higher Maravar caste refused to let her enter the *Panchayat.* She persevered, first moving the *Panchayat* meetings to the neighboring hamlet library, in Venkalapoddal, where "it was attended in huge numbers by women" despite the boycott by men from the dominant caste. Subsequently, Muthukanni was able to secure Corporate Social Responsibility funds from the largest local factory, India Cements, to build a proper, air-conditioned *Panchayat* office open to all constituents – male and female, high and low caste – in Madhavakurichi.

A third female *Pradhan* in rural Maharashtra exemplifies how opening public space to women increases not only their physical mobility to demand rights but also their access to information about the explicit content of these rights:

Women should be informed about various things. They should be told that unless they move about, mix with people, they won't know how things are, how the atmosphere is. Let them say anything behind our backs, or criticize us, we should walk ahead. We shouldn't retreat.[38]

According to a female lawyer, the impact of such information campaigns is clear:

"Formally, no one educates women about their [legal inheritance] rights, [except] those [female political] leaders and the [local] women's groups [they support]." In contrast, when women are not the political gatekeepers, *"it is all about [women] being proactive and coming forward to contest their rights"* alone.[39]

These strategies by female *Pradhans* are directly linked to a broader commitment by many (albeit not all) to invest in the hard work of ensuring women know about their rights, that women's awareness of these legal entitlements is public knowledge, and that women are able to secure enforcement of their rights. Here, I'm most interested in enforcement of women's rights to inherit land.

For example, Pasupathi, a female gatekeeper based in the Madurai district of Tamil Nadu, "a region infamous for its girl-killing," put these strategies to extremely effective use. She obtained government approval and funding for a women's community center on the village's common land. Once at the helm, young and old women from Pullaneri village met together to be educated about their legal prerogatives and how to fight for social change "from cradle [against female infanticide, which as a result of their efforts is no longer common] to the classrooms [where there still are pressures]" and marriage, by countering expectations for expensive dowries.[40]

Such public promotion of women's rights changes family dynamics. As another woman in the same district explains: *"After the meetings, women have*

---

[38] Interview with Satyabhama "Nani" Lawand by Joshi (1998, 60).
[39] Personal interview with R. B., January 7, 2017 at AV College, Hyderabad, AP.
[40] Girls Count (2016).

demanded their rightful share of property. In fact, brothers have given [shares] to their sisters. This happened because they know we're aware of our rights."[41] The combination of legal acumen and opportunities to farm agricultural land has leveled the prior hierarchy in this woman's family. In her words: *"When we were young, father used to eat first at home. Now, all of us sit around and eat together"* (ibid).

I observed similar outcomes across many interviews. For example, in a mandal (subdistrict) of rural Khammam District with a female *Pradhan,* a critical mass of women were able to request and receive land rights from the local state. In particular, of the 16 women I interviewed there, all were members of Scheduled Castes who had recently received land in their name with the state's help. This contrasts dramatically with a neighboring mandal led by a male *Pradhan,* where VROs explained that women and their claims to ancestral land were virtually invisible.

What varied? Here, centrally imposed quotas mandated that the local government's elected *Pradhan* be a woman in the latest electoral round. When I arrived, the female *Pradhan* proudly introduced herself, and a group of women quickly gathered around her on the local government office's porch. The women introduced themselves and discussed the benefits of receiving their land with local government help: *"It [the land] makes a difference for [us]. It yields good crops (cotton) and profits for [us]."*[42]

Indeed, women reflect that while they were skeptical at the initial implementation of the quota system through the *Panchayati Raj* Constitutional reforms, things have changed now that they have a female *Pradhan:* *"Day by day we are having more land. We have [gained] a bit of land for some time now [since the female* Pradhan's *ascension in this village]. By this Act [the expansion of women's political leadership through reservations], we will have more land."*[43]

According to the female gatekeeper I interviewed in Khammam District, the combination of ancestral land in her name and political voice has changed her life: *"Four years ago, I became the Sarpaunch* [Pradhan]. *Before, I was a housewife. Now, I attend meetings and do my work actively, which brings me new respect. Now, regarding land, I take the decisions by sitting with my husband"* (ibid).

For one of her female constituents whom I will refer to as M., the income she receives from land titled in her name enables her to provide security for

---

[41] Documented by ibid.

[42] Personal interview with Pradhan and 16 women on March 30, 2010 in Mathapuram Village, Mudagonda Mandal, Khammam District, AP.

[43] Personal interview with women in Mathapuram Village Mandal Samakhya Meeting on March 30, 2010 in Mathapuram Village, Mudagonda Mandal, Khammam District, AP.

her extended family and stands in direct contrast to the danger of distributing women's inherited wealth through dowry instead of land. When asked about the small portion of land (20 goondas) she owns, the woman shares a larger story:

We both (my husband and I) make decisions about the land. We have a daughter and two sons, but our daughter expired. She married in Muzzaffarnagar district (in Uttar Pradesh). Her husband murdered her six years ago over the issue of dowry. We promised dowry, and paid Rs. 5000. For [another] 3000 Rupees he harassed her, said false things about her, and eventually murdered her. My daughter had two children [who are still in school]. They are staying with us. While we are alive, we will look after our daughter's children with the support of [my] land. After then, others will decide.[44]

As M.'s case illustrates, distribution of monetary dowry can initiate vicious cycles of violence against the very women such resources are meant to empower (Bloch and Rao, 2002; Bhalotra et al., 2018). In contrast, land inheritance in women's names provides them with the agency to support entire families, including survivors of violence, and a greater ability to exit fraught households prior to experiencing violent assault (Panda and Agarwal, 2005).

This brings us to the third and most crucial way in which female gatekeepers catalyze social change. Willingness by female gatekeepers to publicize and support women's rights often alters the intrahousehold distribution of rights and resources. Indeed, one of the greatest benefits of quotas (or reservations) is to make the state an appropriate avenue for women to not only demand property rights but also to gain support for conducting private (as well as public) negotiations of what are often high-stakes conflicts over the distribution of valuable, scarce rights.

Female representatives are responsible for social transformations in large part because they bridge what are typically considered private and public spaces. As Datta (1998b, 114) explains, female-led *Panchayats*, in conjunction with the women's movement, have *"redefined the conventional idea of "politics", bringing into the public, formal, political domain issues which were earlier located in a private, informal, apolitical domain.... Women[-led] Panchayats offer a chance to visibilize women's concerns."*

Once in gatekeeper positions, women indicate their willingness to act as catalysts: contesting a broader system of economic and social norms that disadvantage all members of their communities. Yet they often do so against a broader template of men's resistance. For example, amidst a large public interview in a tiny village elsewhere in Khammam district, when I asked a female official who came to power through women's reservations why she chose to run for office, men jumped to answer my question before she could respond,

---

[44] Personal interview with Respondent Number 10, on March 30, 2010 in Mathapuram Village, Mudagonda Mandal, Khammam District, AP.

claiming: "We chose her as our leader."[45] The female official then stepped in to assert her perspective:

"I chose to run on my own," she declared, with the first caveat: *"Of course, my husband agreed to it first. I don't want to have a bad reputation."* When pushed as to whether she has decision-making power over her responsibilities independent of her husband, she became more assertive: *"As long as my village is better, I don't care what happens to my husband."*[46]

Despite her initial hesitation to openly contest traditional norms, this female politician used her position to muscularly advance her village's development in the face of powerful competing interests. When the central government, along with large landholders and corporate interests set out to build water plants that would severely pollute local agricultural land and groundwater, she mobilized public opinion, drawing large numbers of women and men to protest the construction.

As a result of female political leadership, we see shifts in the private sphere, where women meet female elected "representatives at their homes and [confide] their problems" (Brown, Ananthpur, and Giovarelli, 2002, 45). Women clearly benefit: sisters and daughters claim rights to parental property without any "visible value judgment or social censure attached" (ibid.).

Accounts from across India confirm that reservations simultaneously alter women's public and private identities. For example, as gatekeepers, women have the power to alter parental attitudes about marriage, such as in Haryana where a mother notes she *"not only gave up the ghunghat [veil] but also married off her two sons without taking dowry [from brides]" due to her female Pradhan's influence"* (JaagoRe, 2014).

It is crucial to note that women's public behavior is reinforcing these changes within private, familial life. One member of an all-women's Self Help Group (SHG) in AP – whose colleague from her SHG was elected to be the village's *Pradhan* when reservations were in place – explains how quotas alter female constituents' willingness to make a much broader range of what Kruks-Wisner (2018) calls "claims" on the state:

After women's entry into the public space via reservations for female Pradhans, women's public voice was reinforced by women joining Self Help Groups and village Social Action Committees. As a result, "the village officials [Pradhans] became also responsible for certain [public] works in the village. So they, [Pradhans] invite us to their meetings, and we invite them to ours. In the past, we used to say something to the Sarpaunch [Pradhan] but [he] didn't hear it. Today, women's voices are heard. Now Sarpaunches also council parents [as we demand] to stop child marriages .... In some villages, Sarpaunches make many committees to improve sanitation, schools, road construction, and janmabhoomi

[45] Personal interview with the Mandal-level *Panchayat*'s elected head, along with approximately 30 members of a 2,000-inhabitant village two hours outside Hyderabad, AP, on January 8, 2017.
[46] Ibid.

(teams ensuring local enforcement of pensions, health, and empowerment programs).[47]
*If people do not have the right records (aadar, for jobs or ration cards), they now inquire,
make committees, and take action."*[48]

In fieldwork, I consistently found female *Pradhans* transformed women's
expectations and actions. Take the case of Padmawathi, the female *Pradhan* in
a coastal AP village whom I introduced in the preceding chapter. In addition
to keeping a watchful eye on all relevant documents in the village, she has
successfully helped women claim land inheritance rights and acquire titles from
the state.[49]

During my visit to Padmawathi's *Panchayat*, women filled her office, pointing
out the ways in which she had helped them secure property rights, including
plots for new homes in their names, and connections to electrical grids and road
networks. Indeed, each meeting I conducted with female *Pradhans* included a
solid contingent of women who proudly occupied seats near the *Pradhan* and
myself. This stood in stark contrast to my interviews with male *Pradhans,* where
men dominated the physical and verbal space.

Throughout my research, I found that women's willingness and ability
to make claims for rights upon the local state was entirely different where
reservations for female *Pradhans* were in place. It is often women's acute
understanding of how challenging it is to navigate public space and at the
same time how important the state's resources are for *all women,* as Kruks-
Wisner (2011) provides striking evidence of in post-Tsunami in Tamil Nadu,
that motivates them to run for public office. Once reservations open the door,
women's recognition of the long history of repression combined with their
resolve to forge a more equitable path that forward – for themselves personally
as well as women more generally – often propels a vibrant activism on behalf
of their female constituents.

Of course, I am speaking here in general terms. Not every woman is a
stalwart advocate of female empowerment, and such "commitment" may be
generated primarily by the interest to win competitive elections (as women do
successfully) or by persistent demands raised by female constituents upon a
given woman's assumption of this role. Regardless of the motive, this does not
dilute the importance of the changes I found where political power changed
hands from men to women.

---

[47] Personal interview in Krishna District, AP, Spring 2015. In AP this is a recently implemented program, which the government describes as "a people centered development and
welfare programme 'Janmabhoomi–MaaVooru." For details on this scheme's form in AP, see:
http://jbmv.ap.gov.in.

[48] Personal interview with Padmawathi and colleagues in March 2015, Krishna district, AP.

[49] Personal interview, first with Jamuna Paruchuri, Former SERP Gender Head on January 21,
2014 in Hyderabad, AP; confirmed by personal visit and interview with Padmawathi, on
January 18, 2016 at her office, Kanchikacherla Mandal Headquarters, Krishna District, AP.

2.5 MAPPING IMPACT: WHAT ABOUT BACKLASH?

Transformative social reforms almost inevitably have unintended consequences.

Here, I consider when we should expect female gatekeepers' enforcement of gender-equalizing property rights reform not to tilt economic agency toward women, but rather prompt resistance by those who traditionally inherit property (men) and the family members who rely on their care (parents). Resistance is significant because it has the potential to mitigate female economic autonomy or nullify it altogether.

To consider when resistance to reform may dominate any positive influence of female gatekeepers, I focus on the main actors in determining inheritance: natal families, whom I define as parents and children. This is a clean way to model the standard organization of interests in ancestral property: prior to reform, title has traditionally been passed from fathers to sons, who jointly own land. Gender-equalizing inheritance reform, of course, changed that in law but not necessarily in practice. Inheritance strategies and decisions affect not just the natal family but also the subsequent pool of marital alliances. I conclude by considering the consequences of these decisions for a daughter's marital options and her subsequent well-being. To consider how inheritance reform should change behavior, let me begin with a brief discussion of inheritance coordination prior to legal change.

Life before Gender Equalizing Reform

I characterize the collective interests of families as twofold: coordination of production (to maximize wealth) and optimization of social status (as a source of prestige, security, and fulfillment).[50] This is a simplification that I make to consider whether these two sets of interests create mutually reinforcing or mutually undermining dynamics (Greif, 2006, 15–17).[51]

Prior to land inheritance reform, I argue that the equilibrium behavior dictated by social institutions has been to provide ancestral wealth to daughters exclusively as monetary dowry and to sons as property. Hindu families typically distribute a daughter's "share" of her natal family's ancestral property as monetary dowry. Historically, traditional forms of dowry varied across locales

---

[50] Advice from Jon Bendor was integral to the organization of this section. All errors are my own.

[51] Greif posits that institutions can either reinforce or undermine themselves; that is, they can reinforce (or undermine) the relevance of the "rules of the game," such that they become self-enforcing for an increasingly larger (or smaller) set of parameters. For example, consider a case in which individuals use the more efficient agricultural production spurred by the Green Revolution to lobby for social prestige, adopting more socially conservative patterns of behavior such as relegating women's movement (part of what Srinivas [1956] calls "Sanskritization"). Here, as wealth requires less coordination, more individuals adhere to "conservative," gender-inegalitarian social norms, making these institutions self-reinforcing. In contrast, greater wealth could improve information and human capital, enabling the critique and disavowal of socially conservative barriers to individual agency as Shami (2017) finds proximity to roads enables in Pakistan, making coordination of production and conservative social norms self-undermining.

and families. In many parts of Southern India, the practice of giving *Stridhan* or "women's wealth" was widespread. However, pressure by British colonial administrators altered the practice of transferring wealth directly to the bride. As a result, wealth held by the bride has virtually disappeared. Today, dowry is seen as the groom and his family's possession rather than the bride's property.[52]

The arrival of female *Pradhans* prior to reform enabled daughters to be more comfortable and confident in claiming notional rights to ancestral land. Where a daughter made such a claim, I predict it was unlikely to upset traditional, gender-specific norms about wealth distribution because her share of inheritance was only a small, symbolic fraction compared to that of a son, and thus not comparable to – or able to substitute for – dowry.[53]

I argue traditional norms were inefficient (Pareto suboptimal) strategies for distributing ancestral wealth. Why? The practice of "early" (premortem) distribution of familial resources to daughters as dowry has alternatives that could optimize family resources: giving *property* to all children could improve familial wealth.

Dowry is materially inefficient for three reasons: it inhibits the optimal strategy of specialization based on comparative advantage; it is more costly – in terms of material transfers, economic coordination, and productivity – and it has a greater risk of resulting in turbulent marriages, with greater probability of harm for daughters and extortion of the family's wealth for additional dowry. I address each in turn.

First, by excluding daughters from property inheritance *ex ante*, support for the institution of dowry reduces the likelihood that the child with the greatest skill in managing property and other facets of family wealth will be able to specialize in this task (by artificially halving the set of children allowed to manage property).

Second, the cost of dowry – which is high enough to encourage female infanticide[54] and by many estimates growing – frequently requires sales of property (Anderson and Bidner 2015).[55] According to Anjali Dave, Associate Professor of Women's Studies at the Tata Institute for Social Sciences in Mumbai: *In order to pay for dowry: "People sell land and get bankrupt after marriage .... Globalization and the market economy have escalated dowry prices to an amount that you and I can't comprehend"* (Ramakrishnan, 2013).

---

52 Uberoi (1994).

53 Desai (2010).

54 For recent articles on the extent of dowry-related violence, see: Bloch and Rao (2002); Srinivasan and Bedi (2007); Bhalotra et al. (2019); and Bhalotra, Chakravarty, and Gulesci (2018). Also see: Gentleman (2006), Sukumar (2017), and Jha (2014).

55 On the magnitude of dowry, Anderson (2007, 154) cites evidence, likely a lower bound, that it amounts to "several times more than total annual household income." Anukriti, Kwon, and Prakash (2018) find families whose first-born child is a girl start saving immediately at birth to pay dowry; those with a first-born boy, who plan to receive dowry, save at much lower rates. Dowry in Maharashtra's rural villages can be 5–7 lakh Rupees (US $7,900–11,000) for well-educated grooms (Ramakrishnan, 2013).

The phenomenon of liquidating valuable property to pay for dowry is not limited to rural areas. According to Rashmi Misra, who founded a Delhi-based nongovermental organization (NGO) for women's empowerment and education: *"The richest in Delhi pay for their daughter's husband in the form of a Mercedes, furnished apartments and hard cash."*[56]

Selling sizable amounts of ancestral property to finance dowry payments reduces both the acreage the family owns and the returns to investment on such property, the main source of wealth with the highest rate of return in India.[57] Thus, considering the material trade-off between selling property (and potentially incurring debt) for a daughter's dowry versus redistributing property titles within the family, between sons and daughters, and maintaining the integrity of jointly held land, the benefits of the latter strategy – complying with gender equal inheritance law – are clear. While social norms traditionally deemed married daughters to be members of a separate, patrilineal family (the groom's), there is notable evidence of change on this front, which has led to "beti villages" where grooms join the families of brides, even in bastions of conservatism such as Haryana, north India (Chowdhry, 2005).

Yet even if gender equal land inheritance is less costly in terms of material transfers, could it create a second form of cost: reducing the efficiency of agricultural production? Agarwal (1994, 34–7) provides evidence that the answer is no: including female inheritors does not lead to less efficient, smaller farms; multiple owners do not preclude effective coordination. While women farmers may be less efficient than men, data suggests this is due to women's limited access to productive inputs, which greater female inheritance should diminish (Goldstein and Udry, 2008).

The third and final consideration of dowry's material inefficiency concerns the quality of marital alliances it imposes on daughters. The provision of dowry frequently leads to threats of violence or "terror as a bargaining instrument," to extract further monetary transfers from a bride's natal family after marriage (Bloch and Rao, 2002). Such intimidation is widespread and, when most severe, results in murder. Indeed, the National Crime Records Bureau of India reports statistics of "dowry deaths," estimated at 8,233 in 2012. This is equivalent to the murder of one woman every 60 minutes (Ramakrishnan, 2013). Due to widespread social stigma against divorce, wives are unlikely to leave their marriages in the face of violence. When considering dowry in its most popular, one-dimensional, liquid monetary form, payments from a daughter's natal family to her marital family, it is potentially limitless. This suggests that the abusive pillaging of resources by the marital family is also potentially boundless. Furthermore, as such transfers are usually made directly by the

[56] Ramakrishnan (2013).
[57] Land has tended to accrue value over time since the green revolution, which has made agricultural land more productive and more valuable independent of its productive capacity, in light of India's increasing land scarcity with an associated rise in demand for both agricultural production and residential property.

authority figures in each family, there is no way of knowing whether a daughter will benefit from the exchange.[58]

In contrast, distributing inheritance as title to ancestral land gives a daughter autonomy separate from both (natal and marital) families, increasing her agency about whether to marry, whom to marry, and whether to remain in a marriage. Such independence translates into lower levels of domestic violence against women with property rights (Panda and Agarwal, 2005). It also limits the prospective pool of prospective marriage partners (Anderson and Bidner, 2015). However, given the potential of dowry to contribute to turbulent marriages where violence becomes a tool to coerce further payments from a bride's natal family, another way to interpret this smaller pool is to consider it a higher quality subset of potential grooms.

What Does Reform "Buy" Families?

If this assessment of equilibrium behavior is correct, inheritance reform enables families to choose a Pareto-superior distribution of resources, shifting away from less efficient transmission of ancestral wealth to daughters through dowries in favor of more efficient wealth transmission through rights to ancestral property. Such distribution increases the likelihood that families maximize wealth by concentrating their investment in their most lucrative (property) resources. While not all families will be able to choose this Pareto-superior outcome, those who are able and willing to do so should anticipate accruing larger stocks of wealth than families who follow the prereform equilibrium behavior of distributing dowry to daughters. In other words, there are good reasons for eligible families to anticipate material benefits from reform and voluntarily comply.[59]

Are reform's advantages limited? Inheritance reform enables families *who have not yet distributed dowries to daughters* to successfully coordinate around provision of land rather than dowry as female inheritance. However, reform does not help *families who have already distributed dowry* shift behavior accordingly. Given that roughly 90 percent of Indian marriages in contemporary India involve the exchange of dowry, I assume that most married daughters have already received dowry. Such families are unable to repossess these resources and, as such, likely view an additional distribution of land inheritance to the same daughter as unjust and financially nonviable. For these families, reform represents an accumulation rather than an adjustment of obligation. This creates a testable hypothesis: I expect backlash when reform creates a *double material burden* on the distribution of familial resources, rather than *reducing* material burdens.

---

[58] Indeed, the only certainty is that a daughter's worth has been calculated in monetary form, with troubling implications for responses to dissatisfaction within the marriage (Bloch and Rao, 2002).

[59] Note that this logic does not imply that all possible outcomes postreform will be Pareto-superior to prereform equilibrium outcomes for families.

When are the wealth-optimizing opportunities of reform clearest? My gatekeeper theory suggests that the most optimal, advantageous circumstance is for families with daughters who are eligible for reform and *entering marriage negotiations in the presence of female gatekeepers*. As women, these gatekeepers can and do encourage discussion of alternative resource distribution strategies when they are most relevant: at the time marriages are being brokered.

Yet, backlash may not be grounded solely in material motives. If behavior is driven exclusively by monetary incentives, we would expect backlash to be limited to families who already distributed dowry. However, concerns about social status may also drive behavior. Here, I refer to social status as something intrinsically valuable, to the extent that individuals may be willing to sacrifice material payoffs to enhance it (Shayo, 2009). Borrowing from social psychology, "status" can be defined through social comparisons with other groups along socially significant categories.[60]

In India, as in much of the world, marriage is one of the most significant points for signaling and reinforcing social status. Here, the high-status reference group is frequently drawn from the upper castes (in particular, *Brahmans* in North India) whose traditional use of dowry gives this practice particular social value for members not only of upper castes but also, more importantly, lower castes aspiring to increase their social prestige across Indian regions and religions today (Srinivas, 1956; Uberoi, 1994, 232–4). Thus, gifts of monetary dowry signal – and reinforce – the social status of the natal family who distributes them (and, by extension, that of the daughter given in marriage). Amongst families for whom concerns about social status dominate, the mandate to give daughters equal shares of ancestral property, as dictated by reform, would not eliminate the social relevance of monetary dowry. Thus, recognizing a daughter's rights to inherit property could easily become prohibitively expensive in addition to socially stigmatized as a deviation from the norm of dowry provision.

For families concerned with optimizing social status, the more uncertain they are about whether reform will be enforced, the more likely they are to evade it. For these families, attempts by female *Pradhans* to facilitate the move from dowry to property inheritance will be effective only to the extent families believe that the cost of evasion will be higher than the cost of compliance.

We now have a rough map of when to expect backlash, based on the strength of conflicting motivations for behavior postreform. This is essentially an argument about behavior "in the shadow of the law," where individual willingness to voluntarily comply with reform depends on both the material rewards of compliance and the likelihood that they will be punished for noncompliance.[61] If information on enforcement is limited, this suggests noncompliance with reform – that is backlash – is plausible *even if reform were to materially benefit all families*. Why? Coordination of behavior around a single,

---

[60] Shayo (2009, 50–1).   [61] Dixit (2007).

equilibrium strategy – here, compliance with reform – requires the probability of enforcement to be common knowledge. For families to collectively agree to comply, everyone must know not only that reform will be enforced, but also that everyone else knows that reform will be enforced. This exacting level of knowledge is unlikely given initial expectations that gender-equalizing inheritance reform would *not* be enforced, and the lack of foresight that female gatekeepers *would* enable enforcement.[62]

This leads to three hypotheses about variation in familial responses to reform:

H1. For families with eligible daughters entering marriage negotiations, the presence of a female gatekeeper should increase compliance with reform.

H2. For families with eligible daughters who have completed marriage negotiations, the presence of a female gatekeeper should increase resistance to reform.

H3. For families with eligible daughters entering marriage negotiations, where information about reform's enforcement is incomplete, the greater the value they place on social status, the more female gatekeeper presence should increase resistance to reform.

The value of social status presents the greatest challenge for measurement. As a first attempt, I hypothesize that the importance of social status may vary in direct proportion to socioeconomic inequality. I consider such inequality as a barrier to coordination around more egalitarian social norms of inheritance – just as inequality can constrain support for egalitarian political norms of democracy.

From studies of democratization, we know that transformation of political institutions from elite to mass control is particularly unlikely at high levels of inequality, such as when a monarch can unilaterally expropriate, and hence concentrate wealth without bounds (North and Weingast, 1989). As inequality diminishes, nonelites are able to make credible threats to overturn the existing political order, thus making redistribution of formal power by elites – that is democratization – worthwhile in exchange for their survival (Acemoglu and Robinson, 2005).

I hypothesize that a similar dynamic exists within social institutions. Where socioeconomic inequality is "too" high, we should expect demands by nonelites (such as women and/or members of lower castes or classes) for redistribution of social and material rights – here, to property inheritance – to lack credibility. I assume the penalty of deviating from social norms to claim new rights is a loss in social status (sanctioning for inappropriate behavior), with possible material consequences (ranging from temporary ostracism to expulsion, which limit socially-facilitated opportunities to accrue material resources). I expect higher levels of inequality to be associated with a greater reliance on social identity as well as social precariousness, such that even a slight "fall" down

---

[62] In sum, I expect backlash to reform amongst some families in the effort to reach a stable equilibrium. That is, backlash is the result of out-of-equilibrium dynamics.

the ladder results in marked changes in a family's social prestige. Here, the cost of social sanctions for deviation outweigh the highly uncertain benefit: a daughter's ability to claim and control ancestral property.

In contrast, at moderate levels of inequality, the potential to coordinate around new, more egalitarian social norms may gain traction as a growing percentage of individuals with not insubstantial levels of socioeconomic power have sufficient voice and resources to bear the consequences of social sanctions over the long term – thus making demands for social change credible. At these intermediate levels of socio-economic inequality, the presence of female gatekeepers may enable fundamental changes in young women's willingness to demand inheritance rights as they enter marriage negotiations.

Finally, at the highest levels of equality, the ability of female gatekeepers to support "integrative bargains" around egalitarian norms may not present a relevant new channel for negotiation of rights. This logic should hold if socioeconomic equality enables both women and men to pursue alternative, nonconflictual processes of negotiating rights and resources. If this set of predictions linking the impact of social status with levels of socioeconomic inequality holds, an inverted U-shaped relationship should exist between inequality and claims to ancestral property rights by eligible women entering marriage markets in the presence of female gatekeepers. This would mirror the Acemoglu and Robinson (2005) theory of the relationship between inequality and the probability of transitions to democracy, such that political change is unlikely to occur in either highly inegalitarian or highly egalitarian societies.

In subsequent analysis, I test the importance of social status as a predictor of backlash by considering whether the impact of reform varies alongside socioeconomic inequality. Given its relevance to this book, my focus here is on landownership within one's village as a meaningful dimension of status and agency. This is an early attempt. I do hope this work opens the door to future research that measures the impact of inequality more holistically, following work by Baldwin and Huber (2010), Huber and Suryanarayan (2016), Huber (2017), Kasara (2013), Kasara and Mares (2017).

2.5.1 Choice Bracketing: Transforming Backlash to Support

How exactly can female gatekeepers catalyze change in decisionmaking, such that parents and brothers become willing to deviate from traditional norms and the certainty (material and social) that following the status quo provides? Negotiation around integrative bargaining – where all parties benefit – generates space for parents to accept and benefit from daughters' rights.

To explain, let me return to the larger question motivating my theory: How does a low-status group challenge and destabilize an inegalitarian order? Where members of the group enter positions at the apex of the relevant power structure, their ability to facilitate negotiations of integrative bargains between low- and high-status groups enables coordination around new, more egalitarian equilibrium strategies. This is possible for two reasons: young women entering marriage markets have a valuable commodity to trade – monetary dowry – at a time when they have a powerful ally who can not only lead negotiations on their behalf but ensure everyone identifies real, concrete advantages from the resulting bargains: a female head of local government.

To illuminate how this happens, I employ the language of choice bracketing. According to Read et al. (1999, 172–3), choice bracketing is one piece of decision-making. Specifically, choice bracketing studies whether we cast the net of alternative strategies we consider at a given moment narrowly or broadly. The major point is that sequential decision making over a complex issue (using narrow choice bracketing) leads to a far narrower, more conflict-prone set of options than integrative bargains (using broad choice bracketing).

Figure 2.2 illustrates the varied choices that result from narrow versus broad choice bracketing. Note that narrow choice bracketing is default behavior. Individuals tend to frame choices as one-dimensional trade-offs. This has two downsides: it limits the set of available options and encourages perception of decisions as "zero sum," where one party gains at the other's expense. In the case of a brother considering whether to accept his sister's request for an equal share of ancestral property following gender-equalizing land inheritance reform, "narrow" choice bracketing leads to separate decision-making processes about how to distribute wealth as dowry versus as land inheritance (Scenario A, Figure 2.2). The result of such bargains is often that a brother will see his sister's

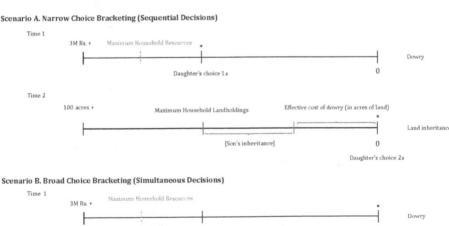

FIGURE 2.2. Choice Bracketing

demand for equal inheritance rights purely as an economic loss for himself, and hence be unlikely to support her request (especially if the family has already liquidated property to pay for her dowry).

In contrast, broad choice bracketing frames choices in a more comprehensive context, including overlapping decisions, each of which has the potential for loss *or* gain (Scenario B, Figure 2.2). As a result, all concerned parties have an opportunity to benefit. In the case of the brother mentioned previously, using a "broad" choice bracket would enable him and his sister to simultaneously negotiate the distribution of inheritance, dowry, and, potentially, responsibility for elder parents. Within this larger framework of options, a brother may be willing to cede significant inheritance rights if his sister *simultaneously* offers not only to deny any groom who demands dowry but also to choose a marriage that enables her to share the duty of caring for elder parents. The brother benefits by offsetting the loss in exclusive property rights by minimizing other monetary obligations (to transfer land for dowry) and social obligations (shared care for elder parents).

In Figure 2.2, Scenario B illustrates this welfare-enhancing shift for a daughter – who receives enduring rights to ancestral property *in her name* rather than transitory dowry *given directly to in-laws,* as in Scenario A. There is also a welfare gain for the household. The family has avoided selling valuable ancestral land to pay for a daughter's dowry, and is able to distribute inheritance rights equally to a daughter and a son, without reducing a son's quantum of inheritance. In the language of bargaining theory, this allows for "integrative solutions" where "the good parts of some alternatives compensate for the bad parts of others."[63] Such solutions minimize the likelihood of backlash and maximize benefits for all parties.

2.6 INVESTIGATING RESISTANCE: EVIDENCE FROM FIELD RESEARCH

The question is, can women overcome the anticipated social and material costs to deviation from status quo inheritance with help from female gatekeepers? To answer this, I let my respondents speak for themselves as much as possible.

Over the course of my field research, women's most frequent concern about demanding property inheritance rights was resistance by brothers, the status quo beneficiaries of (traditional, patrilineal) land inheritance, first and fore- most, as well as with parents who were secondary but still crucial guarantors of female welfare. Again and again, my interviews revealed that compliance with

---

[63] Read et al. (1999, 177). This work draws from a larger literature on negotiation that supports the benefits of "integrative" negotiations – that is, negotiations across multiple issues – relative to "distributive" negotiations where only a single issue is discussed, where negotiators are more likely to view benefits and costs as a zero-sum game where only one party can "win" a given negotiation (Babcock et al., 2003, 166).

gender-equalizing reform is seen as a direct threat to the brothers of women now guaranteed equal shares of property inheritance. Prem Chowdhry states the case bluntly:

"[R]ural patriarchal forces" have worked to limit the property insecurity that results from women's new property inheritance rights by a variety of means. An important way has been to pose the inheritance right of a daughter and a sister to be against that of the brother.... For this the brother-sister bonds of love have also been greatly encouraged as seen in the noticeable revival of Raksha Bandhan *festival [where sisters tie a sacred thread or* rakhi *on their brothers' wrists and pray for brothers' well-being, in return for brothers' promise to protect sisters] and the renewed sanctity it has claimed in north India.*[64]

Brothers regularly cite the monetary burden of dowry payments as justifying opposition to gender-equal land inheritance. Additionally, as women's participation in the labor force declines, the size of dowries must increase to compensate a husband's family for accepting ever-more-dependent women as wives.[65] Recent accounts suggest that extended families residing outside India make demands for dowries totaling as much as a half a million US dollars.[66] As one mother explains: *"We're spending a huge amount on her ... marriage ... why should we give land? This is not required."*[67]

Virilocal marriage norms dictate that sons remain in their natal homes, enabling them to cultivate and manage ancestral property while providing long-term care for aging parents. In contrast, daughters bring monetary dowry (rather than land inheritance) into their husbands' homes, which are commonly not in their natal village, where ancestral land is nearly always located (Rosenzweig and Stark, 1989). In addition, sons are traditionally the sole practitioners of the sacred Hindu death rites for their parents that "propitiate their souls after death."[68] These deep-seated norms and practices legitimize the property inheritance claims of sons while contesting or denying outright those of daughters. As a result, a consistent theme across my two years of field research was the fear frequently expressed by sisters that any demand they might make for inheritance would result in backlash by brothers. In one woman's words: *"As a boy [inheritance] is his right. So if [my parents] give [inheritance] to me, others will tell the boy he got less [than he should], so he will quarrel, litigate, fight. So they [parents] won't give and we won't ask."*[69]

Such fears are at least in part the result of pressure that is consistently placed on daughters from early childhood onward to renounce rights. This can range from "encouragement" to sign away inheritance, with support from a panoply of repurposed cultural practices – such as Chowdhry (1997)'s example

---

[64] Chowdhry (1997, 1026).   [65] See, for example, Barry (2016).   [66] See Sukumar (2017).
[67] Personal interview, FGD 3, Respondent 1, November 29, 2010, Rotarypuram, Anantapur, AP.
[68] Gough (1956).
[69] Personal interview No. 13, November 14, 2010, Chompi Village, Araku, Vishakapatanam, AP.

of annual *Raksha Bandhan* celebrations – to explicit challenges: court cases or possession of land by force (Gowen, 2016).

Overall, the belief that demanding rights decisively destroys a daughter's relationship with her natal family explains the most widely expressed rationale for women remaining silent *despite* understanding the value of inherited land and the scope of law entitling them to claim it on par with sons. A widely circulated story (rural myth?) epitomizes the fear of consequences:

A woman successfully litigated for her legal inheritance share, *"but when she dragged [her family] to court her elder brother died of cardiac arrest, while her parents suffered badly. They severed their relationship with [her]. . . . The people say that she had won the property but had lost the [brother and] parents."*[70]

Even women's activists claim such resistance to be unavoidable, explaining: *"Everyone agrees that 'Only because of love [fear of losing brothers' support] women (sisters) are not asking brothers for land.' In order to cover or smooth over problems in the family, women won't ask for land."*[71]

Survey work by Landesa confirms these patterns: 53 percent of 1,440 female respondents to their recent survey in AP, Bihar, and Madhya Pradesh do not believe their brothers would "agree with the idea of their sisters receiving land" (Sircar and Pal, 2014, 12). Of 360 male respondents, 45 percent confirm they would not accept parental transfer of ancestral land to sisters.

A number of lawyers who have spent decades litigating inheritance claims provide additional support for the notion that these "bonds of affection" between siblings are acutely important for women's welfare.[72] This widespread viewpoint was articulated most clearly by a group of women, several of whom were born or married into landholding families, all living in rural village in Ibrahimpatnam Mandal, just a few hours journey outside AP's capital:

We know of women's legal rights . . . recently we are hearing about this but no one is fighting with their family. . . . [We know about this because] land rates are rising these last four to six years. [As a result] discussions about land are more amongst families. . . . We learn [about legal rights] from court cases . . . but no one is courageous enough to stand up for themselves amongst women.[73]

But why exactly is courage required to demand rights? According to Vindhya Undurti, a professor at the Tata Institute of Social Sciences, Hyderabad campus, AP:

[70] Author and SERP's survey of T. S., SERP Gender Unit Training, February 21, 2011, Krishna District, AP.
[71] Personal interview with Social Action Committee members and Mandal Samakhya Presidents, in particular with N., April 11, 2010, Krishna District, AP.
[72] Personal interview with Male Lawyers #1 and #2, January 7, 2017, AV College, Hyderabad, India.
[73] Personal interview, Focus Group #3 on February 17, 2011 in Ibrahimpatnam Mandal, Ranga Reddy District, AP.

The language of "rights" rather than "responsibilities" for women is threatening to society in India. This threat seems bigger now given that women are seen as not discharging their responsibilities [beginning with deference to male familial authorities]. Thus mentioning "rights" is seen as destabilizing the present social or domestic balance. People who worry about such destabilization make a clear demarcation between India's glorious past and the present where women demand rights and cause [problems].[74]

A leading family lawyer who has practiced for nearly three decades in AP and Telangana's capital, Hyderabad, explains opposition to gender-equal inheritance rights in extremely concrete terms:

Do you think pre-amendment [HSAA] there were true affections between brothers and sisters? If yes, then this amendment is bad. It doesn't mean that there was no sharing [of familial resources] pre-amendment. When there [was] the marriage of a daughter, an agriculturalist [would] spend 10 laks [about US $15,000] for his daughter. Post-amendment, women will demand 50 percent [of ancestral property], but by then the family already spent 10 lakhs on the daughter. There is a sentiment that women are getting more than brothers if they get dowry and inheritance.[75]

A Maharashtra-based District Court Judge provides a similar perspective: "*We cannot detach the social issues from the legal issues. [Each of our] mindset[s are] required to be changed. The mindset is not an easy thing to be changed*", [in particular, for brothers traditionally entitled to inherit property rights].[76]

Taken singularly or collectively, these powerful influences radically temper expectations of which women – if any – will initiate legal claims to inheritance. In an experienced female lawyer's account of such cases: "*Only those women whose relationships with their families are already broken [and have nothing left to lose in terms of 'the traditional bonds of affection'] will dare contest their legal inheritance rights in court.*"[77]

Other women attempt to contest inheritance rights informally, she suggested – as opposed to approaching the court – yet the risk of breaking familial relationships by demanding rights that contradict traditional norms remains severe.

An Odisha-based woman's case exemplifies both the magnitude of the conflict and the possibility of its resolution when a female *Pradhan* is present: in 2016 Sunana, 36, demanded her share of her recently deceased father's nine-acre farmland. With the female-led *Panchayat* in the background, she made a straightforward claim to inheritance: "*Land had been sold to finance the marriages of my two sisters. Since I had not married, I had an equal claim to a*

74 Personal interview with Professor Vindhya Undurti, November 15, 2010, Andhra University, Visakhapatnam, AP.
75 Personal interview with R. M. on January 7, 2017 at A. V. College, Hyderabad, AP.
76 Personal interview with Maharashtra District Court Judge on January 10, 2017 in his Court Office, Maharashtra.
77 Personal panel discussion with female lawyer #1, January 7, 2017, in Hyderabad, AP.

portion of the remaining land." Her brothers disagreed. *"Die or run away – they would say every day."*

Two months later they chased her out, battering a wooden rod against her head until she lost consciousness. The *Panchayat* intervened, negotiating a portion of the ancestral home for Sunana and her mother. They procured a state pension and subsidized food, and made space for Sunana's tailoring shop in the community center. *"Life would have been so different if I had known my options [i.e.* Pradhan-*led negotiation of rights] earlier,"* says Sunana (Awasthi, 2017).

What is important to note in Sunana's case is the fragility of "affection" by brothers. Indeed, the much-lauded provision of care and consideration by brothers to sisters can shift quickly from protection to exploitation. Another lawyer I interviewed presented a less violent but equally bleak accounting of the difficulties of negotiating rights within the family. Recounting his personal experience, he began with his aunt's story:

*My maternal uncle (*māma*) is my grandmother's only son. When my* māma's *younger sister married, about twenty years ago, my grandparents (her parents) gave her four acres of mango gardens. However her parents and her brother cultivated this land continuously throughout this time. Her parents later decided that they wanted to sell this land in order to pay the education expenses for my* māma's *son. The [property] title is still in her parent's name, and her parents merely gave an informal promise in front of [village] elders that they would gift the land to their daughter. Unfortunately, this is a common practice, such that no registration occurs of gifts to daughters. However, parents usually, traditionally, abide by these promises. Now this tradition is getting ruined.*

So then this girl's parents and her brother agree to give her some amount of land. Her brother offers to "purchase" the land from his sister at a rate of 5 lakhs [Rs. 500,000, or US $9,000] per acre, e.g. for 20 lakhs [$36,000]. If the sister was to sell this land on the open market she would get about 60 lakhs [$108,000], but she does not have a formal title deed so her parents and her brother would need to sign the exchange deed and then they would break their promise to her [to gift the land]. Additionally the sister needs money. So she agreed to this exchange orally, without ever entering a court.

Male revenge against a sister for merely asserting formal rights to ancestral property is apparent when we step back one generation, following the same AP property lawyer's maternal grandmother's (*ammamma's*) case:

My ammamma's parents had two sons, four daughters, and 18 acres of land. At my ammamma's marriage, she received 50 cents (half an acre) of land. Her other sisters received this amount of land along with gifts in cash and in kind because they married into other villages, whereas her marriage was inside her mother's village. From her mother's registered will, she received one acre of land and 35 cents house site. Her father died intestate [without a will] with six acres of land, after having given six acres to each son.[78]

[78] Note that this reflects the probability that none of the daughters' possession of the land they "received" from their parents at the time of their marriages was recognized as legitimate. Indeed, it is highly unlikely that any of the daughters residing in other villages ever gained physical possession of their land.

After my ammamma's father's death, the sons [her brothers] forcibly occupied the remaining six acres of property, thinking this is their right 'because they are males.' His sons [her brothers] say they will give cash to their sister as maintenance, but they also kicked her out of her home and off her property with nothing.

My ammamma came to her daughter [my mother] and asked for help. I filed a case on my ammamma's behalf for maintenance by her brothers. The case was disposed for [in favor of] my ammamma, but her brothers didn't pay her maintenance. So in 2009, in Khammam District ... in the Senior Civil Judge's Court, I filed a second case on my mother's behalf after my ammamma transferred her own property (1 acre and the 35 cents house site) to her daughter by registered will. I also filed a suit for eviction of my [grand] uncles from the property and main profits [due to their unlawful enjoyment of the property].

Within the single Hindu joint family's experience described in the preceding text, daughters evidence a varied ability to occupy and benefit from bequeathed ancestral property. In the younger generation, a sister bargains with her parents and brother, accepting monetary compensation for her legal rights, albeit at a grossly undervalued amount. Alternately, in the older generation, a sister's expectation that she will receive her formal share of ancestral land without bargaining for associated rights and responsibilities is the probable cause of backlash by her brothers: their malicious eviction of her from "their" rightful property without compensating her physical and monetary losses. In the face of this, the sister has no good will to salvage with her brother and is thus willing to approach the courts, with her grandson's help, to demand validation of her own and later her daughter's formal property rights.

Although the final verdict of this later case was still pending when we spoke, the direct consequences of the lawyer's *ammamma*'s demands for formal rights were clear: backlash from her brothers left her without either home or property. The apathy of courts in assuring that women's legal rights are fully realized is also clear from this case. Despite her grandson's profession and energetic support, she is unable to gain direct access to either the property to which she has been granted rights or the monetary profits from its cultivation.

To summarize, gaining meaningful resources through public engagement openly challenges women's traditional familial roles, resources, and the existing hierarchy. As a result, political quotas for women and subsequent enforcement of their economic rights by female representatives are often vilified as unacceptable breaches of culture. In such a challenging context, what makes gender-equal inheritance legislation welfare-improving rather than welfare-reducing? It is to this question that I now turn.

2.7 BARGAINING AWAY BACKLASH?

I assume that female representation is a precondition for women's effective bargaining power. I argue that female gatekeepers do not simply muffle backlash. When effective, they divest resistance of its political power by augmenting women's agency to frame integrative solutions to the struggle for control over property.

As one woman explains, the process of claiming land rights alone is a process of claiming power:

[When] *the wife asks for her land as her right – her* "hakka", *she consciously demands that she be made part-owner of the land. This is a* "hakkachi bhakri" *(literally, rightful bread), and so tastes quite different from the bread received out of* daan *(charity, donation).*[79]

Why are female *Pradhans* so effective at enabling women to raise their voices for scarce, highly valued rights in the hierarchical domain of the household? They are particularly attuned to the multiple and challenging ways in which young women need support during critical junctures. For instance, intervening when women are too young to marry legally (18 is both the legal marriage age and the mean for REDS 2006/9 round). One female gatekeeper in Krishna District, AP, temporarily sheltered an underage, 14-year-old girl whose parents tried to force her out of school and into marriage, negotiating a return of her monetary dowry to fund future land inheritance.[80]

Why is marriage such a pivotal moment? When I asked mothers to assess their daughters' future welfare, marriage stood out as the main determinant: *"our daughters aren't married yet, so we don't know yet [as to whether their lives will be better or worse than ours]."* [81]

The importance of a dowry to a family's stock of lifetime resources cannot be overestimated. Often parents start putting away money for a dowry from the time of a daughter's birth, and this significantly impacts the financial assets available for other things, including the acquisition or maintenance of land.[82] More broadly, a growing literature identifies the relevance of norms related to marriage in determining women's welfare across a range of outcomes in the developing world.[83]

However, as one VRO explained, parental investments in daughters are malleable around the time of marriage. While "dowry" is often comprised of money or material goods, this is a point where women can advocate for land instead: *"At the time of marriage, parents [may] consider giving daughters land (in place of monetary dowry). This land may be given at the time of marriage or during partition [at a father's death when rights are formalized]."*[84]

Female gatekeepers also use their physical presence to ensure that land titles for plots divided equally between brothers and sisters at the time of a sister's marriage are properly documented and recorded by the VRO.[85] For example, in one village run by a female *Pradhan* in rural AP, half of 48 women I interviewed

---

[79] Sathaye (1998, 104).
[80] Personal interview, Y. W. & class, January 18, 2016, Krishna District, AP.
[81] Personal interview with Focus Group #3, with specific responses from interviews #4 and #5, as conducted on February 17, 2011, in Ibrahimpatnam Mandal, Ranga Reddy District, AP.
[82] Browning and Subramaniam (1995); Bhalotra et al. (2019).
[83] Ashraf et al. (2016); Borker et al. (2017); Corno, Hildebrandt, and Voena (2017); Lowes and Nunn (2017).
[84] Personal interview with Tehsildar, March 25, 2010, Khammam District, AP.
[85] Personal interview with N., April 11, 2010, Krishna District, AP.

have land in their names, many through inheritance their parents gave equally to daughters and sons.[86]

As gatekeepers, women also alter broader parental attitudes about marriage. These negotiations are radically different when a female gatekeeper is not involved. Days before K. Bina Devi was married in Rajasthan, the typically all-male cadre of village elders assembled in her house as witnesses. They watched as she and her sister signed away their land inheritance shares to four brothers in exchange for receiving dowry. The ceremony is so common it has a (tragic) name: *haq tyag,* meaning "sacrifice of right." Ms. Devi explains that noncompliance with this "voluntary" ritual has a cost: "If we don't do it, our family will boycott us. Our relationship with the family will break, and people will speak ill of us" (Chandran, 2016).

Yet, my broader fieldwork suggests that even such hardened attitudes are indeed changing, in part, one can assume, as the culture acclimates itself to the presence of women in the public sphere and their growing assertiveness in private life. A good example is the case of one woman I interviewed. She and her sister each received a monetary dowry of Rs. 10,000 when they married 20 years ago. Their brother was given the entirety of the family's land, five acres, which he controls "from olden days."[87] In contrast, when this woman and her husband arranged their daughter's marriage a year ago, they made entirely different choices:

We gave her Rs. 1 lakh as cash (used for marriage festival), Rs. 50,000 in gold (which she keeps), and 50 cents [half an acre] of land. [As an aside, she adds] Our son-in-law has 10 acres of land. We wanted to give some land for our daughter's honor. This land was transferred orally, and we will decide later about the formal title transfer. Right now we are leasing the land from our daughter. We give her half of the returns to production." For the remaining 1.5 acres of their property: *"We will divide the land equally between our two sons, we've already given 50 cents of land [worth about Rs. 1.5 lakhs] and Rs. 1.5 lakhs to our daughter.*[88]

A group of mothers in a rural village just beyond the border of AP and Telangana's capital, Hyderabad, voice cautious optimism about the capacity of their daughters to shift social norms. When I ask them whether they expect their daughters to take care of them in the future, they respond:

"We want them to!" One older woman who leads a local Self Help Group adds: *"Daughters-in-law won't give love, but daughters will.... The love your daughters show you, your sons will never show you.... Daughters will at least give you four Rupees if you need it, sons won't give you anything. I have three sons, I know. You must have daughters! They will love you and visit you.... If I have a daughter I'll have some courage!"*[89]

[86] Personal Interview, April 7, 2010, Bachugarigudem, Khammam District, AP.
[87] Personal interview with Respondent Number 2 on April 10, 2010 in ibid.   [88] Ibid.
[89] Personal interview with Focus Group Number 3, including longer discussion with Respondent Number 9 on February 17, 2011, in Ibrahimpatnam Mandal, Ranga Reddy District, AP.

These positive examples of fluidity suggest room for hope about familial adjustment to legal change, particularly through incremental experimentation with alternate norms as younger generations are born and raised with the understanding that a daughter's legal rights are equal to those of sons. We see such radical about-faces in beliefs that translate into political action around the world. Most recently, Ireland's 2018 vote to reverse the long-standing ban against abortion exemplifies the possibility for sea change.[90] Here, young people are leading the way in reenvisioning each woman's agency and autonomy to decide what is right and best for herself.

In sum, marriage negotiations are decisive moments for formalizing or waiving women's property rights, and the time at which *Pradhans* have the opportunity to play a life-changing supporting role. Figure 2.3 maps the implications of this "gatekeeper theory" for women's access to gender-equal land inheritance. In Chapter 5, I explore the hypotheses presented here: the importance of female gatekeepers – and the timing of women's access to them – for inheritance, and two mechanisms central to their impact: their ability to mobilize female public participation in *Gram Sabha* meetings and to mediate private, intrahousehold disputes. In Chapters 6–7, I analyze whether the gate-keeper theory I develop can accurately predict whether political representation will spark resistance to or support for gender-equalizing reform.

2.8 CONCLUSION

I have argued that when political institutions open representation – and the authority and power of the state – to women, it gives rise to a fundamental reordering of power. With this new authority, female heads of local government revolutionize how women occupy the public sphere, create *new* public spaces for women's benefit, and repurpose the private sphere. This strains existing social institutions. Such productive conflict is particularly clear where legal reforms provide women equal rights to inherit land. This change presents the potential for a low-status group (women) to destabilize a broader traditional order that relies on their limited economic, political, and social rights, in favor of a more egalitarian system. Unsurprisingly, those who are historically advantaged recognize and resist challenges to their dominance.

This theory starts by mapping the paradoxical politics of backlash to women's successful empowerment. It also suggests female gatekeepers can provide a pathway through this resistance. Where gatekeepers encounter young women at critical junctures in their lives – as they enter marriage negotiations – female *Pradhans* can leverage their authority and acumen to move familial negotiations toward integrative solutions than enable young women to claim inheritance rights in ways that benefit the entire family. It's important to note that these negotiations are about far more than just land. They are fundamental

[90] McDonald, Graham-Harrison, and Baker (2018).

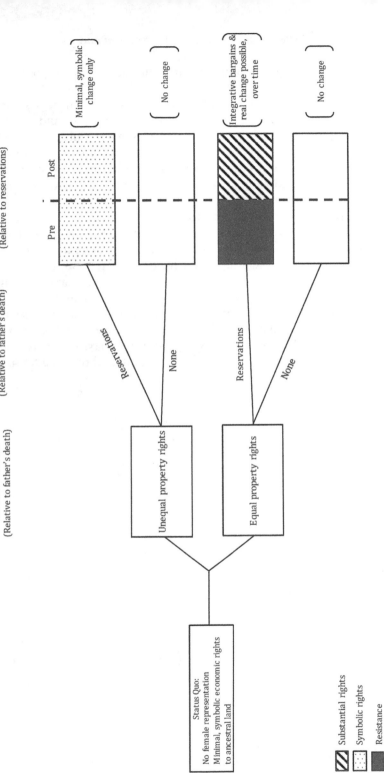

FIGURE 2.3. Gatekeeper Theory: A Diagram

Experience of Gender Equal Inheritance Reform (Relative to father's death)

Experience of Reservations (Relative to father's death)

Time of Marriage (Relative to reservations)

Status Quo:
No female representation
Minimal, symbolic economic rights to ancestral land

Unequal property rights

Equal property rights

Reservations

None

Reservations

None

Pre Post

Minimal, symbolic change only

No change

Integrative bargains & real change possible, over time

No change

Substantial rights

Symbolic rights

Resistance

moments for reimagining the family unit and, through that microcosm, society as whole.

My field research spells out Hindu women's dynamic strategies for navigating social norms and legal rights amidst the messiness and discord of asserting unorthodox forms of power. This generates seismic shifts in social, political, and economic subsystems that individuals and organizations are unprepared to arbitrate. My scrutiny provides a window into how these crucial sources of social connection, obligation, and authority can be navigated as an interconnected ecosystem.

The next two chapters step back to consider the historical evolution of India's social norms in colonial and contemporary time, with particular focus on the political economy story about why gender equalizing inheritance reform and national legislation mandating quotas for female representatives exist. The remaining chapters analyze a larger dataset of individuals across 17 Indian states with regard to land inheritance, family formation and division, and political participation. In these chapters, I zero in on how female representatives catalyze enforcement of legislation altering a single element of this ecosystem – inheritance reforms. I document how this affects behavior across political, economic, and social domains in both the short term and the long term.

3

Property and Power

A Political History of the Hindu Joint Family

The numerous live social questions of the day in India have their origin in [the Hindu home's] seclusion of all domestic life within four walls.
—(K. Viresalingam and Hutchinson [2009], Preface)

The father guards her during virginity, the husband guards her in youth, the sons guard her in old age; the woman is never fit for independence.
—(*Manu smriti*, Chapter 9, Verse 3)[1]

When people were totally free without property in land, I do not think there were these slavish practices of women's oppression and compulsory marriage contracts. *When there was no concept of accumulating private property ... there could not have been any compulsion for acquiring heir for the family – property – through child-birth.* Only when the desire for private property came into practice the concept of marriage and imprisoning women to protect the family property also came into practice. Once a woman was made the guardian of a man's property, she herself became his property to produce heir for the family ... women lost their right to worship their gods but only their husbands. The private property which has been the main reason for women's oppression has to be totally destroyed in order to achieve women's liberation.
—(*Periyar*, c.f. Anandhi 2003: 144)

Family structures a person's first vision of power, and creates the most durable institution for defining and adjudicating rights amongst partners and siblings, and across generations of parents and children. Property and social privilege are two of the most enduring forms of authority, and families often jealously guard the control and transfer of these sources of influence.

---

[1] Source in Sanskrit, transliterated, and English.

This chapter tells a story about the social conventions around the Hindu extended family (encompassing control of property, social alliances, and the politics of mobility and public voice) that provide the anchor and color of life for both men and women. I will explore how they have been constructed, challenged, and either reaffirmed or altered over the past several centuries. This history of social norms about property ownership is political in its very bones because, for many, as John Locke (1988, 329) argued: "Government has no other end but the preservation of property."[2]

The tale starts with a brief glimpse into what religion and its dictates about the family looked like prior to British colonialism. The British attempted to homogenize diverse religious, spiritual, and pragmatic traditions into a single code with a tiny elite of highly educated *Brahman* men at the top. Comfortably, the elite's sense of "tradition" looked much like the male British colonial ideal of "classical patriarchy" in terms of control of property and social authority. Ironically, this British-*Brahman* imposition has seeped into the seams of Indian history.

The remainder of this chapter details the changes to the ecosystem of norms around women's traditional property rights from independence to contemporary India. In doing so, I ground the prior chapter's "gatekeeper theory." The subsequent chapter jumps from the outer edges of the colonial empire's history into the core of state-level attempts at inheritance reform. That chapter will conclude by circling back to the essence of gatekeeper theory: investigating the emergence of the national legislation that made such rights viable. But first, I will provide context.

3.1 RELIGION AND INHERITANCE NORMS

In India, no less than in other countries, the question of property has been eternally preeminent, present in the earliest social, and political texts as well as in contemporary commentary on the crux of social, economic, and political conflict. This is because, in Sanjoy Chakravorty's (2015) words, "Land is India's scarcest resource and the source of livelihood for over half of its population."

As a result, land is also India's most contested resource. A study of just under half of India's major ongoing land conflicts finds they affect 3.1 million people, and are worth about $178 billion (12 trillion rupees).[3] More than half of contemporary legal disputes over land and property occur within the family (DAKASH, 2016). Traditional familial authority is intimately conjoined with power over land, both of which are particularly contested in contemporary India due to legislation upending long-standing statutes and mores.

[2] Locke ([1690] 1991: 329).   [3] Times of India (2016).

The form and content of contemporary legal rights owe much to British colonialism. Prior to British control, Mughal rulers and their antecedents respected the right of each community, be it religion or caste based, to regulate all "kinship" matters, which remained the domain of *jat* or *birdari* (subsets of caste-based lineages) community elders.[4] Mughal regulation focused on the relatively narrow set of actions deemed to be of the regime's interest: crimes against the rulers and their fiscal administration.[5] In contrast, the British Empire's political leaders entered on the heels of traders working for the British East India Company with a financial interest in broader state regulation.

Both private and public British entities worked to standardize the body of local law and authority to simplify and delegate management responsibility.[6] Their strategy was derived from the assumption that laws about familial matters from marriage and divorce to ancestral inheritance were drawn from religious texts, just as European marriages and questions of "testaments and distribution of goods, ... all matters of religious worship and discipline, excommunication and so forth were within the exclusive jurisdiction of the Bishops' courts, and the law was ecclesiastical law."[7] Thus began the tradition of partitioning "family law" – legislation of marriage, divorce, inheritance, and adoption – into the authority of distinct religious communities and their texts.

In Islamic communities, the central textual authority became the *Shari'a* law compiled by Mughal rulers, primarily using the Koran and supplementary texts.[8] In Hindu communities, developing a decisive text was more difficult. As a result, in 1772, the first British Governor-General of India, Warren Hastings, sought to assemble a definitive code with the help of *Brahman* scholars.[9]

While the texts used to codify diverse Hindu traditions varied over subsequent years, British bias in favor of upper caste, *Brahman* practices with some of the most severe prohibitions on women's social, economic, and political rights remained strikingly consistent. The most prominent legal compilation exemplifies this pattern: William Jones's 1796 *Institutes of Hindu Law, or, the Ordinances of Manu* was a translation of the *Manu Smriti*, literally "that which is remembered," or a body of Hindu teachings attributed to Manu. The text

---

[4] Kishwar (1994, 2145).   [5] Ibid.

[6] Kishwar (1994); Cohn (1996); Robins (2017). As Cohn (1996, 5) documents: "Starting in the 1770s in Bengal, the British began to investigate, through what they called 'enquiries,' a list of specific questions to which they sought answers about how revenue was assessed and collected. Out of this grew the most extensive administrative activity of the British, which they termed the land-settlement process. Entailed in this enterprise was the collection of 'customs and local histories,' which in the British discourse related to land tenure. The process culminated in the production of [district-level] settlement reports."

[7] Derrett (1968, 233–5) c.f. Kishwar (1994, 2145).   [8] See Anderson (1993).

[9] This was published as of 1776 in London with the title: *A Code of Gentoo Laws, or, Ordinations of the Pundits*, as noted by Derrett (1968, 240), c.f. Kishwar (1994).

dates roughly to 200 BCE–200 CE. Hindu authorities originally considered Manu the son of the divinity Brahma, to whom all of creation is attributed. Chakravarti (1993, 582) calls Manu "the most prominent ideologue of the *brahmanical* system." The *Manu Smriti* promotes strict norms governing not only patrilineal inheritance but also the regulation of women within the Hindu joint family. Indeed, it exhorts men to guard what they conceive of as the most important category of women – wives – night and day to maintain the purity of their children, family, selves, and spiritual advancement.[10]

Overall, British colonial division of the legal regulation of familial dynamics into religion-specific codes created a more rigid system. In the case of Hindu law, the system was particularly biased against the broader sets of rights women received outside the domain of high-caste *Brahman* Vedic texts. Ironically, despite initiating significant change in the nature of Indian legal regulation, Galanter (1978a, 494) notes: "the British were reluctant to institute any large scale innovations in the personal law of the Hindus." As a result, while early-nineteenth-century reforms attempted to dismantle a few practices that British and Hindu elites agreed were intolerable – female infanticide, immolation of widows and slavery – they left the "basic structure" of strict *Brahmanical* Vedic codes about the Hindu joint family unchanged.[11]

With this structure of colonial regulation in mind, we return to precolonial gender relations as the Hindu joint family establishes its roots. The initial focus is on female inheritance, with an overview of what *Brahman* Vedic codes enjoined. This is followed by a consideration of related norms about marriage and dowry, elder care, and death. We then circle back to norms about the disparate value of sons and daughters within the traditional Hindu joint family.

From there, we move to the British East India Company's attempt to codify existing practices as a means to exercise greater judicial and political control.[12] I leverage this discussion of legislation's impact on norms and behavior to explain the analytic foundation of my gatekeeper theory developed in Chapter 2 and to facilitate interpretation of subsequent empirical analysis.

3.1.1 The Hindu Joint Family's Precolonial Roots

According to one of the oldest forms of documentation, cave paintings, women's role in prehistoric culture was one of great value, both in productive

---

[10] *Manusmriti IX.*7, c.f. Chakravarti (1993, 582).   [11] Galanter (1978a, 494).
[12] In the words of Kishwar (1994, 2145): "The attempt to codify Hindu law was begun in the late 18th century because the colonial rulers wanted to bring under their judicial purview aspects of the social and political life of diverse communities which all erstwhile rulers had never encroached upon." On the religious basis of codification: "They assumed that just as the European marriage laws were based on Biblical tenants, so must the personal laws of various communities draw their legitimacy from some fundamental religious tenants."

and reproductive terms.[13] Society in this phase is defined by Neumayer (1983, 21) as "matristic," that is "one in which women were not subjected to the authority of men, or of other women."[14] By the time of the *Rig Veda*'s writing, however, around 1500–1200 BCE, female sexuality had become a problematic concept.[15] The portrayal of *apsaras,* or mythical, demoniac women "free from male control ... [who] even set stringent conditions for any long-term cohabitation with men" as a "threat to men and to their rituals" embodies this altered mindset.[16] By 800–600 BCE, with the advent an agricultural economy, came sharper distinctions around caste, class, and gender-specific social roles.[17]

As mentioned, the British were particularly reliant on the *Manu smriti* (circa 200 BCE–300 CE) and its stringent caste and gender prescriptions to map the "traditional" Hindu joint family. Once the structure of control had been established, the state, prioritized punishment for "crimes against the family." These were clearest around adultery and crimes against property.[18] Control over women's sexuality was a primary concern. According to Manu: "By adultery [particularly with lower caste men] is caused the mixture of castes among men, hence follows sin, which cuts up even the roots and causes the destruction of everything."[19] By *everything,* Yalman (1963, 27) posits, Hinduism means the "closed circle" around which people draw boundaries "to preserve land, women and ritual quality [caste] within it." Thus social norms about property ownership became intimately intertwined with concerns about controlling women and the other crucial marker of social status: caste.

According to Chakravarti (1993, 579), as the caste structure coalesced, it was safeguarded through extreme restriction over women's movement, culminating

---

[13] Chakravarti (1993, 580) notes in "a recent study of cave paintings at Bhimbetka (circa 5000 BCE) it has been argued that women were engaged in gathering fruit and other wild produce and in hunting small game using baskets and small nets. They combined their roles as mothers with their activities as gatherers during this hunting-gathering stage of society. The paintings include those of a woman with a basket slung across her shoulders with two children in it and she also carries an animal on her head; women carrying baskets and nets often depicted as pregnant; a woman dragging a deer by its antlers; and women engaged in catching fish (Roy, 1987, 3–4). In group hunting scenes too the paintings include women. From the elaborate headdress that they wear it is possible to argue that their presence in the hunt might indicate both a symbolic and an actual participation in ensuring the success of the hunt. Evidence from the cave paintings in central India thus suggests that in the hunting-gathering stage there was no rigid sexual division of labor as has sometimes been postulated, i.e., men hunt and women gather. In the case of central India in the Mesolithic period, it is likely that women participated in the hunt apart from the all important task of gathering which in any case accounted for the major source of food in tropical climates. The rule of women in the economy was thus equal if not more than that of men ... the important role of women in the hunting-gathering economy, which was highly valued, was enhanced by the importance attached to the reproductive role of women. Pregnant women, women in their nurturing roles as mothers, and women portrayed in the act of childbirth are sometimes depicted in the paintings and the last has been identified as the figure of a mother goddess."

[14] C.f. Chakravarti (1993, 580). [15] Flood (1996, 37). [16] Chakravarti (1993).
[17] Ibid., 581. [18] Ibid., 584. [19] Manusmriti VIII: 353, c.f. Chakravarti (1993, 584).

in their seclusion. Indeed, as "gateways – literally points of entrance into the caste system" – women's choices around marriage and sexuality became the most important markers of the caste system's integrity as well as crucial determinants of the wealth and status associated with caste markers. These imperatives supported a broader kinship system to maximize male control over female autonomy in these domains, with the result of limiting a woman's direct control over property throughout her lifetime.

Yet, notable exceptions to this rigid framework existed in Kerala, parts of Karnataka, Andhra Pradesh (AP), and throughout Northeast India, particularly in Meghalaya where norms reversed women's and men's relative entitlements to land and the natal home.[20] Even in the generally patrilineal domains of mainland India, records exist of temple donations made by women in South India from across the social spectrum.[21] However, as already stated, colonial codification resulted in homogenizing regional laws "on the basis of Brahminical tradition."[22]

3.1.2 Colonial Rule's Ossification of the Hindu Joint Family

A legal sea change occurred with Governor-General Warren Hastings's Judicial Plan of 1772, which made British law preeminent in commerce and Qur'anic or "Shaster" (*Shastras* or Hindu scripture) law central in resolving "civil" and religious matters.[23] The plan sparked a frenzy of scholarship on Hindu texts, beginning with the commission of 11 pandits (*Brahmans*) to compile and translate *Shastra* from Sanskrit to Persian and English, followed by British-authored work to standardize regulations based on *smritis* (rules compiled by sages, privileging popular customs).

This system was biased toward those at the top of the social ladder, with unbalanced patronage by the British exacerbating bias in its legal application.[24] The particular texts selected for translation, such as William Jones's translation of *Manu smriti*, were particularly adept at simplifying and streamlining British

---

[20] Chowdhry (2008, xvii); see also Agarwal (1994) and Basu (2005a).

[21] According to Agarwal (1994, 94) these women came not only from royal families but also among homes of peasant leaders, warriors, herders, or merchants. Inscriptions also reveal that a number of South Indian women from wealthy families were given landed property through inheritance or gifts, which they could donate for religious purposes. While a few donations suggest that permission had to be obtained by the donating parties, the fact that many did not indicates that South Indian women had a greater rights of alienation of property than deemed appropriate by the Hindu *shastras* (ibid., 96). However, Agarwal adds a caveat that temple donations have historically enjoyed broad social and legal sanction, which precludes their interpretation as a holistic indication of women's autonomy over property in other domains (ibid., 97).

[22] In particular, see Nair (1996, 66).

[23] Newbigin (2013, 31).

[24] Specifically, "the use of these Sanskrit pandits to interpret the customary laws for the benefit of [British East India Company] courts inevitably brought in a heavy Anglo-brahmanical bias" (Kishwar, 1994, 2145).

control in partnership with *Brahman* authorities, particularly around gender and caste.[25] According to the social reformer and constitutional author, Bhimrao Ramji Ambedkar: "Inequality was the soul of the Law of Manu. It pervaded all walks of life, all social relationships and all departments of state."[26]

After the *Manu smriti*'s publication in English, Colebrooke's translation of *smriti*, which categorized inheritance as following one of two sets of commentaries, Jimutavahana's *Dayabhaga* (the "Bengal" school) or Vijnanesvara's *Mitakshara* (the "Banaras" school), became the most cited source in colonial court judgments.[27] Most notably, Colebrook's work established the "default position of the Hindu family ... [as] that of a joint, or undivided, property-owning collective."[28] The British applied *Mitakshara* tradition to all Hindus except for those in one region: Bengal. It was a particularly attractive concept to British legislators because of its resemblance to English common law's joint property-holding structure: the coparcenary. There was one notable difference. Whereas English common law allowed women to be members of the coparcenary, the *Mitakshara* included only men.[29]

Once the British standardized the male-only coparcenary, it was a short leap to Sir Henry Sumner Maine's highly influential *Ancient Law*. This text held up Hindu law as exemplary of backward societies because the Hindu joint family "reflected the survival 'in absolute completeness' of the Roman doctrine of

[25] According to Kishwar (ibid. 2146), this was "one of the most favored texts of the British."

[26] Ambedkar (1979, 358), c.f. Newbigin (2013, 169). For details, see this chapter's first page.

[27] More specifically, the Dayabhaga school of law is observed across North Eastern and Eastern India, in what used to be the Colonial Presidency of Bengal, whereas the Mitakshara school is observed throughout the rest of India's Hindu population. The Mitakshara school is traditionally more conservative, considering only men as members of the joint family, with four generations of men (the family's head or Karta, his son, grandson, and great-grandson) as collective co-owners or coparcenors in the joint family's property. Sons acquire their interest in the property by birth, and only realize their distinct "share" upon their demand for partition of the property. According to Desai (2010, 100): "Mitakshara recognizes two modes of devolution of property, namely, survivorship and succession. The rules of survivorship applies to joint family property, and the rules of succession applies to [private] property held in absolute severalty by the last owner." In contrast, the Dayabhaga school sons do not acquire a right upon birth to ancestral property's inheritance, but only upon the death of their father, which is when they acquire rights to a coparcenary. Here, rights are defined and can be alienated at any point, despite property remaining held in common, as a part of the joint Hindu family. Again, according to Desai (2010, 100): "Dayabhaga recognizes only one mode of devolution, namely succession. It does not recognize the rule of survivorship even in the case of joint family property. The reason is that, while every member of a Mitakshara joint family has only an undivided interest in the joint property, a member of a Dayabhaga joint family holds his share in quasi-severalty, so that it passes on his death to his heirs, as if he was absolutely seized thereof, and not to the surviving copartners as under Mitakshara law." While mothers can be heirs in each system, they can only become coparceners in the Dayabhaga school, where all heirs of a given coparcener become coparceners at the death of the given coparcener. For details, see: H. T. Colebrooke (1810) *Two Treatises on the Hindu Law of Inheritance.* Calcutta; J. D. M. Derrett (1968, 247–52); Kishwar (1994, 2146); Newbigin (2013, 36).

[28] Newbigin (2013).

[29] Colebrooke (1810, 242–56); Sir William Blackstone (2001, 151–2), c.f. Newbigin (2013, 37).

patria potestas under which the head of the family held power to the negation of the claims of other members, particularly women."[30] However, upon becoming Viceroy, Maine worked to codify Indian law not to implement "modern" notions of equal access to property rights, but rather to safeguard Indian, and particularly Hinduism's "premodern" inequality from English law.[31] Thus did the British colonial legal system magnify and extend an extremely gender inegalitarian system of familial organization and access to property rights across most of the Indian subcontinent.

3.1.3   Social Norms and the Political Struggle for Independence

One might say that the British colonial political and economic system nurtured the resistance to colonialism that was its own undoing. Janaki Nair (1996, 49) explains this ecosystem as one of extensive deindustrialization, whereby India shifted from being a crucial manufacturer of goods to a site of primarily raw resource extraction managed by large landowners *(zamindars)*. British powers designated *zamindars* extensive property rights and an expanding writ of "feudal powers." Alongside was a parallel system of plantation and mine-based extraction with similarly monolithic authority granted to managers to the detriment of local manufacturing. This *modus operandi* required constant effort by the British to expand their network of indigenous collaborators willing to succeed at the expense of their compatriots.

As local economic entrepreneurship narrowed, the benefits of staffing "the imperial machine" grew for Indian educated men. This subset of new elites was instrumental in crafting both Indian colonial policy and the subcontinent's move for independence. This was also the group amongst which "the ideology of the patriarchal nuclear family" took root most firmly, thanks to the influence of colonial administrators, missionaries, and colonially supported education.[32]

3.1.3.1   The Hindu Joint Family and Property Management

By the time of nationalist movements for independence, the household had become a political and cultural haven from the centralized power of colonial rule. However, authority for the domestic sphere's management was equally concentrated in a single power: the *karta*, or male patriarch with exclusive responsibility for managing the Hindu joint family's property. For example, a mid-nineteenth-century tract on domestic management began: "Just as the King reigns over his dominion, so the head of the household (*karta*) rules over his household."[33] According to another tract: "The *karta* sometimes rules like a King, sometimes needs to legislate like the lawgiver and sometimes he adjudicates like the chief justice." [34]

---

[30] Maine (1861, 153), c.f. Newbigin (2013, 38).
[31] Mantena (2010, Chapters 3–4), c.f. Newbigin (2013, 39–40).   [32] See Nair (1996, 49).
[33] Sarkar (2010, 38)
[34] Cited from ibid., c.f. *Garhashya* [Domesticity] (monthly journal, 1884: 1), Calcutta.

Reassertion of the male patriarch's control was a source of agency for people otherwise dependent on the whims of the colonial regime. Tanika Sarkar (2010, 37–8) explains: "The Hindu home was the one sphere where improvement could be made through personal initiative, and changes wrought whereby education would bring forth concrete, manipulable, desired results. The home, then, had to substitute for the world outside and for all the work and relations that lay beyond personal comprehension and control."

It is no coincidence that the term used to define the household head, *karta*, is directly linked to oversight of property. The *karta's* foremost role is as property manager. In addition, he has another crucial responsibility: performing the funeral rites around a father's cremation that assure peace for departed and security for his descendants.[35] Usually, the eldest male in the family occupied the role of *karta*. Thus, norms about property inheritance have been directly tied to a broader set of social responsibilities spanning the life cycle, from gender-specific investments in children to the appropriate conduct of death rites for parents.

By conflating the *karta's* economic duties with social and political justice, Hindu nationalist activism consolidated power in senior male authorities and reduced the legitimate scope for women's (re)negotiation of economic, social, and political authority. According to Partha Chatterjee, "[T]he nationalists established their hegemony over the home even before they launched their political battles."[36] Indeed, the control of husbands over wives became particularly prized in Hindu nationalism. Sarkar notes that "out of the entire gamut of household relations, conjugality was found to be ideally relevant ... [as it] was based on the apparent absolutism of one partner and the total subordination of the other." Thus, women's complete commitment to their husbands, became "at once a sign of difference [with colonialism] and of superiority, a Hindu claim to power" (Sarkar, 2010, 41).

As the struggle for Indian independence mounted, women were given the opportunity to choose one of two mutuallyexclusive paths: either organize *as women,* in solidarity with Western notions of individual equality to demand new forms of legal rights and political inclusion *within the British colonial regime,* or outside the colonial domain, *as traditional Hindu wives in support of national independence.* In serving the nationalist cause for independence, women's unquestioning obedience to their husbands and overt recognition and acceptance of a subordinate role became imperative.[37]

However, as education became more accessible to women, their voices became more assertive and, thus, harder to ignore. Especially pronounced was women's dissent against legal reforms attempting to safeguard the "traditional" Hindu joint family's property at female expense. Pandita Ramabai Saraswati,

---

35 On this, see *Hindustan Times* (2016); Poleman (1934, 276–8) interpreting the five liturgical hymns of the Rgveda's tenth Mandala, 14–18, using Whitney's *Translation of the Atharvaveda* (1905), 81.34–37. See Mercier (1989, 58) on eldest sons' duties.

36 Chatterjee (1993, 135–57), c.f. Nair (1996, 50).   37 Sarkar (2010).

a highly educated woman widowed at a young age, became one of the most prominent critics of the patriarchy supported by both colonial and Indian nationalism's leaders:

The learned and civilized judges ... are determined to enforce, in this enlightened age the inhuman laws enacted in barbaric times four thousand years ago.... There is no hope for women in India whether they be under Hindu rule or British rule.... [But] We cannot blame the English government for not defending a helpless woman; it is only fulfilling its agreement made with the male population of India.[38]

Indeed, colonial and nationalist support for "the inhuman laws enacted in barbaric times" meant much more than reinforcing hierarchical property management by the male *karta*. Both political actors reinforced a larger set of gender-inegalitarian relationships stretching from marriage norms to children's support of parents in old age and death.

3.1.3.2 *Related Norms: Marriage and Parental Care*

Norms about marriage both constitute and divide extended or "joint" Hindu families. The widespread practice of village exogamy implies that women generally marry strangers in families distant from their natal home.[39] While there is variation, much of Western and Central India follow similar norms.[40] In South India, some groups of *Brahmans* support marriage within extended families.[41] However, marriage within a given clan is forbidden by norms across India, and hierarchy consistently privileges husbands and their lineage.[42]

Despite the generally greater autonomy afforded women in South Indian Hindu marriage norms as opposed to those in the North, Gough (1956, 166–7), studying *Brahman* culture in South India, explains that a girl only attains her social identity at the time of marriage, upon her transfer "as a personal gift, called the 'gift of a virgin,' by her father to her husband." After marriage, a

---

[38] Ramabai (1887, 66–67), c.f. Nair (1996, 70).

[39] According to Karve (1993, 54), this additional practice of clan exogamy is observed by all North Indian castes, based on the ancient interdiction against marrying someone removed less than seven degrees from one's father and five degrees from one's mother. In practice, this is operationalized using subcaste groups or subclans known as *gotras*. Men are traditionally prohibited from marriage within their own *gotra* as well as their mother's *gotra*. For some castes such as the *Jats*, an agricultural caste in Delhi, Punjab, and Haryana, a man must avoid marrying someone from his paternal grandmother's *gotra* as well (ibid, 55).

[40] Karve (1993, 65–6) demarcates Central India as comprising the states of Gujarat, Madhya Pradesh, Rajasthan, Maharashtra, and Orissa. In Rajasthan, Gujarat, and most of Maharashtra and Orissa, North Indian marriage practices are the norm.

[41] Again, according to Karve (1993, 67–8), while non-Brahman castes prohibit a brother's marriage to a younger sister's daughters, this is the preference amongst a number of South Indian *Brahman* subcastes, alongside marriage to first cousins: men to their mother's sisters' or brothers' daughters.

[42] Karve (1993, 69). Chapter 8, Table 8.2 provides greater detail on intra-India variation in norms about female autonomy in colonial and contemporary India.

woman's salvation comes from daily worship of her husband. According to the well-known proverb "She who on rising worships not G-d but her husband, if she says, 'Let it rain,' it will rain." [43] In the most extreme embodiment of female dependence, the now-illegal practice of *sati* encourages a wife's immolation on her husband's funeral pyre to ensure redemption.

Not surprisingly, folk songs across India identify inherently hostile relationships in marital families, particularly that between a bride and the other woman traditionally reliant on her husband's attention in the marital home: her mother-in-law (*saas*) and sister-in-law (*nanad*). They also lament the agony of the girl parting from her parental home, only to be received by in-laws who are eager to find fault with her.[44]

Yet married women's welfare is not entirely dependent upon the relationship they strike with husbands. Brothers, in particular, are considered sources of inherent support, so much so that songs often refer to them as the *bir*, or champion of a sister, and the one person who provides an unbreakable link to her natal home. Ideally, brothers also provide economic and emotional security, particularly after parents' death.[45]

Fraternal ties not withstanding, the importance of severing familial relationships with a daughter upon her marriage and moving to her husband's family home is taken so seriously throughout much of India that daughters are traditionally considered *paraya dhan* or the wealth of another man's lineage (the husband's family). In contrast, the birth of sons is considered a boon. Whereas daughters leave the natal home at marriage, sons remain inside or nearby, providing the main contribution to agricultural production and caring for parents as they age, enabled and rewarded by patrilineal inheritance.

These traditions are still the default position. As one married woman with four children explained:

I have six siblings, three boys and three girls. My mother's family gave [3 acres of] land to brothers only, and cash dowry to sisters. . . . This is because in [my mother's] family we don't give land to daughters. This is our tradition. . . . I myself had children until I had a boy. In the future I will give land inheritance to my son only because we don't give to girl children, because boys stay here. My son only, and my daughter-in-law will take care of me in my old age. [This is how it is for my generation.] Currently, I am looking after my parents-in-law. My brother and his wife will look after our parents.[46]

Care for aging parents by sons is particularly important in light of traditional norms about death rites. According to *Brahman* Hindu tradition, the eldest son is the sole legitimate practitioner of the sacred Hindu death rites for their parents that "propitiate their souls after death."[47] It is up to sons to assure

---

43 Cited from Gough (1956, 166–7). Note that mothers-in-law, as extensions of their sons, also require wives' strict obedience and devotion (ibid.).
44 Karve (1993, 58).   45 Ibid., 62; Agarwal (1994, 261).
46 Personal interview with Respondent Number 6, Araku District, Vizag, November 14, 2010.
47 Gough (1956).

the correct performance of these rites, not only to bring peace to their parents but also to secure the good fortune and reputation of the lineage and its surviving members. Thus, parental investment in sons, which is most clear through inheritance, contains both a material dimension – assuring current agricultural production and future material and physical wellbeing – and a spiritual dimension.

3.2 BACKLASH TO REFORM IN THE COLONIAL ERA

Colonial attempts to change social norms using legislation were extremely difficult to enforce. For example, in 1829, the British outlawed *sati*. However, the practice continued, and occurs even in the present time. Although recorded cases of *sati* have diminished dramatically, *sati* temples, where prayers, known as *pujas*, are carried out and festivals organized to glorify both the patron goddess, *Sati*, the benevolent avatar of the mother goddess who immolated herself on a funeral pyre in response to her father's insults of her husband, as does the practice of a wife's self-immolation following her husband's death.[48] Today, India has at least 250 *sati* temples, and legal prohibitions are too vague to effectively prohibit *pujas* there.[49] Whereas new legislation may be able to effectively criminalize behavior promoted by social norms, such legislation may explicitly mobilize support for social traditions like *sati* in direct resistance to state enforcement of legislation to eradicate social norms.

Sati is a particularly relevant social practice because it is often used as a means to prevent inheritance of property by widows.[50] In parallel, widows are also sometimes branded as witches – and subjected to violent expulsion from their homes – as a means to prevent their inheritance.[51] Compounding the issue, enforcement became both more possible and more problematic following legal reforms driven by women. Women's collective legal activism took shape in the All India Women's Conference (AIWC) established in 1927. In addition, women's simultaneous actions within the Congress Party helped bring about the Child Marriage Restraint Act of 1929, raising the minimum age of women's legal marriage from 12 to 14 years.[52] When opponents cited Hindu shastras to argue against any increase in the minimum marriage

[48] Recorded cases have dropped from 8,135 between 1813–28 in the British East India Company's Bengal Presidency ledgers, to roughly 40 since India's Independence (ibid.).

[49] Times of India (2009).

[50] Assessments of "successful" enforcement competes with reports of "violent protests" that follow "police action to prevent immolation," such as in a Rajasthani village where "a few dozen supporters of the *sati* ritual pelted the police with rocks [and] smashed windows in nearby buildings and cars" leading to over 20 injured persons and 30 arrests in 2006 (Gravchev, 2006).

[51] "Old and young widows are easy targets. The mixing of old superstitions [about women as witches] with modern material desires has proved deadly for these women, as many brandings are now done to disinherit them from family property" (Sharma, 2012).

[52] Women speaking to the Select Committee tasked with drafting legislation urged a minimum age of 16–18 years. Details in Nair (1996, 79–82).

age, the AIWC members retorted: "We want new *sastras*."[53] Yet the British colonial government was not in accord. As soon as the legal reform passed, the government "warned against vigorous prosecutions under the new act since it would 'unnecessarily disrupt family relations and ruin the wife's prospects for life.'"[54]

AIWC attempts to encourage enforcement enabled backlash. As chronicled by a 1936 editorial in the *Indian Social Reformer*: a "veritable stampede" to register (child) marriages occurred between the bill's passage in September 1929 and April 1930, the date when it became enforceable. The result of this enthusiasm for child marriage was "a hideous legacy of a large increase in child widows in one year so as to be clearly reflected in the census of 1931."[55] To summarize, women's demands for revising what was widely regarded as the "traditional" Hindu joint family at the dawn of independence became a source of backlash led by social authorities, specifically patriarchal heads of the joint Hindu family.[56]

Overall, India's arc of experience from independent kingdoms to colonial rule and toward a more unified, autonomous state suggests that gender equal norms were neither widely followed nor effectively legislated prior to India's independence. If anything, colonial rule and the transition to independence strengthened Hindu traditions supporting patrilineal inheritance of ancestral identity and property.

---

53 Forbes (1979, 415), c.f. Nair (1996, 82).
54 This passage is based on colonial discussion on the dangers of using the police to implement regulations derived from the plague of 1898, quoted in David Arnold (1987), c.f. Nair (1996, 82).
55 *Indian Social Reformer*, August 1936, c.f. Nair (1996, 83).   56 Nair (1996, 84).

4

Where Are the Women?

Investigating Reform's Roots

Reform does not drop fully formed from the sky, but rather emerges from a constellation of political, social, and economic interests of stakeholders, legislators, and opponents. We can learn a great deal about the design, enforcement, and impact of reform based on its origins. This chapter considers the dynamic relationships between actors, interests, and shifting sources of power and constraint through the perspective of the individuals and coalitions that shape legislation. The focus is on three states situated at unique points in the spectrum of gender, caste, and land inequality. We will examine how each legislated rights for women on par with men. We will conclude with a study of the constitutional amendment mandating quotas for women's political representation.

We begin with Kerala, which entered Independent India with one of the highest levels of caste and landholding inequality, along with small perches of matrilineal communities in which women experienced greater autonomy than nearly anywhere else in the subcontinent. Here, women's rights to land were weaponized as a source of injustice (to men). Those in favor of change – mainly men excluded from inheritance in matrilineal communities – worked to shame women with the greatest economic and social autonomy as uncivilized and exploitative. For them, inheritance reform promised the opportunity to rise in the colonial system by liquidating female wealth to benefit their own careers and build nuclear families. The result was a reform to ostensibly facilitate "gender equality" by dispatching with the Hindu joint family – including matrilineal women's traditional, exclusive entitlements to own ancestral property – in favor of a patriarchal model of male-headed nuclear families that enabled well-educated men to fragment ancestral property and quickly consolidate nearly exclusive control over land.

We move next to Andhra Pradesh (AP), which also entered independence with high caste and landholding inequality, yet without the strong tradition of women's autonomy notable in pockets of Kerala. Activism by radical, caste-based movements to undercut traditional caste dominance enabled rethinking of power in other domains. In this "moderate" example of reform – which became the nationwide model for equalizing women's inheritance rights – legislation was largely symbolic, with little hope of enforcement but resonant with newly pivotal female voters. Within AP, women were neither "dangerous" (i.e., entitled) enough to merit attempts to redistribute their traditional sources of autonomy – as was the case in Kerala – nor powerful enough to merit redistribution of traditional authority in their favor – as occurred in Karnataka. Yet women's potential as an electoral coalition that could provide decisive victories encouraged a first round of legislation with the potential, once widespread, to yield foundational economic rights. In AP, agrarian agitation forced the reduction of caste and landholding inequality, which led to a reconsideration of property rights for women, albeit in a way intended to increase their power more on paper than in reality.

In one of the last states to reform women's inheritance rights, Karnataka, moderate levels of caste and landholding inequality enabled a newly empowered party and its chief minister to legislate and enforce redistribution of political power in favor of marginalized groups, including women and members of lower castes. Here, two factors were at play, women's enhanced status as pivotal voters (as was true in AP) and the promise of a fundamental restructuring of political agency. Thanks to Karnataka's uniquely low levels of landholding inequality, this resulted in meaningful political reform: the creation of local elected governments with quotas for women. Once in possession of local political agency, women were able to translate this power into economic and social currency. Thus, while Karnataka's inheritance reform was intended to be symbolic, as in AP, its timing *after* women received real political power led Karnataka to experience the highest level of reform enforcement across all states, which legislated change in advance of national policy.[1]

A very different picture of reform emerges in the run-up to the constitutional amendments mandating nationwide elected local governments with reservations for women and members of Scheduled Castes and Tribes (SCs and STs). Unlike the tepid activism around earlier inheritance reform, women now mobilized in powerful local and national movements to debate the value of quotas for their political representation. While the multifaceted women's movement was never defined by a single, unified position, a growing infrastructure of highly articulate, determined, powerful women committed to changing exploitative hierarchies of caste, community (religion), and gender burgeoned across India from the nineteenth century onward. Women's increasingly pivotal role as well-informed voters willing to reward and punish parties for their demonstrated commitments to political, economic, and social empowerment made reform an attractive tool for national figures such as Rajiv Gandhi

---

[1] See Chapter 8, Table 8.2 for details.

and Narasimha Rao to amass new sources of political authority independent of the Congress Party's traditional local intermediaries: landed, upper caste élites.[2] Overall, this chapter explores the diverse forms of female agency required to renegotiate inegalitarian authority structures across historical and contemporary India.

4.1 ON THE ORIGINS OF INHERITANCE REFORM

To illuminate the political dynamics of legislation, I commissioned the first translations of debates concerning the passage of reforms in three state legislative assemblies. These debates stretch from the earliest to the latest state amendments. In this chapter, I combine analysis of debates with first-hand interviews of individuals involved in the legislative process, electoral dynamics, and contemporaneous discussion and interpretation of reforms by scholars of history, gender, political economy, and the media. I conclude this section with comparative analysis of the reform processes across states to pinpoint critical variation in each state's capacity and interest in enforcing – versus blocking – inheritance reform.

I develop case studies for three Indian states: the first two reformers, Kerala (1976) and AP (1986), and the final state to legislate gender equalizing land inheritance reform, Karnataka (1994). I consider the three states as models for the range of political processes through which reform was legislated. The content and scope of their reforms are diverse, yet all possess the political infrastructure necessary to support implementation. In each state, divergent social coalitions promoted reform and aligned to advance or block progressive content in the legislative process. However, this did not include women's political mobilization for inheritance reform. This paucity of female political pressure translated into minimal incentives for politicians to ensure the existence of robust enforcement mechanisms, despite explicit concerns raised in each legislative process.

First, in Kerala, a "voluble minority" of élite, English-educated Nair men stood to gain from the dismantling of matrilineal family structures. This group was visible as the prime movers and authors of reform from precolonial times until the final round of legislation in 1976. Legislators possessed a clear understanding of the disadvantages reform was likely to create for women from matrilineal families. However, in the legislation they made no attempts to include formal systems to enforce women's rights.

In AP, women actively mobilized to eradicate dowry in the years preceding inheritance reform. Yet, this did not include demands for gender equal inheritance reform. The governing Telugu Desam Party (TDP), cognizant of this disinterest in inheritance reform, perceived no incentives to design and implement the costly legal and bureaucratic mechanisms necessary for

---

[2] See, in particular, masterful analysis of decentralization by Bohlken (2015).

substantive enforcement. With neither agitation nor oversight provided by women, the party's self-propelled move to pass reform was sufficient to produce significant political capital with immediate benefits.This legislation formed a crucial foundation for the TDP's reputation as a progressive party with deep commitment to improving women's welfare. Widespread publicity gave the TDP credit as a "revolutionary" party likely to "transform" women's role in society. In addition, the party relied upon visual imagery to maintain this reputation, even producing an illustrated booklet of the programs it had initiated for women between 1984 and 1988 to win subsequent elections.

In Karnataka, Chief Minister Ramakrishna Hegde proposed inheritance reform in line with the "Andhra" model in form and strategy: garnering female votes to transform a regionally based political upstart into a victorious governing party. This strategy was explicit; Rajasekhariah et al. (1987, 591) attribute the decisive victory of Hegde and his Janata Party in the Assembly Elections of March 1985 to their last-minute supplementary manifesto, which targeted populist-style resources directly to women, who voted decisively for Hegde. Hegde also successfully claimed credit for his prior work to benefit women's welfare, most notably securing the first reservation of seats for women through an early version of *Panchayats* in 1987.

Congress wrested power back from Hegde's Janata Party in 1989. Under the leadership of S. Bangarappa, they proposed the inheritance reform that Hegde had initially advocated. As the next round of elections loomed large, Chief Minister Veerappa Moily successfully shepherded inheritance reform through to passage. This had taken two iterations of leaders to achieve, but yet it was not enough to keep Congress in power. Hegde's Janata Dal won subsequent elections thanks to his identification with effective use of quotas (reservations) to advance the interests of women and a broader, deeper coalition of castes.[3]

Thus, across states, early reform equalizing women's inheritance rights appears to have been an effective means to mobilize female votes to bolster new parties. However, such reform was motivated by elite male politicians rather than female agriculturalists or voters more generally. Nor did it include follow-through in the form of effective enforcement mechanisms.

4.2 KERALA

4.2.1 Historical Context: Caste, Land, and Gender

Kerala, occupying India's southernmost tip, is oft viewed as synonymous with social, economic, and political equality, distinct from the rest of India. Yet precolonial and colonial sources suggest that society in what now comprises

---

3 India Today (1994); Gould (1997, 2343), Raghavan and Manor (2009, 267).

Kerala – the Princely States of Travancore and Cochin and British-administered Malabar[4] – was organized around a fine-grained social hierarchy with elaborate restrictions for the lowest ranks. Indeed, the nineteenth century reformer Vivekananda called Kerala's system a "madhouse of caste."[5] As of an 1875 survey, Travancore had 420 relevant Hindu castes, with social inequality directly tied to landownership inequality.[6] Those at the bottom of the hierarchy were prohibited not only from direct contact with upper tiers (untouchability) but also from mere proximity (unapproachability), and many were tied to upper caste families as bonded labor.[7]

With British rule, those at the top of the caste hierarchy, *Brahman janmis* were declared absolute landowners, making the system more exploitative.[8] Even with "radical" land reform in 1969, agricultural land inequality was worse in Kerala than in all but two other Indian states.[9]

Amidst its once-rigid caste system, Kerala's distinctive versions of gender egalitarian social organization are particularly striking. Records of matrilineal society amongst the *nair* caste exist from at least 300 years prior to British rule over Malabar.[10] Matrilineal groups across Kerala followed versions of *marumakkatayam*, defined broadly as a system of "vest[ing] property in the females of the family."[11] The kinship group or *taravad*, traced through a common female ancestor, held property jointly. The *taravad's* head, known as the *karanavan* was widely considered responsible for property management; because this role was usually male, Kerala's matrilineal systems are not considered matriarchal – that is, run politically by women.[12]

---

4 Contemporary Kerala also comprises the Madras Presidency's South Canara district, in which the same broad historical patterns discussed in the larger colonial units of Malabar and the princely states apply.
5 See Franke and Chasin (1994, 75).
6 Report on the Census of Travancore (1875) Trivandrum, 185: c.f. Vasudhevani (2002, 9).
7 See Thomas (2004, 6–7).
8 Nair (1996, 153).
9 Thomas (2004, 56). Statistics from a 1971 survey conducted prior to land reform's full implementation.
10 See Miller (1954, 416), cited in Kodoth (2002, 17).
11 Kodoth (2002, 12) notes that the later terminology was used to harmonize *marumakkattayam* and *aliyasantana* systems. The former is defined as inheritance by one's sister's children; the latter is also matrilineal and recognizes women (rather than men) as customary family heads. I cannot do justice to the "plurality of practice" in Kerala's matrilineal societies alluded to by Kodoth (2002, 11), but point readers to Kodoth as well as to Schneider and Gough (1962); Arunima (1995); Thomas (2004); and Jeffrey (1993, 2010). Kodoth (2002, 23–4) notes that studies of matrilineal practices are drawn from central Kerala, where Nambudiri Brahmins are concentrated, a patrilineal group that traditionally dominated in the region socially and economically, as the largest landholders, and whose marital relationships with matrilineal groups were the subject of much critique by social reformers.
12 In contrast, female *karanavan* operated in *aliyasantana* systems, mainly concentrated in South Canara. Gough notes that senior women had significant control over property and kin in some *marumakkattayam* systems, with variation in seniority's origin. ("Nayars: Central Kerala," 338–41, c.f. [Kodoth, 2002, 25]).

Matriliny had clear benefits for women: despite hierarchical, increasingly formalized male control over de jure property rights, women wielded a great deal of de facto influence over the use of property and the distribution of its benefits.[13] However, matriliny remained tied to a broader, patriarchal system of caste dominance with many sources of exploitation.

In particular, "liaisons" between Kerala's matrilineal castes and the patrilineal, *Brahman nambudiri* men drew attention and scorn from outside observers.[14] These relationships, known as *sambandham* alliances, were hypergamous, linking *nair* women to *nair* or *nambudiri* men for any mutually agreed upon length of time.[15] This was often beneficial for a *nair* woman, who gained status from *sambandham* with *nambudiris*, had all children born of unions accepted into and raised by her mother's *taravad*, and ended relationships as she wished by putting a man's sleeping mat outside the door of her house.[16] Such alliances were less kind to *nambudiri* women, who were barred from formal marriage to anyone except *nambudiri* eldest sons. As families' sole inheritors, eldest sons were also permitted to practice polygamy. This limited *nambudiri* women's options to intracaste polygamy or celibacy and – most importantly for catalyzing reform – barred *nambudiri* younger sons from marriage and inheritance.

Notably, the rulers of Cochin and Travancore's princely states hailed from matrilineal castes. Within this structure, men held political authority.[17] Roughly one-third of Malabar's population followed *marumakkatayam* law as of 1881, and another 20 percent followed versions of matrilineal inheritance; 56 percent of Travancore's population was classed as matrilineal in 1891.[18] Matrilineal practices were highly flexible and varied at the advent of colonial rule, after which British judges and jurists assembled an increasing rigid body of law, which made customary partition and management particularly challenging.[19] Coordination that had worked in the past no longer did.

---

[13] See Kodoth (2002).

[14] See Jeffrey (2010, 93) and Thomas (2004, 9–12).

[15] As Jeffrey (2010, 93) notes, relationships could be for life but changing partners was not stigmatized.

[16] See Thomas (2004, 11–12), and Jeffrey (2010, 93) for the details of ending *sambandham* alliances.

[17] Heirs were sons of the ruler's sister, with sisters of deceased rulers acting as state caretakers until heirs were old enough to rule. Female regents ruled Travancore in 1809–29 and 1924–31 (Jeffrey (2004, 648).

[18] *Nair, Mapilla,* and *Tiyya* communities all followed *marumakkathayam* matrilineal law (Nair 1996, 150). On Malabar, see Thomas (2004, 12); on Travancore, see the Census of India (1893, 252), c.f. Jeffrey (2004, 649).

[19] In Madras High Court Judge P. R. Sundara Aiyar's words, "While the law of property among the *marumakkatayis* was based entirely on usages, British exponents of the law allowed little weight to the views of the people and were guided by their own notions of a perfect system of *marumakkatayam* law" (Variar, 1969, 13). The direction of change was significantly biased against matrilineal practices (Kodoth 2002, 7).

4.2.2 Inheritance Reform's Origins

By 1869, a combination of economic and political incentives had created a "voluble minority demanding changes in the existing system" of matrilineal inheritance in Kerala.[20] Elite, English-educated *nair* men who stood to gain from dismantling the Hindu joint family became the prime movers of inheritance legislation from pre-colonial times until the last round of reform in 1976.

Colonial education, the opportunities associated with it, and the economy's monetization were particularly central to catalyzing legal reform. English language education was a prerequisite for entrance into Malabar's colonial administration. This became more relevant as growing monetization increased incentives to sell land and work in urban colonial centers. Because salaries associated with such professions quickly eclipsed those from traditional livelihoods tied to agriculture, colonial position became an increasingly important determinant of social status.[21]

Pursuit of this education required young members of the *taravad* to study in colonial administrative centers, increasing their exposure to colonial values and prestige at the cost of the *taravad's* resources and influence. This fostered internal competition that further weakened *taravads*, which could only afford to send a few members for this grooming. Eldest males were most likely to receive the privilege, bringing a wife with them when possible. With their education complete, these young men looked increasingly to nuclear patrilineal families and careers in colonial administration as the definition of success. In comparison, reliance on jointly owned, landed matrilineal wealth held by others appeared much less enticing, and thus easy to denigrate as the relic of a premodern system.[22]

With a burgeoning market for well-educated, high-caste colonial administrators, the individuals who saw themselves as best suited to pivot into this new socio-economic landscape – male members of matrilineal communities – were amongst the main constituents demanding inheritance reform.[23] As these men gained political clout, they reconsidered the value of traditional matrilineal property inheritance institutions. These prohibited all men from inheriting, but gave senior *nair* men control over ancestral property as the managerial head or *karnavan* of the matrilineal *taravad*. As a result, junior *nair* men were in a particularly disadvantaged position, possessing neither rights to own nor to control property. "In contrast, *karnavans* stridently opposed reform."[24]

---

[20] Thomas (2004, 128).   [21] Ibid., 122–3; Nair (1996, 153).

[22] Thomas (2004, 124–6). Nair (1996, 153) emphasizes that matrilineal property ownership was particularly galling for the high numbers of well-educated Nair men who accumulated significant property through careers in colonial bureaucracy because "self-earned incomes, even when unrelated to the land, reverted to the joint property of the man's tarawad.... Nayar men strained their resources to educate their sons at their own expense. It was this class, with its increasing exposure to English language education, which was also most susceptible to the Victorian moral onslaught of the missionaries."

[23] Jeffrey (2010, 85–6).   [24] Nair (1996, 157).

As a member of Travancore's Assembly argued with clear frustration, demands for reform were mainly motivated by men's desire "to keep self-acquired property out of the hands of one's *taravad* and rightful heirs" and "to use it to make ample provision ... for the wife and children."[25]

The most organized proponents of reform were also its clearest beneficiaries. In 1869, *nair* men, likely junior, established the *Malayala Sudrachara Parishodana Sabha* society, demanding *marumakkathayam* marriage reform. This was followed formation of the Malabar Marriage Association in 1879.[26] These and similar societies circulated proreform government petitions and filled local papers with "sustained propaganda."[27]

At the same time, pressure to restrict the power of large landlords encouraged the British government to mount the legal infrastructure for caste and inheritance reform.[28] In 1880, William Logan was appointed special commissioner in the regard. Logan argued for weakening the joint family and promoting wills for self-acquired inheritance, such that "individual industry and thrift" would blossom.[29] After legislation for marriage reform on these terms failed, the colonial government appointed the Malabar Marriage Commission of 1891, comprised of "six leading men."[30]

Responses to the commission's queries on what reform should entail are instructive: out of 38 petitions, 13 were signed by 2,723 men favoring reform and 25 signed by 2,131 men opposing any change. Four petitions were signed by 245 women supporting reform and 387 opposing change. The commission argued: *"'it was not in their [women's] power to express their opinion otherwise than through their karnavans and husbands,' and it was therefore difficult to ascertain their general feeling."*[31]

The commission's final decision was *not* based on popular demand. It admitted that few witnesses supported reform, but claimed: *"we believe that the uninstructed majority will rapidly follow the lead of the enlightened classes [in accepting reform]."*[32]

The result was the Malabar Marriage Act of 1896, passed by the Madras government to allow *sambandham* registration as marriage. Registration gave women and children legal rights to support by husbands or fathers and to one-half of the husband's property if he died without a will.

The act's success is questionable; in the decade following reform only 100 marriages were registered.[33] To the extent that women preferred a nuclear family, with men as the primary owners and managers of resources over prior

---

[25] Jeffrey (1976, 188), c.f. Nair (1996, 156).
[26] See Nair (1996, 154); K. N. Panikkar (1992, 177), c.f. Thomas (2004, 128).
[27] Thomas (2004, 128). [28] Nair (1996, 154). [29] Saradamoni (1982, 62), c.f. Nair (1996, 154).
[30] Nair (1996, 154). *Brahman* social reformer T. Muthuswami Aiyar was selected as president of the MMC.
[31] Nair (1996, 155), with reference to memo of T. M. Aiyar in Report of the Malabar Marriage Commission (MMCR) with enclosures and appendixes (1892, 11).
[32] MMCR (1892, 4), c.f. Nair (1996, 156). [33] Nair (1996, 156–7).

tradition (matrilineal for *nairs*, patrilineal for *nambudiris*), both of which vested significant de facto power in women, reform was a boon. On balance, reform appears costly for *nair* women: it reduced their sexual independence, autonomy, collective property ownership, and security in the natal home.[34] Despite clear identification of the disadvantage legal reform was likely to create for women from matrilineal families, no attempts were made to include enforcement of matrilineal women's legal rights within the legislation.

Subsequent reforms replicated the 1896 process. In 1897, male *nair* social reformer Pattom Thanu Pillai failed to pass a similar bill in the Travancore Legislative Council, after which committee work led to the Travancore Maru-makkattayam Act of 1912. Jeffrey (2010, 86) suggests this act was "welcomed by élite Nair women," 350 of whom gathered in November 1912 to pass a resolution affirming the act "will materially add to the self-respect of the Nairs generally and Nair ladies particularly."[35] Yet *nair* men remained the strongest promoters of reform. The Nair Service Society (NSS), founded in 1915, made the most strident demands for the abolition of matriliny.[36] In the ensuing decades, momentum built for the legal dissolution of matriliny, buoyed by broader demands for social reform to limit *Brahman* privileges. These demands were not inclusive: *"women's voices were rarely heard" and "newspapers scrupulously avoided seeking women's opinions"* on reform.[37]

Piecemeal reforms did succeed in making matrilineal inheritance increasingly liminal. As of Malabar's 1931 census, the *taravad* had disappeared as the center of the *marumakkathayam* community. With the Malabar Marumakkathayam (Matriliny) Act of 1933, the entirety of a father's property and inheritance became divisible amongst his children rather than the *taravad's* joint property, leading to the *taravad's* "brisk" disintegration.[38] National reform of women's inheritance occurred through the Hindu Succession Act of 1956, which pro-vided a only weak buffer for matrilineal inheritance.[39]

In more than 20 pieces of legislation passed in Kerala between 1896 and 1976, the unifying theme was the systematic dismantling of matrilineal inheritance, driven by elite *nair* men. Despite the promotion of reform as

---

[34] Jeffrey (2010, 86). [35] Ibid., c.f. Madras Mail, November 14, 1912, p. 3. [36] Jeffrey (2010, 87).
[37] Nair (1996, 159), c.f. Saradamoni (1982, 79), and Panikkar (1992, 46), respectively.
[38] Panikkar (1992, 46), c.f. Nair (1996, 159).
[39] For detailed analysis of relevant legislative debates see Kishwar 1994. Matrilineal inheritance received a small but notable concession in India's 1956 Hindu Succession Act thanks to elite pacts that exempted women "who would have been governed by matrilineal law" from inheritance distribution along patrilineal rules. The 1956 Act specifies sons, daughters, and the mother as primary heirs for matrilineal women who die intestate, versus sons, daughters, and husband for others. Jeffrey (2010, 95) argues that legislation was likely influenced by "many senior Nairs near the heart of government in New Delhi at that time – KPS Menon (1898–1982), VP Menon (1894–1966), VK Krishna Menon (1897–1974), to name three of the best known." Professor Devika J, at Trivandrum's Center for Development Studies identifies former Law Minister Ambedkar as a strong proponent of Nair women's rights (interview conducted by Rajiv Naresh, Fall 2015).

benefiting women, it is clear that changes in inheritance laws were in no way propelled by these parties.

Yet, to fully understand the chronology of Kerala's reforms, its final piece of inheritance legislation is key: the 1976 Abolition of the Joint Hindu Family. Even today, assessments of its impact inspire diametrically opposed views. Historians cite 1976 as matriliny's final moment, when "Kerala's Legislature abolished the matrilineal system" (Nair, 1996, 163). In contrast, lawyers, legislators, and economists identify 1976 as the beginning of radical state-level reforms for gender equity.[40] This reform increased equality by abolishing any birthright guaranteeing inheritance, both for men in patrilineal systems and women in matrilineal systems. There was additional support provided for individuals who had been disadvantaged in the past to negotiate inheritance rights in the future.

The paucity of scholarship on the reform's origin suggests a great puzzle: What was its purpose of the 1976 reform? Did it change anything and, if not, what cause did it serve? A number of scholars assert that by 1976, partition of matrilineal *taravads'* property was the rule rather than the exception.[41] Yet, the language of the legislation clearly laid out that all *taravads* and other forms of joint landholdings were now to be divided, such that each member was a "co-tenant in a common [divisible] tenancy."[42] According to Jeffrey (2010, 94–5), that stipulation was relevant only for the remaining families "that had not explicitly divided themselves [who were] still regarded as joint-families and deemed to hold joint-family property."

I argue that this reform served an important political purpose for the parties who advanced it. For the left, redistributing control over land was a means to solidify traditional alliances with landless groups and build new relationships with political élites. This benefited the Communist Party of India (CPI), which held the position of Kerala's chief minister. The center, namely the Indian National Congress Party (INC, or Congress), acting as the CPI's coalition partner, facilitated initial reforms to solidify its weak ties to landless groups.

4.2.3 Political Context: Strange Bedfellows

Kerala's 1971 elections that had brought the CPI–Congress coalition to power occurred amid extreme frustration with a decade and a half of stalled "land to the tiller" reforms. In 1959, radical reforms aimed at redistributing excess landholdings to landless cultivators were enacted under the state's first chief minister, the CPI's E. M. S. Namboodiripad. However, they were derailed by

---

[40] Most notably, see the Law Commission of India's 174th Report on "Property Rights of Women: Proposed Reforms under the Hindu Law" (2005), which identifies the "Kerala" and "Andhra" models of reform. See also: Deininger et al. (2013); Deininger et al. (2015); Anderson and Genicot (2015); Rosenblum (2015); Roy (2015).

[41] In particular, see Jeffrey (2010, 95).   [42] Ibid.

court rulings and other obstacles.[43] Severe inequality had prompted these reforms; by 1962, roughly 31 percent of Kerala's rural households were still landless, versus 12 percent nationally.[44] Little had changed by the late 1960s. A 1967 food crisis elevated stress caused by stagnant agricultural productivity and high underemployment.[45]

Land redistribution was particularly important for the CPI as the majority of its support derived from landless laborers, sharecroppers, and small cultivators.[46] For Congress, whose traditional supporters were Kerala's landed groups, land reform was a method of expanding its weak support among landless groups.[47]

By 1972, despite multiple attempts to redistribute land, the Land Board responsible for implementation had identified a mere 40,000 acres of surplus land available for redistribution, of which only 1,200 acres had been distributed to landless individuals. Challenges in court, limited bureaucratic capacity, and "excess land agitation" mobilized by political opponents (the Communist Party of India-Marxist or CPM) kept the pace of state-led land redistribution "painfully slow."[48] Nationally, the Congress Party faced a similar dilemma. In 1971, Indira Gandhi was elected on a wildly popular agenda of *garibi hatao* ("Stop Poverty") with land reform a core component.[49] The Congress Party quickly passed the 24th and 25th constitutional amendments addressing the Supreme Court's prior rulings limiting the scope of state-legislated land redistribution.[50] However, in the wake of the Oil Crisis of 1973, popular unrest in the form of strikes and mass protests began to mount. Critiques of Indira's regime came from within Parliament, through 10 no confidence votes, and also from Supreme Court rulings. When the Court declared electoral malpractice by the PM in *Indira Nehru Gandhi v. Raj Narayan*, Indira's tolerance for democratic dissent broke. She declared a state of internal emergency, known as the Emergency, which lasted from June 25, 1975 until March 21, 1977.

Despite its draconian costs, the Emergency had surprising benefits for redistribution. India overall suffered from extreme curtailment of civil and political liberties, widespread censorship, police detention and torture, and a

---

[43] Nossiter (1982, 292–306). In 1963, Congress passed the Kerala Land Reforms Act, 1963, which attempted to revive the 1959 reform, but rather than compulsory vesting of landlords' and intermediaries' land rights in the government, the 1963 Act required cultivators to apply to purchase land rights using a Land Tribunal. By the *Land Reforms Survey in Kerala 1966–7*, only 3 percent of tenants had applied for new land rights, and no tenants had purchased title to the land (s)he cultivated via the Land Tribunal.

[44] Nossiter (1982, 294). [45] Ibid.

[46] See Gough (1967, 86–7); Murthy and Rao (1968, 69–72), c.f. Nossiter (1982, 335); Dasgupta and Morris-Jones (1975).

[47] Ibid. [48] Nossiter (1982, 297). [49] Pillai and Ghurye (1976, 168).

[50] These amendments asserted Parliament's right to amend the fundamental rights enumerated in the Constitution, in line with the Constitution's directive principles. The amendments explicitly claim that legislation along these lines does not contradict constitutional article 31 (ensuring no person shall be deprived of his or her property save by the authority of the law). See Pillai and Ghurye (1976, 169).

brutal mass sterilization campaign by Indira Gandhi's son Sanjay. Yet, in Kerala, Congress and the CPI used this period to push land redistribution forward at an artificially fast pace. Whereas only 8,600 acres of land had been redistributed pre-Emergency, by the end of 1976, the government identified 106,000 acres of surplus land. The state acquired possession of 52,000 surplus acres, from which it redistributed 26,000 acres.[51]

The Emergency's massive land redistribution destabilized traditional sources of privilege and brought remaining power disparities into sharper focus. According to Mr. K. R. N. Menon, land redistribution empowered the Communist Party to unite low-caste, formerly landless cultivators against the matrilineal joint family as a source of "concentrated pockets of power and land ownership ... that created a landed gentry."[52] Emergency-facilitated land redistribution brought the continued, albeit diminished, control of land and power by matrilineal joint families once again into the public eye. *Such frustration provided "the Communist movement [with] the necessary catalyst to create [the] groundswell of support that was needed to pass" inheritance reform.*[53]

According to Professor Devika J., the CPI-led abolition of the Hindu joint family served two purposes: it performed the powerful symbolic act of dismantling feudalism by ending joint families' inherited privileges,[54] while it also quietly consolidated new CPI alliances with elite men from *nair* and other matrilineal groups (*ezhava*). Reform advanced these relationships by eliminating legal constraints to the partitioning and selling of landed wealth. As a result, "[V]ast tracts of land were sold off by subsequent [*nair* and *ezhava*] generations post 1976 to this day."[55] This final destruction of matrilineal practices was possible, in large part, because "women were still dispensable, disposable, and invisible" in Kerala's politics.[56]

To summarize, the CPI successfully legislated Kerala's final round of inheritance reform using Congress-led land redistribution to mobilize popular resentment around the core concern of land inequality. The CPI was the main political force behind reform, directing anger and blame to the matrilineal joint family to win a symbolic victory with its base – formerly landless agriculturalists – and to build a new set of supporters – elite matrilineal men aiming to transfer jointly held property into private assets and solidify their social standing.[57] This latter concern was ostensibly to benefit matrilineal women and the patrilineal *nambudiri* women tied to them. However, reform mainly benefited "junior" men (younger brothers) in matrilineal *(nair* and *ezhava)* groups.

[51] Nossiter (1982, 297).
[52] This hierarchy was solidified through *nambudiri – nair* marriage alliances, according to interviews with Mr. K. R. N. Menon during Fall 2015 by Rajiv Naresh on my behalf.
[53] Ibid.   [54] That is, through *nambudiri – nair* marriage alliances.
[55] Interview with Professor Devika J., Fall 2015 by Rajiv Naresh on my behalf.   [56] Ibid.
[57] In the prior 1967 elections, *nair* social reformers' NSS supported Congress (Nossiter, 1982, 211).

If my conclusions about reform's motivation are accurate, legislators should not only raise rhetorical concerns about dismantling exploitative social systems as well as economic concerns about eliminating constraints to accessing ancestral property in parliamentary debates about inheritance reform. Additionally, if women's influence was minimal, references to their interests should be primarily rhetorical, with few to no indications of women's direct influence over reform's proposed content or implementation.

4.2.4 Legislating Reform: Motives, Voices, and Silence

I found that the importance of dismantling exploitative social and economic traditions along the lines of concerns raised by ambitious young *nair* men seeking to destroy the socially "backward" matrilineal traditions dominated Kerala's legislative debates. At the outset of the 1975 legislative session, Congress Minister of Agriculture and Labor Shri Vakkom Purushothaman began with the message: *"Kerala, which has made many progressive laws has a black spot; we are here today to remove [it]."*[58]

This echoed his argument in 1973's preliminary discussion of the bill:

the old joint family system is not apt for the modern outlook. I won't go into detail on the accursed customs that were going on in the name of joint family systems and matriliny. ... Things are changing now. The government has brought this new law to abolish this system completely.[59]

Throughout the debate processes, legislators made clear their commitment to equality to justify abolishing the Hindu joint family. As G. Gopinathan Pillai put it:

"Even though we say we are a secular nation and we are journeying towards socialism, we still give prominence to religion and caste ... men and women should have equal rights. I welcome both these laws."[60]

Legislators supporting reform as a matter of justice typically belong to the ruling coalition – members of Indira Gandhi's "New" or "Ruling" Congress, the Communist Party of India, and minority parties including the Praja Socialist Party (PSP), dominated by *nairs*, to which Pillai adhered.[61]

---

[58] Government of India, Kerala State Legislature proceedings of August 1, 1975 on "The Kerala Joint Hindu Family System (Abolition) Bill, 1973 and the Hindu Marriage (Kerala Amendment) Bill, 1973."

[59] Government of India, Kerala State Legislature proceedings of July 11, 1973 on "The Hindu Marriage (Kerala Amendment) Bill, 1973 and the Kerala Joint Hindu Family System (Abolition) Bill, 1973."

[60] Ibid.

[61] According to the Nossiter (1982, 223) summary of the Indian Electoral Commission Report on the General Election to the Kerala Legislative Assembly 1970, Kerala's ruling coalition included the CPI, RSP, PSP, ML, and New Congress: the branch of the INC led by Indira Gandhi (INC(R)). See Nossiter 1982, 207 for the characterization of the PSP as dominated by nairs.

Members of opposition parties also supported reform to further economic interests. According to Shri K. M. Mani from the (opposition) Kerala Congress:

if an individual from a joint family starts a new industry, he would be unable to do so without getting his share from the property.... It is difficult to approach other family members regarding share division.... So it is usually better to choose each person's tenancy [individual shares] in common over the Coparcenary [Joint Family system.[62]

Notably, Mani's Kerala Congress was the main contender with the INC for matrilineal *nair* men's votes.

Where are the women, from either matrilineal or patrilineal groups in this debate? In 1975, there were no women in Kerala's legislative assembly.[63] Thus, concern for women by male members of parliament took two forms. The most frequent conceded women's severe constraints to accessing inheritance, and proposed state paternalism as the only contemporary solution to "dirty, pre-modern concept[s]," along with the hope of women's increased political participation in the future.[64] In the words of Samyukta Socialist Party (opposition) party member Shri V. K. Gopinathan:

Gender equality is a deception. Because it will take many centuries before women achieve equality in society or come into ruling positions that men have secured their authority over. So, to achieve equality, we have to give reservations – even in appointments – to women.... We don't yet have rules for fighting against the loss of inheritance rights of women after marriage and the dirty, pre-modern concept of dowry.... I conclude by requesting ... the bill so as to rescue women from the cruelty of divorce.

The second form of concern for women recognized their particular constraints to benefiting from legal rights. The CPM's Shri K. Chathunni Master explains:

this new bill will bring forth many knotty problems that are unfit for this age ... it is the women who will suffer more as anyone can guess from their present day condition. Men will find many loopholes to escape while women won't ... no protection has been meted out to [women] ... [the law] has the potential to destroy the inheritance rights, social and familial relationships and can throw man-woman relationships into the sewer.[65]

While such critique was moderated in the final round of debates, it was not totally abandoned. K. Pankajakshan of the opposition Revolutionary Socialist

[62] Government of India, Kerala State Legislature proceedings of July 11, 1973 on "The Hindu Marriage (Kerala Amendment) Bill, 1973 and the Kerala Joint Hindu Family System (Abolition) Bill, 1973."
[63] In 1970, no women were elected to any of the State Legislative Assembly's 133 seats. One woman was elected in 1967's elections, and one woman elected to one of the 140 seats in 1977's elections. See the Electoral Commission of India data on elections to Kerala's Legislative Assembly.
[64] Shri V. K. Gopinath, 1973 proceedings, 2814–15. [65] Ibid.

Party raised this concern briefly, but with little effort to alter the proposed bill before passage: *"Where changing conditions that were in existence for a long time, due diligence should have been given. I conclude my words by giving my opinion that the government should reform the bill further even if it is passed now."*[66]

The final critique, presented by N. E. Balaram, the ruling CPI's party leader in Parliament, advocated further revisions prior to legislating reform to alleviate concern about women's ability to benefit from the current legislation: *"Can this law [for inheritance which may spur divorce] be revised ...? Because women will suffer till their breaking point before they go to court, while men will go whenever they want."*[67]

Given legal reform's fundamental challenges for women, what alternative avenues existed for their participation and agency? K. Saradamoni (1982, 156) writes:

the struggles and fights of the period [to reform land rights, including inheritance] which were motivated by a sense of freedom, equality and fairness pushed women to a position of subordination ... non-participation in economic activity as well as socio-political organizations outside the home, insufficient economic development ... and growing class interests prevented women even from realizing what was happening.

Interviews confirm this bleak view. According to Professor Praveena Kodoth at the Centre for Development Studies, "[S]ocio-political [inheritance] reform movements were not women-controlled in any manner."[68] Devika J. characterizes Kerala as having "an almost complete absence of civil society during that [the reform] period that would answer to female oppression."[69] The one exception, according to Kodoth, occurred within the *namboodiri* community in which "women were terribly oppressed and the reform was designed to give them more humane forms of marriage.... [However] in reality, all subsumed in the framework of caste and community and women's rights were incidental or ancillary [to reform movements]."

Despite legislators' clear understanding of the disadvantage legal reform was likely to create for women from matrilineal families, no attempts were made to formalize structures that would enforce women's legal rights within the legislation. As a result, it is not surprising that reform's dominant impact on women was to dispossess them of ancestral land, according to Professor Kodoth. Saradamoni (1982, 161) suggests that the main impact of land reform was to give individuals wishing to partition the joint family leverage; a claim made by legislators in debates: *"With the introduction of private interests in*

---

[66] Government of India, Kerala State Legislature proceedings of August 1, 1975 on "The Kerala Joint Hindu Family System (Abolition) Bill, 1973 and the Hindu Marriage (Kerala Amendment) Bill, 1973."

[67] Ibid., 133–4.

[68] Interview with Professor Praveena Kodoth, Fall 2015 by Rajiv Naresh on my behalf.

[69] Interview with Professor Devika J., Fall 2015 by Rajiv Naresh on my behalf.

land which permitted division and alienation the joint family and the shelter and security they offered to women withered away."

Professor Kodoth elaborates further:

[T]he idea of marriage [and separation from the matrilineal taravad] became entrenched – it became the organizing mode of society and women were being increasingly defined in a dependent relationship with their husbands. Nair women were actually losing their rights since they were married to men outside their hometown – their native land was sold and the liquidated asset was then re-invested and often under the husband's control.[70]

Jeffrey (2010, 86) suggests a more positive interpretation, arguing: "[D]uring the transition from matriliny to patriliny, they [women] acquired positions in salaried employment that gave them importance to a family as earners and as people of some (however limited) influence in public and private institutions." He concludes that the Joint Hindu Family (Abolition) Act and its precursors were successful because they were *"demanded,* not imposed."[71] Yet, it is noteworthy that these demands came not from female beneficiaries, but from matrilineal men. The ideal of social equality was powerful enough to attract supporters from both the landless groups that traditionally supported the Communist Party of India and the male social elites who typically supported Congress.[72]

For women, the results of reform fell far short of equality, further marginalizing them. In the words of one *nair* woman who lived through most of this process, postreform:

People were unhappy – the rights of ladies had gone. There was no use of women fighting this and there was no such organised movement in our village despite women being unhappy. When I was growing up, in our side, the girls were not working and were not in politics at all.[73]

4.3 ANDHRA PRADESH

4.3.1 Historical Context: Caste, Land, and Gender

The recent bifurcation of the former AP state, located at the south eastern edge of the Indian subcontinent, is indicative of its deep divisions since formation in 1956. Much variation can be explained from the state's binary division into water-rich, broadly prosperous "wet areas" – from which the TDP responsible for legislating reform drew its *Kamma* supporters – and water-poor, extractive "dry areas" – from which the Congress traditionally picked

[70] Interview with Professor Praveena Kodoth, Fall 2015 by Rajiv Naresh on the author's behalf.
[71] Jeffrey (2010, 87).
[72] Interview with Professor Praveena Kodoth, Fall 2015 by Rajiv Naresh on the author's behalf.
[73] Interview with Mrs. Saraswathi Nair, born in 1933, in Pudupurriyaram, South Palakkad District, Fall 2015 by Rajiv Naresh on the author's behalf.

leaders and the Communist Party identified those who could mobilize dissent. Unsurprisingly, the breakaway Telangana province now occupies most of the arid area's landmass.[74]

Each of these regions shares important similarities with Kerala's precolonial and colonial historical milieu. The wet areas, districts bordering either the coast or the Krishna and Godavari Rivers, benefitted from "centuries old" irrigation infrastructure extended by the British within the Madras Presidency.[75] This, in turn, resulted in prosperous rice cultivation that facilitated high levels of mobility between urban and rural centers and autonomous development of credit societies that fueled a range of investments, including in literacy. This generated "widespread popular participation in political movements."[76] Similar to Kerala and much of India, a small set of *Brahmans* comprising about 5 percent of the population occupied traditional elite caste in this region, while the main peasant cultivator castes, here *Kammas* and *Kapus*, gained the most from colonial rule.[77]

The dry areas were comprised of two regions ceded from the Nizam of Hyderabad's Princely State at the end of the eighteenth century: Ryalaseema and the remains of the Nizam's domain ceded in 1948 to Independent India, known as Telangana.[78] Limited access to water and investment in agricultural development, coupled with a rigid, hierarchical distribution of political authority, produced a small, *"extremely powerful rural élite which kept localities tightly controlled under it and monopolized access to government institutions"* (Washbrook, 1973, 523).

Under the Nizams, religious and linguistic differences separated rulers (a small Urdu-speaking Muslim elite) from subjects (mainly Hindu, speaking a mixture of Telegu, Marathi, and Kannada languages). In addition to "total absence" of political and civil freedoms, subjects endured "the grossest forms of feudal exploitation."[79] While caste hierarchy was similar to Kerala's, repression was significantly more severe, particularly in Telangana where both Muslim and high-caste Hindu landlords (*deshmukhs*) and *jagirdars* (holders of lifetime, Nizam-granted land titles) extorted forced labor (*vetti*) and debt bondage from

---

[74] For extensive historical examination of the region according to these divisions, see Washbrook (1973).

[75] See ibid., 508–18.

[76] See ibid. Notably, on p. 513: "between 1891 and 1931, the literacy rate in Kistna and Godaveri districts rose faster than anywhere else [in India]." On "public politics," see p. 518: "The ease of communication, the existence of obvious centres for organization, and, above all, the large number of wealthy people in the countryside, made it possible to develop, and, for the government, impossible to prevent, widespread popular participation in political movements."

[77] Ibid., 508–12. *Kamma* and *Kapu* subcastes invested and gained most from increasing access to irrigation and literacy under British colonial rule.

[78] Rayalaseema, or "land of the kings" comprises Chittoor, Cuddapah, Anantapur, and Kurnool districts, with the *Reddi* or *Reddy* subcastes dominant; and Telangana, or "land of the Telugus" includes Mahabubnagar, Ranga Reddy, Hyderabad, Medak, Nizamabad, Adilabad, Karimnagar, Warangal, Khammam, and Nalgonda districts, as of 2002 boundaries. See Suri (2002, 4).

[79] See Sarkar (1983, 442–3).

peasants of lower castes and tribes.[80] As independence neared, land grabs by the landlord classes reduced peasant welfare even further (ibid.).

In response to the INC's unwillingness to "take up the struggle of the people against the 'princes and *nawabs*' of the native states" prior to independence, communists led an armed revolt against Hyderabad's Nizam and his Raza-kar bands.[81] Between July 4, 1946 and October 1951, the Communist-led movement waged the largest peasant guerilla war in contemporary Indian history.[82] The movement created significant change, eliminating forced labor and enforcing land redistribution. It also set a hard political agenda for more extensive land reform postrevolt. Congress's first act following the national army's intervention to end the armed rebellion was to abolish all *jagirdars'* land titles in 1949, alongside similar reforms in the former Madras Presidency.[83]

Telangana's armed struggle is significant because it catalyzed land redistribution and set expectations for reform that Congress could not ignore. The Communists also benefitted from their ability to navigate peaceful politics, retaining popular support in the first elections postrevolt. As of 1952, Communists won every Assembly seat from Nalgonda and Warangal districts under the pseudonym of the People's Democratic Front.[84] In 1953, concerns about the communists' militant agenda waned once the Congress Party agreed to create AP as a linguistic state for Telugus. Yet, as in Kerala, land redistribution's slow initial pace led to popular mobilization in the late 1960s. As of October 1967, a clash between landlords and tribal *Girijans* marching to a Communist Party of India (Marxist) meeting in rural Srikakulam sparked an armed conflict across the state that lasted until 1972 (Sarkar 1983, 424; Singh 1995, 238). This also marked the passage of new land redistribution legislation: the AP Land Reforms (Ceiling on Agricultural Holdings) Bill of 1972. Again, the state made limited implementation efforts in the following decade.[85] Political competition over commitment to land reform and social empowerment returned to the fore around AP's inheritance reform a decade later.

4.3.2 Inheritance Reform's Origins

AP's inheritance reform has two remarkable characteristics: First, the stark contrast between women's active mobilization around social reform in the years preceding inheritance reform and the absence of women's demands for legislating gender-equal inheritance. Second, the TDP aggressively publicized its support for and passage of inheritance reform on women's behalf. This strategy

---

[80] See ibid. 443.   [81] See Sundarayya and Chattopadhyaya (1972, 4).
[82] See Sarkar (1983, 442). At its height, the armed struggle affected about 3,000 villages with a population of three million people occupying an area of 16,000 square miles.
[83] Sankaran (p. 20) "Introduction" in Yugandhar, (1996). Reforms include the Madras Estates (Abolition and Conversion into Ryotwari) Act 1948, and the Abolition of Jagirdari Act of 1949.
[84] See Sarkar (1983, 445).   [85] Suri and Raghavulu (1996, 43).

of promoting the TDP's "revolutionary reform" produced significant political capital with immediate benefits for the TDP's ability to mobilize women voters.

AP was revolutionary as the first state to amend Nehru's problematic attempt to equalize women's inheritance rights: the Hindu Succession Act of 1956.[86] Whereas the "Kerala model" of reform abolished the Hindu joint family with collective ownership by the coparcenary, the "Andhra model" kept the Hindu joint family and gave women equal rights with male coparceners. Under AP's amendment, the daughter of a coparcener became a coparcener by birth, entitled to the same share of inheritance as a son in the event of collective property's partition. If a given daughter died before partition, the amendment granted her children entitlement to her share.[87]

AP's TDP proposed the HSA Amendment (HSAA) in the state's legislative assembly on March 18, 1983. As in Kerala, preliminary debates led the assembly to appoint a Select Committee, which collected opinions from a number of districts. Remarkably, consultations explicitly included not only social organizations but also women. In 1985, after Nandamuri Taraka Rama Rao (popularly known as N. T. R.) returned to power in a new TDP-led government, the act was reintroduced as the "Hindu Succession (Andhra Pradesh Amendment) Bill, 1985." Ultimately the bill was passed, effective from September 5, 1985.

Why did reform emerge at this moment? NTR served as chief minister of AP for the major part of the years between 1983 and 1995, and is widely considered the act's main architect and sponsor. A former film star who acted in more than 300 Telugu films with a sizable female fan base, NTR launched his political career by founding the TDP in 1982.[88] One year later, in 1983, his party achieved historic electoral victory against the Indira Gandhi–led National Congress Party, which had dominated AP politics for more than 30 years.[89]

The TDP identified its creation as a "historical necessity" to right the injustice that AP's Telugus endured under decades of Congress leadership.[90] Yet it also required an autonomous voter base to survive. While the Congress Party had implicitly courted women voters, fielding the most women candidates of any party in prior elections, they rarely mentioned women explicitly in party manifestos.[91] NTR and the TDP sought to gain women's votes by explicitly addressing women's issues in the TDP manifesto and its marketing.[92]

---

[86] See Kishwar (1994) for detailed analysis. The 1956 Act marginally improved widow's inheritance, at the cost of introducing the "testamentary power" of wills to distribute inheritance outside reform's domain.

[87] Note that this reform explicitly applies to Hindu joint families governed by *Mitakshara* law, where inheritance of ancestral, joint family land is traditionally allocated at birth to sons only. In contrast, Hindu joint families governed by *Dayabhaga* law base inheritance on survivors' rights, rather than birth rights. In these cases, both sons and daughters inherit equally at the time of *kartas'* death. For details, see the 174th Law Commission Report (2005) or Desai (2010).

[88] Prasad (2014).   [89] Shatrugna (1984, 98).

[90] Naidu (1984, 131).   [91] Singer (2007, 143).   [92] Ibid., 143–8.

4.3.3 Political Context: Credit Claiming

Despite Andhra Pradesh's status as an "old Congress stronghold," citizens' patience with Indira Gandhi's growing personalization of the party and its machine broke by 1982.[93] In the space of the prior four years, she had replaced Andhra Pradesh's chief minister four times.[94] As of 1982, the disintegration of Congress (I)'s main opposition, the Janata Party, gave credence to the assertion that no alternative to Indira Gandhi's party existed.[95] Amidst rising frustration with the frequent imposition of president's rule and the open appointment of governor positions for party patronage, NTR launched the TDP.

NTR's campaign style and content were geared to attract a new voting constituency. In both his speeches and his campaigns, he directly sought out and addressed women. He garnered large audiences in rural villages, where women rarely joined political rallies, by creating his own chariot – a *padyatra* bus – in which he and his wife, Laxmi Parvati, rode.[96] Prasad (2014) credits NTR and his TDP as the most successful practitioners of "cine-politics": elite use of the cinema as a tool for political expression and mass mobilization. As a film star at the peak of his career, NTR produced drama by harnessing "home-grown images and idioms" – from reminding voters of the charismatic power he embodied in his divine stage presence to the importance of regional leadership: "self-respect for the Telugus" – to communicate the party's commitments to new constituents: poor rural voters, female voters, and *Kamma* co-elites. In addition to rousing speeches, the TDP distributed cassettes, pamphlets, and "life-sized posters" of NTR portrayed as the mythological and historical roles he took on in cinema.[97]

NTR's dual support bases in mass media and elite literary circles[98] facilitated his ability to communicate his willingness to commit to women's welfare and empowerment to them directly. This communication was crucial for mobilizing women, as traditionally less engaged voters.[99] The TDP's 20-point election manifesto specifically addressed women's land inheritance within its "women's welfare" plank:

"Telugu Desam" will see that women's welfare does not remain a mere slogan. It will guarantee their legitimate rights. It condemns the feudal culture which only views women as objects of pleasure. It would initiate action for equal share for daughters in the paternal property along with the sons. It would establish a separate University for women and would ensure a respectable place for women in society. The evil practice of dowry will be curbed.[100]

---

93 Guha (2007, 548). 94 Ibid. 95 Shatrugna (1984, 96). 96 Singer (2007, 143).
97 Naidu (1984, 133–7) and Rajasekhariah et al. (1987, 591).
98 NTR launched the TDP's campaign by touring AP on his "chariot," the Chaitanya Radham. Giant cardboard cutouts of NTR as the god Krishna emerged everywhere, portraying him "blowing the conch to sound the start of the war." Messages proclaimed: "Telugu Desam pilustondi, lea. Kadaliraa" (Telugu Desam is calling; arise; join [us])." For details: Guha (2007, 549); Juluri (2013, 97–8); Shatrugna (1984, 98); Prasad (2014, 67–8).
99 Mehta et al. (1981, 106); Bardhan and Mookherjee (2000). 100 See Shatrugna (1984, 108).

Supporting such legislation had several political advantages as a signal of the TDP's responsiveness to female voters. First, legislation was a concrete commitment to advance women's "legitimate rights," but as a symbolic gesture only. This leads to a second benefit: given the lack of women's demands for such change, costly investments in its implementation were unlikely to be necessary.[101]

As of the 1983 elections, women's political allegiances shifted dramatically. While the majority of female voters had supported Congress in 1980, only 39 percent voted for them in 1983.[102] Instead, a majority of women supported the TDP.[103] Analysts claim "the women's vote edged the Telugu Desam into office."[104] Postelections, Singer (2007, 149) presents evidence that the TDP's victory encouraged similar shifts in opposition party strategies, as articulated across manifestos.

The diffusion of political strategies is clearest around women's political and economic inclusion. The TDP proactively instituted reservations (9 percent) for women as members of *Panchayats* following their 1983 electoral victory.[105] As of the 1991 elections, Congress, the BJP, and the TDP's partners in the National Front coalition began directly addressing women's interests in their own party manifestos. Indeed, this piecemeal reform of local governance set the stage for more comprehensive institutional changes in Karnataka shortly thereafter. While AP again set an agenda for pro-women reforms, the structure of legislation left many loop holes. By 1989, they went further, reserving 9 percent of heads of local government *(Sarpaunches, Pradhans, or Presidents of the Panchayat)* to be female. However, there was a catch: if no women were elected, they could be co-opted.[106] After the TDP's historic victory of 1983, recognition of women's pivotal role prompted the party's newly elected representatives to act on their campaign promises. The TDP's position in debates emphasized their interests in ensuring their party received sole credit as women's benefactor.

Within two months of elections, the TDP proposed a legislative reform in line with its pledge "to initiate action for equal share for daughters in the paternal property along with the sons." The party introduced a bill to the state

---

[101] Despite extensive interviews with NTR on the nature and source of his policies toward women, Singer (2007) presents no evidence of women's demands for inheritance reform. Personal interviews with NTR's daughter by the author, in Hyderabad during January 2014 confirm that pressure from women did not drive NTR's support for inheritance reform.

[102] Preelection Survey of A. P. Assembly elections 1983, Political Science Department, Osmania University, Hyderabad. Reported as Table 4.5, p. 69 of Telugu Desam Party (1984, 104–12).

[103] See Singer (2007, 148) and Suri (2003, 66). Suri only provides figures on women's votes for TDP and Congress in 1996 and 1998, but states: "The women's vote for the TDP had been on the higher side in all the previous elections." Vakil (1984).

[104] Analysis in *Eenadu*, August 15, 1983, cited on Suri (2003, 148).

[105] Singer (2007, 103).

[106] Ibid.

Legislative Assembly proposing to amend the Hindu Succession Act 1956 to give daughters equal property inheritance rights.[107]

4.3.4 Legislating Reform: Motives, Voices, and Silence

Members of the TDP framed reform as a symbolic victory for all women, and for progressive society more broadly. In fact, they saw reform as a specific source of political capital for the TDP, emphasizing the party's political ownership of the act. In contrast, members of the TDP's main opposition, Congress, argued that the TDP's proposal was a flawed attempt at reform.

The TDP's Minister for Law and Courts, Shri Rajesam Gaud, framed the importance of reform as all encompassing: *"this Bill ... brings a lot of good name to the society."*[108] Shri D. Chinnamallayya, member of TDP ally the CPI, added similar support: *"it is happy news that for the first time in Andhra state, this Bill is bringing equal property rights to women. Our women are going to United Nations Organization and throwing light on the whole clan of women."*[109] Congress's Shri. A. Dharmarao cast doubt on both the substance and veracity of the TDP's claims: *"this Telugu Desam Government is showing off saying that it is striving for women's welfare. This party once said that it is going to give key importance to women, but so far one woman got place in the ministry. Same way, the motive of this Bill might not get fulfilled."*[110] The TDP's Srimathi Prathi Manemma pushed back: *"nothing good was done to these women during Congress regime, people should feel happy that during the regime of Annagaru [NTR], we are striving to better the status of women."*[111] The immediate response, we can presume from a member of Congress, indicates that Congress also worried about their reputation: *"We should not forget that it is Mother Indira who brought out this Equal Rights Bill."*[112] Law Minister Shri Rajesam Goud makes clear that the TDP deserves sole credit: *"Hon. Chief Minister Rama Rao Garu introduced this Bill to give equal right in property sharing ... this is the first time ever in India, for a Bill like this be introduced .... In order to fulfill the promise [we] made [in our manifesto], Telugu Desam has brought in this Bill."*[113]

Congress's response, by Shri P. Ramachandrareddy, made clear how crucial the cultivation of women's votes through the promotion of pro-women reform had become for both parties: *"Nobody should use this for his or her political gains.... We all should praise this Bill.... After getting this Bill passed here, let this be continued in the Central Government too.... [Please do not] give speeches that the [Congress-led] Parliament is not doing it."*[114]

---

[107] See Sri Rajesam Goud's explanation of the Bill's timeline in AP, State Legislative Assembly (1985, 423–4).
[108] Ibid., 433. [109] Ibid., 430. [110] Ibid., 431–2. [111] Ibid., 427.
[112] Ibid. This is the only response attributed to "A Respectable Member" rather than a specific MP.
[113] Ibid., 423. [114] Ibid., 425.

In contrast to Kerala's dearth of female members of parliament, AP's 1985 legislative assembly included four women, notably all elected within the TDP. One of these representatives, Shrimati Y. Sithadevi, lauded the TDP's commitment to women: *"we, all women support this Bill in its totality. We discussed our fundamental rights in our Constitutional law, but because of 1956 Hindu Succession Act, due its gender differentiation, a daughter is deprived of participation in a joint family ... till today no one ever protected their equal rights."*[115]

Yet even amidst her praise, Shrimati Sithadevi voiced a note of concern about the potential ineffectiveness of reform absent enforcement that spanned multiple legal domains: land inheritance and dowry. *"This government is bringing a lot of laws.... I congratulate the Telugu Desam Government for coming forward bravely in bringing the Dowry Banishment Law ... after passing this Bill, see to it that the law is certainly followed.... If ever anybody tries to take dowry, let them be punished severely."*[116]

The final female TDP legislator to speak, Srimathi A. Bhanumathi, echoed a similar concern: *"Law alone cannot take women to noble position. If this law followed true to its words ... then this will be a backbone for the progress.... Women will develop a lot of strength to take their own decisions when they have rights for the properties."*[117]

Thus, women directly and indirectly raised two concerns. The first emphasized the need for enforcing reform. The second was about monitoring reform's subsequent application, which could foster either egalitarian behavior or traditional, inegalitarian practices such as dowry. These concerns fit into a larger pattern of prior demands to reduce violence against women, particularly around dowry "harassment."

Notably, NTR's daughter, Congress MP Dr. Daggubati Purandeswari, suggested that women's *political* organization was not driving her father's vision of reform: *"Yes, women were involved in his campaign, but women played a very silent role.... There was no political awareness in the early days of his campaign. Later, women gained greater political awareness, thanks to his work."*[118]

Dr. Tripurana, a TDP female legislator and member of the Select Committee that had structured inheritance reform, insisted it was women's *social* campaigns that had influenced legal reform's passage.

A brief history: in 1974, Hyderabad, AP's capital, had been the site of the first "contemporary feminist" women's group: the Progressive Organization of Women (POW) (Kumar, 1999, 345). Comprised of women from the Maoist movement, POW dedicated itself to comprehensively addressing gender oppression (ibid., 345–6). In 1975, POW mobilized against dowry, drawing as many as two thousand people to demonstrations (ibid., 349). Following the Emergency's imposition, most activists went underground, only to emerge with the formation of a new, post-Emergency Janata government in 1978.

[115] Ibid., 425–6.   [116] Ibid., 426.   [117] Ibid.
[118] Interview with the author on January 24, 2014, at Purandeswari's residence in Hyderabad.

At this point, Delhi became the focal point for agitation and reform. National legislation criminalizing dowry passed in 1980, although it was subsequently heavily contested by rulings from the Delhi Sessions Court and the Supreme Court from 1982 to 1985 (ibid., 347, 350–1).

After the Emergency, Hyderabad's POW took up a second concern: rape. The city exploded after the rape of a Hyderabadi woman, Rameeza Bee, by several policemen, and the murder of her husband following his protest:

Twenty-two thousand people went to the police station, laid the man's dead body in the station veranda, set up road blocks, cut the telephone wires, stoned the building, and set fire to some bicycles in the compound. The army had to be called in, and the uprising was quieted only after the state government had been dismissed and a commission of inquiry into the rape and the murder had been appointed.[119]

In this context, the early 1980s emerged as a moment of unprecedented visibility for the women's movement and their two major issues, dowry and rape.[120]

Decades later, during my personal interview with her, former TDP legislator Dr. Tripurana argued that NTR had introduced inheritance reform to respond to these concerns: *"he wanted to end the dowry system … if parents give a share of land equally to boys and girls, they will not give dowry."*[121]

NTR's daughter affirmed this in a segment of our interview, explaining: *"If women are given equal rights to property, he believed dowry will eventually go away."*[122]

Such an attitude was highly optimistic, given the failure of dowry to disappear "on its own" many decades after its legal abolishment. Indeed, the relationship between dowry abolishment and property inheritance reform was never obvious.[123]

According to Jamuna Paruchuri, a female activist who headed an initiative through the National Rural Development Program to empower women, NTR and the TDP were acting on behalf of the *Kamma* elites who funded, publicized, and provided the political vision for the party's lightning quick ascendancy

---

[119] Compilation of reports in the *Times of India, Statesman, Indian Express, and Patriot*, April 2-12, 1978, c.f. ibid., 352–3.

[120] In 1979, a number of women's demonstrations mobilized around protests against police- and landlord- or employer-initiated rape around the country. Women's protests coalesced as a movement against rape in 1980, when four senior lawyers authored an open letter against a judgment in Maharashtra regarding a case of police rape. For a cogent summary, see ibid., 353. Growing scholarship around issues of gender justice, such as the Indian Ministry of Education and Social Welfare's 1974 toward Equality Report (Guha, 1974) helped these movements take shape.

[121] Interview with the author on January 24, 2014, at the Andhra Pradesh State Commission for Women, Hyderabad.

[122] Interview with the author on January 24, 2014, Hyderabad.

[123] On relevant legislation, the Dowry Prohibition Act of 1961, Dr. Tripurana explained: "Yes, there was this Act, but people are taking [dowry] and giving a glass of water. This was a total failure of an act." Personal interview on January 24, 2014, Hyderabad.

94 *Where Are the Women? Investigating Reform's Roots*

to power. Following Congress-led land reform policies that dominated the 1950s–1970s, a class of small landholders, particularly the *Kamma*, gained valuable landholdings with which they were disinclined to part. *"This was why NTR declared land for daughters as compulsory. This was a strategy to help this new segment of landowners keep their land."*[124]

As the Maoist revolutionary Varavara Rao further explains: while the *Kamma* had traditionally allied with the CPI and CPI (ML) to fight *Brahman* oppression, their interests changed as they benefited from the combination of irrigation projects along the Krishna and Godavri Rivers and land redistribution. *"NTR used Naxal slogans (land reform) to come to power, but once he came to power he acted to protect his class. Where there were [water] resources in Telangana, they [Kamma] came and settled, and these people were the vote banks of NTR."*[125]

Elite *Kamma* men's interests appear similar to those of elite *Nair* men in promoting Kerala's abolition of the Hindu joint family. In other words, we should not expect to see mechanisms drafted to enforce women's entitlements, as daughters, to inherit land. Instead, we would expect majority-male legislators to invest very little, if any, resources for this purpose.

Indeed, both Paruchuri and Rao argue that inheritance reform was "mainly on paper."[126] Even Dr. Tripurana, head of AP's State Women's Commission, argues that even today reform is not being vigorously enforced: *There are acts, very good acts, but strict implementation is necessary. If so, if these acts are implemented, this is a great safety mechanism for the girl. [On inheritance reform] they [the executive and judiciary] don't implement the law. Property share is totally a civil issue – family elders are there, but if they don't agree, then [women's use of] civil litigation is hopeless – it takes years.*[127]

Despite women's active mobilization around social reform in the years preceding inheritance reform, they did not demand gender equal inheritance rights.[128] In the absence of such a demand from politically mobilized women, the party who legislated these reforms, the TDP, perceived no incentive to put in place the costly legal-bureaucratic mechanisms necessary for enforcement.

In fact, even the 9 percent reservation for women as heads of local government that NTR pioneered did not transform women's ability to enforce rights. This was because the legal statute included a means for men to avoid giving

[124] Personal interview on January 21, 2014, Society for the Elimination of Rural Poverty, Hyderabad.
[125] Personal interview on January 22, 2014, at Varavara Rao's home, Hyderabad.
[126] Ibid.
[127] Personal interview on January 24, 2014, Hyderabad.
[128] This contrasts with examples of other reforms enacted in other states during the same period, where women played a rather active and direct role in bringing about substantive changes toward gender equality. Examples, both regressive and progressive, include the Nikahanama Group that drafted the "nikahanama," a Muslim marriage contract in India's Muslim Women (Protection of Rights in Marriage) Bill in 1986, and the Women's Action and Research Group (WRAG) and Joint Women's Programme (JWP), who drafted a reformed Christian law with involvement from various church-based functionaries.

women electoral power (by appointing a woman of their choice as a figurehead rather than one that was autonomously elected, instead of encouraging women to form autonomous electoral bases). With no agitation and oversight from women, the party's self-propelled move to pass reform produced significant political benefits for the TDP. It formed a crucial part of the TDP's reputation as progressive and committed to women's welfare. Publicity credited the TDP as "revolutionary" and likely to "transform" women's role in society.[129] However, the party used visual imagery rather than bureaucratic enforcement mechanisms to maintain this reputation, even producing an "illustrated booklet depicting the schemes it had initiated for women between 1984 and 1988" to win subsequent elections.[130]

4.4 KARNATAKA

Karnataka, along with its most distinct pre-independence precursor, the Princely State of Mysore, is alternately lauded as "one of the few states in the Indian union to have evolved radical land reforms"[131] and derided as the "child of imperialism"[132] or "puppet sovereignty"[133] that failed at reforms, particularly around land.[134]

Independent of this debate, Karnataka is widely understood as unique in its "comparatively cohesive society" with much lower levels of economic and social inequality than either of the early reformers studied in the preceding text: Kerala and AP.[135]

4.4.1 Historical Context: Caste, Land, and Gender

Until the eighteenth century, a "patchwork of little kingdoms of quite restricted scale" with widely dispersed power occupied most of what became Karnataka state.[136] Between 1761 and 1799, the military regimes of Haidar Ali and his son Tipu Sultan created a sharp break from the past. This followed the broader pattern of "thrusting centralization" dictated by military imperatives across South India.[137] To raise revenue for increasingly expensive wars, especially as the British East India Company worked to extend their influence across South India's peninsula from Madras, their efforts were largely focused on centralizing the revenue collection process.[138] Estimates suggest they were quite effective: Haidar Ali raised about 0.8 million British pounds in revenue as of 1770, which soared to 2.8 million in 1792 in light of Tipu's victories.[139]

Upon defeating Tipu Sultan in 1799, the British parceled his territory between their allies – the Nizam in Hyderabad and the erstwhile royal family of Mysore, the Wadiyars (or Wodeyars) – who were positioned outside of

[129] See legislative assembly debates. [130] Singer (2007, 148).
[131] Thimmaiah and Aziz (1983, 811). [132] Hettne (1978, 43), c.f. Ikegame (2013, 10).
[133] Ray (1981, 99), c.f. Ikegame (2013, 10). [134] Kohli (1982, 311). [135] Manor (1989, 322).
[136] Ibid. 327. [137] Stein (1985, 391). [138] Roy (2010, 32); Manor (1989, 327).
[139] Calculations from Sanjay Subrahmanyam (1989, 203–33), c.f. Roy (2010, 18–19).

the regions where the British maintained direct control.[140] This led to six autonomous territories later amalgamated to form Independent Karnataka: the Princely States of the Maharaja of Mysore, the Nizam of Hyderabad, and Sandur; the British colonial governments of the Bombay and Madras presidencies; and the territory of Coorg, run by the chief commissioner of Coorg who doubled as the British Resident at Bangalore.[141]

While power remained largely dispersed at the level of rural villages, these units were increasingly well integrated into the structures of formal states.[142] However, the widespread institution of the *ryotwari* system of individual land cultivation promoted by British colonial rule led to a decline in the central state's revenue.[143] This was in part due to the gap – linguistically and socially – between bureaucracies largely staffed by *Brahmans* from other parts of India or civil servants from Britain and the local, non-*Brahman* landowners and cultivators whom they sought to regulate.[144]

These "not-too-intrusive *ryotwari* systems" led to relatively stable extensions of regional variations in equality through colonial times and into independence. "An extremely high proportion of owner-cultivators and an extremely low incidence of landless labourers" existed in what was princely Mysore, whereas levels of inequality were closer to the national mean in what had been Madras Presidency, and higher-than-average levels of tenants with low percentages of owner-cultivators in the former Bombay Presidency.[145]

The final, crucial event shaping Colonial Karnataka was the series of revolts by landowning peasants across what had been princely Mysore in the first part of the 1830s. These uprisings were in response to British attempts to aggressively intervene in local revenue extraction.[146] While the British initially imposed direct rule on Mysore until 1881, after the revolt they avoided interfering with local control by dominant owner-cultivator castes (ibid.). This meant that across Karnataka, power remained distributed between three castes: the "dominant castes" who owned and cultivated land: the *lingayats* and *vokkaligas*; princely rulers who came from a modest caste (either the cow-herding *yadav jati* or the potter *jati*); and those responsible for lending money, often controlled by members of the mercantile *banajiga jati*.[147]

After 1881, the royal family of the Princely State of Mysore adopted a new approach to circumvent British control: building a model state. This meant using a merit-based system to staff the Princely State's civil service, which inadvertently produced another bastion of *brahman* power.[148] The resulting bureaucracy coordinated publicly-financed industries, including the generation

---

[140] Manor (1989, 327); Ikegame (2013).   [141] Manor (1989, 326).
[142] Frykenberg (1977); Manor (1989, 327–8).
[143] Roy (2010, 19) estimates that a revenue of 1.4 million pounds was produced within "the territory carved up by the alliance between the Company, Nizam, and the Marathas after the fall of Tipu" along with a revenue of 0.4 million collected by the Wodeyar king.
[144] Manor (1989, 328, 338).
[145] Ibid., 328–9. See especially "Table 1: Karnataka's Agricultural Population in 1951" from the Census of India of the same year in ibid., 329.
[146] Ibid., 330.   [147] Ibid., 330, 334.   [148] Ibid., 39.

of hydro-electric power, which made Bangalore the first city in India with electric light, along with educational institutions and representative government well ahead of British India's provincial legislatures. It also supported freedom of the press and speech, which made it "a rare liberal island in the autocratic sea that was princely India."[149]

The unintended consequence of Mysore's unique openness was a non-*Brahman* movement that began with limited facilitation by the state in 1910, significantly opening the public service to non-*Brahmans*, and progressed to increasingly assertive associations of non-*Brahmans* that organized outside the state as of 1930.[150] Surprisingly, the long-term legacy of this mobilization was cooperation with another strong, yet largely *brahman* political association – the Mysore State Congress – to create the first substantive Congress movement as of 1937. This movement was initially mobilized by interest in channeling political resources from the national center to the state. However, as time passed it solidified around the dominant *lingayats* and *vokkaligas*, who successfully compelled the Maharaja to concede power to popular sovereignty as of 1947.[151]

Karnataka's history made such change uniquely possible. In the precolonial period, the *lingayat* or *virashaiva* sect of *Shaiva* accomplished major social reform. As early as the twelfth century, they "actively attacked religious hypocrisy," questioning the *brahman*-led system of caste hierarchy.[152] The sect preached radical rejection of many core principles of *Brahmanism*, most notably the idea that some groups could be socially polluted or "untouchable." In addition, its followers promoted practices to improve women's status, including relatively late (postpuberty) marriages and widow remarriages.[153]

Overall, a consistent trend that ties Karnataka's historical social landscape to the present appears to be its relatively fertile ground for tolerance with minimal support for large-scale concentration of wealth according to social hierarchy. As Manor (1989, 322–3) explains, it was the only region of British colonial India without mass conversions to Christianity by groups dissatisfied with Brahmanism. Despite its significant Muslim community (10.6 percent of the state population), violence between Hindus and Muslims has been extremely rare (ibid.). Additionally, Karnataka boasts relatively low proportions of landless laborers in its largest regional subsection: the former princely state of Mysore.

4.4.2 Political Context: Equality and Incremental Change

Karnataka's unique level of land equality played a central role in the process of inheritance reforms for gender equality. Notably, the old Mysore Princely State boasted the lowest levels of landlessness in all of South Asia for at

---

[149] Ibid.; Raghavan and Manor (2009, 4).
[150] Manor (1989, 339–40); Raghavan and Manor (2009, 4).   [151] Manor (1989, 340).
[152] The *lingayats* worshiped Shiva using the phallic symbol of the *lingam*, with "each member of the sect carrying a miniature *lingam*" (Thapar, 2002, 399).
[153] Ibid. Rather ironically, the movement evolved into its own caste, with earlier divisions later reasserting themselves in more muted forms (ibid.).

least two centuries.[154] Upon consolidation of a unified administration over Independent India's Karnataka, the INC Party took effective control of state politics. On its face, it looked similar to Congress in much of the rest of India, with the leadership held by members of the dominant castes – *vokkaligas* and *lingayats*.[155] Again, along the lines of work on Congress,[156] this led to a "Congress system" with clear, but limited grounds for inclusion (ibid.).

In the case of Karnataka, Congress was more committed to incremental change than elsewhere. They implemented a policy of "very modest reform and very limited representation for and concessions to less prosperous groups."[157] However, there was one notable exception to this pattern of tokenism: land reform of 1961, which set a precedent for future land reforms with a real capacity for enforcement.

Capturing the historical dynamics of landholding inequality is difficult given broad skepticism in the available data. However, two important, contradictory trends appear as of 1961. First, a doubling of landless laborers between the 1961 and 1971 Census of India: from roughly 13–26 percent.[158] Second, the proportion of owner-cultivators with small or marginal plot sizes increased in this same period, from 43.6 to 54.1 percent.[159] Manor (1989, 345) points out that tenants, rather than the landless, were the primary beneficiaries of this early reform. Clearly, there was resistance to radical redistribution of property to the landless, but early reforms made incremental improvements for the smallest landholders.

The first round of real redistribution came at the tail end of the Congress Party's political dominance. In 1972, Chief Minister Devaraj Urs rode into power "on the coattails of a popular and populist Indira Gandhi."[160] Unlike prior occupants of the office, his was the caste of the former maharajas who ruled the Princely State of Mysore rather than the dominant, landed *vokkaligas* and *lingayats,* who largely supported the separate arm of Congress that had broken with Indira Gandhi.[161] For the sake of political survival, Urs cultivated a "rainbow coalition" of groups drawn mainly from nondominant castes, which comprised three-quarters of Karnataka's society.[162]

Devaraj Urs is best known for the land reform of 1984, which increased the pace at which large landholdings (those more than 10 acres) were divided and sped up the creation of smaller holdings (less than 5 acres).[163] In addition to ensuring that political resources reached poorer individuals, Urs implemented a broad umbrella of programs to build support from disadvantaged voters. These measures also included provision of houses for the poor, pensions for the elderly,

---

[154] As reported by Raghavan and Manor (2009, 7).   [155] Ibid., 5.
[156] Kothari (1964); Morris-Jones (1967); Weiner (1967).
[157] Manor (1989, 342).   [158] Kohli et al. (2006 [1987], 164).
[159] According to Rajapurohit (1982, 293, 306), cited from Manor (1989, 344).
[160] Kohli et al. (2006 [1987], 96).   [161] Raghavan and Manor (2009, 6).
[162] Ibid., 6–7.
[163] See Manor (1989, 346) table 3, from the Ministry of Agriculture, Government of India, *Agricultural Census, 1970–71*, 171; and *Agricultural Census, 1980–81*.

monetary resources for families dependent upon seasonal labor, and investment in children from antenatal care to educational support, particularly for children from poorer groups. Urs also worked to enforce minimum wages, lower rural debt, increase sources of credit, and promote the dignity of members of SCs, both in labor and their treatment by police.[164]

The most enduring legacies of Urs stem from his intuition about the local changes required "to give his programmes some prospect of success."[165] This meant recruiting large numbers of individuals from "disadvantaged communities" into the state's Administrative Service and subsequently appointing them, along with others deemed sympathetic to his aims, into "key positions where they might expedite implementation" (ibid.). Three years after this bureaucratic restaffing, he implemented the land reform for which is most well known. Two years later, he announced his intention to implement the 1975 recommendation of the Karnataka Backward Classes Commission to "reserve" seats in schools and government service for members of these socially and economically disadvantaged classes (ibid., 351). In tandem, he supported the establishment of caste associations for groups with limited socio-economic resources or electoral mobilization capacity, and ensured his supporters had enough influence to monitor and report their functioning (ibid., 353). He timed these initiatives sequentially, to give each "some time to make an impact at the grassroots" (ibid., 351).

Such programs did not result in "major social change."[166] However, they did create a popular template for redistributing political influence and resources across a much broader segment of Karnataka's population.[167] This model was driven by political necessity for Urs, as a leader "determined to oust the older ruling alliance by creating an alternative and broader political base. The strategy was to exclude some, but co-opt most of the social influentials, albeit from different backgrounds, into a large network of patronage."[168] The next highly competent chief minister to alter political power, Ramakrishna Hegde, was clearly inspired by the success of Urs's strategy.

In the aftermath of Urs's regime, Congress planted the seeds of its own demise by working to reduce the authority of Karnataka's chief ministers.[169] This became particularly clear once Indira Gandhi regained power post-Emergency, in 1980, and appointed Gundu Rao as chief minister. In July of that year, Karnataka experienced "one of the most militant peasant agitations in the country" (ibid., 171). Motivated around the struggle for linguistic, Kannada autonomy, the insurgents maintained a strong front against a violent response by the state.[170] This overly violent response by the state, coupled with the popular perception that Gundu Rao was "basically a lover of Sanskrit and that he did not want Kannada to get primacy," eliminated the lion's share of

---

[164] Ibid., 346–9. [165] Ibid., 350. [166] Ibid.; Kholi (2006). [167] Manor (1989, 350–1).
[168] Kohli et al. (2006 [1987], 178–9) [169] Mathew (1984, 170).
[170] There were 139 incidents of police firing between July 1980 and December 1982, with more than 100 deaths, mainly amongst farmers. *The Other Side*, February 1983: 5, c.f. Mathew (1984, 171).

support Rao may have secured from his identification with the once-wildly popular *Indramma,* Indira Gandhi.[171]

When Congress (I) prioritized national unity over responsiveness to pro-Kannada agitation, support swung to the regional political party explicitly founded to advance Kannada interests: the *Kannada Kranti Ranga* (KKR), led by Devaraj Urs following his break with Indira Gandhi in 1979 (ibid.). The combination of a surge of support for the KKR following the death of Urs in 1982 and the group's support for the Janata Party enabled a narrow Janata victory as a minority government in 1983. However its first two years in power were precarious, with the potential of "sudden political extinction" of the government and removal of its chief minister throughout.[172] This fragility stemmed from the 1983 elections, "a negative vote" against "Gundu Rao's vile Congress regime" that brought the Janata Party and Chief Minister Hegde into government.[173]

The 1985 state election stood out as the first "overwhelmingly positive vote" for the Janata Party and its leadership by Hegde (ibid.). The dynamics of this election are essential, given its preeminent significance as a "colossal swing" between the majority vote for Congress in the parliamentary election of 1984, and a reversal that favored the Janata Party in 105 of 224 assembly constituencies a year later.[174]

The major factor in the Janata Party's decisive 1985 victory was the support of women. According to Rajasekhariah et al. (1987, 591): *"the Janata party could get an edge over Congress(I) at the last minute when it put out its supplementary Manifesto promising populist measures such as Rs. 2/- a kilo of rice, Janata Sarees and Dhotis at subsidised rates etc., which swung the women voters in favour of Hegde."*

Such a radical shift – the reversal of nearly half of state assembly constituencies – was not merely the result of populist promises. Indeed, Hegde had been an astute student of the Congress Party's past failures to deliver on its dual promises of poverty eradication and political empowerment for constituents who he saw as crucial: women.

Hegde used his first two years in office to legislate and implement a promising record of change that spoke directly to women. He made extraordinary progress on two fronts: decentralization with explicit reservations for women and expansion of the rural drinking water infrastructure.[175] Hegde's priority of transferring authority to the local level had been clear since his work as Karnataka's Minister for Co-operation and Panchayati Raj in the 1960s. While he failed to legislate change at that time, he now partnered with his Minister of Rural Development and Panchayati Raj, Abdul Nazirsab, who began to draft

---

[171] Mathew (1984, 171).   [172] Raghavan and Manor (2009, 201).   [173] Ibid., 199.
[174] Ibid., 200. These calculations are based on E. Raghavan's work following the 1985 Karnataka elections.
[175] Raghavan and Manor (2009, 154).

a viable bill for decentralization of power through local *Panchayats* (councils) within 24 hours of taking office in 1983.[176]

These efforts eventually translated into the Karnataka *Zilla Parishads, Taluk Panchayat Samithis, Mandal Panchayats*, and *Nyaya Panchayats* Act of 1985. This legislation initially included a quota – or reservation – for 50 percent of seats to be occupied by women. While the scope was reduced to 25 percent, it remained pathbreaking.[177] In addition, Hegde and Nazirsab ensured representation for the broader umbrella of disadvantaged groups, including an 18 percent reservation for members of SCs and STs, and one seat in each council for a woman who was also a member of a SC or ST.[178]

Elections for the newly legislated *Panchayat* positions were not held until 1987 (ibid., 156). However, once in place, they resulted in the expansion of Karnataka's elected offices from 224 legislative seats to more than 55,000 offices from the local revenue body (Mandal) up to the state level (ibid.). This achievement became the model for India's 1993 Constitutional Amendments mandating decentralization to elected *Panchayats* with reservations for women and members of SCs and STs.

The Janata Party mandated urban elections across the state for civic offices that had been run by appointed bureaucrats rather than officials elected by voters since the early 1970s.[179] In another unprecedented move, the Janata Party set aside 30 percent of seats in these elections for women. According to Raghavan and Manor (2009, 156), this policy "inspired extremely favorable political and popular responses, first in Karnataka and later elsewhere in the country." Altogether, Hegde's reservations for women across urban and rural governmental bodies led to a remarkable surge of women into politics. Almost 9,000 posts were created for women across Karnataka (ibid., 157).

According to Devaki Jain (1996, 9), c.f. Kudva (2003, 448), "complex" reasons lay behind Karnataka's bold political stroke: *"Women's entry in large numbers into local government arose from a mixture of political opportunism and an ethical sensibility that regarded the implications of gender as integral, rather than peripheral, to the creation of a more just society. Critically, it arose from the actions of both women and men."*

In addition to bringing about effective women's representation in local government, collaboration between Minister Nazirsab and Chief Minster Hegde enabled a second successful program that was particularly meaningful for women: alleviation of enduring rural drought by catalyzing the expansion of drinking water sources. During his first two years in office, Nazirsab became a legend known as "Neersab,"[180] providing an autonomous source of drinking water for every 200 persons in the rural regions (ibid., 155). While

[176] Ibid., 152–4.   [177] Ibid., 155.   [178] Aziz (2000, 3523); Raghavan and Manor (2009, 157).
[179] Raghavan and Manor (2009, 156). Chief Minister Urs had suspended civic elections in the early 1970s, fearing they would result in Congress losing power.
[180] *Neersab* is a combination of *neeru*, or "water" in Kannada, and *sab*, or the Urdu *saheb*, a deferential term meaning sir or master, as explained by Raghavan and Manor (2009, 155).

this action did not translate into votes amongst the urban elite, it was an extraordinary improvement for rural women who could easily spend the better part of their work day walking to secure clean water from distant sources (ibid., 154). In the 1985 elections, Hegde made explicit, convincing references to his first two years of work on behalf of women. Again, according to Rajasekhariah et al. (1987, 591):

In his speeches, Hegde asked women as to why they always voted for Congress (I), though that party had done pretty little for them in 35 years, even with a woman Prime Minister. He used to high-light the Janata Party's programme for the welfare of the women, such as the [first] pregnancy allowance [for informal workers] of Rs. 100/- a month for three months, widows pensions of Rs. 50/- a month, the Mangalasutra *scheme [providing support wedding expenses] and* reservation of seats for women in local bodies. *This helped in getting the women's votes, which was actually the deciding factor. Thus women did vote for him and contributed largely to the success of the Janata Party. (Final emphasis mine)*

And yet, despite this articulate focus on women's interests, one piece of legislation is marked in its absence: support for women's property inheritance. Why?

A quick look back to AP's chief minister responsible for legislating gender-equalizing property inheritance rights – NTR – provides insight into Hegde's direct but quiet support for these reforms. Much of the rhetoric that mobilized the broadest coalition of voters in 1985 had a clear parallel in NTR's upstart victory of 1983. Just as Rama Rao advocated "self respect of the Telugus," Hegde asked voters: "Do you want to be ruled by Delhi or from Bangalore?"[181]

Hegde borrowed from Rao's successful strategy to mobilize female voters as his key – unexpected – tool to pivot control away from Congress. This meant advocating for the same sorts of empowering legislation that NTR had, including monetary support for widows and women in the rural and urban labor force, with use of electoral "reservations" for women to bolster their political influence.[182] Hegde's contemporaries argued that he also "promise[d] to provide the female children share in the property through the governor's speech after Andhra Pradesh enacted reform."[183]

Given NTR's ability to gain reelection with only negligible attempts to implement reform, it is likely that Hegde surmised that advocating gender-equalizing inheritance reform from a purely symbolic platform with a low priority for implementation would be an adequate complement to his other work to secure votes by his female constituents. Indeed, Hegde's policies

---

[181] See Rajasekhariah et al. (1987, 591).

[182] According to Amarnath K. Menon (1984), in January 1983 the government of AP passed an order reserving 30 percent of all government jobs for women, "but so far all it has achieved is divide opinion on its efficacy, even among women." For more details, see Menon (1984).

[183] Koujalagi (1990: 369), Karnataka State Legislative Debates of 1990. For the debates in Kannada and the translation into English I commissioned, see the Chapter Appendix.

changing women's systemic access to crucial resources – both drinking water in rural areas and political power in urban areas – appear to have been enough to secure electoral victory.

What also became clear from the electoral politics of Karnataka was that pro-women legislation absent investment in enforcement was an inadequate tool for sustaining political power. By the 1989 elections, Hegde and his successor in the Janata Dal Party, Bommai, had "woefully neglected" engaging the local *Panchayats* created by Hegde as a means to reach electoral constituents and create a strong local structure for the Janata Party.[184] Struggles for power and its employment for personal, material benefits gave the state party a reputation similar to its national counterpart, as "interested more and more in positions and perquisites and less and less in affecting society."[185] As a result, the Congress Party (I) "rode an anti-Janata Dal wave in the state."[186]

Upon its return to power in Karnataka, the Congress (I) Party worked to regain its footing "as a saviour of the poor, the tribals, the Scheduled Castes, and [most importantly here] women."[187] This included transparent legislative attempts "to catch votes."[188] In particular, the chief minister installed following the Congress victory, S. Bangarappa, introduced the first round of legislation for gender-equal inheritance rights. Overall, this marked the beginning of intense competition for political dominance both in Karnataka (with the Janata Dal Party as a clear alternative to Congress) and across all of India.[189] Political power in Karnataka pivoted, at least in part, on whether reforms for women's advancement were real and credible versus symbolic. Female constituents appear to have rewarded clear records of decisive investments in their political and economic advancement (bringing the Janata Party to power in 1985 and its successor, the Janata Dal Party, in 1994), and to have punished parties for rhetorical commitments that lacked substance (cinching electoral defeats by the Janata Dal Party in 1989 and the Congress Party in 1994).[190]

What explains women's unique role in Karnataka's politics? According to Sen (2002, 504), while Karnataka was the site of "the major breakthrough" for women's political inclusion – through the Janata's passage of the 1983 Panchayati Raj Act reserving 25 percent of seats for women in local, elected councils – political reform was not due to pressure from an organized "women's

---

[184] EPW Special Correspondent (1989, 961).

[185] *Himmat*, January 6, 1978, c.f. Guha (2007, 537).

[186] Rajghatta (1989).

[187] Guha (2007, 534).

[188] Nayak (1990: 367) *4th Legislative Session, Karnataka Legislative Assembly Debates*, with translation from Kannada I commissioned.

[189] In the words of Manor (1989, 357–8), "[T]he people in Karnataka demonstrated their political sophistication and assertiveness in March 1985, when in over one hundred state assembly segments they reversed the pro-Congress(I) vote which they had cast only nine weeks earlier and produced pro-Janata majorities."

[190] Gould (1997, 2340). For an insightful analysis of women's importance as undecided "swing" voters in the 1994 elections, see India Today (1994).

movement." Sen (2002, 504–5) argues that the Janata Dal's ideology is responsible for women's political inclusion – specifically, the combination of its democratic socialism and Gandhian values directed toward a "pro-people agenda."

I suggest a more pragmatic rationale for the Janata Dal's path breaking legislation, based on the importance of female votes for the party's political survival and authority. Here, the absence of women's active organization in party politics is balanced by the presence of politically astute women in polling booths willing to punish parties for "cheap talk" just as much as rewarding them for substantive commitments, as Jain (1996) explained earlier. This made women's inclusion a core priority in the Janata Dal's political platforms and policy implementation, despite the absence of women as primary advocates for reform.

Finally, to understand how women's political empowerment created momentum for legislating gender-equal property rights, it is worthwhile to note the broader impact of the first round of *Panchayat* elections catalyzed by the Janata Dal, again according to Jain:[191]

On 1 May 1987, the Janata Dal (the party that won the elections) called a convention of all the 56,000 elected representatives, of whom 25 percent were women. It was a wonderful sight to see 14,000 women in the audience, shining bright, 80 percent of whom were participating in politics for the first time, thrilled with their victory at the hustings. Even those who had passed the law, and advocated for positive discrimination in the interests of gender equity, were stunned [emphasis added].

Yet, it was not the Janata Dal but Congress who legislated economic reform in Karnataka upon defeating the Janata Dal in 1989, as an attempt to ensure female voters' loyalty.

4.4.3 Legislating Reform: Motives, Voices, and Silence

In their attempt to claim credit for amending the Hindu Succession Act to advance women's rights, Karnataka's Congress Party borrowed language from the debates in AP. In the first round of debates, in 1990, Shri N. G. Nayak, Congress representative from Molakalmuru, stressed, albeit in paternalistic terms, that the aim of the legislation was to ensure the universal good of gender equality:

For a father female children and male children are the same but the parents will have a special love and affection for the female children. … It will be remembered that such a law was made in your period [of the Congress Party governance] hence I pray to you for making this amendment and thank you for giving this opportunity.[192]

---

[191] Jain (1996, 4), c.f. Kudva (2003, 449).

[192] Nayak (Molakalmuru) (1990, 372) 4*th Legislative Session, Karnataka Legislative Assembly Debates,* with translation from Kannada I commissioned. Note that the party affiliation is garnered from India Votes, whose record provides a different transliteration of the surname [Naik rather than Nayak].

Minister of Law and Social Justice, Shri B. Shivanna, the Congress representative responsible for advancing the law, extended Shri Nayak's argument by referencing the foundational importance of equity in India's Constitution. Again, this parroted language from the 1985 AP debates:

For parents, sons and daughters are equal. Our Constitution says that under fundamental rights all are equal. Before law – opportunity should be given to all ... [therefore] we have brought Section 6A and B [as amendments to the Hindu Succession Act of 1956] giving equal protection.[193]

This can be construed as a sharp, if subtle dig at the prior, Janata-led government (as well as Hindus more generally) for their inability to pass such reform. Specifically, Congress representative Shri B. M. Idinabba from Ullal emphasized the "delay":

I feel that the Hindu sisters should have got the share in their father's property long back ... It is there in Muslim law rights to the female and male children has been provided as per the 1400 years old Mohammadian law, it is a very happy thing.... Though delayed this law has been brought here now and its very important to implement it at the earliest.[194]

As in the case of AP, opposition party members worked to moderate any credit the governing party received. However, the opposition possessed an additional weapon in Karnataka: members of the Janata Party redirected the debate to their earlier attempts at reform. As Janata Party representative Sri R. V. Deshpande of Haliyala explains: *"I welcome this, we [the Janata Party] also wanted to bring this amendment hence we had decided to prepare this when our party was in power. I feel that in today's society economic status to women can only be provided through this amendment."*[195]

Following this, Janata Party representative Shri Shivanad H. Koujalagi of Bailahongala took the floor:

Andhra Pradesh is the first country which passed an act for providing share to the female children in their father's property. After ... the then Karnataka chief minister Shriman Ramakrishna Hegde ... announced to provide the female children share in the property. As per that announcement Honourable Law Minister has introduced this act in our state on this day... I am really very happy that the objective of our previous chief minister Shri Ramakrishna Hegde is successful on this day[196]

These comments paved the way for a much sharper, Janata Party critique of Congress-led reform as a rushed, opportunistic measure to gain votes. The Janata Dal's Shri P. G. R. Sindhya from Kanakapura argued:

Read the Hindu Succession Act, an act of government of India. It does not appear that this [Bill] is made in concurrence with it ... if this bill becomes act then it would only remain on paper and cannot be implemented. ... What is the need to bring this bill in urgency[?]! As I know your government will remain in power ... do not bring this bill for the sake of votes and publicity. ... Please refer the bill to the joint select committee,

[193] Ibid., 374. [194] Ibid., 370–1. [195] Ibid., 365. [196] Ibid., 369–70.

we all will think completely about it and pass this in the next session and you will get the credit for this.[197]

Along these lines a stricter critique argued that the Congress-led reform prioritized votes over resolving structural flaws, which doomed attempts at enforcement. Shri B. H. Bannikod of Hirekerur argued that the legislation provided no legal redress for mothers or daughters to claim their share of ancestral property:

It seems that this amendment is brought as a populous measure for showing that we are providing share in property to female children but in reality if the objective has to become successful then the defects in this should be rectified and they should get their share in complete and easy way as the male children get their share.[198]

In Bannikod's opinion, even with equal legal redress, the current process of claiming rights posed grave problems for women:

The system of the law is that where in during the property partition if a mother approaches court to claim her share in property then it would take so much time that she may get her share but she might [not] be alive. This is the reason why the system of partition through the revenue system should be discontinued. Amendment should be made so that there is equal division of property through court [decree instead of revenue department]. There should not be a system wherein they approach the court for property then they lose the property as well as also money and enmity grows between father and children leading to many problems in life.[199]

In Karnataka, unlike in AP, critique about reform's structural flaws was not only acknowledged but offered openly as a reason to postpone passage until its unintended consequences had been thought through and rectified. In the words of the INC's Shri Mallarigouda S. Patil from Sankeswar:

we are reading in the everyday newspapers about dowry deaths and also we see dowry is being given. I fear that more people will approach female children who get more share in property due to this [law] … amendments have to be made regarding marriage of children and those who marry the female children who get their share in property because it should not be understood as dowry plus property share … we all agree that female children should get share in their ancestral property but in future many dangers can occur.[200]

In the final moments of debate, even the INC Minister of Law and Social Justice responsible for introducing the legislation appeared convinced by the strength and articulation of critiques about technical flaws in the law. Accordingly, he acquiesced and requested the measure be referred to a Joint Selection Committee for further review.[201]

Just more than two years later, the INC presented the reworked Hindu Succession (Karnataka Amendment) Act for passage, at the ninth session of the State Legislative Assembly in January and February 1993. This represented

[197] Ibid., 373–4.   [198] Ibid., 371–2.   [199] Ibid.   [200] Ibid., 372–3.   [201] Ibid., 482–3.

the culmination of attempts by the Karnataka Congress Party to advance women's equal property inheritance rights as evidence of their commitment to female voters. Their relatively quick work on the project was thanks to the combination of a new, more collaborative chief minister representing Congress, Veerappa Moily, and the Joint Review Committee's efforts. Between December 27, 1990 and the submission of their report on August 29, 1992, the committee had met 22 times and visited the prior reforming states of AP, Tamil Nadu, and Kerala. However, their vision of women's concerns may have been limited by the committee's composition, as only 2 of the 12 representatives were female.

In this final round of debates, members of the opposition Janata Dal Party did their utmost to block Congress' reform. Their claims were two fold: technically, according to a member of the Joint Review Committee, Mr. Mallikarjun, quoted by Janata Dal representative Shri D. B. Chandregowda: "the state government has no authority to make this amendment" because of its intention "to change the basic principle" of prior law.[202] In defense, the INC argued that there were precedents for state attempts to legislate women's rights to property. In the words of Congress representative Shri Harnahalli Ramaswamy:

> *this is the 3rd time such an effort has been made. [First] The Hindu Women's Right to Property Act, 1933 in old Mysore.... After which, it was decided to give the girl child some [1/4] portion of the property [at the time of partition].... [Second] After our Constitution was enacted on 26 January, 1956, the Central Government through [Congress-led] Lok Sabha and Rajya Sabha brought the Hindu Women's Right to Property Act.... Yet, the female children would get 1/4 part to 1/8 part which was less compared to the male children.... [Third] To remove this discrimination the bill proposes to provide equal property rights to the female children as that of male children.[203]*

In response, the opposition Janata Dal had only one more tool remaining to impede an amendment that the party "basically welcome[ed]":[204] the difficulty of implementing and enforcing the legislation. As Shri R. V. Deshapande argued: *"this Act has already been introduced in the State of Andhra Pradesh but is not being implemented. Hence... it is not enough that the Government just passes the bill but it has to take appropriate measures to implement [it].[205]*

In response to Shri Deshapande's critique of the reform's ineffectiveness due to the lack of enforcement mechanisms, the sole woman to speak in the debates – Congress Party Representative Smt. Motamma of Mudigere – mounted an impassioned defense:

> *on behalf of all women I urge all the honourable Legislators to completely welcome this bill which has been introduced by the Government of Karnataka.... Chandregowda has said that this bill should not be passed as the honourable member Mallikarjun has found*

---

[202] Page 245 in the 8th Legislative Session of the Karnataka Legislative Assembly, January–February (1993), vol. 2, p. 245–50, with quotes from the translation I commissioned.

[203] Ibid., 2–3, English translation of 1993 debates.   [204] Shri D. B. Chandregowda, ibid., 245.

[205] Ibid., 3, English translation of 1993 debates.

a small flaw. Mr. Chandregowda has 4 girl children. [So] you should welcome the bill by ignoring the flaw and should have asked all others to approve this ... it is not correct to say that discussion is needed because of such a small issue ... No one should raise objections against this revolutionary bill which intends to provide social and financial security to women[206]

Smt. Motamma drives home the importance of women's minority status as requiring a unified front of support by the men who comprise the majority of legislators: *"you are the majority, we are minority and I spoke because women should not face problems."*[207]

The effectiveness of her argument on behalf of the Congress Party's act was clear from the final opposition statement made by the BJP's Shri K. S. Eshwarappa. He acknowledged his discomfort, as a man, voicing any dissent but sought to emphasize the potential moral high ground of non-passage while claiming credit for the BJP as a supporter of women:

I am not a member of the committee and neither a woman.... [Smt. Motamma] has spoken in a way that she is the voice on behalf of all women in the state. The revolutionary move that the Government has taken should not take long time in its implementation.... I congratulate on behalf of the Bharatiya Janata Party[208]

Does the forcefulness of the arguments made by a single, female legislator relate to the influence of women more broadly as advocates for reform in Karnataka? Unlike the Janata Dal, the INC appeared to ignore the importance of including women in competitive electoral politics. Once the Congress Party returned to power in Karnataka, in 1989, they suspended *Panchayat* elections for the duration of their rule (until 1994). Congress substituted symbolic, economic reform with little probability of enforcement in place of substantive, political empowerment (political quotas for women in local government). This policy did not endear women to Congress, which endured decisive defeat at the hands of female voters in 1994.[209]

When the Janata Dal returned to power, they proudly reinstalled the *Panchayat* system for which they were responsible. While reservations for women within local government were not overtly intended to enforce women's new, Congress-legislated land inheritance rights, they created the very leverage over the revenue system that INC opponents such as Shri B. H. Bannikod had advocated as necessary.[210]

4.5 ON THE ORIGIN OF THE 1993 CONSTITUTIONAL AMENDMENT FOR WOMEN'S RESERVATIONS

We now leave the state-level reforms of Kerala, AP, and Karnataka to consider the origin of the 1993 national constitutional amendments mandating the

[206] Ibid., 4, English translation of 1993 debates.
[207] Ibid., 5, English translation of 1993 debates.   [208] Ibid., 6, English translation of 1993 debates.
[209] India Today (1994).
[210] Karnataka Legislative Assembly, 4th Legislative Session Debates, November (1990): 371.

inclusion of women as well as all members of SCs and STs in newly mandated local government. This story is a much more optimistic one – of women organizing for representation and fundamental change of exploitative political, social, and economic structures – than the prior narratives. Yet there are also parallels that lead us to a coherent understanding of how, when, and why institutional reforms improving women's rights and representation have such varied impacts on women, their families, and the collective organization and flourishing of the communities in which they reside.

This is not a harmonious narrative where women possess a unified collective vision either of how the world is or how it should be. Many analyses point to the diversity of women's opinions as indicative of a weakness of political strength or vision. Yet, such arguments ignore two significant factors: the importance of political mobilization in determining the salience of a given identity and its value in addressing multiple forms of oppression.

As Menon (2000, 3839) argues, the identity of "women" is not primordial, but a product of collective engagement. The greater numbers of political and social entrepreneurs invested in mobilizing individuals around caste and religion helps explain the frequency with which caste and communal identities (as well as about family), complicate – and fracture – women's responses as a unified entity (Menon 2000; Sen 2002, 511). And yet, the repeated commitments made by women to bring about justice across multiple domains, all of which tend to bind women's agency more severely than men's, suggest a broader interest in equality that requires a longer, more circuitous path to achieve.

4.5.1 Historical Context: Caste, Political Parties, and Gender

Women's mobilization around the reservations nationally mandated by the 1993 constitutional amendments stands in contrast to a theme running from the beginning to end of the origins the HSAA, which we have thus far followed from colonial times to the mid-1990s: "reform from above."

Indeed, such practices were clear from the first moments of British colonial social reforms, where women's silence resounded in movements ostensibly for their betterment, such as for the abolishment of *sati*, that is widow burning.[211] From the *sati* debates of the 1820s onward, colonial campaigns around practices from marriage to education focused exclusively on the lives of women from upper castes.[212] This emphasis is important not only because it failed to acknowledge the "hard" exclusion and exploitation faced by women from lower castes or religious minorities, but also because it permitted what Uma Chakravarti (2003) identifies as the "*brahmanical* patriarchy," which undercut demands for more radical change.

According to Tanika Sarkar (1993, 1869), "colonial structures of power compromised with, indeed learnt much from indigenous patriarchy and upper

---

[211] Mani (1998).   [212] Rao (2003, 15).

caste norms and practices."[213] As the earlier sections of this chapter on inheritance reform show, new opportunities for advancement in British colonial administration created competition between men of different castes. This encouraged greater efforts by men with lower social status and resources to "leapfrog" ahead by increasing their control over women in their families, while opening the door for "modern" achievements of Western education and social mobility amongst women from upper castes.[214] Thus, reforms ostensibly designed for women's empowerment – legalizing widow remarriage in 1856 or prohibiting child marriage – often narrowed the boundaries of some women's autonomy, while undermining opportunities for female intercaste solidarity.[215]

Yet, when it comes to women's political representation, there is a contradictory narrative that carries equal weight. This is the replacement of the upper caste, largely male political concern for the "woman's question" – to use the colonial terminology for problematic social traditions aimed at controlling women's behavior – with the explicit political activism of women with radical goals, many of them from lower castes. According to Anupama Rao (2003, 21):

"the precise period of social reform's disappearance from the upper-caste agenda is that of its appearance on other agendas – in the emerging political activism of women themselves (whether we wish to call it feminist or not), as well as the debates over the "woman's question" in anti-caste movements."

Indeed, the dalit or non-*Brahman* political movements across Southern and Western India, including those led by B. R. Ambedkar and Periyar (E. V. Ramaswamy Naicker) understood the struggle for equality to require overturning both caste and gender hierarchies.[216] In both cases, women's political mobilization was critical. Ambedkar supported the organization of women's conferences in parallel to events such as the First Round Table Conference with the British colonial regime as of 1930, which included only men.[217] Such spaces enabled the dalit female leaders emerging in the 1920s and 1930s, including Shantabai Dani, Sulochana Dongre, and Radhabai Kamble, to establish firm grounding as speaking not only on behalf of women but also the broader dalit community.[218]

In addition, the Dravidian *Suyamariathai Iyakkam* or Self Respect Movement launched by Periyar in 1926 sought an even more radical democratization of Tamil society that required "radical reconstructive work which would *destroy the traditional structures* [emphasis added]" of religion, caste hierarchy, and patriarchy.[219] In contrast to the Gandhian nationalist movement, Periyar was unequivocal that women's efforts were central, arguing: "As of

---

[213] For a masterful overview of "the troubled relationship of feminism and history," as well as this citation, see the EPW article of the same name by Nair (2008b, 59).
[214] O'Hanlon (1985); Rao (2003, 19–20).
[215] Carroll (1989); Sarkar (1993); Nair (1996, 2008a, 59); Chowdhry (1998)
[216] Pardeshi (2003, 356). [217] John (2008, 45); Rao (2003, 22). [218] Rao (2003, 22).
[219] Anandhi (2003, 141–2).

now, men's struggle for women's liberation has only strengthened women's enslavement."[220]

The Self Respect Movement that developed was structured on partnerships between women and men. Participating women not only ran their own "special" all-women's conferences but were also active in general conferences, frequently delivering the inaugural speech. The movement's content reflected the strength of women's voices: explicitly politicizing the practice of marrying as well as the form of marriage (as intercaste, "self-respect" decisions by both partners), with women occupying integral roles leading and justifying mass agitations.[221] The independence of women's approach is particularly clear in a transcript published between a woman and a prosecuting inspector at a Madras Court in the of wake mass anti-Hindi agitation that resulted in the arrest and jailing of 73 women, including 32 children. As recorded by Anandhi:

Prosecuting Inspector: *"You are with your small children, prison is painful and your husband will suffer. If you promise you will not do similar things in the future (i.e., participating in such agitations), we shall pardon you."*

Woman activist: *"We are willing to bear any suffering for the progress of our language, our nation.* Our husbands have no right to interfere in this. *They are not the ones to do so."*[222]

Women also organized and ran influential political organizations in the service of the nationalist cause as of the 1920s, including the All India Women's Conference (AIWC), established in 1926, as well as the Women's Indian Association in Madras (WIA), and the National Council of Indian Women (NCIW). These groups initially included women who held diverse opinions on the goals of female inclusion in politics. This outspokenness was in part thanks to what had occurred within the largest political organization, the INC, where, since 1889, "every meeting of the INC included some women, a few of whom were delegates and many observers. Their participation was often 'token' and symbolic, but the women were educated and politically knowledgeable and they were seeking (or being given) very new public roles."[223]

From the 1920s onward, the INC began actively building ties with peasants, workers, and women's organizations to demonstrate the universality of its demands. By the 1930s, Sen (2002, 475) notes that women's organizations had built a base broad enough to credibly represent "Indian women" and "participated in every committee and planning group set up to discuss India's future."

---

[220] Sami Chidambaranar (1983, 218) *Tamilar Thalaivar* (leader of the Tamils), c.f. Anandhi (2003, 149). Indeed, Periyar's more radical views on systems of power are equally clear on the topic of property. He is quoted as arguing against property altogether as necessary to end the subjugation of women, as cited at the start of this chapter.

[221] Anandhi (2003, 145, 150).

[222] *Kudi Arasu,* November 20, 1938, cited by Anandhi (2003, 153), with emphasis hers.

[223] Sen (2002, 475).

This radical (if brief) opening of political organization to women encouraged a range of views on their appropriate role in politics.[224] In one camp, Sarojini Naidu, a widely renowned, upper-caste woman from north India, categorically opposed reservations as an implicit admission of women's "inferiority."[225] This view held that any sort of reservation opened the door to the "wrong" sort of women. In Rajkumari Amrit Kaur's words: *"there is no question as to the reality of unity amongst us women. We want to send our best women and our best men to the councils – therefore we do not want the canker of communalism amongst us. Once we are divided into sects and communities all will be lost."*[226]

From this elitist perspective, support for reservations of any sort by women – be it according to religious community, caste, or gender – is lumped into a broader concern that such support would be tantamount to an admission of vulnerability relative to the dominant (male, upper-caste Hindu) community.

Muthulakshmi Reddi, who hailed from a devadasi family in the Madras Presidency and had been trained as a medical doctor before becoming one of the first (reluctant) female representatives nominated by the WIA in 1926 to sit on the Madras Legislative Council, saw a very different role for women in politics. She agreed to join the council to use this power with the explicit agenda to improve women's economic independence and inheritance rights, reform marriage law, abolish the *devadasi* system, and legislate reservations "to represent the women's point of view." However, she did not want to separate women's and men's electoral decision making, explaining: "[W]e do not want to form a separate caste [as] men and women rise and fall together."[227]

However, even this limited diversity of opinion was soon squelched as the national struggle for independence took hold in the early 1930s.[228] Mary John (2008, 45) notes that Gandhi's protest against granting special electorates to "members of depressed classes," known as his "fast against untouchability" that began on September 20, 1932 "dramatically broke [the WIA's] demand for reserved seats and nominations." As a result, "[O]ne by one, women who had previously supported nomination and reserved seats [such as Muthulakshmi Reddi] added their voices to the demand for 'equality and no privileges' and 'a fair field and no favour.'"[229]

Pressure by Gandhi to sacrifice the collective interests of women in favor of unified support for the advancement of untouchables and the broader (Hindu) community culminated by 1932 in an official stance by all three major women's organizations against "privileges" for women.[230] The Poona Pact, signed upon the conclusion of Gandhi's fast, supported a two-tier electorate for untouchables and the general population. This quickly translated into a formal

---

[224] Sen (2002, 475–6).   [225] John (2008, 38–9).

[226] AIWC (233, 51) in opposition to the British attempt to provide separate electorates and reserved seats to different religious communities, c.f. John (2008, 40–1).

[227] John (2008, 35–7).   [228] Nair (2008a, 61).

[229] Forbes (1996, 107–8), c.f. John (2008, 38).   [230] John (2008, 38–46).

support for those who had suffered the historical injustice of untouchability, with an understanding about "backwardness" as exclusively caste driven, which evolved out of broader movements in Mysore and Madras.[231]

In parallel, women were denied any special provisions for representation, but instead were lauded as "model bearers of political unity and universal citizenship." Renuka Ray provides insightful critique of the Government of India Act of 1935 that provided the template for women's political exclusion post-Independence as a moment where "the social backwardness of women had been sought to be exploited in the same manner as the backwardness of so many sections in this country by those who wanted to deny its freedom."[232]

Thus, during the initial decades of Indian Independence, the all-India women's movement consolidated around a "harmonious alliance" with the male national leadership.[233] Urban, educated, modern, self-avowedly progressive women accepted and even advocated exclusion from institutional remedies as a signal of their commitment to the (initially aspirational) Indian nation, as well as "an impediment to our [women's] growth and an insult to our very intelligence and capacity."[234] In this period, new organizations with more diverse agendas – the *Mahila Atma Raksha Samiti* (Women's Self-Defense League) in Bengal and the National Federation of Indian Women within the Communist Party of India (CPI) – were also created. They provided opportunities for women's collective mobilization while setting limits on the unity of women's voices.[235]

Many women from peasant and working-class backgrounds became radicalized post-Independence, joining Communist groups and movements for land and labor reform inspired by them: the Tebhaga movement in North Bengal, Telangana movement in AP, and a campaign by cotton textile workers in Western India. Yet their agendas did not explicitly include "women's issues."[236]

The reflections of numerous female CPI members in the Telangana movement suggest that "revolution" was not yet broadly construed as important for women. According to Mallu Swarajyam:

sacrifices have to be made [for the Telangana movement]. But the question came up of why it was always the women who had to make the sacrifices. The reply was "if you consider this struggle as a whole though it is a struggle of the working classes, the peasantry is also involved and they are making sacrifices that will ultimately benefit the proletariat. That is how the women should also regard this sacrifice." It was difficult to swallow this.... What did we fight for all these days? ... But gradually it became necessary for us to give it up. We never got the freedom we wanted.[237]

[231] Galanter (1984); John (2008, 47).

[232] John (2008, 49), citing Constituent Assembly Debates (1947, 668).   [233] Sen (2002, 481–2).

[234] See John (2008, 48–9); quote from the Constituent Assembly Debates (1947, 669).

[235] Sen (2002, 482).   [236] Sen (2002, 479–80).

[237] Stree Shakti Sanghatana (1989: 240), recorded in *We Were Making History...*, cited by Nair (2008a, 62).

4.5.2 Political Context: Women's Unmistakable Electoral Voice

What changed to formalize guarantees of women's political representation? The 1970s marked an extraordinary upswing in women's political salience, within India as well as globally. This transformation started with the confluence of support for "New Feminism" in the Global North and a vehicle for organizing change – the United Nations – that in partnership led a movement for development grounded in women's empowerment: the International Year of Women in 1971, which inaugurated the International Decade of Women. As part of these larger gestures, the Government of India appointed a Committee on the Status of Women in India. Their report in 1974 brought national clarity as to women's sustained disadvantages or "backwardness" that their large-scale mobilization had thus far not generated. Rather than improving, women's condition relative to that of men had worsened in labor, health, education, and politics.[238]

In the wake of this realization, Indian women organized across many domains. They provided "a driving force" for uprisings against economic and social exploitation, starting with the Shahada movement by Bhil (Adivasi or tribal) landless laborers in Maharashtra, which sparked women's explicit organization to assert their own power. Within the Shahada movement this became the Shramik Sangathana to confront domestic violence as of 1972. This was followed by a rapid proliferation of women's organizations grounded in economic concerns: the Self-Employed Women's Association led by Ela Bhatt in 1972, the United Women's Anti-Price Rise Front catalyzed by Mrinal Gore in 1973, and the Progressive Organization of Women (POW) organized by female Maoists in 1973–4.[239] The bridge between domestic and international support for women is clear in one of the most visible, unified actions by Maoist "women's organizations": their organization of the first major celebration of International Women's Day on March 8, 1975.[240]

Whereas the women's movements around Independence saw the state as an ally, the events of the mid-1970s to 1980s destroyed any remaining faith in the state as an altruistic actor. Initially, Indira Gandhi had appeared to be a willing partner in inclusive development. In 1971, she ran on a platform of *Garibi Hatao* (remove or end poverty) and was re elected chief minister of the ruling Congress Party by a spectacular margin thanks to strong support from landless, lower-caste, and Muslim Indians.[241] At first, her victory translated into support for expanding the beneficiaries of economic progress – through land reform, Green Revolution technology, and abolishing the privileges princely rulers had obtained since colonial times.[242]

---

[238] Sen (2002, 482–3).   [239] Ibid.   [240] Kumar (1995), c.f. Sen (2002, 483).
[241] Indira Gandhi's Congress (R) won 352 out of 518 seats in Parliament, with the next largest party being the Communist Party of India-Maoist (CPI-Maoist), who won only 25 (Guha, 2007, 447).
[242] Guha (2007, 448).

However, Indira's declaration of Emergency rule in 1975 pushed many radical women's organizations underground.[243] What emerged after the Emergency's removal was an array of women's groups, including urban "autonomous" organizations – broadly concerned with "consciousness-raising" about gender issues – and rural struggles for land rights – which brought women's demands for independent rights to the fore, most notably the Chipko and Bodhgaya movements.[244]

A more organized political opposition emerged in 1977, with strong motivation to expand local political autonomy. When the new Janata Party was elected, they used the Asoka Mehta Committee to push for specific proposals on how to "re-institute local self-government."[245] Just as the post-Emergency women's movements became more focused on the political struggle of reshaping the state, the Asokha Mehta Committee recommended reworking the political terrain of local government: giving *Panchayats,* as local elected councils, the power to tax citizens, run schools, and identify and solve core problems in rural villages. In the committee's perspective, this meant shifting the balance of power away from the fiefdoms of local bureaucrats who "would not easily be adjusted to working under the supervisions of elected representatives" and toward local elected representatives.[246]

What is important here is the mechanical significance of breaking up status quo local power structures – typically operating in partnership with local landed elites – in the service of creating alternative forms of political accountability (or loyalty) that new entrants to higher levels of government could harness. Such concerns loomed large for both Rajiv Gandhi, when he proposed the *Panchayati Raj* Constitutional Amendments (mandating "reservations" for women and members of SCs and STs), and Narasimha Rao, in his successful push to write these changes into law.[247] For both leaders, establishing an autonomous base of local intermediaries who could mobilize votes independent of existing (Congress Party) power structures was crucial for their political survival.

Both women and members of SCs and STs played a crucial role in this project. Members of "the backward classes" (SCs and STs) are widely identified as politically pivotal, dating back to their ability to mobilize separate electorates pre-Independence and reservations (or quotas) in proportion to their local population share post-Independence.[248] In contrast, reservations for women are seen as a separate matter of "the government's commitments to women's uplift."[249] However, this ignores their decisive electoral significance within the newly competitive democratic polity of post-Emergency India.

---

[243] Whether or not explicitly for development; Sen (2002, 483–4).
[244] Manimala (1983); Patel (1985); Shiva (1986); Sen (2002, 484).   [245] Singer (2007, 101).
[246] Asokha Mehta (1978) *Report of the Committee on Panchayati Raj Institutions,* c.f. Singer (2007, 101).
[247] Bohlken (2015, 85–91).   [248] Singer (2007, 121).   [249] Ibid.

This significance is documented as of the 1980 elections, "when Indira Gandhi focused serious attention on attracting women voters" who did indeed help bring about the victory of her Congress Party, according to a 1980 survey by Mehta, Billimoria, and Thakkar.[250]

Furthermore, the importance not only of women voters but also of commitments to ensure their representation in local politics is unmistakable by 1983, when the newly formed TDP's leader, NTR, professed his commitment to implement the women's reservations that the Ashoka Mehta Committee recommended in his election plank. This, in turn, helped him garner the "mass support from women voters" that propelled him into power.[251] Singer (2007, 148) notes that "despite the fact that only two of the 30 Members of Parliament [elected in 1983] were women, the TDP had gained a reputation as the party which overtly courted women voters." As previously discussed, NTR imposed a first round of women's reservations immediately after his first election (9 percent), and expanded them upon his re election (to 20–5 percent at the village level and 9 percent for elected heads of village councils).[252]

According to Singer (2007, 149), the success of the TDP convinced other major parties to make "comparable changes" in the language of their party manifestos, the commitments they made to development for women, and the strategies they used to attract female voters. This is clear in the prior examination of Karnataka's inheritance reform, where Hegde employed a similar strategy – introducing women's reservations in 1983 to successfully attract and reward voters. By ensuring the implementation as of 1987, Hegde secured his viability in future elections. In addition, by 1991, the National Front (a broad coalition of parties that included the TDP) advocated 30 percent reservations for women in all government jobs, and by 1996, all party manifestos supported 30 per cent reservations for women in state legislatures and Parliament.[253]

Thus, the consensus that "the demand for reservations did not arise from the women's movement" – divided on quotas since before Independence – but rather "from institutional/male sources" requires an amendment, as Sen (2002, 501) and Singer (2007, 122) explain. In fact, reservations owe a great deal to the effectiveness with which women have employed their power as voters. They have used this leverage to identify and support new political entrants with a strong commitment to increasing women's political voice. In addition, women have demonstrated their willingness to punish politicians who fail to implement commitments to women's political empowerment, as is clear in the varied fortunes of Karnataka's Janata Dal Party, and AP's TDP, and the national Congress Party. This shift away from legal advocacy to focus on explicit demands for powerful electoral representation was the result of a major lesson during the mid-1980s. Then, national mobilization around the

[250] Mehta et al. (1981), c.f. Singer (2007, 146).
[251] Singer's personal interview with N. T. Rama Rao "On Policies for Women," Hyderabad, November 16, 1995, c.f. Singer (2007, 103); *Eenadu*, August 15, 1983, c.f. Singer (2007, 148).
[252] Singer (2007, 103).   [253] Ibid., 149–50.

problems of violence against women – rape and dowry deaths – led to a series of legislative changes criminalizing these two acts, as well as increasing protections for Muslim women around divorce. However, legal reform did not lead to measurable improvements in women's welfare. Counter productively, legislation did increase communal (Hindu-Muslim) tensions as well as women's reluctance to request support from the state to combat domestic violence.[254]

Women's importance for the political survival of successive chief ministers,[255] coupled with their political mobilization beyond the voting booth,[256] explains the state's decision to mobilize substantial political and material resources. This came in the form of creating not only a new structure of elected local government in which women were required to play a central role, but also in the commitment to direct funds to the elected *Panchayat* leaders.[257]

4.6 CONCLUSION

This chapter illustrated how a radical mandate for formal equality of inherited property rights emerged across two states at the vanguard of this movement, and a third that lagged behind. I compared the legislative process in each state, where women play an important role as an electorate to be mobilized, but were not at the center of agenda setting, except around reservations. While the prior chapter investigated social norms about marriage, inheritance, and parental care pre- and post-death, this chapter focused on the evolution of two legal institutions – one around inheritance, and the second responsible for distributing political authority (using "reservations").

These twin historical contexts help interpret my gatekeeper theory of change, which argues that when new political institutions open representation – and authority over wielding government power – to women, we see more effective enforcement of their legal rights. This, in turn, challenges social institutions and generates resistance.

These chapters explored the historical scope and substance of laws and norms about inheritance and the extent to which a mandate for female political representation evolved such that enforcement of women's economic rights became real and credible. Subsequent chapters investigate the appropriateness of my "gatekeeper" theory to explain the enforcement of economic rights, the subsequent behavioral responses by individuals, and women's resulting ability to overcome resistance when they can strike integrative bargaining solutions that benefit the entire family.

---

[254] Basu (1992, 498–9); Agnes (2000, 498); Sen (2002, 484–95)
[255] Bohlken (2015, 99–103, 111). [256] Sen (2002, 501–16). [257] Singer (2007, 106–7).

5

The Politics of Property Rights Enforcement

In Hinduism, it is said, "Gods are pleased in a land where women are revered." But this is an empty slogan, unless the state promotes the welfare of women citizens. Therefore, Telugu Desam Government fought for reserved seats for women in government posts, promoted bank loans for women, ensured them inheritance rights and reserved seats in Panchayats.[1]

New woman came into the Panchayats [thanks to reservations] — they bring lots of ideas and energy to address problems of education, health, girl children's education, nourishment, and so on. Prior to women's entry in Panchayats, [these issues were] not considered important. Now [they are] considered very important — women will bring much more force.[2]

How exactly can we know the impact of women's political representation on gender equality beyond formal politics? This question – whether or not democratic institutions can further social and economic equality in tangible ways – is hotly contested around the world.[3] Some studies find representation increases women's ability to voice policy preferences and secure public goods. Others find evidence of inefficiency, backlash, and political disengagement.[4]

---

[1] Interview by Wendy Singer with NT Rama Rao, former Chief Minister of Andhra Pradesh and founder of the Telugu Desam Party, on November 23, 1995, "On Women's Politics," c.f. Singer (2007, 157–8).

[2] Personal interview with Dr. Daggubati Purandeswari Rao, Member of Parliament for Andhra Pradesh and Minister of State in Ministry of Human Resource Development, on January 24, 2014, in her Hyderabad constituency office.

[3] Bush (2011); Piscopo (2015); Clayton and Zetterberg (2018).

[4] On the optimists, see: Mansbridge (1999a); Burns, Schlozman, and Verba (2001); Chattopadhyay and Duflo (2004b); Bhavnani (2009); Beaman et al. (2010); Reingold and Harrell (2010); Iyer et al. (2012). For pessimistic outcomes, see Mayaram (2002); Bardhan et al. (2005); Clayton (2015). For those who suggest mixed outcomes, see Franceschet and Piscopo (2008).

Here, I will first introduce the research method devised to design this project as well as to collect and analyze a combination of qualitative and quantitative data – including more than two years of field research – built upon my collaboration with two unique centers of research and development: the Andhra Pradesh (AP) – based Society for the Elimination of Rural Poverty (SERP) and the Delhi-based National Council of Applied Economic Research.

With this strategy in mind, I will present and analyze the central tests of the "gatekeeper theory" developed in Chapter 2. To remind readers, my hypothesis is that quotas mandating women's political representation can increase enforcement of their property rights by changing the gender of pivotal local officials: "gatekeepers." Male gatekeepers typically lack incentives to shift property rights from traditional, male holders to females. Where representatives are female, they may increase women's capacity to demand property rights and secure enforcement. Yet quotas are often a double-edged sword. Female representation can spark resistance when quotas occur alongside legislative reforms that materially reduce men's long-standing rights.

This chapter provides the first component of this book's broader empirical project: resolving the debate over whether and when female representation enables enforcement of economic reforms and produces durable change sufficient to alter patterns of exclusion.

5.1 RESEARCH METHOD

We have studied power from the earliest records of civilization. The Mesopotamian epic of Gilgamesh chronicles the enduring nature of exploitative power, where even divine intervention was not enough to overthrow oppressive rule by Gilgamesh two thousand years before the common era (BCE). By 400 BCE, Thucydides was more optimistic about the merits of Athenian power based on impartial institutions: "If we look to the laws, they afford equal justice to all in their private differences."[5]

The measurement of power has been a persistent problem. Dahl addressed this eloquently by defining power simply as "a relation among people,"[6] where "power" is measured as the ability of one person to induce change in the other's behavior.[7] Contemporary analysis of power has gained greater analytic traction by recognizing the importance of more systemic influences on behavior: institutions or "the rules of the game in a society" according to North (1990, 3–4). The relevant set of institutions that influence the

---

[5] Thucydides (c. 431–428 BCE: 2.37.1–2.37.2), Pericles's Funeral Oration in *History of the Peloponnesian War*.

[6] Dahl (1957, 203).

[7] March (1955, 434) formalizes this theory explicitly around measuring behavioral change. Many other mainstream contemporary theories of power are built upon this core theory, such as Dahl (1957), with later work extending theory to less easily observable forms of influence: inducing change in individual agendas or beliefs, such as Bachrach and Baratz (1962) and Lukes (1974).

individual-level distribution of power is nearly infinite. In North's (1990, 3–4) terms, institutions encompass "the humanly devised constraints that shape human interaction. In consequence, they structure incentives in human exchange, whether political, social, or economic."

Despite the expansive breadth of institutions, the scope of political science research has been surprisingly circumscribed. Work abounds on the importance of formal institutions, that is, legal rules governing the structure of states – including decision making in legislative bodies, property rights, and trade. Yet there is more limited scholarship on informal institutions: norms or social conventions "created, communicated, and enforced outside of officially-sanctioned channels."[8]

This distinction often migrates into methodological design. We have sharper, better-honed procedures to study formal institutions than informal rules, despite acknowledgments that the latter are responsible for driving much of political behavior.[9]

Where informal institutions are explicitly studied, these are most often norms about formal political action, such as agreements amongst legislators about how to detect and remedy Executive branch noncompliance with the legislative goals of Congress in the United States,[10] or the common, global practice of "clientelism" that is linking citizen receipt of public goods – which the state is legally (formally) obligated to provide – to political loyalty.[11] A growing body of work begins to expand this focus by investigating the complex relationship between formal and informal political organization.[12]

The enduring focus on archetypal forms of political behavior in mainstream political science results in two crucial errors of omission.

First, scholarship frequently ignores the problem of enforcement: "Who watches the watchman?" or, more formally, "why some behavioral rules, originating either inside or outside the state, are followed while others are ignored."[13] It is inherently problematic to ignore processes of enforcement outside the prototypically *political* domain because what we think of as prototypically political decisions – such as those about how and when to punish individuals for breaking rules – are intimately linked to identities and experiences in social and economic domains.[14]

Second, the widespread focus on "traditional" forms of political behavior reinforces artificial barriers between "public" versus "private" spheres – or political versus personal, "intimate" household action – that are explicitly

---

[8] Helmke and Levitsky (2004, 725–6). Exceptional studies of informal institutions include those by Levi (1988); North (1990); Ellickson (1991); Knight (1992); Libecap (1993); Evans (1995); Scott (1998); Grindle (2000); Greif (2006); Tsai (2007); Ellickson (2010); Singh (2016); Kruks-Wisner (2018).

[9] Evans (1995); Helmke and Levitsky (2004); Singh (2016).

[10] McCubbins and Schwartz (1984).   [11] Helmke and Levitsky (2004, 727).

[12] Boone (2003); Tsai (2007); Scott (2014); Baldwin (2015); Cooper (2018); Risse and Stollenwerk (2018).

[13] Greif (2006, 8).   [14] Ellickson (1991); Cooper (2018).

gendered. As Trotsky explained in lectures he delivered to workers, *Problems of Life:*

Unless there is actual equality of husband and wife in the family, in a normal sense as well as in the conditions of life, we cannot speak seriously of their equality in social work or even in politics. As long as woman is chained to her housework, the care of the family, the cooking and sewing, all her chances of participation in social and political life are cut down to the extreme.[15]

Ignoring "private" political behavior has a clear impact on gender-based notions of agency and efficacy. However, this bias also radiates across the many dimensions of privilege. For example, Anoll (2018) notes that race and spacial organization influence how much American citizens value "traditional" forms of political participation such as voting versus less formal modes of engagement such as rallies or protests.

5.1.1 Applying Feminist Analysis to Informal Institutions

In line with a growing body of research,[16] I break down the barriers between the "personal, private" and informal economy where female interests are widely assumed to center, versus the "public," male-dominated arenas of politics and the formal economy, where women are increasingly scarce.

My research method and content aim to advance the argument that the specific act of claiming rights within the household – here, to inherit property – is *political* behavior. In particular, one's ability to claim property rights within the family depends upon political agency and is an exertion of political power, which, if successful, further augments one's political resources and voice.[17]

As a result, I tailor my research method to identify how conferring new property rights translates into individual willingness to claim them. In doing so, I pay particular attention to the processes – both public and private, in elected council meetings, on porches, and in kitchens – by which property ownership is negotiated. Asking these questions brings my work, in many ways, closer to Ensminger's (1996) economic anthropology or Goldstein and Udry's (2008) development economics than to traditional political science research. I follow Ensminger's (1996, 4) assumption that "to comprehend these changes [in economic, political, and social institutions] we must look both at individual motivation (institutional patterns that result from individual choices) and at the socially determined constraints and incentives that influence what individuals strive for and how they go about realizing their goals."

---

[15] Trotsky (1924, 48), c.f. Rowbotham (1974, 144).

[16] In particular, see Iversen and Rosenbluth (2008); Ellickson (2010); Mabsout and Van Staveren (2010); Khan (2017); Prillaman (2017); Bleck and Michelitch (2018); Gottlieb, Grossman, and Robinson (2018); Teele, Kalla, and Rosenbluth (2018); World Economic Forum (2018).

[17] Sen (2001a); Folbre (2009).

In particular, I seek to understand the extent to which changes in the formal rules of the game can alter social norms – that is, ideology or "what people value" in Ensminger's (1996, 4) terms. Such changes usually occur at a near glacial pace, and are "lumpy," that is they "are indivisible and operate across numerous frontiers" – social, political, and economic.[18]

My contribution is to recognize – and explicitly study – how changes in political institutions alter individual behavior within the often-invisible "domestic economy" of the household, and to examine how such changes translate into meaningful behavioral shifts at larger levels of organization: participation in local political councils, articulation of personal and collective political demands, and national trends in women's property inheritance, sex-selective abortion, and care for elder parents.

5.1.2 Design-Based Research Is More than Just Research Design

To capture the impact of formal institutional change on "lumpy" behavior across social, economic, and political domains, I employ three sets of research design strategies. First, I use what Dunning (2012, 4) defines as a "design-based" method of research. What I mean is that I began my research with interlinked motivations concerning content and design.

One motive was substantive: to understand the impact of expanding access to formal, state-enforced property rights. I chose this focus because prior to beginning my PhD, I interned for the Sri Lanka–based Consortium of Humanitarian Agencies to help investigate and propose methods of voluntary return and resettlement for citizens who were displaced during Sri Lanka's then-ongoing multidecade civil war. The project was my first experience with policy-relevant field research. The displaced persons I interviewed gave a consistent, surprising response about their fundamental requirement for return: formal property rights to the land on which they would reside. During subsequent work with the Abdul Latif Jameel Poverty Action Lab, in particular for Sendhil Mullainathan, I began observing the conflicts over property rights in rural North and South India. The individuals hardest hit by the lack of secure – if any – property rights were usually the most vulnerable community members – Tamil citizens in Sri Lanka, and women along with members of Scheduled Castes and Scheduled Tribes (SCs and STs) in rural India. I entered my doctoral studies determined to figure out how the state could expand access to property rights in ways that would benefit those most likely to be discriminated against in multiple spheres.

My other motive for this research was design based. To analyze the effectiveness of state policies, I searched to locate a "natural experiment," where individuals gained access to formal rights or resources in a random or as-if random way. If individual eligibility for an intervention is indeed as good as random, this would allow me to analyze a group of "treated" individuals who

[18] North (1990, 16); Ensminger (1996, 11).

are directly comparable to those untreated by the intervention – the "control" group.[19] Comparable treatment and control groups allow the researcher to causally identify a given policy's impact on individual behavior. In Dunning's (2012, 4) language, design-based research methods offer a decisive advantage: they enable control over confounding variables such as wealth or social connections, to "come primarily from research-design choices rather than *ex post* adjustment using parametric statistical models."[20]

In my case, the central policy intervention is the "as-if random" assignment of one-third of all elections for heads of village-level councils in India to be eligible for only female candidates, a random draw that is repeated every new round of elections following the constitutional mandate's passage in 1993. Chattopadhyay and Duflo (2004b) published the first systematic study of these quotas for female representation across two Indian states (Rajasthan and West Bengal). They find significant impact: where quotas require women to head local government, public goods such as roads and water are distributed in line with female citizen demands. Where there are no quotas – hence, no women heads – public goods are distributed in line with male citizen priorities.

Since then, we have learned a great deal more about the impact of quotas – known as "reservations" – on a number of explicitly political behaviors. They reduce the likelihood of bribes paid for access to public goods (Duflo and Topalova, 2004). They also increase educational activities (although not other actions) taken by elected local councils (Ban and Rao, 2008), as well as the likelihood of women competing in elections (Bhavnani, 2009), and long-term voter support for female candidates (Beaman et al., 2009). However, they also do a poorer job of ensuring that state development resources reach socially disadvantaged groups (Bardhan, Mookherjee, and Parra Torrado, 2010). A smaller set of work examines how quotas alter behavior in related domains, such as encouraging women to report crime (Iyer et al., 2012), and young women to have higher career aspirations and educational attainment (Beaman et al., 2012).

What we do not know is how quotas alter women's "authority" in the broader domain of politics.[21] I am particularly interested in women's ability to

---

[19] Examples of natural experiments where random assignment determines access to new resources include lotteries for eligibility to attend a well-resourced school or to take up a comprehensive health insurance plan, where every relevant citizen is eligible to receive these opportunities.

[20] This is because as-if random procedures for selecting who receives treatment versus who does not mean that there is just one source of randomly applied variation that separates all individuals in the treatment group from those in the control group. In contrast, where access to benefits is not as-if randomly distributed – for example because it requires expensive applications, is driven by word-of-mouth information, and/or requires recommendations from influential individuals – those who successfully access benefits are likely to be different from those who do not on many dimensions beyond access, including wealth, social ties, and connections, in particular, to influential individuals.

[21] See Paluck (2008) for a broader argument about the importance of qualitative research to understand the impact of "reservations" in India.

successfully claim formal rights to the most highly valued resource – ancestral land – within and across households.

Remarkably, India's roll out of quotas for female heads of local government overlapped with the roll out of a second, relevant policy change: equal inheritance rights for women governed by Hindu law (more than 80 percent of India's population). A constitutional amendment mandated quotas for women's political representation across all major states as of 1993, whereas individual states began equalizing Hindu women's inheritance rights earlier, as of 1976. However, national legislation for gender-equal inheritance took substantially longer than local-level political quotas, occurring only in 2005.[22] Daughters whose fathers die postlegislation have equal rights as sons to inherit ancestral property.[23] I leverage within- and across-state variation in women's access to these legal rights to identify the impact of female representation on women's ability to successfully claim gender-equal inheritance rights, as follows (Figure 5.1).

While this book focuses more attention on the "cleaner" natural experiment – quotas for women's local electoral representation – I began my research by investigating a policy intervention with messier eligibility criteria: legislative reforms giving Hindu women equal rights to inherit ancestral property. My initial descriptive analysis of nationally representative data suggested little if any direct effect of legal reform. As a result, I used the latter portion of my field research to search for additional natural experiments that would provide analytic leverage to explain the contrast between the significant local effect of reform identified by earlier studies,[24] and the significant resistance to reform I found across many of my field research sites.

I raise these points here to acknowledge the often frustrating, incomplete nature of research design that seeks to evaluate policy interventions in isolation from their context. While experiments that approximate "laboratory conditions" for analysis minimize potential distractions for analysts and readers, treating policy interventions as experiments increases the dependence on extremely simplified working models of *how, where, when, and why* citizen behavior changes around state policy interventions.

In my research, I have done my utmost to conduct in-depth critical analysis, both of the gaps between legal and practical implementation criteria for relevant policies and of the diverse ways that citizens negotiate the "rules of the game" inside *and outside* the explicit sphere of the state. I now turn to how I address this challenge.

---

[22] I would be remiss if I did not acknowledge the difficulty of legislating quotas for women's higher-level electoral representation; despite several decades of attempts to expand quotas above the district level, no such legislation has been accepted as of yet.

[23] This is a simplification that focuses on the main eligibility requirements. I provide a more detailed discussion of these criteria later in this chapter.

[24] Deininger et al. (2013).

Reservations for Women (Political Change)

		First	Second
Gender Equal Land Inheritance (Economic Change)	**First**	*Maharashtra (*same year of legislation for reform and reservations*)	Andhra Pradesh Kerala *Maharashtra (*1st elections postreform legislation*) *Tamil Nadu (*1st elections postreform*) *Bihar (*1st elections postreform*) *Jharkhand (*1st elections postreform*)
	Second	*Bihar (*legislated reform after reservations*) Chhattisgarh Gujarat Haryana Himachal Pradesh *Jharkhand (*legislated reform after reservations*) Karnataka Madhya Pradesh Orissa Punjab Rajasthan *Tamil Nadu (*legislated reform after reservations*) Uttar Pradesh West Bengal	

FIGURE 5.1. State-Level Timing of Political vs. Economic Reform

5.1.3 Measuring Women's Political Power

I employed a second set of research design strategies to develop appropriate theory and measurement of women's political power on the ground in contemporary India. I conducted field research primarily in a pioneer state of property rights reforms: Andhra Pradesh, in south India.[25]

To select districts for field research, I prioritized variation due to political geography. Following seminal work by Scott (1998, 2014) and Herbst (2000), I posit that geography affects not only the state's ability to project power over its citizens but also citizen interest in engaging the state and its formal legal structures.

If political geography does indeed matter, I expect the presence, accessibility, and subsequent influence of the state to be strongest in flat, densely populated terrain with close proximity to centers of state power. In such places, the state ensures it reaches citizens by building extensive infrastructure – including roads and irrigation. Scott (1998) argues populations in such sites are most "legible" for states. In Andhra Pradesh, I consider two sets of "highly legible"

---

[25] For more detail, see Chapter 4 on the origins of gender-equalizing property inheritance reforms.

FIGURE 5.2. Qualitative Interview Districts, Andhra Pradesh State as of 2001
Source: Census of India, 2001 political boundaries

populations: first, in the state's arid capital district,[26] Ranga Reddy, and second, the well-irrigated Krishna district, in Coastal Andhra Pradesh (with its capital, Vijayawada, located just 18 miles [29 km] from what would soon be Andhra Pradesh's new state capital, Amravati). In contrast, the state's power over – and accessibility to – its citizens should be weaker in predominantly rural, poorly irrigated, and less densely populated districts. I consider two such districts, Anantapur in the arid region known as Ryalaseema, and second, Khammam in the relatively impoverished Telangana region (now an independent state).

Finally, I expect the central state's power to be minimal and its resources nearly invisible for citizens in remote, hillier regions, both at the edges of the Khammam district and in Visakhapatnam and Srikakulam districts, both of which are densely forested and with a history of antistate, Maoist activism.

I map my field research sites in Figure 5.2. If political geography matters, this selection of sites should allow me to observe the varied strategies individuals employ to access – or avoid – state power. I expect these strategies should vary in direct proportion to the distance between individuals and the state.

Next, I hypothesize that individual capacity to engage the state is also a function of locality-specific biases in support for particular population groups. One central measure of state investment in citizen capacity is literacy. In India, achieving total literacy has been a persistent challenge: only 20 percent of the population was literate at Independence, and an half century later, just under two-thirds were able to read and write (Reddy and Rao, 2003).

I used village-level rates of female literacy relative to male to determine in which villages to conduct my interviews. This allowed me to identify a local spectrum of variation in women's relative ability to engage the state. I focused

[26] Hyderabad is currently the joint capital of AP and Telangana states, soon to be solely Telangana's capital.

on women's relative literacy because it is a crucial measure of individual access to information and the ability to make formal claims on the state. It is also a proxy for multiple socioeconomic disadvantages. In AP, as in most of India, women face higher constraints to achieving literacy than men. For men, the greatest hindrance to individual ability to achieve a basic education – measured as literacy – is scarce household resources: poverty is the main source of school dropout for all caste groups. For women who are members of disadvantaged ("backward") castes, poverty also predicts dropout rates. However, amongst women from advantaged caste groups, the greatest predictor of dropout is the common priority that women should take care of the home.[27] AP's per capita expenditure exacerbates individual constraints: the state spends significantly less on women than men, and less on members of disadvantaged versus advantaged castes.[28]

I implemented this criteria by drawing half of each district-level subset of villages from areas with high levels of women's relative literacy and half from areas with low levels. I did this in collaboration with state- and district-level representatives of AP's SERP.

Lastly, I selected two criteria to account for intravillage variation in women's capacity to claim resources and exercise a political voice: whether or not women are members of families who own land, and whether or not they participate in all-female Self-Help Groups (SHGs) organized throughout AP by the state to distribute microcredit amongst women.

I used membership in SHGs, as did Prillaman (2017), as a measure of whether a given woman's access to female-centric networks improved the likelihood that she would claim rights from the state. In each village, I sought to meet equal portions of women from landowning and landless families, as well as equal subsets of each group who were and were not members of SHGs. I expected women in landholding families who were SHG members to have the greatest set of resources to engage the state, and women from landless families who were not SHG members to possess the least. I anticipated the remaining two categories of women to possess moderate capacity to make their voices heard by the state.

Once I had assembled my pool of potential interviewees, I developed a core set of interview questions to understand individual, household, and community-specific access to land inheritance. I wanted to investigate how such rights were distributed, formalized, and contested at each level and what

---

[27] Reddy and Rao (2003, 1249).

[28] AP consistently lags behind other Indian states in this regard. In 1971, 25 percent of the population was literate in AP as opposed to 34 percent nationally; as of 2001, this comparison was 61 percent in AP compared to 65 percent nationally (Reddy and Rao, 2003, 1242–3, 1249). As of the 2001 census, the state ranks 22nd among 28 for adult literacy despite ranking 11th from the top in terms of per capita state domestic product. It also registered the lowest growth rate in net public educational expenditure by a federal state, as well as consistently ranks in the lowest 2–3 states for per capita expenditure between 1980 and 2000 (Shariff and Ghosh, 2000, 1397, 1403).

Distance from State Center

	District	None		Moderate		Extreme	
		Ranga Reddy	Krishna	Anantapur	Khammam	Srikakulam	Visakhapatnam
High/Equal			✓	✓	✓		✓
Low		✓	✓	✓	✓	✓	✓

Women's Literacy (Relative to Men)

FIGURE 5.3. Field Research Selection Criteria (District and Village Level)

role, if any, the state played in mediating information and dispute resolution. To this end, I relied heavily on the advice and support of my field research partner, SERP, in particular their Director of Advocacy, Jamuna Paruchuri. I explain more on this partnership in the following text. After the first few months of my field research, I adjusted my questions significantly because of what I had learned from initial interviews with activists, academics, lawyers, and public servants. My insights were gained not only from content but also by noting which questions elicited silence and which prompted reflection and conversation.

To conclude, Figure 5.3 summarizes the central criteria I used to select the sample of districts and villages in rural AP where I conducted my interviews. Overall, this strategy allowed me to examine the varied political, economic, and social channels through which women decide *how, when, and with what effect* to claim gender-equal rights to ancestral property.

5.1.4 Essential Collaboration

After deciding *what* to study – how policy changes enabled or prevented women from claiming valuable economic resources – I had to decide *how* to explore and analyze the impact of these changes. Collaboration, starting years before I began data collection and continuing in many cases up to the present day, has been essential at every step of the research design and implementation process. The acknowledgments section highlights the core relationships through MIT's Abdul Latif Jameel Poverty Action Lab (JPAL), particularly thanks to Esther Duflo, Abhijit Banerjee, Sendhil Mullainathan, and the core staff of their Udaipur office, as well as dear friends and colleagues in Yamuna Nagar, Haryana; Delhi; Lucknow, Uttar Pradesh; and Hyderabad and Vijayawada, in

AP, which were fundamental to my understanding of basic concepts: what the phenomena I cared about *in theory* looked like in practice, and how to construct appropriate measurement devices that could span the Indian subcontinent.

The main skill I garnered from this work was how to conduct "street smart" or rather "community wise" field research. I learned early on to never take for granted access to a given community. I worked to build trust with research partners and subjects before attempting to gather meaningful information, constantly reflecting on what knowledge I sought to obtain and listening to what people said about the appropriateness and accuracy of my research strategies, even when the information was difficult to digest. I constantly attempted to see the "big picture" of what I considered ideal research design while not forgetting to attend to the edges of daily life. The greatest insights individuals shared with me were often over the informal parts of our day together – pounding spices for tea before breakfast or sitting together over hours of bumpy rural roads to reach the real "research site." These initial conversations and relationships provided the model for interviews later organized around women's land inheritance in rural AP, South India.

In addition, two key graduate mentors, Beatriz Magaloni and Saumitra Jha, helped me find my way to the most important questions and data. Saumitra Jha pointed me toward the most comprehensive dataset on land inheritance in contemporary India, the Rural Economic and Demographic Survey (REDS), which led me to Andy Foster at Yale University, who along with Mark Rosenzweig at Harvard had designed REDS for its first round in 1968/9 and painstakingly continued expanding the panel dataset through to the latest comprehensive survey in 2006/9. I was lucky to meet Andy at the Delhi-based National Council of Applied Economic Research (NCAER), where he advised me on how to navigate REDS and research in rural India. My experience with JPAL also brought me into contact with Hari Nagarajan at NCAER, who led challenging implementation of the REDS 2006/9 round. After a number of helpful conversations about research on inequality, he invited me to apply to, and later join, NCAER on a Canadian IRDC-NCAER fellowship for an enlightening year of analyzing REDS.

It was thanks to these mentors that I was able to access an essential piece of this research project: survey data for more than 8,500 households collected by the NCAER in the 2006/9 round of REDS. This dataset compiles information on inheritance, marriage, political participation, representation, and the nature of economic, social, and political disputes for more than 100,000 individuals in rural locations of 17 major Indian states: the multigenerational members of the 8,500 families mapped in the 2006/9 survey. This is the data I used to test the hypotheses that I developed through my field research.

Finally, I began my field research design in earnest by approaching two pioneers of study in Indian women's inheritance rights: Bina Agarwal, who generously advised me on how to select optimal field research sites, and Nitya Rao, who helped me tackle big conceptual issues about how to study women's inheritance rights using a tenuous Internet connection. She opened my eyes to the dynamics of claiming rights that became essential to this manuscript.

Introductions from World Bank–based scholars also opened up what became the essential partnership for my field research, with SERP.[29] In particular, Jamuna Paruchuri spearheaded their substantive work on women. She and her "right-hand woman," Aruna, helped me implement individual and group interviews in villages across the state using SERP's federated structure. Jamuna worked tirelessly to help me locate the relevant data to select villages for study. In large part, we retrieved data from the national census, World Bank surveys, and/or SERP's local- and district-level surveys, some of which she invited me to help design and field, in collaboration with relevant local bureaucracies and elected bodies.

In interview selection, I relied as much as possible on objective criteria to avoid collecting a biased sample of exceptional over- (or under-) performing SERP-affiliated communities. This was essential given the vast scope of SERP's mobilization across AP – as of 2011 they had organized nearly 630,000 SHGs federated into 28,080 Village Organizations (VOs) and 864 *Mandal Samakhyas* (MSs). I did my best to work in districts with varied tenures of collaboration with SERP. A significant portion of the locales I studied had no SERP-based VO, and between one-third and one-half of the women I interviewed were not members of SERP SHGs. Jamuna's extraordinary assistant, Aruna, accompanied me directly to translate and navigate, and helped locate effective local assistants when necessary.

Throughout my interviews, individual privacy was a priority. This meant first obtaining Institutional Review Board approval from my home research institution,[30] asking permission of relevant local authorities – including family members if interviewees requested – and assuring each person I met that any conversation was voluntary and that I would keep their identities private unless they requested otherwise. Given that the majority of my interviewees were female, my translators were usually also women, although male SERP employees helped when circumstances required. When possible, I interviewed individuals separately. However, when large groups of women – and sometimes men – were enthusiastic enough to speak, I interviewed them as a group. For some of the more isolated villages I visited, and for some women in more tense communities, my very presence was too conspicuous to be left alone with a single individual, who felt too scrutinized by me or neighbors to speak in isolation. In these cases, translators, local authorities, and I composed focus groups in public and then interviewed each group privately.

---

[29] These first conversations were possible because of the longstanding relationship between the World Bank and SERP, which is an autonomous, AP organization with a significant portion of its funding originating with the Bank.

[30] My relevant institution was either Stanford University (IRB Protocol 18558), the National Council of Applied Economic Research, or New York University in Abu Dhabi and New York (IRB Protocol 114–2016).

5.1.5 Assumptions

Entering the first round of fieldwork, I expected that rights were clear and citizens well informed about their basic contours, with bureaucrats acting as willing partners to implement rights upon receipt of requests. I attributed the variation in access to rights to individual incentives to demand authorities to formalize nontraditional rights. I expected group-level socioeconomic identities – related to caste or economic resources – to be the main sources of women's differential access to land inheritance rights. To check this assumption, I supplemented my interviews by assembling archival evidence on 40 years of property rights disputes registered in the most litigious district in AP: Krishna. The parties included both women and men who disputed inheritance and ownership rights over plots of land of varied sizes and values with varied success.

What I found contradicted my initial expectations and led to a fundamental reassessment of my project. Women's knowledge of rights varied. Local officials were usually informed, but none I met were enthusiastic about implementing gender-equal property inheritance. Most women expressed pessimism about the state's attentiveness to their rights.

In the second round of research, I expanded my interviews with politicians, bureaucrats, lawyers, academics, and activists – including an additional survey of 55 female activists employed by SERP – to better understand *how, when, why, and with what effect* women renegotiate rights in families and broader political, economic, and social communities. I made three additional trips to AP for in-depth conversations with politicians and their constituents. Where possible, I conducted similar interviews across the north Indian states of Uttar Pradesh, Haryana, and the National Capital Region centered around Delhi as well as the western state of Maharashtra.

By the end of two years, I had conducted interviews in 48 villages of six districts in AP. Altogether, I completed more than five hundred individual interviews and discussions with a roughly equal number of people in larger groups. I then sought to broaden my interlocutors over a handful of extended visits over the following half decade. The conversations provided me with insight into how and why women's access to property inheritance varies across rural India. While I expected the cost of demanding formal "rights" to be enormous to women, what I learned throughout these years was that obtaining recognition from a disinterested or even hostile state was the most difficult obstacle to overcome.

What results is a pioneering study of women's ability to harness political voice to claim fundamental economic rights. This panoramic scrutiny is possible because of my combination of three types of design-based research methodology: first, at the project's inception; second, through my systematic organization of in-depth qualitative interviews from key actors inside and outside the state; and third, through on the ground collaboration that enabled me to analyze nationally representative quantitative data on individual political representation and economic, social, and political resources and action. The next section explains the data I use, my hypothesis tests, what I find, and why it matters.

5.2 DATA

My primary dataset is the NCAER's REDS. I rely on the most recent 2006/9 round, which covers 8,659 households from 240 rural villages across 17 Indian states. In addition to standard demographic questions, the nationally representative survey records all land transfers between the household head, their siblings, parents, spouse, and children, plus adult household residents' political participation and perceptions of local governance. In other words, this data provides a rich and comprehensive accounting of individual property inheritance in contemporary India.

I study all female respondents born between 1956, when women gained symbolic property rights, and the year their state equalized their property rights, culminating in the national mandate of 2005 (1976–2005).[31] In total, the sample comprises 31,729 women with a mean age of 31 years, 48 percent of whom have fathers whose death occurs after their village *Pradhan* seat is reserved for women. On average, 4 percent of women inherit land (Tables A.9.6 and 5.1).

5.3 CAUSAL IDENTIFICATION STRATEGY

I utilize India's quasirandom implementation of "reservations" for women as elected heads of village councils – constitutionally mandated as of 1993 – to identify the impact of female representation on enforcement of women's property inheritance rights. These rights were legislated at different times by the various Indian states. Thus the year of "reform" varies from state to state. All culminated in the 2005 passage of a national mandate equalizing property inheritance rights for men and women.[32]

I compare daughters with fathers who die at or after the year their village *Pradhan* seat was reserved for a woman with those whose fathers died prior. If the father's village (where ancestral property is typically located) has been reserved for a woman in any election occurring up to the year of his death, I code his daughter as *"treated"* by reservations. I focus on the time of paternal death as the relevant point for inheritance reform enforcement, as it determines a daughter's eligibility for gender-equal inheritance: she is eligible if her father dies post reform. Reform timing varies by state, from 1976 to 2005.[33] Specifically, I estimate the equation:

$$y_{isk} = \alpha_s + \beta_k + \gamma_{sk} + \delta' R_{is} + \delta'' D_{isk} + \delta''' D_{isk} * R_{is} + \theta X_{isk} + \epsilon_{isk} \quad (5.1)$$

[31] Roy (2015) finds parental investment changes post-HSAA, so I exclude these births.
[32] See the note to Figure A.9.4 for details.   [33] Figure A.9.4.

TABLE 5.1. *Descriptive Statistics, Main Dependent, and Independent Variables*

	All	Women	Men
Age < 20 at reform	0.38	0.37	0.39
	(0.49)	(0.48)	(0.49)
Pradhan seat ever reserved for a woman	0.69	0.69	0.69
	(0.46)	(0.46)	(0.46)
Latest *pradhan* seat reserved for a woman	0.33	0.33	0.33
	(0.47)	(0.47)	(0.47)
Father died postreservations	0.42	0.48	0.34
	(0.49)	(0.50)	(0.47)
Father died postreform	0.31	0.41	0.20
	(0.46)	(0.49)	(0.40)
Father died postreform and postreservations	0.36	0.44	0.25
	(0.48)	(0.50)	(0.43)
Aged 1–20 at reform * Father died postreform	0.12	0.15	0.10
	(0.33)	(0.35)	(0.30)
Aged 1–20 at reform * Father died postreservations	0.14	0.15	0.14
	(0.35)	(0.35)	(0.34)
Aged 1–20 at reform * Father died postreform and postreservations	0.14	0.15	0.13
	(0.35)	(0.35)	(0.34)
Inherit land?	0.13	0.04	0.24
	(0.34)	(0.19)	(0.43)
Area of inherited plot fragment	3.46	3.57	3.45
	(5.10)	(7.93)	(4.76)
Any dowry given (for a woman)	0.34	0.48	–
	(0.48)	(0.50)	–
Last gram sabha: attended? (%)	0.23	0.10	0.34
	(0.42)	(0.30)	(0.47)
Current *pradhan*: How able to resolve social problems (scale of 1–3)?	1.96	1.95	1.97
	(0.73)	(0.73)	(0.74)
Observations	61,569	31,729	29,840

Source: Rural Economic and Demographic Survey, 2006. The sample includes all men and women born post-HSA and pre-HSAA in their state. Standard deviations are in parentheses.

The dependent variable of interest, y_{isk}, is a binary indicator of whether or not a daughter i, born in state s, in year k, inherits any land. It takes a value of 1 if a given woman inherits any land and 0 otherwise. This outcome is the most parsimonious measure of impact. The independent variables of interest identify whether or not individuals are *treated* by reservations and eligible for gender-equal inheritance. D_{isk} is a binary indicator of *treatment*: whether a given daughter i, born in state s-specific cohort k, has a father who died at or after the first year his village *Pradhan* seat was reserved for a woman. R_{is} is a binary indicator of *eligibility:* whether daughter i's father dies after his state s legislates gender-equal inheritance rights. δ'''''s coefficient indicates the impact of representation on daughters eligible for reform. Women whose fathers die before village-level reservation and state-level reform are the control group.

α_s is a placeholder for state fixed effects, to account for state characteristics that are invariant across birth cohorts. β_k represents birth year fixed effects, to capture changes in the economy, policy, or society that occur at the macrolevel, affecting particular birth cohorts. γ_{sk} symbolizes state-year of birth fixed effects. These account for temporal variation in relevant state-level actions, such as pro-female legislation that may have coincided with inheritance reform, including the establishment of Women's Commissions studied by Anderson and Genicot (2015).[34] X_{isk} is a vector of predominantly household-level control variables: number of male and female siblings, caste status, total number of children, region, and wealth status (measured by parental land). Standard errors are clustered at the village level, which is the level at which reservations are applied in this dataset. This helps address concerns about geographic correlation of responses within locations sharing the same government (and gatekeeper), and allows for heteroscedasticity. I present OLS analysis throughout for ease of interpretation.[35]

To identify the causal impact of reservations, I assume that these quotas are rolled out according to procedures that are as-if random. In other words, whether or not a given village receives a quota for a given electoral cycle should be as good as random selection at making the assignment of quotas independent of that village's characteristics or relevant political agendas. To test this assumption, I first confirm balance across villages with and without reservations for female *Pradhans* (Table A.9.3).[36] I find that villages look similar across all specifications except for the percentage of women in sub-district populations prior to reservations. To understand whether reservation implementation procedures might result in a biased sample of villages receiving female representatives, I compiled the first comprehensive summary of the mechanisms for implementing these quotas. I found that a number of states use the proportion of women as a mechanism for reserving villages and rotating reservations, as Table 5.2 indicates. To eliminate this source of bias in calculating the effect of quotas, I compare states when I exclude those that use a non-random mechanism for reserving villages. This results in a balanced sample on all relevant characteristics (Table 5.3). I also check and confirm that individuals whose fathers die pre- versus post-implementation of reservations are similar (Table 5.4); and that REDS records of reservation status

---

[34] State-birth year fixed effects also absorb economic influences on parental incentives to recognize a daughter's inheritance rights, such as the state-specific increase in returns to agricultural land, and account for any differential state-level prereform trends in female inheritance.

[35] For logit analysis, see Tables A.9.8, A.9.10, A.9.11, and A.9.12.

[36] All analysis is based on REDS 2006/9 round, which collects information on reservation status for the past three *Gram Panchayat* elections in each village.

TABLE 5.2. *Women's Reservations' Timing, Selection, and Rotation, by Indian State*

State	Panchayat Act (Year)	First Election	Random	Selection Method	Rotation	Increase to 50% Quota
Andhra Pradesh	1994	1995	Not Random	Sex ratio	Unknown	2011
Bihar	1993	2006	As-if Random	Population size	Without replacement, every 10 years	2006
Delhi	1993	Unknown	Unknown	Unknown	Unknown	No
Chhattisgarh	1994	1995	Random	Draw of lots	Without replacement, every 5 years	2008
Gujarat	1994	1995	Unknown	Unknown	Unknown	2009
Haryana	1994	1994	Random	Draw of lots	Unknown	No
Himachal Pradesh	1994	1995	Not Random	Proportion of women in population	Without replacement, every 5 years	2010
Jharkhand	2001	2010	Unknown	Unknown	Unknown	2005
Karnataka	1993	1993	As-if Random	Population size: *panchayat* seats	No two consecutive reservations	2010
Kerala	1994	1995	Not Random	Proportion of women in population	No two consecutive reservations	2010
Madhya Pradesh	1994	1994	Random	Draw of lots	Without replacement, every 5 years	2009
Maharashtra	1994	1995	Random	Draw of lots	Without replacement, every 5 years	2011
Orissa	1994	1997	Random	Alphabetical order (every 3rd)	Without replacement, every 5 years	2011
Punjab	1994	1998	Unknown	Unknown	Every 10 years	2017
Rajasthan	1994	1995	Random	Draw of lots	Without replacement, every 5 years	2008
Tamil Nadu	1994	1996	Not Random	Proportion of women in population	Without replacement, every 10 years	2016
Uttar Pradesh	1994	1995	As-if Random	Population size	No two consecutive reservations	No
West Bengal	1994	1998	Random	Legislative Assembly numbers (every 3rd, ascending)	Without replacement, random number table	2012

Main Sources: Panchayat Raj Acts, Election Rules, and Department of Rural Development and Panchayat Raj.

TABLE 5.3. *Descriptive Statistics: Villages without vs. with Reservations, Excluding Nonrandom Implementers*

	(1) All Villages Mean	(2) With Reservations Mean	(3) Without Reservations Mean	(4) Difference of Means Difference (t-score)
District population, 1991 census	294,652.41	299,450.78	299,793.30	342.52 (0.01)
% women in subdistrict (tehsil) population, 1991 census	0.51	0.53	0.46	−0.07 (−1.91)
Village population: first *panchayat* period	4,096.88	3,999.12	4,383.50	384.38 (0.49)
Number of *panchayat* members: first *panchayat* period	12.56	12.58	12.49	−0.09 (−0.12)
% SCs *panchayat* members: first *panchayat* period	0.22	0.23	0.20	−0.03 (−0.94)
% STs *panchayat* members: first *panchayat* period	0.11	0.12	0.11	−0.00 (−0.07)
% OBCs *panchayat* members: first *panchayat* period	0.38	0.41	0.30	−0.10 (−2.03)
% Hindus in village population currently	0.87	0.88	0.86	−0.02 (−0.44)
% Muslims in village population currently	0.07	0.06	0.08	0.01 (0.51)
% SCs in village population currently	0.05	0.05	0.04	−0.01 (−0.74)
% STs in village population currently	0.06	0.05	0.10	0.05 (1.35)
% OBCs in village population currently	0.09	0.08	0.12	0.04 (1.09)
% own <2 acres of land in village population currently	0.26	0.25	0.27	0.02 (0.61)
% own land in village population currently	0.51	0.50	0.51	0.01 (0.22)
Average price: unirrigated land now (Rs.)	87,992.70	98,526.88	68,153.85	−30,373.04 (−1.34)
Average price: residential land now (Rs.)	417,477.12	419,767.86	447,702.70	27,934.85 (0.31)
% villages experienced drought, 1999	0.19	0.18	0.25	0.08 (1.13)
% villages experienced flood, 1999	0.14	0.11	0.24	0.12 (1.83)
% villages experienced pests, 1999	0.14	0.15	0.12	−0.03 (−0.50)
Number of villages	189	131	51	

Source: Rural Economic and Demographic Survey, 2006 village-level means are provided. Column (4) displays beta coefficients, *t* statistics are in parentheses.

TABLE 5.4. *Balance Test: Father's Death Pre- vs. Post-reservations*

	(1) All States	(2) Father Dies Postreservations	(3) Prereservations	(4) Difference (t-score)
Exogenous Variables				
Grandmother: secondary or more education	0.01	0.01	0.01	−0.00 (−0.33)
Grandfather: secondary or more education	0.06	0.07	0.07	0.01 (1.15)
Deceased Patriarch: top 20% landholders	0.28	0.28	0.28	0.00 (0.11)
Deceased Patriarch: low caste	0.73	0.71	0.73	0.02 (1.29)
Married Individuals: landed natal family	0.83	0.83	0.84	0.00 (0.22)
Potentially Endogenous Variables				
Father: secondary or more education	0.40	0.40	0.41	0.01 (1.07)
Mother: secondary or more education	0.12	0.12	0.16	0.03 (4.73)
Living Patriarch: top 20% landholders	0.32	0.36	0.28	−0.08 (−8.93)
Living Patriarch: low caste	0.73	0.73	0.71	−0.03 (−3.06)
Living Patriarch: land (acres)	10.42	11.49	8.86	−2.63 (−8.52)
Endogenous Variables				
Age (years)	30.26	31.23	37.07	5.83 (25.56)
Education (years completed)	5.61	4.27	5.13	0.86 (8.69)
Siblings: proportion sisters	0.41	0.39	0.46	0.08 (17.84)
Land Inheritance (%)	0.05	0.02	0.09	0.06 (13.87)
Total Land Inheritance (acres)	0.20	0.08	0.33	0.24 (8.35)
Observations	19,396	5,984	4,774	

Source: Rural Economic and Demographic Survey, 2006/9. The sample includes all landed Hindus who were born pre-HSA and pre-HSAA in their own state. For parental landholdings, I~consider the subset of children with fathers who are no longer living to ensure reported wealth is not strategically reported to influence future inheritance distribution. I take age as endogenous as older fathers are likely to pass away sooner. Prior work also shows that parents' investment in education and proportion of sisters is affected by property rights reform (Anderson and Genicot 2015; Rosenblum 2015; Roy 2015; Lawry et al. 2016; Bhalotra et al. 2018). Finally, this work shows that land inheritance and the amount of land inherited are also affected by reform. Column (4) displays beta coefficients, *t* statistics are in parentheses.

consistently predict the *Pradhan*'s gender for each electoral cycle in each village (Table A.9.4), and at the time of paternal death (Table A.9.5); and map village- and state-level variation in the implementation of reservations (Figures A.9.2, A.9.3, A.9.5).

Next, I test whether female gatekeepers are more effective at enforcing inheritance reform when female constituents have the greatest intrahousehold bargaining power. To investigate this, I exploit the leverage women gain over resource distribution at the time they enter marriage negotiations, that is critical junctures in women's lives, when a daughter is typically given her "share" of ancestral resources as monetary dowry. If female *Pradhans* are effective advocates for women who enter marriage markets eligible for gender-equal inheritance – when they can assist women in negotiating integrative bargaining solutions with families, where women secure land titles in their names rather than dowries – access to female representatives should be particularly valuable for these unmarried, eligible women.

Here, I analyze the differential effect of reservations and reform for daughters aged less than 20 at the time of reform (the treatment group) versus 20 or more (the control group). I choose a cutoff point of age 20 because this is the time by which three-quarters of daughters have begun marriage negotiations (Figure A.9.6).[37] In line with "gatekeeper theory," I expect a daughter's marriage status at reform – and thus whether or not she can use her traditional entitlement to monetary dowry as a bargaining chip – is the best measure of her bargaining power over rights to ancestral land.[38] As a reminder, Chapter 2's Figure 2.3 illustrates the predictions of "gatekeeper theory." If reservations enable female *Pradhans* to catalyze negotiations for a daughter's

---

[37] I use the following equation to estimate the impact of reservations and reform, conditional on women's age at reform:

$$y_{isk} = \alpha_s' + \beta_k' + \gamma_{sk}' + \delta' R_{isk} + \delta'' D_{isk} + \theta' B_{is(k'-20 \leq k \leq k'-1)}$$
$$+ \delta''' R_{isk} * D_{isk} + \theta'' B_{is(k'-20 \leq k \leq k'-1)} * R_{isk} + \theta''' * B_{is(k'-20 \leq k \leq k'-1)} * D_{isk}$$
$$+ \delta'''' B_{is(k'-20 \leq k \leq k'-1)} * R_{isk} * D_{isk} + \lambda X_{isk} + \epsilon_{isk}$$

$$(5.2)$$

The main coefficient of interest measures the impact of reservations for women entering marriage markets as they become eligible for reform (δ'''').

[38] In contrast, other widely used measures of bargaining power, such as education and sibling composition, are likely to be less accurate proxies of women's bargaining power for several reasons. First, evidence documents variation in both the quantum of parental investment in a daughter's education and their willingness to give birth to daughters alongside their exposure to reform (Roy, 2015; Bhalotra et al., 2018). This makes it difficult to separate the impact of such types of bargaining power from that of reform. In addition, gatekeeper theory predicts bargaining to be most responsive to a woman's marital status, as explained in Chapter 2. To verify that these potential influences are not driving results, I check and report the robustness of all main results to specifications where I include controls for both parental education and sibling composition.

inheritance rights in a manner benefiting all members – *by renouncing monetary dowry in favor of land inheritance* – I expect to see behavior change most dramatically in the group of women who are likely unmarried at reform. The next section tests these hypotheses.

Finally, I conduct subsample analysis of village-level inequality as a preliminary test of my hypotheses predicting where female gatekeepers are most likely to spark resistance: that is, households should be more willing to engage in backlash where the value of social status is particularly high. If social status is more valuable where socio-economic inequality is high, we should observe resistance to reform correlated with inequality. At elevated levels of inequality, the social benefits of maintaining status are likely to outweigh the material gains from compliance with gender-equalizing inheritance reform. If so, resistance should vary alongside levels of inequality.

To assess village-level inequality, I focus on the total amount of land owned (in acres) for each household recorded in the REDS 2006/9 dataset. I use this information to calculate village-level Gini coefficients. Land-based Gini coefficients have also been used by Deininger and Squire (1998) as well as Erickson and Vollrath (2004) to assess land inequality for country-level analysis. In addition, Bardhan (2000, 2005) calculates Gini coefficients at the *ayacut*-level (the unit relevant for irrigation systems) of farmer landholdings to measure economic inequality.

While Gini coefficients typically rely on individual-level income, I use the most comprehensive form of income included in the REDS 2006/9 round: household-level records of landownership. I employ this measure because it is least likely to overestimate inequality by inflating the number of landless individuals.[39]

The Gini coefficient takes a value between 0 and 1, where 0 represents perfect equality and 1 represents perfect inequality. To illustrate this concept with reference to landownership, consider a scenario in which all households in Village A own the same amount of land. If so, the Gini coefficient for this village would be equal to 0. In contrast, consider another hypothetical Village, B, where no household owns any land except for one household, which owns 100 percent of the land. In this case, the Gini coefficient would take a value of 1. I calculate intravillage landownership Gini coefficients by utilizing *indeco*, a Stata package for analyzing measures of inequality (Jenkins, 2015).[40] This package uses the following formula to calculate the Gini coefficient, which is essentially a

---

[39] While individual-level measures are available, the problem of disentangling whether nonreporting of landholdings is representative of zero land is particularly difficult for younger individuals.

[40] I include all households in the REDS 2006/9 sample, setting landholdings equal to zero for landless households. This avoids overestimating equality that might arise when only calculating the Gini coefficient for landholding households. Such estimates would clearly miss an important dimension of land inequality (Erickson and Vollrath 2004).

measure of how equal the interhousehold distribution of landholdings is within a given village:

$$G = 1 + \frac{1}{N} - \frac{2}{m \times N^2} \sum (N - i + 1) y_i \qquad (5.3)$$

Here, y_i is a measure of landownership for a given household i, calculated in acres, within a given village.[41] Households are ranked in ascending order of landownership (that is, for all y_i within a given village). N represents the number of households within a given village, while m is a placeholder for the mean landownership within a given village. I calculate this index for a total of 8,660 household-level observations. Within this sample, the mean household landholding is 4.8 acres, for a household of five individuals. Landholding size ranges from 0 to 300 acres. The lowest quartile of households possess at most 0.5 acres; the median own 2.8 acres. The mean village-level Gini coefficient is 0.55, with a standard deviation of 0.15. Overall, Gini values range from 0.21 to 0.96. The final section of my analysis will consider whether the impact of reservations on women's inheritance and associated behavior varies alongside village-level inequality.[42]

To provide a concrete picture of landholding inequality in the sample of villages I analyze, I utilize the Lorenz Curve, shown in Figure 5.4. This is a graphical representation of the intravillage distribution of wealth, which maps the cumulative distribution of landownership and population for each village. The horizontal axis represents the cumulative percentage of the population (measured here as the number of households in the village), ordered in increasing amount of wealth (typically income, here as acreage of household landholdings). The vertical axis captures the percentage of cumulative wealth (landholdings) accrued by a given fraction of the population. The 45-degree line of equality represents a perfectly equal distribution of wealth. This curve is relevant not only purely as an illustration of inequality but also because it can be used to calculate the Gini coefficient.[43] Figure 5.4 plots the Lorenz Curve for three relevant villages, compared to a hypothetical case. The black diagonal line represents the hypothetical case of completely equitable land distribution. The medium gray, solid line located closest to the black diagonal represents the Lorenz curve of the most equal village, with a Gini coefficient of 0.21. The lighter gray, dashed line indicates the Lorenz curve in the village with the median Gini coefficient (0.52). The dark gray line farthest to the right of

---

[41] On average, 35 households are sampled in each of the 241 villages included within the REDS 2006/9 dataset.

[42] Dividing the sample into three categories, with an equal number of villages in each, yields the following three tiers of Gini coefficients: 0.2101–0.4782 for the most equal villages; 0.4784–0.6076 for moderately equal villages; and 0.6096–0.9600 for the least equal villages.

[43] Such calculations estimate the ratio of the area (a) between the Lorenz curve and the line of equality, versus (b) the triangle occupying the space below the line of equality.

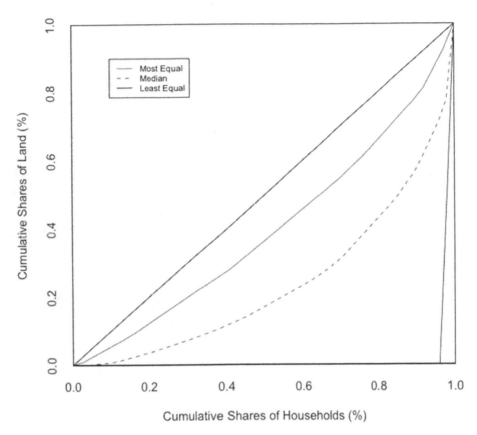

FIGURE 5.4. Lorenz Curves: Landownership Inequality

Source: REDS 2006/9

the figure, which is nearly vertical, represents the least equal village (0.96 Gini coefficient).

5.4 ANALYSIS

I begin by mapping variation in women's land inheritance alongside treatment by reservations and eligibility for reform, respectively, in Figure 5.5. There is a sharp, discontinuous jump in the likelihood of inheritance for women whose fathers die after reservations are implemented in their village, suggesting female gatekeepers are relevant for enforcement of inherited property rights.

5.4.1 Reservations and Women's Inheritance

I first test the impact of reservations on the likelihood of female inheritance for women who have versus lack gender-equal rights. I focus on the group of

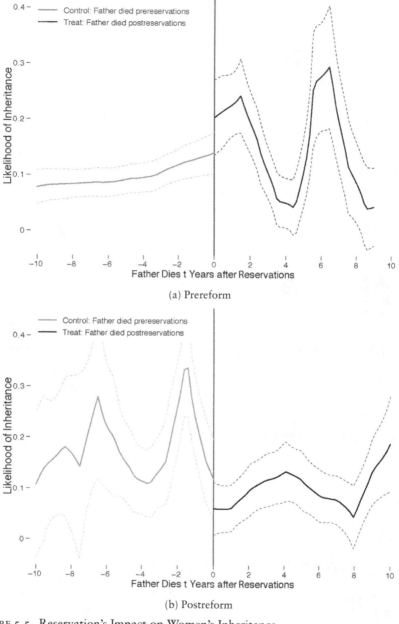

(a) Prereform

(b) Postreform

FIGURE 5.5. Reservation's Impact on Women's Inheritance

Source: NCAER Rural Economic and Demographic Survey, 2006/9. The sample includes landed, Hindu women who were born prior to state-level reform and post-HSA. The first figure includes women whose father died prereform, and the second postreform. Women are excluded whose fathers reside in states that do not assign reservations randomly. The x-axis represents when an individual's father passed away relative to the introduction of reservations in the father's village. The y-axis represents the probability of inheritance. Each point on the graph represents the average probability of inheritance for individuals whose fathers passed away *t* years after reservations

"target" women whom reform was intended to benefit: those with landowning parents who are subject to Hindu law. I consider three samples: the full sample, the sample excluding women residing in states that use biased mechanisms to implement reservations, and the sample excluding those who reside in states that were late to implement quotas.

The regression results using Equation 5.1 are presented in Table 5.5.[44] Prior to gender-equal inheritance reform, reservations are a positive, statistically significant predictor of women's inheritance.[45] Indeed, the impact of reservations is significant at the 90 percent confidence level across all specifications.[46] Absent reform, women whose fathers die after reservations (i.e., who are likely to have a female gatekeeper to help negotiate claims to ancestral land) are 6 percentage points more likely to inherit land – increasing the frequency of female inheritance from 10.3 percent (for landed Hindu families in states that implement reservations as if randomly) to 16.3 percent. This magnitude is small but meaningful: an increase of 6 percentage points in a population of 1.34 billion, where more than 92 percent of the rural population – 67 percent of India – live in landholding families,[47] implies 23.6 million more women would inherit land. Absent reservations, daughters eligible for gender-equal inheritance (i.e., whose fathers die after reform) do not inherit more land than others after controlling for family characteristics (Columns 2–4). Political representation is thus a powerful tool motivating women to claim symbolic land inheritance prereform (as Figure 2.3 illustrates is in line with "gatekeeper theory").[48]

In contrast, the impact of reservations postreform is negative and significant for all specifications. Amongst women eligible for gender-equal land inheritance rights, those with access to female gatekeepers – thanks to reservations – are 8–9 percentage points *less likely* to inherit land (Table 5.5, Columns 1–4, *p-values* = 0.006–0.009). As Figure 5.6 shows, amongst eligible women – those with fathers who die post-reform – inheritance is predicted to be only half as high for those with female representation versus those without. Thus, representation in fact works most consistently in favor of women with rights to tiny, symbolic shares of ancestral property. For these women with female gatekeepers as advocates, predicted inheritance rates rise about 30 percent for them, relative to those without a female at the helm of the local state.

---

44 Figure A.9.8 summarizes results.
45 Women not eligible for gender-equal land inheritance rights under the HSAA possessed tiny, mainly symbolic rights to inherit their natal family's ancestral property. See note to Figure 9.4 for details.
46 Table 5.5, Columns 1–4, *p-values* = 0.058–0.087.
47 As of the National Sample Survey Office's national survey of "Land and Livestock Holdings" in rural India for its 70th round (January 2013–December 2013), landless families comprise only 7.41 percent of the population (Press Trust of India, 2015).
48 In contrast, reform eligibility does not change women's probability of land inheritance (Figure A.9.7).

TABLE 5.5. *Reservation's Impact on Women's Inheritance*

	(1) Target	(2) Target	(3) Target-NR	(4) Target-NR-Late	(5) Target	(6) Target	(7) Target-NR	(8) Target-NR-late
Father died postreservations	0.06+ (0.03)	0.06+ (0.03)	0.06+ (0.03)	0.06+ (0.03)	0.06+ (0.03)	0.06+ (0.03)	0.06+ (0.03)	0.06+ (0.03)
Father died postreform	−0.05*** (0.01)	0.01 (0.02)	0.02 (0.02)	0.02 (0.02)	−0.04** (0.02)	0.02 (0.02)	0.03 (0.03)	0.03 (0.03)
Father died postreform and postreservations	−0.09** (0.03)	−0.08** (0.03)	−0.09** (0.03)	−0.09** (0.03)	−0.10** (0.03)	−0.09** (0.03)	−0.09** (0.03)	−0.09** (0.03)
Age < 20 at reform					0.00 (0.04)	0.01 (0.04)	0.01 (0.05)	0.01 (0.05)
Age < 20 at reform * Father died postreform					−0.02 (0.04)	−0.02 (0.04)	−0.02 (0.05)	−0.02 (0.05)
Age < 20 at reform * Father died postreservations					−0.13** (0.05)	−0.17** (0.06)	−0.17* (0.07)	−0.17* (0.07)
Age < 20 at reform * Father died postreform and postreservations					0.15** (0.05)	0.18** (0.06)	0.19** (0.07)	0.19** (0.07)
Controls	No	Yes	Yes	Yes	No	Yes	Yes	Yes
State FE	Yes	Yes	Yes	Yes	Yes	Yes	Yes	Yes
Birth year FE	Yes	Yes	Yes	Yes	Yes	Yes	Yes	Yes
State trends	Yes	Yes	Yes	Yes	Yes	Yes	Yes	Yes
Adj. R-sq	0.05	0.07	0.08	0.08	0.05	0.07	0.08	0.08
N	11,826	11,826	10,698	10,259	11,826	11,826	10,698	10,259

+ p < 0.10, * p < 0.05, ** p < 0.01, *** p < 0.001

Note: Robust standard errors clustered at the village level in parentheses. The dependent variable is a binary indicator of whether or not women inherit. "Target" includes only landed, Hindu women who were born post-1956 HSA, but prior to their state-specific HSAA's passage. "Target-NR" excludes states that do not assign reservations for female *pradhans* randomly (AP, Himachal Pradesh, Kerala, Tamil Nadu). "Target-NR-Late" excludes nonrandom implementers of reservations and the two states to implement women's reservations over 10 years after constitutional amendments: Bihar (2006) and Jharkhand (2010). Controls include caste status, total number of children, total female children and male children, wealth status, and binary indicator for Western Indian states.

Source: REDS 2006/9, NCAER.

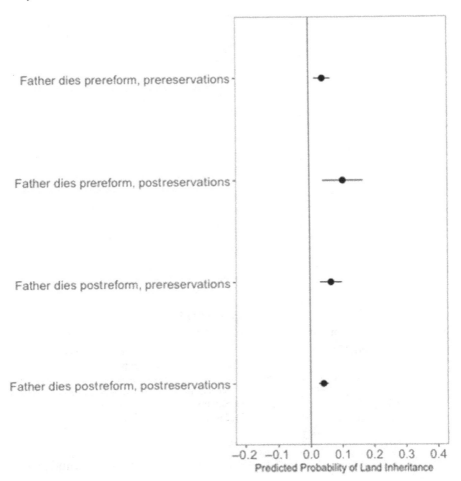

FIGURE 5.6. Impact of Representation on Women's Inheritance: Predicted Values

Source: Data from NCAER REDS 2006/9. The sample includes landed, Hindu women who were born prereform in their respective states and post-HSA. Women whose fathers reside in states that do not assign reservations randomly (AP, Himachal Pradesh, Kerala, and Tamil Nadu) are excluded. Each point on the graph represents the predicted frequency of inheritance for individuals belonging to the given group, with analysis using Equation 5.1's format. Lines represent 95 percent confidence intervals

How do we interpret this finding? I posit it indicates forceful resistance when women receive rights in parity with men that are real and credible, that is at maximum likelihood of being enforced. This suggests that while female political representation initially enables women to effectively demand tiny rights to ancestral property, it also catalyzes backlash when those demands are more sizable: for equal shares. Results are robust to use of alternate samples (excluding sisters without brothers), logistic regression analysis, genetic

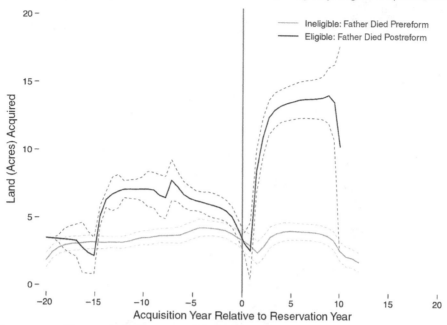

FIGURE 5.7. Reservation's Impact on Women's Land Inheritance Area (Acres)

Source: NCAER Rural Economic and Demographic Survey, 2006/9. The sample includes landed, Hindu women who were born prereform in their respective states and post-HSA. Those women are excluded whose fathers reside in states that do not assign reservations randomly. The x-axis represents when an individual's father passed away relative to the introduction of reservations in the father's village. The y-axis represents the probability of inheritance. Each point on the graph represents the average acreage of inheritance for individuals whose fathers passed away *t* years after reservations

matching following Sekhon and Titiunik's (2012) replication study, and placebo tests.[49]

In addition to changing the likelihood that women inherit land at all, does female representation change the amount of land women inherit? If legal rights are relevant, women who are eligible for equal rights should inherit larger plots than ineligible women. If female gatekeepers are successful facilitators, the size of ancestral plots should be larger for those women eligible for equal rights when they inherit land after as opposed to before reservations. In contrast, if resistance by brothers dominates, it should block the influence of female gatekeepers – in particular for eligible women – and the acreage women inherit should not increase.

Figure 5.7 maps variation in women's land inheritance before and after reservations using the raw data. This initial review – which here is restricted

[49] See Tables A.9.8, A.9.13, A.9.14, and A.9.15, respectively. All logit regression analysis results are robust to use of village-level fixed effects; the same holds for OLS analysis except for the interaction term, for which standard errors increase in some specifications, reducing its statistical significance. Results are available upon request.

to only those women who inherit any land – presents an optimistic picture. First, it suggests that legal inheritance rights do have some purchase. Eligible women consistently inherit larger plots than ineligible women. Second, women who inherit *after* reservations acquire plots markedly larger than women who inherit prior (to the right versus the left of the solid vertical line, which indicates the village-specific year when reservations guaranteed women access to a female representative).

Regressions using Equation 5.1's format, with the area of land a given woman inherits as the outcome of interest, indicate that, prereform, women's exposure to female representatives increases female inheritance by 0.08–0.09 acres.[50] In landholding Hindu families, women's mean ownership is 0.03 acres. Where a woman occupies the local seat of power, women inherit three times as much land *pre-gender-equal rights*. In other words, prereform, female gatekeepers enable women not only to claim rights more frequently but also to push for larger shares. However, once the state mandates equal rights, women do not inherit larger shares. This suggests significant male resistance to reform when female representatives make rights salient.

Figure 5.8 illustrates how women's predicted acres of inheritance vary alongside access to female gatekeepers and gender-equal inheritance rights. Absent reservations, eligible women are predicted to inherit slightly larger plots than ineligible women. However, once reservations install female gatekeepers, only ineligible women will benefit, inheriting larger plots.

5.4.2 Reform, Reservations, and Marriage Markets

Does resistance to gender-equalizing reform vary with women's ability to strike integrative bargaining solutions within families, as gatekeeper theory predicts? If so, we should see resistance and its impact on women's inheritance change based on when women gain access to female gatekeepers. To test this hypothesis, I exploit women's influence over intrahousehold resource distribution at the time they enter marriage negotiations. If female *Pradhans* enable unmarried women to trade monetary dowry for land inheritance in their own names, this should lower the net cost that brothers and parents expect to "pay" for recognizing a sister (or daughter)'s equal inheritance rights, and reduce resistance.

I present the results in Table 5.5[51] Notably, reservations have a significant, negative impact on women's likelihood of inheritance for those who have exited marriage markets by the time they gain equal rights. Paternal death postreservations and reform decreases these women's inheritance by 9–10 percentage points, significant at the 99 percent confidence level across all specifications.[52] This confirms that female representation spurs resistance to inheritance reform, which is most pronounced amongst women whose demands

---

[50] See Table A.9.9, Columns 2–4, (*p-values* = 0.038–0.060).
[51] Results are summarized in Figure A.9.9.   [52] *p-values* = 0.004–0.007.

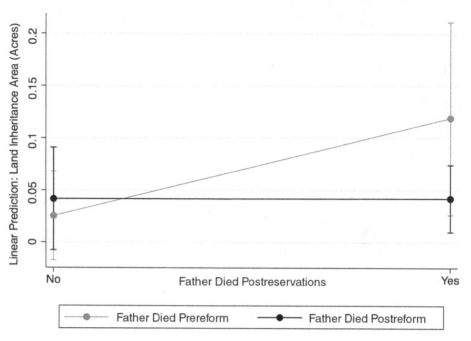

FIGURE 5.8. Impact of Representation on Women's Land Inheritance (Acres): Predicted Values

Source: NCAER REDS, 2006/9. The sample includes landed, Hindu women who were born prereform in their respective states and post-HSA. Those women are excluded whose fathers reside in states that do not assign reservations randomly (AP, Himachal Pradesh, Kerala, and Tamil Nadu). Each point on the graph represents the predicted acreage of inheritance for individuals belonging to the given group, with analysis using Equation 5.1's format. Hatch marks represent 95 percent confidence intervals

are perceived as costly to natal families who have already distributed dowries on their behalf.

Next and most importantly, I consider women who are entering marriage markets when they gain gender-equal rights (i.e., less than 20 at reform with fathers who die postreform: δ''''). Female gatekeepers make these women 15–19 percentage points more likely to inherit land, significant at the 99 percent confidence level for all specifications.[53]

To better understand the importance of age at the time women gain equal inheritance rights, consider Figure 5.9. This graph maps the heterogeneous effect of age at the time of reform on the probability women in landed Hindu families will inherit property.[54] As expected, the younger a woman is at the time

[53] *p-values* = 0.002–0.007.
[54] Each dot represents the impact of reservations and reform on inheritance (the vertical axis) for individuals of a given age at reform (the horizontal axis).

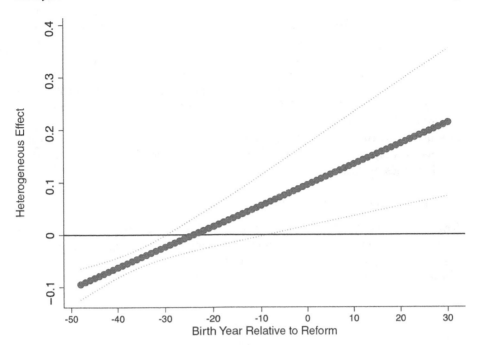

FIGURE 5.9. Heterogeneous Impact of Representation and Reform on Women's Inheritance

Source: NCAER REDS, 2006/9. The sample includes landed, Hindu women who were born prereform in their respective states and post-HSA. Analysis uses the form of Equation 5.2. Each point on the graph marks the average effect of being a given age at reform on the frequency of inheritance, for the group of individuals whose fathers died postreservations and reform. The thinner dotted lines on either side of the thicker, dotted regression line represent 95 percent confidence intervals

she receives equal rights, and hence, the less likely she is to be married when she gains substantial rights, the more able she is to leverage female political power in the service of inheritance.

Overall, Table 5.5 and Figure 5.9 support the hypothesis that where women can utilize female representatives to negotiate gender-equal land inheritance rights through striking integrative bargaining solutions with natal families (to everyone's benefit) while their marriages are being brokered, they experience a lasting gain: property in their name.[55] In contrast, placebo tests that measure the simple or complex impact of reservations find no significant effect.[56]

---

[55] Results are robust to excluding sisters without brothers (Table A.9.13), logistic regression analysis of the target, full, and matched samples (Table A.9.10), and OLS analysis of the full and matched samples (Table A.9.16). Results are also robust to use of village-level fixed effects, and are available upon request.

[56] Tables A.9.15, A.9.17.

In sum, quotas are a powerful inducement for women to claim equal property rights. Prereform, reservations increase the frequency and magnitude of female inheritance. Postreform, reservations result in fewer women inheriting land *but only where reform is costly to natal families.*

I next investigate the mechanisms through which female political representation may directly alter enforcement of women's inheritance rights and subsequent behavior. I consider three channels: political (participation in and responsiveness of the local government), social (parental willingness to use violence to punish a daughter's independent marriage choice), and economic (the dynamics of dowry exchange).

5.4.3 Reservations and Political Participation

How exactly does local female political representation catalyze enforcement of women's inheritance rights? I begin by exploring the political impact of female representation. Specifically, do reservations encourage women to voice their priorities and demands by increasing their willingness and/or ability to engage with local government? Prior research finds conflicting evidence based on studies of distinct regions of India.[57] I disentangle these results with NCAER's REDS 2006/9 data for 17 major Indian states.

Here, I examine the impact of *current* reservations for the gatekeeper on women's *current* participation in local governance to ensure maximum accuracy of recall about participation.[58] For this and subsequent tests of how reservations affect enforcement of women's rights, I use the following estimation equation:

$$y_{ivsk} = \alpha_s + \beta_k + \gamma F_{ivsk} + \delta r_{vs} + \gamma' F_{ivsk} * r_{vs} + \mu X_{ivsk} + \epsilon_{ivsk} \qquad (5.4)$$

The dependent variable (outcome of interest), y_{ivsk}, is a binary indicator of whether a given adult citizen, i, residing in village v, located in state s, born in year k, acknowledges participating in the most recent meeting of the *Gram Sabha* convened by the gatekeeper (*Pradhan*). I study two factors: gender and representation. I measure this in the following way: F_{ivsk} equals 1 when a given individual is female. A village's treatment by the latest round of reservations, r_{vs} is 1 when the *Pradhan* is currently reserved for women. I study each factor's separate influence as well as their joint impact on political participation. Given the importance of state institutions in implementing reservations, all the following tables use fixed effects for an individual's state of residence and year of birth as well as the vector of household-level control variables used in Equations 5.1–5.2.

If reservations improve women's engagement with the state, I expect to observe heightened attendance by women at *Gram Sabha* meetings where villages are currently reserved for a female *Pradhan*. Table 5.6 presents the

[57] Chattopadhyay and Duflo (2004b); Ban and Rao (2008).
[58] The prior treatment – tied to paternal death – captured gatekeeper impact on inheritance.

TABLE 5.6. *Reservation's Impact on Women's Participation in* Gram Sabha *and Willingness to Conduct Violence vs. Daughter's Marital Choice*

	(1) Attendance Target	(2) Attendance Target	(3) Attendance Target-NR	(4) Attendance Target-NR-Late	(5) Violence Target	(6) Violence Target	(7) Violence Target-NR	(8) Violence Target-NR-Late
Female	-0.27***	-0.19***	-0.16***	-0.16***	-0.07***	-0.08***	-0.08***	-0.08***
	(0.02)	(0.02)	(0.02)	(0.02)	(0.01)	(0.01)	(0.01)	(0.01)
Latest *pradhan* seat reserved for woman	-0.05+	-0.05+	-0.05+	-0.05+	0.03	0.03	0.04	0.04
	(0.03)	(0.03)	(0.03)	(0.03)	(0.03)	(0.03)	(0.03)	(0.04)
Female * Reservations	0.07*	0.07*	0.06+	0.06+	-0.05*	-0.05*	-0.05+	-0.05+
	(0.03)	(0.03)	(0.03)	(0.03)	(0.02)	(0.02)	(0.02)	(0.02)
Controls	No	Yes	Yes	Yes	No	Yes	Yes	Yes
Statee FE	Yes	Yes	Yes	Yes	Yes	Yes	Yes	Yes
Birth year FE	Yes	Yes	Yes	Yes	Yes	Yes	Yes	Yes
Adj. R-sq	0.32	0.34	0.30	0.30	0.03	0.03	0.03	0.03
N	15,361	15,361	13,458	13,234	11,355	11,355	10,187	10,047

+ p < 0.10, * p < 0.05, ** p < 0.01, *** p < 0.001

Note: Robust standard errors clustered at the village level in parentheses. For Columns (1)–(4), the dependent variable is a binary indicator of whether or not adults attended the latest *gram sabha*. For Columns (5)–(8), the dependent variable is a binary indicator of a respondent's response willingness to "engage in violence" in response to the following hypothetical scenario: "Your daughter has eloped with a person who belongs to a family whom you do not approve. Would you involve in violence with that family?" For maximum relevance, analysis is restricted to the time their state legislated the HSAA. "Target-NR" excludes states that do not assign reservations for female *pradhans* randomly (AP, Himachal Pradesh, Kerala, Tamil Nadu). "Target-NR-Late" excludes nonrandom implementers of reservations and the two states to implement women's reservations over 10 years after constitutional amendments: Bihar (2006) and Jharkhand (2010). Controls include caste status, total number of children, total female children and male children, wealth status, and a binary indicator for Western Indian states.

Source: REDS 2006/2009, NCAER.

results of OLS regression analysis. Figure 5.10 indicates the magnitude of these effects by presenting the predicted levels of participation for women and men in the presence versus absence of reservations.

Across all specifications, women are significantly less likely to participate in local government, confirming that men dominate local governance in rural India.[59] Women are 16–27 percentage points less likely than men to report participating in the most recent village *Gram Sabha* meeting.[60] Reservations reduce participation of all citizens by 5 percentage points, significant at the 90 percent confidence level, across most regressions.[61] The additional effect of reservations on women is to increase participation by 6–7 percentage points, significant at the 95–99 percent confidence levels for all samples.[62]

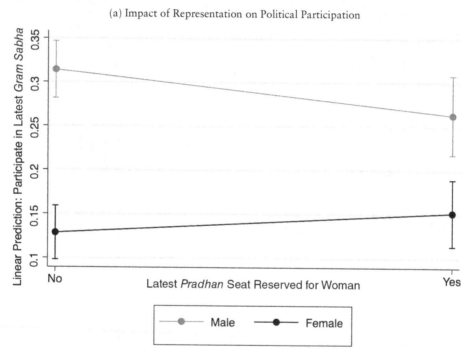

(a) Impact of Representation on Political Participation

FIGURE 5.10. Impact of Representation on Political Participation and Violence: Predicted Values

Source: NCAER Rural Economic and Demographic Survey, 2006/9. The sample includes adult members of landed Hindu households born post-1956 HSA. The x-axis represents when an individual's father passed away relative to the first time reservations were introduced in his village. The y-axis represents the probability of attending the latest *gram sabha* meeting. Each point on the graph represents the average probability of attendance by a group. Hatches indicate 95 percent confidence intervals

[59] Chhibber (2002).   [60] F_{ivsk}, Table 5.6, Columns 1–4, *p-values = 0.000.*
[61] r_{vs}, Table 5.6, Columns 2–4, *p-values = 0.072–0.098.*
[62] γ', Table 5.6, Columns 1–4, *p-values = 0.013–0.055.*

(b) Impact of Representation on Violence

FIGURE 5.10. (Continued)

Source: NCAER REDS, 2006/9. The sample includes adults (18 years or older) residing in surveyed households who are born into landed, Hindu families before state-specific reform. It excludes women born in states that do not assign reservations randomly (AP, Himachal Pradesh, Kerala, and Tamil Nadu). Analysis uses the form of Equation 5.4. The outcome of interest is based on the following hypothetical scenario: "Your daughter has eloped with a person who belongs to a family [of] whom you do not approve." Individuals who "Would involve in violence with that family" are coded as willing to use violence. Hatch marks represent 95 percent confidence intervals

Female gatekeepers nearly halve the gender gap in participation, as the predicted participation levels in Figure 5.10(a) make clear. However, this gain for women comes at the cost of men's political engagement: in the presence of reservations, men's participation decreases at a similar rate to the increase by women.[63] This supports the consistent finding of increased intrafamily distributional conflict over scarce property resources where reservations are in place.[64]

These results support my proposed political mechanism: reservations differentially increase women's participation in local government, exposing

[63] Figure 5.10. The negative, statistically significant coefficient on reservations (R_{vs}) in Table 5.6, Columns 1–4 confirms this effect.

[64] As in Tables 5.5, A.9.9.

gatekeepers to greater contact with their female constituents. This increases women's capacity to exert public pressure on gatekeepers to be responsive (positively correlated with inheritance, Appendix Table 9.19). Indeed, citizen demands in political fora frequently center around requests for rights' enforcement (Kruks-Wisner, 2011). The Head of Andra Pradesh's State Women's Commission, Dr. Venkataratnam Tripurana, confirms that reservations induce women's public participation, while emphasizing the challenges for intrahousehold coordination that ensue: *"social empowerment must occur within the household – husbands must accept wives' power and independence and not interfere with politics. ... This takes time."*[65]

How can one be absolutely certain that greater political engagement improves women's welfare within the household? To answer this question I turn to an additional, related and more severe measure of potential backlash: parental willingness to carry out violence against daughters for independent marriage choices.

5.4.4 Reservations and Violence against Daughters

Here, I consider the ability of reservations to alter *private,* intrahousehold relationships. India, according to the United Nations, is a major site of what are known as honor killings, that is the death of daughters (or, rarely, sons) at the hands of family members for the crime of dishonoring familial social reputation. In UN records, India is home to one in five cases worldwide, tallying 1,000 out of 5,000 such killings annually; nongovernmental organizations estimate the worldwide figure is four times higher.[66]

I hypothesize that familial willingness to conduct such violence against daughters and their marital families represents backlash in one of its most violent forms. Indeed, Chowdhry (2005, 5194) argues that anxiety over honor or "morality" is directly linked with women's changing inheritance rights:

The elder generation, "checkmated in certain spheres ... wants to retain its hold over certain matters – marriage and morality is one such domain. The anxiety to maintain this domain is in its essence connected with the wider male concern with the upkeep of patrilineal inheritance [in light of reforms increasing women's inherited property rights]."

I test whether access to female political representatives makes women – compared with men – more or less willing, as parents, to use violence to control marital choices by daughters.

If my gatekeeper theory is correct, female *Pradhans* will actively mobilize political participation amongst their female constituents. If so, I expect that female political representation will increase female solidarity, which should

[65] Personal interview, January 24, 2014, Hyderabad, AP.   [66] Basu (2013).

differentially encourage women to recognize the enhanced welfare daughters experience when they have more autonomy to negotiate a broad set of rights (around marriage and inheritance). Specifically, I predict that reservations will increase the value women place on giving a daughter voice in negotiating marriage choices as beneficial for a daughter's and the family's collective well-being. If so, women with female *Pradhans* should be more willing to support a daughter's independent marriage choice and less willing to use violence when a daughter's volition diverges from their own.

I hypothesize that men's response to reservations in this domain will reflect the depth of male resistance. If men perceive political support for women's autonomy in marriage markets as harmful to the "traditional family" either in terms of status, material well-being, or both, the presence of a female representative is likely to increase the willingness to violently punish a daughter for marriage choices of which they disapprove. In Chowdhry's terms, this would indicate men's active enlistment in the battle by the "elder generation" to maintain control over "marriage and morality" in the face of women's expanding inheritance rights. However, the more men can identify a daughter's independent choice as beneficial to themselves and the family, the more reservations should diminish their support for using violence to punish a marriage choice that contradicts traditional norms.

To study this form of resistance in more depth, I leverage a hypothetical question from NCAER's 2006/9 round of the REDS:

"Your daughter has eloped with a person who belongs to a family [of] whom you do not approve." Respondents are then asked to choose whether they: (1) "Would not keep any kind of relationship with the daughter;" (2) "Would file a civil suit in the court;" or (3) "Would involve in violence with that family."

I code a respondent as willing to conduct violence against his or her daughter due to disapproval over marriage choices if the response is (3), and code any other response as unwillingness to employ such violence. As in prior tests directly related to inheritance, my analysis uses the form of Equation 5.4 to test how reservations affect parental willingness to use violence as a punishment for a daughter's independent marriage choice. Results are presented in Table 5.6.

Figure 5.10 translates the OLS regression analysis into parents' predicted willingness to use violence as punishment for a daughter's independent marriage choice, comparing women and men where reservations for female gatekeepers are absent versus present. In line with gatekeeper theory, where villages are reserved for female heads, women become significantly less likely to sanction violence as a punishment for a daughter's autonomous marriage choice, by 5 percentage points (Table 5.6, Columns 5–8).[67] As Figure 5.10 makes clear, reservations widen the divergence between men's and women's willingness to use violence. Absent reservations, women are already 8 percentage points less

---

[67] Significant at the 90–95 percent confidence interval.

likely than men to support violence.[68] In the presence of reservations, men become more willing to use violence in response to a daughter's autonomous marriage choice than they would otherwise. Thus, where women head local government, 30 percent of men would use violence in comparison to about 18 percent of women.

This analysis finds that women's political empowerment does appear to encourage female solidarity, increasing support by mothers for autonomous decision making by daughters. However, this political empowerment also causes backlash by men in their role as fathers. The analysis here is particularly pertinent because men's resistance is focused on a key mechanism through which women harness political voice to access economic rights: greater autonomy in negotiating marriage decisions. In the next and final section, I test whether resistance responds to economic incentives, by varying alongside a daughter's willingness to renounce monetary dowry.

5.4.5 Reservations and Dowry

I theorize that female gatekeepers are significant sources of support for women because they have the capacity to alter private, economic bargaining within families as well as public, political behavior. In particular, I posit that women who enter marriage markets with equal inheritance rights and access to female *Pradhans* will be able to negotiate a broader set of entitlements, trading monetary dowries for *personally* receiving titles to ancestral property. I test this hypothesis with help from NCAER's 2006/9 REDS question about the amount of monetary dowry each married female respondent received.

I analyze women's binary receipt of monetary dowries using OLS regression analysis in the form of Equation 5.2.[69] Table 5.7 presents the results. If female gatekeepers increase women's ability to demand land inheritance rights at the time of marriage negotiations *in exchange for renouncing dowry*, I expect to see fewer monetary dowries for the subset of women who enter marriage markets with gender-equal inheritance rights when reservations exist (δ''''). Indeed, these women are 10–28 percentage points less likely to receive dowry

---

[68] Significant at the 99 percent confidence interval (Table 5.6, Columns 5–8).

[69] This question requests respondents provide the net amount of "Gifts given at the time of marriage (total value, Rs.)." This question should lend itself to capturing both monetary dowries and payments in kind (such as expensive saris, linens, or other relevant household, agricultural, or luxury goods including motorcycles or cars). To avoid underestimating the quantum of dowry, I use a binary measure (any dowry receipt). While it is possible that social bias may color reporting of dowry, two factors suggest dowry should be consistently under reported across time and exposure to reservations and gender-equal land inheritance rights. First dowry has been illegal since India's Dowry Prohibition Act of 1961, nearly half a century prior to REDS 2006/9 survey. Second, women's widespread mobilization in campaigns to end dowry has extended across India since the early 1980s. Together, these factors should discourage all survey respondents from reporting dowry, biasing my estimates of reservations' impact toward zero. Thus, I expect that any results I find from this analysis to be a lower bound.

TABLE 5.7. *Reservations' Impact on Women's Dowry*

	(1) Target	(2) Target	(3) Target-NR	(4) Target-NR-Late
Age < 20 at reform	−0.01	0.03	0.05**	0.04*
	(0.04)	(0.02)	(0.02)	(0.02)
Father died postreservations	0.03	−0.00	−0.01	−0.01
	(0.02)	(0.02)	(0.02)	(0.02)
Father died postreform	−0.65***	−0.18***	−0.19***	−0.18***
	(0.03)	(0.02)	(0.02)	(0.02)
Father died postreform and	−0.11**	0.00	0.01	0.01
postreservations	(0.04)	(0.02)	(0.02)	(0.02)
Age < 20 at reform * Father died	0.05	0.03	−0.02	−0.02
postreform	(0.05)	(0.03)	(0.02)	(0.02)
Age < 20 at reform * Father died	0.27***	0.11**	0.09*	0.09*
postreservations	(0.04)	(0.04)	(0.04)	(0.04)
Age < 20 at reform * Father died	−0.28***	−0.14**	−0.10*	−0.10*
postreform and postreservations	(0.06)	(0.04)	(0.04)	(0.04)
Controls	No	Yes	Yes	Yes
State FE	Yes	Yes	Yes	Yes
Cohort FE	Yes	Yes	Yes	Yes
State trends	Yes	Yes	Yes	Yes
Adj. R-sq	0.55	0.78	0.80	0.80
N	11,826	11,826	10,698	10,259

+ p < 0.10, * p < 0.05, ** p < 0.01, *** p < 0.001
Note: Robust standard errors clustered at the village level in parentheses. The dependent variable is a binary indicator of whether or not women receive dowry from their natal families. "Target" includes only landed, Hindu women born post-1965 HSA, but prior to state-specific HSAA. "Target-NR" excludes states that do not assign reservations for female *pradhans* randomly (AP, Himachal Pradesh, Kerala, Tamil Nadu). "Target-NR-Late" excludes nonrandom implementers of reservations and the two states to implement women's reservations over 10 years after constitutional amendments: Bihar (2006) and Jharkhand (2010). Controls include caste status, total number of children, total female children and male children, wealth status, and binary indicator for Western Indian states.
Source: REDS 2006/9, NCAER.

than women who enter marriage markets without gender-equal inheritance rights and a potent political voice.[70] In contrast, women who enter marriage markets with access to female representatives but without gender-equal inheritance rights[71] are significantly, substantively more likely to receive monetary dowries, by 9–27 percentage points.

[70] Results are significant at the 95–99.9 percent confidence levels, and robust to OLS analysis of the full and genetically matched samples (Table A.9.16) and logit analysis for all samples (Table A.9.12).

[71] These are the mothers most likely to carry out violence against daughters for "bad" marriage choices.

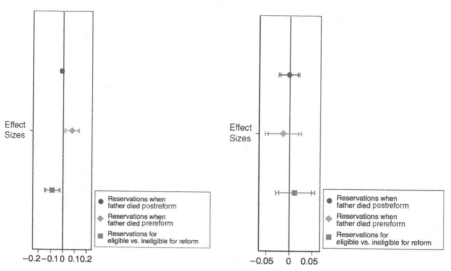

(a) Women entering marriage markets   (b) Women exiting marriage markets at reform.
at reform.

FIGURE 5.11. Net Effects of Reservations on Dowry (Table 5.7)

Source: NCAER REDS, 2006/9. The sample includes women born into landed, Hindu families after 1956 HSA, but before state-specific HSAA. It excludes women born in states that do not assign reservations randomly. Net effects are based on Appendix Table 5.7's OLS regression estimates

We can see the significant, negative net effect of female representation on women's receipt of dowry for those entering marriage markets *with* gender-equal inheritance rights in Figure 5.11a: these women are much less likely to receive dowries than women entering marriage markets *without* gender-equal rights.[72] In contrast, Figure 5.11b indicates that female gatekeepers have no net impact on the receipt of dowry by women who have already exited marriage markets – and hence concluded negotiations of dowry – prior to receiving gender-equal inheritance rights.[73]

Overall, analysis presents a nuanced picture of how female representation improves enforcement of gender-equalizing land inheritance reform in India. When women's property rights are limited, reservations that exogenously impose female gatekeepers enable women to demand and receive effective enforcement of tiny, symbolic land inheritance rights (Tables 5.5, 9.9).

[72] For Figure 5.11a, the net effect of reservations preform is calculated using as: $\delta'' + \theta'''$, the net effect postreform is calculated by $\delta'' + \delta''' + \theta''' + \delta''''$, their difference is given by $\delta''' + \delta''''$ from 5.2.

[73] For Figure 5.11b, the net effect of reservations preform is given by δ'', the net effect of reservations postreform is $\delta'' + \delta'''$, and their difference is calculated as δ'''.

Reservations increase women's ability to demand effective enforcement of economic rights through political participation (Figure 5.10).

However, representation-enabled enforcement of gender-equal inheritance rights bears a higher cost for men, potentially decreasing their access to scarce ancestral resources and their political engagement (Table 5.6). Reservations may thus catalyze intra family conflict, leading men to resist their daughter's greater autonomy in marriage decisions. This is meaningful as decisions around marriage provide the critical juncture at which women eligible for gender-equal inheritance, with support from female *Pradhans*, can successfully renegotiate traditional entitlements – exchanging dowry for rights to substantial ancestral land (Table 5.6, Columns 5–8). Thus, the presence of female heads of local government is particularly valuable for women as they enter marriage negotiations, when female gatekeepers can shift familial decisionmaking to consider integrative bargaining solutions that benefit the entire family. This diminishes the cost of reform to parents and brothers, reducing resistance while increasing the realization of women's economic rights (Tables 5.5, 5.7).

Female political agency is less helpful for women who enter marriage markets without gender-equal inheritance rights. Here, female representatives can help women receive monetary dowries (as Table 5.7 and Figure 5.11 indicate), but not land inheritance (Table 5.5). Given women's typical lack of control over dowry and its potential to initiate cycles of violence (known as "dowry harassment") against brides, this is likely a poor substitute for substantial land inheritance titled in a woman's name.

5.5 DISCUSSION

In brief, this analysis suggests that women are able to leverage female gatekeepers and equal economic rights to bargain away welfare-reducing traditional inheritance (monetary dowry) in exchange for property inheritance that enhances individual and family welfare. If so, they may avoid internalizing resistance to women's agency[74] at this crucial point of social change. However, only women able to access *Pradhan*-facilitated bargaining over marriage negotiations when they gain these credible rights are able to make and benefit from these integrative bargaining solutions.

My findings support the first two hypotheses I proposed in Chapter 2's gatekeeper theory. Yet what about my hypothesis that resistance should vary alongside the value of social status? If higher levels of socio economic inequality are indeed associated with a greater role of social identity in one's daily life, along with a more precarious position on the social ladder, such that traditional social identity – that is, refusing to distribute land inheritance to daughters –

---

[74] Measured here as willingness to enact violence following a daughter's unsatisfactory marriage choice.

may indeed be increasingly "worth fighting for" as levels of inequality increase. If so, resistance should be most pronounced once inequality passes a certain threshold. In addition, if demands for social change are too costly to be credible when inequality is very high, we should see resistance disappear in the most unequal locales.

To investigate the plausibility that socioeconomic inequality may be a relevant channel for enhancing or moderating resistance, I return to the Gini index of landholding inequality within villages explained in the Causal Identification Strategy. Here, I analyze the impact of reservations on the likelihood of female inheritance for eligible versus ineligible women across the three terciles of Gini values (relatively low equality: 0.21–0.48, moderate: 0.48–0.61, and high: 0.61–0.96).

Responses to female representation do indeed vary with levels of inequality (Table A.9.20). As predicted, we see the most significant variation at moderate levels of intra village landholding inequality – in the second tercile of Gini coefficients (Panel B). Following the main findings, the presence of female gatekeepers creates significant leverage for women to successfully claim inheritance rights, increasing their likelihood of inheriting land by 7–8 percentage points (Table A.9.20, Panel B, Columns 1–4).[75] This is also where resistance to women's enforceable demands for substantial rights is most pronounced. In the presence of female gatekeepers, eligible women are 8–9 percentage points less likely to inherit, relative to ineligible women without female representation (Table A.9.20, Panel B, Columns 1–4).[76] At the highest levels of equality, resistance to female gatekeepers is similar, but with limited statistical significance (Table A.9.20, Panel A). In contrast, at the highest levels of inequality, female gatekeepers do not alter inheritance for eligible or ineligible women (Table A.9.20, Panel C).

As Figure 5.12 illustrates, where female gatekeepers are present, the net effect of eligibility for gender-equal inheritance rights is to significantly reduce inheritance *only at moderate levels of landholding inequality*. Female representation sparks resistance for the second tercile of villages (with intermediate levels of landholding inequality), reducing the likelihood that eligible daughters will inherit land by 11 percentage points, relative to ineligible daughters.[77] At this point, inequality is high enough to make enforcing social status outweigh its material costs, but not so high as to preclude credible demands by women for coordination around a new, gender-equal strategy of inheritance distribution in partnership with female *Pradhans*. Who bears the brunt of such resistance? Individuals at the highest rung of the caste ladder (members of other castes, Table A.9.22, Panel C) and women in families with the largest landholdings

---

[75] Results are significant at the 90 percent confidence interval.
[76] Results are significant at the 95 percent confidence interval for all but Column 2.
[77] Results are significant at the 95 percent confidence interval.

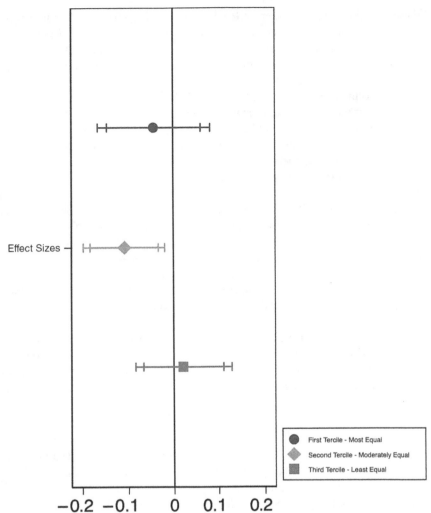

FIGURE 5.12. Net Impact of Reservations on Women's Inheritance, by Inequality

Source: NCAER Rural Economic and Demographic Survey, 2006/9. The sample includes women born into landed, Hindu families after 1956 HSA, but before state-specific HSAA. It excludes women born in states that do not assign reservations randomly (AP, Himachal Pradesh, Kerala, and Tamil Nadu). Net effects are based on Table A. 9.20's OLS regression estimates. The net effect of reform postreservation is calculated using the following formula: $\delta' + \delta'''$ from Equation 5.1.

(Table A.9.23, Panel C), that is families with the highest socio-economic status, who thus have the most "status" to lose.

Do political behavior and social attitudes – two mechanisms through which I hypothesize female gatekeepers create new opportunities for women – also vary with landholding inequality? Female citizens appear most politically responsive to female gatekeepers at moderate levels of inequality: consistently increasing their attendance in local government *(Gram Sabha)* meetings by 8 percentage points where elected heads are female (Table A.9.21, Panel B, Columns 1–4).[78] While women respond similarly in highly unequal villages, such action is met with significant male resistance: in the presence of reservations, women are 11 percentage points more likely to attend *Gram Sabha* meetings, but this is offset by a 7 percentage point (male-driven) decline in village-wide participation, relative to nonreserved villages (Table A.9.21, Panel C, Columns 1–2).[79] Thus, moderate levels of inequality appear to create the most robust incentives for women's political engagement.

Finally, inequality appears to operate differently concerning its ability to moderate the impact of female gatekeepers on social attitudes, measured as a parent's willingness to violently sanction a daughter's independent marriage decision. Female representation significantly increases women's solidarity – making mothers 5–7 percentage points less likely to support violent sanctions against daughters – only at the highest levels of equality (Table A.9.21, Panel A, Columns 5–8).[80] This lends support to the notion that high levels of equality may be more fertile ground for slower, less conflict-ridden and possibly more enduring shifts in social support for equality as a result of female representation. In contrast, where inequality is more pronounced, in moderately unequal villages, women may be more willing to make costly investments in political engagement – seeking help from female representatives – to demand land inheritance because they realize that absent such engagement, progressive changes in social attitudes are unlikely.

5.6 CONCLUSION

Quotas that increase women's local political representation provide an effective channel for them to demand enforcement of the property inheritance rights that have been theirs nationally since 2005. Representation enables women to lobby pivotal local officials – gatekeepers – for such enforcement by engaging families in broader forms of bargaining with integrative solutions that can benefit all. Across India, where "reservations" are in place, women are more likely to inherit property. However, political representation coupled with enforcement of gender-equalizing property inheritance rights has an unintended consequence – male resistance – which decreases women's inheritance. Backlash is strongest against women unable to negotiate acceptable trade-offs within families.

---

[78] Significant at the 90 percent confidence interval.
[79] Results are significant at the 90 percent confidence interval. Note as well that the significance of results for high inequality villages disappears for the best-specified analysis (Table A.9.21, Panel C, Columns 3–4).
[80] Results are significant at the 95 percent confidence interval for all but Column 6.

Female gatekeepers fundamentally change economic opportunities for one group of women: those entering marriage negotiations around or after reform (aged less than 20 at reform). These women can leverage reservations at this critical juncture to effectively demand rights that benefit everyone: reducing the "cost" of gender-equal rights to parents and brothers by renegotiating entitlements to household wealth across multiple domains. This represents a net gain for women, who part with dowry in favor of land titled in their own names.

In sum, women's descriptive representation can improve local access to property rights in democracies with limited enforcement capacity such as India. However, there is a paradox. When representation occurs alongside meaningful enforcement of female economic entitlements, resistance occurs that can make women worse off than they were prior to these policy changes. This is particularly likely in the short term, immediately following legislation of new rights. In the case of India's inheritance reforms, legislators expected gender-equal inheritance rights would increase the value and position of daughters.[81] Yet this first quantitative chapter provides evidence of resistance that may diminish women's welfare in the domains of land inheritance and the likelihood of intrahousehold violence for daughters who gain rights "too late" – after marriage, when they have lost a major bargaining chip (authority over the allocation of dowry). Overall, this chapter's analysis suggests that quotas for female representation will be successful at incentivizing economic gender equality only to the extent they also provide women with resources to pursue enforcement of these rights in ways that provide opportunities for integrative bargaining solutions. As increasingly more women come of age and enter marriage negotiations with equal economic rights, the promise of female gatekeepers should become increasingly evident.

At the end of the day, how do women advance? Connecting economic rights to political voice is not a new concept. Historically, women's suffrage in the West has been tied to property inheritance. In other regions of the world, women have gained the right to political participation without the ability to inherit and control property. The promise of "gatekeeper" theory is that quotas for female representatives open doors for women to claim what may be tiny plots of land, but with transformational power.

The next two chapters examine the impact of gender-equalizing property inheritance reform enforcement by female gatekeepers on two other, highly consequential domains where gender inequality is at the crux of traditional institutions: care for aging parents, and related parental decisions about whether or not to conduct female infanticide.

[81] Personal interview with a member of parliament, Delhi constituency office, January 27, 2014.

6

The Long Arm of Resistance

Refusal to Care for Parents

Can enforcement of India's gender equal property inheritance reform advance equality by bringing about meaningful reorganization of familial responsibilities? The previous chapter provided evidence that quotas increasing women's political representation strengthen enforcement of gender-equalizing land inheritance reform. However, within the family, such enforcement has great potential to increase conflict. Families are more likely to block equal distribution of inheritance to daughters, conditional on the anticipated cost of losing ancestral property rights. This "cost" can be transformed into a benefit for the entire family when female gatekeepers spur integrative bargaining solutions, striking agreements about the distribution of rights and responsibilities across multiple domains simultaneously.

In this chapter, I examine whether the destabilization of traditional norms induced by enforcing inheritance rights spills over into familial organization of care, in particular, care for elderly parents traditionally provided by sons.

Concern about the weakening of reciprocal bonds between parents and children speaks to a broader global crisis of care. As Nancy Folbre (2020, 16) explains: *"Throughout much of the twentieth century, the weakening of familial ties in affluent capitalist countries increased the economic pressure for state provision of care services such as education, health care, pensions, and a social safety net."*

Countries with more limited levels of social heterogeneity than India (along lines of race, class, and ethnicity) – such as those of Northern Europe – were more adept at providing extensive, universal benefits (ibid.). Currently, European and Central Asian countries spend an average of 2.2 percent of GDP to fund social safety-net programs. South Asia invests the least of any global region on care: 0.9 percentage points of GDP.[1] India – which invests slightly more than the regional average at just under 1.5 percent of GDP – makes social

---

[1] World Bank (2018).

security eligibility for the elderly conditional on "destitution," that is absence of familial care.[2] This definition is no accident, but rather a piece of a systematic effort by the state to reinforce filial bonds of obligation as social norms confront rapid shifts in economic, social, and political organization.

Indeed, the state's legal response to the crisis of poverty amongst the oldest portion of India's population – estimates place nearly half (41.6 percent) of India's elderly as working under duress to ensure their daily survival – has been to require children to care for parents. The Maintenance and Welfare of Parents and Senior Citizens Act of 2007 formalizes "the obligation of the children to maintain his or her parent ... so that such parent may lead a normal life."[3] Such obligation is monetized according to property inheritance: where multiple relatives stand to inherit property, each is required to pay maintenance "in the proportion in which they would inherit [a given elder's] property" (ibid.).

Thus, India's attempt to improve the equity of inheritance distribution is inextricably linked with the dynamics of familial rights and responsibilities throughout the lives of children and their parents. Constitutional law reflects mainstream Hindu ideology (if not practice) that the paramount duty of a son to his natal family is to ensure its continuity, both by securing a wife who will produce children and caring for parents as they age. Traditional patrilineal inheritance is organized to reinforce and reward satisfying these obligations.

As one respondent explained when asked about how she will distribute household wealth to her daughter and son – currently both completing secondary education: *"I will give dowry as cash to [my] girl, and half an acre to [my] boy. We only give [land inheritance] to [our] boy because he only looks after us. The girl will go to the groom's house."*[4]

Given the high stakes of inheritance as an incentive for the crucial, increasingly scarce provision of care for elder parents, how is this aspect of family structure affected by reform? Specifically, does enforcement of women's rights to inherit property undermine the son-parent relationship at the core of the Hindu joint family? If legislation indeed weakens these bonds, does it simultaneously present a new opportunity for daughters to care for elder parents? Might the impact of reform in this domain, as in inheritance, be tied to an individual's ability to bargain effectively for new rights with mutual benefits to family members?

Following my "gatekeeper theory," I expect enforcement of women's property rights to increase resistance amongst families whose daughters experience

---

[2] The Indira Gandhi National Old Age Pension Scheme, whereby individuals aged 60 years and older receive a monthly pension, makes eligibility condition on poverty and destitution, whereby a given individual has "no regular source of financial support from family members or any other sources." For details, see India Filings (2007).

[3] The act text is available at http://socialjustice.nic.in/writereaddata/UploadFile/Annexure-X635996104030434742.pdf.

[4] Personal interview with respondent no. 12, on April 10, 2010, in Musumur Mandal, Krishna District, Andhra Pradesh (AP).

gender equal inheritance *after exiting marriage negotiations*. At the same time, I expect reform to generate a potential positive shift from resistance to support for reform in families with daughters who are *entering marriage negotiations* as they receive these rights. As subsequent cohorts of women utilize female *Pradhan*-supported marriage negotiations, where broad choice bracketing enables integrative bargaining solutions, I expect their ability to redefine obligations and the resources they accrue to fulfill them to expand and grow. If this hypothesis proves to be true, this suggests that resistance to women's representation may be a temporary phenomenon, leading to a more progressive equilibrium as daughters become equally valuable guarantors of familial security and wealth. If not true, resistance to women's representation may become more obdurate and pervasive.

6.1 HYPOTHESES

Given the substantial economic impact of enabling daughters to claim and secure property inheritance, I hypothesize that women's political representation will catalyze resistance that alters the very structure of the Hindu joint family. Specifically, I expect sons to perceive daughters' requests for land inheritance as unjustified infringements on their traditional reward for providing parental care. I predict such sons will be less likely to uphold their reciprocal obligation to care for aging parents.

As the impact of female representatives on inheritance distribution is most costly and contested in the presence of gender-equalizing reform, I expect sons will be most likely to deny elder parents care in anticipation of a daughter's claim for substantial, that is gender-equal, inheritance. Thus, I expect resistance to be concentrated in families where daughters eligible for equal inheritance rights have access to female representatives.

Under these circumstances, I predict a significant, negative impact on an adult son's most observable investment in parental care: co-residence with aging parents. Why exactly is such an adverse response so likely? Enforcement of gender-equal inheritance rights creates two distinct sources of conflict with virilocal marriage norms, which bind daughters postmarriage to in-laws rather than natal parents. First, reform forces parents to distribute land inheritance to those children whose loyalty traditionally shifts postmarriage and who are *least likely* to care for them in old age (daughters). Second, reform requires an *ex-ante* commitment to gender-equal inheritance distribution, thus limiting parental ability to provide traditional incentives for a son to care for them as they age. In all probability, so long as virilocal marriage norms persist, reservations will lower the amount of inheritance a son anticipates receiving *without reducing his responsibilities for parental care*. Resistance – here, refusal to care for parents after sons marry – can be considered a rational response.

Might married daughters also be able to alter their care for aging parents in anticipation of gender-equal inheritance rights? Ideally, enforceable rights to ancestral property enable women to negotiate new care obligations: prioritizing support for their own parents such that they become true substitutes for brothers. If so, the presence of female gatekeepers – thanks to reservations – should encourage daughters to invite husbands into their natal homes, making co-residence with elder parents straightforward. Such change should be most pronounced amongst daughters eligible for gender-equal inheritance shares. In these cases, significant redistribution of familial resources should markedly improve the incentives and ability of daughters to bargain for accepting the (traditionally male) responsibility to care for aging parents over the (traditionally female) responsibility to care for a spouse's parents (who are widely considered to make greater demands and provide less respect for daughters-in-law than daughters).

Yet, widespread, tenacious virilocal marriage norms across most of mainland India constrain the majority of women (as explained in Chapter 3). If marriage institutions are not responsive to reform, as Bhalotra et al. (2018) demonstrate, women are unlikely to alter co-residence with parents even in the face of real, substantive rights to inherit property. In addition, Chapter 5's analysis finds that when female gatekeepers enable new claims to land by daughters eligible for gender-equalizing inheritance reform, reservations increase intrahousehold conflict. In particular, resistance – often led by sons – to daughters' demands for gender-equal inheritance rights may make it difficult, if not impossible, for adult daughters to co-reside with parents. Thus, reservations and reform may increase intrafamily conflict with the effect of discouraging a daughter's care for elder parents. If this scenario holds, quotas for female representatives that make reform's enforcement more likely may also have the net impact of diminishing the willingness of all siblings to care for aging parents.

I predict this pessimistic outcome – increased resistance to reform, led by sons, who both refuse to care for elder parents and accordingly eliminate a daughter's ability to substitute as caregivers – will be most likely to occur wherever enforcement is most problematic: that is, where it occurs *after* daughters have completed marriage negotiations, such that parents have already invested significant monetary resources in said marriages. Daughters who marry into distant locales should have the greatest handicap in providing care for aging parents. As a female interviewee said: *"Daughters get married and go away. Only sons stay and look after parents."*[5]

Might there be an exception to this bleak picture? I suggest optimism is possible for daughters with the power to improve familial welfare by simultaneously bargaining for new distributions of rights and responsibilities across multiple domains. Where daughters are *entering* processes of marriage negotiations at the same time they receive credible gender-equal inheritance rights, families might be able to strategically choose marriages that enable

---

5 Personal interview with Respondent 8, Focus Group 3 on November 12, 2010, Gabada Village, Palakonda Mandal, Srikakluam District, AP.

rather than preclude a daughter's parental support.[6] Enforcement of gender-equal rights by female *Pradhans* may encourage daughters as well as parents to consider a broader repertoire of marriage strategies, as Chapter 2 documents. If marriage options broaden for these daughters, they may decide to marry into families closer to the natal home and/or choose partners who recognize and support their long-term obligations to parents. These strategic shifts in behavior could enable daughters to substitute for sons in caring for elder parents. If the reservations that make gender-equal rights credible also motivate parents to reward daughters through inheritance as generously as they reward sons, they may be more willing to bequeath stronger relationships to daughters. To test these hypotheses, I study the distance between a daughter's natal and marital homes, her expected strategies to support parents in old age, and co-residence with parents after marriage. The results are presented in the following text.

6.2 DATA AND IDENTIFICATION STRATEGY

This chapter relies on the same methodology as was introduced in Chapter 5 to identify the causal effect of representation on behavior. I do so by leveraging as-if randomly applied reservations for female elected heads of local government.[7] Here, the outcome of interest is the willingness of children to support aging parents. I first analyze the most widespread and observable form of "care": co-residence by adult, married sons with parents. I consider the subset of sons in families with daughters, where reform is relevant.

I begin by examining the impact of quotas for female representation alone. I next compare the effect of female representation in families where daughters are eligible versus ineligible for gender-equalizing property inheritance reform. I then test whether reservations alter the willingness of adult, married daughters to co-reside with parents in this same set of households. Finally, I consider the impact of female representation on two more attainable measures of a daughter's support for aging parents: the distance between natal and marital homes for daughters, and planned support for parents, which spans co-residence to regular financial contributions. This will help us understand whether daughters' behavior adjusts to new distributions of resources.

---

[6] As discussed in Chapter 3, data from 2014 suggests that 95 percent or more of marriages in India are arranged, according to Rubio (2014), cited in Anukriti and Dasgupta (2018, 4).

[7] As a reminder, my sample includes all respondents to the 2006/9 round of the REDS conducted by the NCAER who are born between 1956, when women gained symbolic property rights, and the year their state equalized their property rights, culminating in the national mandate for gender-equal inheritance as of 2005 (1976–2005). I focus on the group of "target" women whom reform was intended to benefit: those with landowning parents who are subject to Hindu law. I consider three samples: the full sample, the sample excluding women residing in states that use biased mechanisms to implement reservations, and the sample excluding the last states to implement quotas.

6.2.1 Identification Strategy

I study adult, married children who face dilemmas about providing care for elder parents. To do so, I consider a subset of children for whom the question of whether *they or their siblings* will provide care is relevant: individuals with at least one living parent, in families with at least one sibling of the opposite sex. To ensure the independence of each observation when studying co-residence with elder parents – as an action that only one sibling is likely to perform – I narrow my focus to the first-born child in each family.[8] The simplest equation identifies the effect of reservations for female gatekeepers on a child's willingness to co-reside with parents:

$$y_{ihsk} = \alpha_s + \beta_k + \gamma_{sk} + \delta' D_{ihsk} + \theta X_{ishk} + \epsilon_{ihsk} \qquad (6.1)$$

The dependent variable of interest, y_{ihsk}, measures whether or not any parent from a given natal household, h, is cared for by the first-born, adult child, i, residing in state s and born in year k. I define anyone aged 18 or older as an adult.[9]

I capture a child's exposure to reservations as δ'. I code exposure to reservations using a slightly broader method than in the prior chapter, which focused on *postmortem* distribution of inheritance. Here, D_{ihsk} is a binary variable indicating whether a given child, i, from a given natal household, h, born in state-s specific cohort k has a father alive at the time his village *Pradhan* seat is reserved exclusively for female candidates. These regression results capture whether reservations for female gatekeepers shift behavior in households with at least one daughter who can negotiate rights, relative to those with daughters who cannot.

If the most extreme intrafamily conflict is generated by the combination of female gatekeepers and gender-equal rights, as Chapter 5 finds, I predict that sons will be most likely to renounce care for elder parents in families where a daughter is eligible for reform and can approach a female representative for support to claim her rights. I check this hypothesis using the following regression specification:

$$y_{ihsk} = \alpha_s + \beta_k + \gamma_{sk} + \delta' D_{ihsk} + \delta'' R_{ihsk} + \delta''' D_{ihsk} * R_{ihsk} + \theta X_{ishk} + \epsilon_{ihsk} \qquad (6.2)$$

---

[8] Table A.9.26 checks and verifies that birth order does not predict the likelihood that a given child will co-reside with parents postmarriage, either for sons (Panel A) or daughters (Panel B), once controls for familial characteristics are included (Columns 2–4).

[9] As in Equation 5.1, α_k and β_k represent state and year of birth fixed effects, to capture trends due to state-specific legislation and culture as well as birth cohort-specific trends. γ_{sk} uses state-specific linear trends to capture state-level patterns of change *over time*. θX_{ishk} is a vector of predominantly household-level control variables including the number of male and female siblings, caste status, total number of children, region, and wealth status (measured by parental land). Standard errors are clustered at the village level, the unit at which reservations are uniquely assigned in this dataset, to address concerns about geographic correlation and to allow for heteroscedasticity.

I use the same dependent variable of interest, y_{ihsk}, as in the preceding text. Here, I include a binary measure of eligibility for reform, R. As in the prior equation, I code eligibility for reform using a measure that enables me to study each child's ability to care for parents while they are *alive*. R_{ihsk} indicates whether or not a given household h has a child, i, born in state-s specific cohort k whose father was alive at the time his state legislated gender-equal land inheritance rights. The coefficient of interest here is δ''', the impact of reservations for female heads of local government on households with at least one son and one daughter eligible for gender-equal property inheritance, relative to households where no daughter has rights on par with sons.

I begin by considering the behavior of first-born, adult sons. As the traditional care provider, I expect a son to be most likely to reject caring for aging parents where female gatekeepers, who make enforcement of a daughter's gender-equal inheritance rights credible, hold power. I expect the anticipated loss of traditional inheritance entitlements to be a dynamic factor that overwhelms a son's faithful upholding of his time-honored duties.

Next, as in Chapter 5, I consider bargaining power around marriage negotiations. As a reminder, I compare women aged under 20 at the time they receive substantive inheritance rights – those who are likely to be negotiating marriages within such rights – with women 20 years or older when they receive rights. This second set of women is likely both to have married prior to receiving these rights and to have been given monetary dowry in place of land inheritance, honing resistance while also diminishing women's bargaining power to transform resistance into support.

I study bargaining power in two ways. Indirectly, I consider whether sons behave differently in families where a daughter has the opportunity to strike integrative bargaining solutions with the *Pradhan*'s leverage, versus those where a daughter does not. Directly, I also assess whether daughters are able and willing to make different choices about co-residence, marriage distance, and planned support for parents in the presence as opposed to absence of such bargaining power. Here, I am working with a small sample of adult, married, first-born daughters with living parents. As a result, I use a minimally demanding procedure to analyze bargaining power: I split the full sample of women into two groups – those with higher and those lower degrees of bargaining power – and analyze each separately. This allows me to delineate whether the results are driven by women with more or less bargaining power. In addition, to aid comparison with the prior chapter, I also present the results of the more analytically demanding procedure in the appendix. Following Equation 5.2's format, I study the interaction of age at reform (as a proxy for marriage, which determines one's leverage in bargaining over economic rights) with exposure to female representation and gender-equal inheritance rights.

Finally, I consider whether wealth or caste affect a child's decision to renounce the obligation to care for parents as they age. This concluding analysis

TABLE 6.1. *Descriptive Statistics, Main Dependent and Independent Variables*

	(1) All *mean/sd*	(2) Women *mean/sd*	(3) Men *mean/sd*
Adult child in co-residence with parent(s)	0.21	0.03	0.34
	(0.40)	(0.18)	(0.48)
Distance between natal and marital village	69.92	78.98	54.35
	(536.58)	(732.00)	(156.34)
Father died postreform	0.91	0.93	0.89
	(0.29)	(0.26)	(0.31)
Father dies postreservations	0.89	0.91	0.87
	(0.31)	(0.28)	(0.34)
Father died postreform and postreservations	0.88	0.90	0.85
	(0.33)	(0.30)	(0.36)
Aged < 20 at reform		0.26	
		(0.44)	
Sister aged < 20 at reform			0.47
			(0.50)
Observations	6,575	2,797	3,481

Source: Rural Economics and Demographic Survey, 2006/9. The sample presented here is the basis for all co-residence analysis. "All" includes all married individuals, who are the first-born child amongst their siblings, aged 18 or older, born post-1956 HSA, with at least one living parent. The "male" sample includes married sons, first born in their families, aged 18 or older, born post-1956 HSA, with at least one living parent and at least one daughter in the family. The "female" sample includes married daughters, first born in their families, aged 18 or older, born post-1956 HSA, with at least one living parent. Standard deviations are in parentheses.

is helpful for understanding the source of the backlash that I hypothesize results from female representation. Such resistance could originate amongst individuals constrained by a dearth wealth (as in those with limited land holdings) or by a concern over loss in social status (as members of more socially entitled castes). Subsequent analysis tests whether either material or social grievances appear – from this initial, descriptive analysis – to be relevant motivators for resistance (see Table 6.1).

6.3 ANALYSIS

Does women's political representation that activates enforcement of a daughter's nontraditional inheritance rights alter patterns of support for parents in old age? I begin by examining a son's behavior as the primary traditional caretakers and then study the effect of representation on daughters, as nontraditional sources of support.

6.3.1 Representation, Reform, and Son's Parental Care

What can we learn from the raw data on care by adult sons? In Figure 6.1, we see a marked drop in the likelihood of sons co-residing with elder parents (along the vertical, y-axis) to the right of the vertical line (which indicates a father's death in the year reservations were implemented): that is, in families where fathers are alive at the time female *Pradhans* take office versus not. Indeed, an adult son's willingness to co-reside with his parents diminishes the further to the right we move on the horizontal axis, that is, the greater the exposure a son receives to female gatekeepers while his father is alive. This provides initial support for my hypothesis that sons explicitly resist women's political representation as a tool for enforcing a daughter's inheritance rights.

To more precisely study the relationship between quotas for female gate-keepers and a son's care for his aging parents, I begin by investigating whether

(a) Sons' Co-residence with Parents

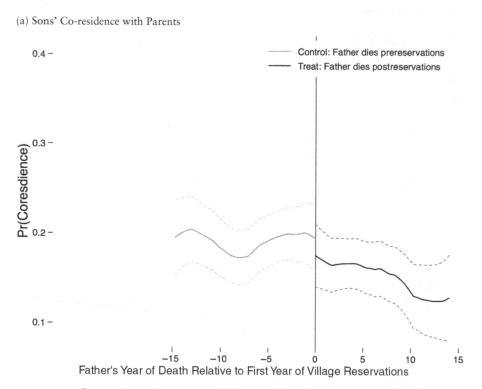

FIGURE 6.1. Reservations' Impact on Children's Co-residence with Parents

Source: NCAER Rural Economic and Demographic Survey, 2006/9. The sample includes married, sons, aged 18 years or more, born post-1956 HSA, with at least one living parent and one sister. The x-axis represents when an individual's father passed away relative to the first time reservations were introduced in his village. The y-axis represents the probability of an adult son's co-residence with his parents. Each point on the graph represents the average probability of co-residence for individuals whose fathers passed away *t* years after reservations

(b) Daughters' Co-residence with Parents

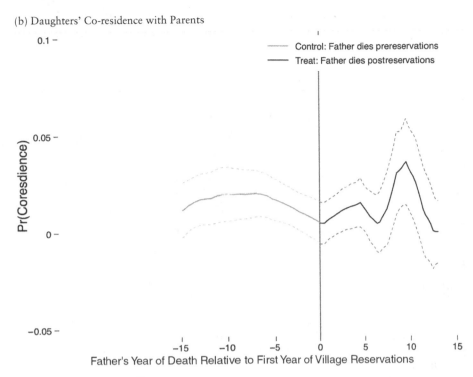

FIGURE 6.1. (Continued)

Source: NCAER Rural Economic and Demographic Survey, 2006/9. The sample includes married women, aged 18 or older, born post-1956 HSA, with at least one living parent. The x-axis represents the year an individual's father died relative to the first time reservations were introduced in his village. The y-axis represents the probability of an adult daughter's co-residence with her parents. Each point on the graph represents the average probability of co-residence for individuals whose fathers passed away *t* years after reservations

women's representation alone has any affects on behavior. Table 6.2, Panel A presents OLS regression results in line with Equation 6.1. Here, we see reservations have a consistent, significant negative impact on the likelihood of sons co-residing with parents. Specifically, once we include controls to account for familial characteristics such as wealth and caste, married adult sons exposed to female representatives are 23–24 percentage points less willing to live with parents (Table 6.2, Panel A, Columns 2–4). Thus, for adult, firstborn, Hindu sons from landholding families, the impact of exposure to a female gatekeeper – who can help women secure inheritance rights regardless of their quantum – leads to a decline in co-residence with parents from 27 percent to only 8 percent. This suggests that parents have justifiable reasons to safeguard a son's traditional, exclusive entitlement to land inheritance.

TABLE 6.2. *Representation's Impact on First-Born Son's Co-residence with Parents*

	(1) Target b/se	(2) Target b/se	(3) Target-NR b/se	(4) Target-NR-Late b/se
Panel A				
Father dies postreservations	−0.06[+]	−0.23***	−0.24***	−0.24***
	(0.04)	(0.03)	(0.03)	(0.04)
Controls	No	Yes	Yes	Yes
State fixed effects	Yes	Yes	Yes	Yes
Cohort fixed effects	Yes	Yes	Yes	Yes
State-specific trends	Yes	Yes	Yes	Yes
Adj. R-sq	0.17	0.63	0.63	0.63
N	2,150	2,150	1,899	1,815
Panel B				
Father dies postreservations	0.01	0.08	0.09	0.09
	(0.08)	(0.08)	(0.08)	(0.08)
Father died postreform	−0.03	−0.04	0.02	0.00
	(0.07)	(0.07)	(0.08)	(0.08)
Father died postreform and	−0.05	−0.29**	−0.36***	−0.35**
postreservations	(0.10)	(0.10)	(0.11)	(0.11)
Controls	No	Yes	Yes	Yes
State fixed effects	Yes	Yes	Yes	Yes
Cohort fixed effects	Yes	Yes	Yes	Yes
State-specific trends	Yes	Yes	Yes	Yes
Adj. R-sq	0.17	0.64	0.64	0.64
N	2,150	2,150	1,899	1,815

[+] $p < 0.10$, * $p < 0.05$, ** $p < 0.01$, *** $p < 0.001$

Note: Robust standard errors, clustered at the village level, are in parentheses. The sample includes all married sons, who are the first-born child amongst their siblings, aged 18 or older, born post-1956 HSA, with at least one living parent and one sister. The dependent variable is a binary indicator of whether a given married, adult son co-resides with a parent. Treatment by reservations is coded as 1 if one's father was alive at the time reservations were implemented in the village. "Target" refers to individuals from Hindu, landholding families. Column (3) excludes sons living in states that do not assign reservations for female *pradhans* randomly (AP, Himachal Pradesh, Kerala, Tamil Nadu). Column (4) excludes nonrandom implementers of reservations and the two states to implement women's reservations over 10 years after constitutional amendments: Bihar (2006) and Jharkhand (2010). Controls include caste status, total number of female and male children of the household head, wealth status, and a binary indicator for Western Indian states.
Source: REDS 2006/9, NCAER.

By now we know that sons and parents both participate in resistance. Is this response more likely when the timing of reservations enables "credible enforcement" of equal rights, as my gatekeeper theory predicts? Figure 6.2 graphs the predicted behavior of sons, using the "target" sample of first-born, adult, married sons residing in states where reservations are applied as-if

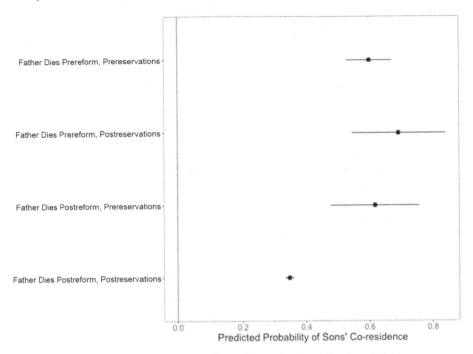

FIGURE 6.2. Representation's Impact: Co-residence by Sons, Predicted Values

Source: NCAER Rural Economic and Demographic Survey, 2006/9. The sample includes married sons, who are first-born amongst their siblings, aged 18 or older, from Hindu, landholding families, born post-1956 HSA, with at least one living parent and one sister. Each point on the graph represents the predicted frequency of co-residence for individuals belonging to the given group, with analysis using Equation 6.2's format. Lines represent 95 percent confidence intervals

randomly. Here, we see the negative, significant impact of quotas for female representation on an adult son's co-residence with his parents *only in families where a son must share inheritance equally with a daughter.* This suggests that a son's behavior is measurably linked to the fear of losing traditional entitlements once his sister can approach her female representative to claim and secure an equal portion of ancestral property.

Table 6.2, Panel B displays the results of regression analysis that takes the form of Equation 6.2. These findings are in line with Figure 6.2. After accounting for familial characteristics, the presence of a female gatekeeper consistently reduces the probability that a son will co-reside with his elder parents by 29–36 percentage points in families where daughters have equal inheritance rights (Table 6.2, Panel B, Columns 2–4). To put this in perspective, consider the sample of sons from landholding, Hindu families in states where reservations are imposed as-good-as-randomly (Table 6.2, Panel B, Column 3). In this sample, a first-born, married son with a sister who has the same rights to inherit as he does, with a female head of the village who can facilitate a sister's claim to these rights is 25 percentage points less likely to care for his parents than is a son in a family untouched by women's political representation and inheritance reform. This translates into a decline from 38 percent of sons co-residing with elder parents – prior to political quotas and inheritance reform – to 13 percent when female gatekeepers and parity of inheritance rights are a factor.

Is it possible for parents and their male and female children to renegotiate care obligations alongside inheritance distribution? If so, we should see the bargaining process become a critically important component of change. Specifically, I hypothesize that brothers may behave differently in families where daughters gain equal inheritance rights alongside the ability to negotiate meaningful redistribution of rights and obligations, versus not. How we interpret behavior depends on the actions of both sons and daughters. I first focus on sons, with the next section examining daughters.

When daughters with gender-equal rights can strike integrative bargaining solutions that materially benefit everyone, I expect sons to choose to respect traditional care norms. If sons are either unresponsive to a sister with such bargaining leverage or even less likely to care for parents, I hypothesize this suggests resistance – unwillingness to accept good faith monetary renegotiations as adequate compensation for the loss of exclusive inheritance rights.

In the face of growing political equality with substantial economic consequences, I find brothers reject caring for elder parents regardless of the bargaining power a sister possesses (Table A.9.28). True, brothers are more likely to renounce care when sisters have – versus lack – leverage to strike mutually beneficial bargains over resource distribution at the time of marriage. Where female gatekeepers enable sisters to secure equal inheritance rights, brothers are 67 percentage points less likely to care for elder parents in the presence of a sister with the opportunity to use broad choice bracketing (eligible daughters aged less than 20 at reform), and the support of a female gatekeeper to do so, as opposed to 27 percentage points less likely to care for parents with a sister unable to do so (aged 20 or older at reform.[10] Table A.9.29 confirms that exposure to female gatekeepers *who can enforce a sister's rights to*

---

[10] See Table A.9.28, Column 5, Panel A versus B, respectively. In the "target" sample of families with daughters entering marriage negotiations eligible for rights at parity with sons, from the set of villages that apply reservations as-if randomly, the net impact of female gatekeepers and gender-equal inheritance rights is to reduce the probability a married, first-born son co-resides with elder parents by 33 percentage points: a drop from 38 percent (the mean for Hindu sons from landholding families) to just 5 percent of sons. In contrast, for families with daughters who exited marriage negotiations before receiving equal inheritance rights, representation and rights cause a smaller net drop: 24 percentage points.

land inheritance – rather than the opportunity to strike integrative bargaining solutions alone – best predicts a son's decision to renounce care.[11]

In the ecosystem of the Hindu joint family, reservations that make the non-traditional, gender-equitable distribution of inheritance credible threaten to break the reciprocal bonds of support – both emotional and material – between parents and sons. A son's adverse response to enforcement of reform undercuts an entire system of reciprocal obligation. In this context, can a daughter provide her parents with an alternate means for establishing their security and welfare in old age? It is to this question I now turn.

6.3.2 Representation and Parental Care by Daughters

If reservations empower daughters to claim land inheritance rights, do daughters then use these rights to renegotiate obligations for parental care? If so, we should see a relevant shift initiated by daughters, whereby the presence of female gatekeepers increases the likelihood of a daughter supporting her parents after marriage.

Alternately, if reservations generate or deepen divisions within a household, a daughter's demand for rights may catalyze destabilizing conflict to the extent that her attempt to renegotiate inheritance rights and marital decisions may unravel time-honored bonds of obligation. If so, the presence of a female representative might encourage a fundamental tension between daughters and parents, making women *less willing* to support elder parents after marriage. In such a scenario, backlash by both brothers and sisters paints a bleak picture for aging parents.

Is either scenario accurate? To begin answering this question with graphical analysis, I return to the raw data in Figure 6.1(b). Here, we see a slight, momentary drop in the already tiny probability that an adult, married daughter will co-reside with parents upon introduction of quotas for female representation (after the vertical line indicating a father's death during the year reservations were implemented).[12]

To the extent we see any impact of female political representation, results run counter to optimistic predictions. Analysis provides no evidence that daughters with equal, credible inheritance rights can or do assume the burden of parental care, at least in the arena of co-residence. After accounting for familial characteristics, quotas for female representation eliminate altogether

---

[11] See the significant, negative coefficient of familial exposure to quotas for female gatekeepers and gender-equal inheritance for daughters and the consistently insignificant marginal impact of eligibility for daughters aged less than 20 at reform (Table A.9.29, Columns 2–5).

[12] Less than 3 percent of adult, married, first-born women reside with elder parents in the subsample of survey respondents from landed Hindu families with fathers who died prior to reservations and reform.

any probability that married daughters co-reside with elder parents (Table A.9.30, Panel A, Column 2).

Thus far, both sons and daughters appear locked into rigid inheritance and elder care roles, which marriage norms reinforce. The default distribution of inheritance – as monetary dowry to daughters who move to the husband's home postmarriage, and property bequeathed to sons – solidifies and rewards children's fulfillment of their traditional care roles. When a female representative enforces a daughter's inheritance entitlement, "rewards" are effectively redistributed without renegotiation of attendant duties. Sons respond en masse by renouncing such obligations. At the same time, daughters do not appear either able or willing to assume this care role.

Yet might this discouraging analysis miss subtle changes encouraged by female political representation? Indeed, studying co-residence by daughters with parents provides a stringent test of the capacity of female gatekeepers to alter physical as well as economic patterns of familial organization in the course of implementing economic reform. The next section considers another way to measure a daughter's adjustment to ensure parental care, based on how far from her natal home she marries.

6.3.3 Representation, Reform, and Daughter's Marriage Choices

Most daughters leave home at marriage, but the distance at which they relocate may be flexible. If so, we might see creative solutions to the issues and opportunities raised by redistribution of inheritance rights. The variety of solutions includes one alluded to by an interview respondent, who posited: *"Daughters sometimes marry in the same village"* even if *"[m]any times they go to outside villages [at least] 5–6 kilometers away."*[13]

This suggests that marriage closer to home may be an option for women, particularly those who stand to inherit ancestral land. For such women, close proximity to the natal family should facilitate greater attention both to property and to parental wellbeing. Negotiating "closer" marriages may allow for a more limited form of parental care, involving periodic visits and deeper emotional connections.

To test this hypothesis, I first investigate the extent to which women's political representation decreases the remoteness of the home into which a daughter marries. Initial regression analysis takes the form of Equation 6.1, with the outcome of interest being the distance in kilometers between a daughter's marital residence and her natal home. If reservations spur women to demand inheritance rights without disrupting familial bonds, they may also create space for women to choose marriages closer to natal families and ancestral land. In this case, reservations should incrementally increase a daughter's ability to replace a son in caring for aging parents and maintaining ancestral land. In

---

[13] Personal Interview with Respondent 2, Focus Group 3 on November 12, 2010, Gadaba Village, Palakonda Mandal, Srikakulam District, AP.

contrast, if, by enabling women to secure equal inheritance rights, reservations expand distributional conflict within families, daughters may move *farther away* from their natal homes. If so, quotas for female gatekeepers would accentuate the physical absence of children in an elder parent's life. Table 6.3 displays the analytic results.

TABLE 6.3. *Representation's Impact on Daughter's Marriage Distance (km)*

	(1) Target b/se	(2) Target b/se	(3) Target-NR b/se	(4) Target-NR-Late b/se
Panel A				
Father dies postreservations	−4.59	1.96	0.03	2.00
	(7.76)	(8.86)	(8.32)	(8.61)
Controls	No	Yes	Yes	Yes
State FE	Yes	Yes	Yes	Yes
Cohort FE	Yes	Yes	Yes	Yes
State trends	Yes	Yes	Yes	Yes
Adj. R-sq	0.02	0.02	0.02	0.02
N	12,878	12,878	11,507	11,084
Panel B				
Father dies postreservations	−9.56	−12.79	−14.36*	−12.55
	(7.20)	(7.99)	(7.89)	(8.01)
Father died postreform	16.38	12.59	−20.15	−18.59
	(22.80)	(23.52)	(12.79)	(13.23)
Father died postreform and postreservations	−7.71	6.70	33.62**	32.48**
	(23.12)	(25.60)	(15.61)	(16.09)
Controls	No	Yes	Yes	Yes
State FE	Yes	Yes	Yes	Yes
Cohort FE	Yes	Yes	Yes	Yes
State trends	Yes	Yes	Yes	Yes
Adj. R-sq	0.02	0.02	0.02	0.02
N	12,878	12,878	11,507	11,084

$^{+} p < 0.10$, $^{*} p < 0.05$, $^{**} p < 0.01$, $^{***} p < 0.001$

Note: Robust standard errors, clustered at the village level, are in parentheses. The sample includes all married daughters aged 18 or older, born post-1956 HSA. The dependent variable is a measure of how many kilometers away a woman's married home is located from her natal home. Treatment by reservations is coded as 1 if one's father was alive at the time reservations were implemented in the village. "Target" refers to individuals from Hindu, landholding families. Column (3) excludes daughters living in states that do not assign reservations for female *pradhans* randomly (AP, Himachal Pradesh, Kerala, Tamil Nadu). Column (4) excludes nonrandom implementers of reservations and the two states to implement women's reservations over 10 years after constitutional amendments: Bihar (2006) and Jharkhand (2010). Controls include caste status, total number of female and male children of the household head, wealth status, and a binary indicator for Western Indian states.
Source: REDS 2006/9, NCAER.

On their own, reservations for female heads of local government do not significantly change the decision a daughter – and her family – make about marriage distance. Across all of Panel A's specifications in Table 6.3, women whose fathers die after reservations are no more likely to select marriages closer to their natal home than women with fathers who die before exposure to female *Pradhans*. In contrast, once we consider the impact of female elected leaders in light of inheritance reform, using Equation 6.2, a more complex story emerges.

As Panel B of Table 6.3 indicates, there is tentative yet suggestive evidence that female gatekeepers may influence women to choose marriages closer to their natal home for women with minimal rights to land inheritance (those ineligible for reform), while the stakes of their inheritance are low and involve notional amounts of land rather than an equal portion (Column 3). Where quotas are implemented as-if randomly, prior to reform, exposure to female gatekeepers reduces the mean distance between women's natal and marital homes by 75 percent – from 20 kilometers to 5 kilometers – roughly an hour walking distance. Thus, when rights are nominal and unlikely to spark familial conflict, female representatives may increase women's inheritance (as Chapter 5 indicates), and their subsequent ability to uphold reciprocal obligations to support elder parents.

In contrast, amongst women eligible for gender-equal inheritance, exposure to female representatives is associated with the choice of marriages that are significantly *farther* from their natal homes (Table 6.3, Panel B, Columns 3–4). For the best-specified samples, adult daughters with access to female representatives and equal rights to ancestral property enter marriages that are, on average, 33–34 kilometers farther away from their natal homes, relative to women without access to female gatekeepers and equal inheritance rights. This is equivalent to a 67 percent increase in the mean marriage distance prior to reservations and inheritance reform (51 kilometers).[14] This declining willingness by women with equal inheritance rights to live in close proximity to their natal home where quotas ensure a female gatekeeper's presence supports the hypothesis that access to female representatives – and women's associated ability to demand substantial ancestral property rights – accentuates a son's resistance to assume responsibility for parental welfare in old age.

Yet what about women's ability to strike integrative bargaining solutions? Might marriage institutions be more amenable to adjustment around the margins, enabling women who enter marriage negotiations with inheritance rights on par with sons – and female gatekeepers who create space for broad choice bracketing around marriage decisions (i.e. women with effective bargaining power) – to select marriages that reweight their obligations to marital versus natal families?[15] Considering the subset of women with effective bargaining

[14] This mean is calculated for Hindu women from landholding families with fathers who die before the first year of village-level reservations and state legislation of inheritance reform.
[15] Analysis takes the form of Equation 6.2, with the sample partitioned into one group of women aged less than 20 years when their state legislated gender-equal inheritance rights, and the second group aged 20 years or greater at this time.

power – those aged less than 20 years at reform who enter marriage markets with gender-equal inheritance rights – Panel A of Table A.9.31 provides no grounds for optimism. Female representation does not alter marriage distance, either amongst women eligible or ineligible for gender-equal rights to ancestral property.

Surprisingly, the subset of women without effective bargaining power – those who are 20 years or older and thus likely to be married when they receive gender-equal inheritance rights – are more consistently responsive to female representation. Pre-reform, exposure to female gatekeepers is associated with a significant reduction in marriage distances by 14–15 kilometers, enabling greater care for elder parents by daughters.[16] This is a sizable difference, translating into a 29 percent reduction in the mean marriage distance amongst women from Hindu landholding families with fathers who die prior to reservations and inheritance reform. In contrast, women choose marriages significantly farther from their natal home, by 36–37 kilometers (a 70 percent increase in marriage distance) once they are eligible for gender equal inheritance rights and have access to a female gatekeeper to help secure these rights.[17]

When directly comparing women with versus without effective bargaining power, there is limited trace evidence – based on the sample of genetically matched women – that those with greater bargaining power can and do choose marriages of closer proximity to natal families.[18] Within this sample, women who are eligible for equal inheritance rights and have access to a female gatekeeper and effective bargaining power choose marriages that are on average 90 kilometers closer to their natal families, relative to ineligible women with neither access to female *Pradhans* nor effective bargaining power (Table A.9.32, Column 3). However, the absence of significant findings across better-specified samples does not warrant strong conclusions from this analysis.

With this caveat in mind, Figure 6.3 maps variation in the effect of female gatekeepers for women eligible versus ineligible for equal inheritance amongst women with versus without effective bargaining power, using the genetically matched sample. Women without effective bargaining power choose marriages farther from home where representatives help them to secure substantial rights to ancestral property. While these effects are insignificant for this sample,

---

[16] Table A.9.31, Panel B, Columns 2 and 4, significant at the 95 percent confidence level.

[17] Table A.9.31, Panel B, Columns 4–5, significant at the 95–99 percent confidence levels.

[18] See Table A.9.32. Analysis takes the form of Equation 5.2, where the outcome variable y_{ihst} is a measure of how many kilometers away a daughter's married home is located from her natal home:

$$y_{ihst} = \alpha'_s + \beta'_k + \gamma'_{sk} + \delta' R_{ihsk} + \delta'' D_{ihsk} + \theta' B_{ihs(k'-20 \leq k \leq k'-1)}$$
$$+ \delta''' R_{ihsk} * D_{ihsk} + \theta'' B_{ihs(k'-20 \leq k \leq k'-1)} * R_{ihsk} + \theta''' * B_{ihs(k'-20 \leq k \leq k'-1)} * D_{ihsk}$$
$$+ \delta'''' B_{ihs(k'-20 \leq k \leq k'-1)} * R_{ihsk} * D_{ihsk} + \theta X_{ishk} + \epsilon_{ihsk}$$

$$(6.3)$$

The genetically matched sample matches villages with and without reservations for female heads of government to ensure they are as comparable as possible across a number of domains, including their treatment of women.

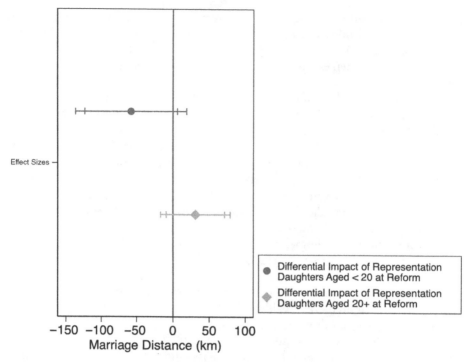

FIGURE 6.3. Representation's Differential Impact on Daughters' Marriage Distance

Source: NCAER Rural Economic and Demographic Survey, 2006/9. The sample includes all genetically matched married daughters aged 18 or older, born post-1956 HSA. The differential impact of representation for daughters aged 20 years or younger is calculated using the following formula: $(\delta'' + \delta''' + \theta''' + \delta'''') - (\delta'' + \theta''')$ from Equation 6.3. The net impact of representation for daughters over the age of 20 is calculated using the following formula: $(\delta'' + \delta''') - (\delta'')$

the distance becomes statistically significant for the better-specified sample of target women that excludes states without as-if random implementation of reservations. This suggests that women's ability to secure rights without the ability to negotiate mutually beneficial resource trade-offs increases conflict within natal households. In contrast, women with more bargaining power can choose marriages closer to home, suggesting a greater willingness and ability to care for elder parents where integrative bargaining solutions around the distribution of rights and responsibilities can make everyone better off. However, these results are just outside the bounds of conventional statistical significance for the genetically matched sample and not significant for better-specified samples.

In sum, there is limited support for the optimistic hypothesis that women's representation may increase the ability of women with effective bargaining power to provide support for elder parents. Yet at this moment – in the first decade following national inheritance reform – the evidence is sparse.

What should we take from this examination of women's bargaining power? The analysis thus far suggests that entering marriage negotiations with substantial rights to ancestral property enables women to strike alternative bargains about the intra-familial distribution of material resources – including land inheritance and dowry – but these bargains do not systematically translate into agency to alter deeper-rooted norms about parental obligation. We observe only one case in which greater bargaining power in the presence of female gatekeepers who increase expectations that gender-equal inheritance will be enforced leads women to renegotiate marriage distance: when studying women in comparable, genetically matched villages with versus without reservations.

The prior analysis suggests reason for concern about familial conflict not only between parents and sons but also between parents and daughters following women's representation that makes enforcement of inheritance reform credible. At best, there is limited evidence that conflicts between parents and daughters occur at lower rates where women are able to leverage gender-equal inheritance rights to negotiate marriages that enable care for aging parents and ancestral property, as opposed to where women cannot strike integrative bargaining solutions.

Given the hurdles women must surmount to renegotiate obligation within their families, I investigate one further, nontraditional form of parental care available to daughters: plans about future levels of financial support. The next section studies this broader spectrum of support daughters can propose to parents.

6.3.4 Women's Planned Support for Parents

What can we learn from asking daughters directly about the care, if any, they plan to provide elder parents? This analysis should improve our understanding of a daughter's ability and willingness to support her parents, as long as a daughter's answer represents a real commitment to pursue this course of action. This is beneficial in two ways. On the one hand, leveraging women's intentions to support of elder parents expands the set of women whose actions we consider from the subset of daughters who have parents already requiring care (in the previous analysis) to the broader set of parents who will require care at some point in the future. On the other hand, this investigation allows us to consider an important strategy for parental care outside the domain of marriage: financial support. For both reasons, analysis of women's support provides complementary insights into the impact of female representation on a daughter's willingness and ability to augment a son's traditional care for aging parents.

Regression analysis follows Equations 6.1 and 6.2. Here, the outcome of interest is based on responses by adult, married women to the following question: "If your parents are alive, what methods will you use to support them?" I analyze only those women who provide a response, which I code according to the scope of financial investment they say they will make in caring for parents, if any. The scale ranges from zero, indicating no support ("Will not be able to support") to three, representing explicit financial investment (which includes "savings," "rely on husband for financial support," or "take an extra job").[19]

If reservations enable women to demand inheritance rights that significantly increase their economic autonomy,[20] do they also encourage women to initiate reciprocal obligations to care for parents financially? Figure 6.4 graphs responses for two particularly relevant groups of women: those without access to either female representatives or equal inheritance rights (Figure A), versus those with both (Figure B). Here, we see that women with access to female gatekeepers who can enforce substantial rights to ancestral property (Figure 6.4 B) make greater financial investments in elder parents than women with neither female representatives nor equal inheritance rights (Figure 6.4 A). Nearly 20 percent more women with the ability and support to claim substantial rights plan to provide financial assistance to parents, relative to women without such capacity. Additionally, such women are roughly 10 percent *less likely to refuse support* for elder parents than those without the ability to effectively claim rights (Figures 6.4 B and A, respectively). This suggests that women whom reservations empower to claim and secure rights to ancestral property are more willing to support parents than others, but the form of such support lies outside the scope of earlier analyses: transferring financial resources directly to elder parents.

Indeed, regression analysis indicates that women with access to female gatekeepers are significantly more likely to claim they will provide financial support for elder parents (Table A.9.33, Panel A, Columns 1–2, 4, significant at the 95–99.9 percent confidence intervals). However, the impact of female gatekeepers is clearest amongst those women who are not eligible for gender-equal inheritance rights.[21] For women with *notional rights to ancestral property,* access to female representatives by the time of their father's death increases the mean financial support they plan to provide parents from 2.2 (a request to live within the household) to 2.6 (more likely to explicitly make a financial commitment to parental care). Women with equal inheritance rights are no more likely to commit to care for parents than women without such rights. As in the prior analysis, this suggests that women whom female *Pradhans* can help secure notional inheritance rights – without increasing intrahousehold

---

[19] I code two intermediary categories of financial investment: "put them in an old age home" as a value of one, only marginally better than no support, and "ask them to live within your household" as a value of two, better than placement in an old age home because of the sustained commitment to provide resources for a member of one's household, but less resource intensive than explicit forms financial investment. To ensure analysis is not sensitive to the order of these intermediate options, Table A.9.34 presents the results of analysis that reverses the value of the intermediate options, with comparable statistical significance of results.

[20] Panda and Agarwal (2005).   [21] Table A.9.33, Panel B, Columns 1–2, 4–5.

(a) Prereform and Prereservations

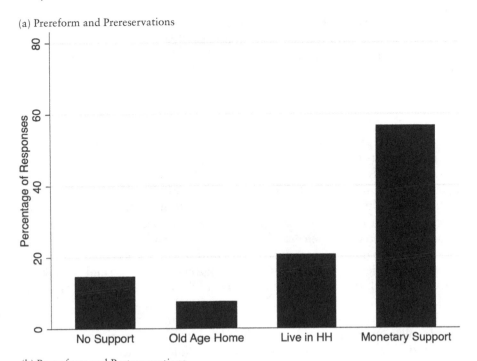

(b) Postreform and Postreservations

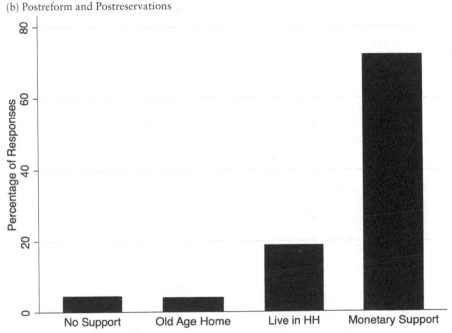

FIGURE 6.4. Daughters' Planned Support for Parents

Source: NCAER Rural Economic and Demographic Survey, 2006/9. The sample includes all married daughters, from Hindu, landholding families, aged 18 or older, born post-1956 HSA. Each bar on the graph represents the relative frequency of the respective response given

conflict – are consistently the most able and willing to care for elder parents. This underlines the difficulties of renegotiating children's obligations to care for parents given the multidimensional conflict that a daughter's claim to rights on a par with her brother can spark.

6.4 DISCUSSION

Overall, this chapter's analysis suggests that quotas bringing female gatekeepers into power fracture important bonds of obligation between parents and children, particularly when they enable daughters to claim and secure fundamental rights to ancestral property. By facilitating inheritance parity amongst a subset of eligible daughters, they discourage a son's customary provision of care for elder parents. In the presence of rigid, virilocal marriage norms, conflict over property initiated by eforcement of gender-equalizing inheritance reform causes sons to punish parents by renouncing their traditional role as caretakers. While analysis in Table A.9.33 suggests that daughters are increasingly willing to provide financial support for parents, this occurs most consistently when female gatekeepers assist them in securing limited, notional rights to ancestral property, that is, prior to gender-equalizing inheritance reform.

In families where daughters gain eligibility for gender-equal property rights after exiting marriage negotiations, intrahousehold conflict between parents and children intensifies. This explains the decreased willingness of daughters to move closer to parents to fulfill the elder care duties their brothers have renounced (Table A.9.31, Panel B). Where daughters gain eligibility at the time they enter marriage negotiations – creating space for integrative bargaining solutions to everyone's benefit – they are no longer resistant to choosing marital residences close to their parents (Table A.9.31, Panel A). In fact, tentative evidence suggests daughters with such bargaining power may instead choose marriages significantly closer to home (Table A.9.32, Column 3). However, at best this change suggests the potential for more daughters to assume responsibility for care of parents at some point in the future rather a strong contemporary trend. Overall, the inability of daughters to consistently substitute for their brothers as care providers means parents ultimately experience effective reform as a source of insecurity in their old age.

To return to Chapter 2's gatekeeper theory, I ask: Does the severity of resistance to enforcement found in this chapter vary alongside the value of social status for families? To answer, I return to the initial measure I propose as a proxy for the value of social status: the level of socioeconomic inequality within each village. I employ the Gini measure of inequality based on the distribution of landownership within villages that I built and explained in Chapter 5. I test whether resistance increases alongside the value of social status, using the proxy of landholding inequality (which I posit has a direct positive correlation with the value of social status). In addition, I query whether demands for social change become incredible beyond a certain threshold level of inequality, making resistance unnecessary.

Let us start by considering the main perpetrators of backlash against elder parents: sons, as the traditional care providers. We see consistent, significant resistance to women's political representation across all levels of inequality. First-born sons are 17–26 percentage points less likely to care for their parents in the presence of quotas for female gatekeepers, as compared to villages without such quotas (Table A.9.39, Panels A–C, Columns 2–4). Specifically, considering the response of sons to representation *as a tool for enforcement of women's substantive property inheritance rights,* in Table A.9.40 we see a ceiling to such resistance. This backlash to female representatives who are able to enforce gender-equal inheritance rights is significant at moderate levels of inequality, and even at low levels, but disappears at the highest levels of inequality (Table A.9.40, Panels A and B versus C). In particular, where a sister is eligible for gender-equal rights, the presence of a female gatekeeper reduces a brother's willingness to care for his parents by 35–40 percentage points for all but the most unequal villages.[22] This suggests that high levels of inequality may impede coordination of backlash by sons just as much as they impede coordination of claims to inheritance rights by daughters.

Which sons are most likely to renounce care of elder parents in response to the presence of female gatekeepers able to enforce a daughter's substantive land inheritance rights? Those who belong to the upper two quartiles of landholders (families who own 2.5 or more acres of land) from any caste.[23] In sum, sons exhibit high levels of resistance against the imposition of quotas that bring women to power who can help daughters claim substantial inheritance rights, even in the most equal villages and as members of the castes at the lowest ranks of the social hierarchy. Yet, as in Chapter 5, high levels of inequality do appear to limit resistance by sons, potentially because the threat of a daughter's demand for substantial inheritance is not credible when inequality – and hence, I posit, the value of social status – is above a certain threshold.

What about resistance to female gatekeepers by sisters? When considering decisions about the remoteness of marital homes, which complicate or facilitate care for elder parents, we find resistance in a surprising locale: the most equal villages. Across villages, daughters with female gatekeepers who can enforce property rights are significantly more likely to marry farther from home, regardless of the specification.[24]

In addition, women in the wealthiest quartile of landholding families (with eight or more acres of land) are most consistently likely to choose marriages farther from the natal home when they have access to female *Pradhans* who can enforce their substantial rights to ancestral property on par with brothers.[25] Finally, women who belong to Scheduled Castes (SCs) are also likely to choose marriages *farther* from their natal families – by 29–56 kilometers – where

[22] Significant at the 95 percent confidence interval, Table A.9.40, Panel A, Columns 2–4 and Panel B, Columns 3–4.

[23] Table A.9.35, Panels B and C, and Table A.9.36, Panels A–C, respectively.

[24] Table A.9.41, Panel A, Columns 1–4, significant at the 99 percent confidence interval.

[25] Table A.9.37, Panel C.

female gatekeepers enable them to secure gender-equal inheritance rights.[26] This analysis suggests that two potential sources of agency for women – relatively large family landholdings or the relatively high economic agency women possess within traditionally disparaged (Scheduled) castes – do translate into greater opportunities to influence marriage distance. However daughters appear to employ this power to increase the remoteness of their marriages, which minimizes, rather than maximizes, obligations to natal families.

Overall, this analysis suggests that high levels of inequality act as a break to resistance – that is, refusal to care for elder parents – as a response female representation that enables enforcement of gender-equal property rights. This holds for both sons and daughters. Sons appear least constrained by levels of social status, here using the proxy of intravillage landholding inequality. Indeed, resistance by sons occurs at all levels of equality. In contrast, daughters exhibit resistance to political representatives only at high levels of equality, perhaps when social status is least valid and sanctions for deviation from social norms are least costly. However, when female gatekeepers enable enforcement of new land inheritance distributions, both sons and daughters are equally likely to translate higher levels of familial power (particularly in terms of family landholdings) into greater-intensity resistance, reducing commitments to care for parents as they age.

6.5 CONCLUSION

I began this chapter with a question: Does women's access to female representatives who enable them to secure property inheritance rights across rural India can give rise to meaningful reorganization of responsibility for a fundamental good, that is, children's care for aging parents? The answer depends on the degree of intrafamily conflict caused by a daughter's demands for land inheritance. When daughters leverage female gatekeepers to exercise symbolic or notional rights to land, such claims are unlikely to cause conflict, and women are accordingly more able to care for aging parents, choosing closer marriages and planning to financially support elder parents.

However, in families where a daughter gains gender-equal property inheritance *after exiting marriage negotiations,* all children revoke support for parents. Here, quotas for female heads of local government (reservations) that facilitate a daughter's demands for substantial land inheritance rights reduce sons' willingness to act as traditional care-providers for parents and lower the already rare likelihood of daughters' care. This supports the cautionary admonition about the ability of reform to immediately alter social norms expressed by a member of India's national Parliament: *"Law without [a] paradigm shift won't work at all."*[27]

---

[26] Table A.9.38, Panel A, Columns 1–5, significant at the 95–99.9 percent confidence levels.
[27] Personal interview with then Member of Parliament for Maharashtra Sharad Joshi on January 20, 2010, in his Delhi constituency office.

Sons are most likely to renounce care in families where daughters have equal inheritance rights and access to female representatives. In other words, a son's expectation that he will lose a sizable portion of his traditional inheritance entitlement is the best predictor of resistance. Yet, in these families, daughters are also significantly less willing to care for aging parents than they were prior to reform and reservations. This lends heft to parental concerns about redistribution of traditional inheritance entitlements. As explained by one lawyer:

> *[Hindu society is based on the patrilineal] tradition of land-holding and protecting the land. When a woman marries, she moves out of the family to the husband's family. [Parents] thought taking the family's land to another family is not right.... [For women, parents think] "Her only right is to ensure that the family gets her married off."*[28]

However, resistance to marriages close to home – a nontraditional form of support for aging parents – may slightly diminish amongst the group of daughters who enter marriage markets with substantial inheritance rights they can credibly enforce.[29] Note this directly follows from gatekeeper theory: these are the women able to strike integrative bargaining solutions that benefit the entire family, and as such their claims should not spur intrafamily conflict. In addition, the increased willingness to financially support elder parents by daughters with access to female representatives but without inheritance rights on a par with their brothers suggests limited grounds for hope that as women's inheritance rights become less politically, socially, and psychologically fraught, daughters may be able to substitute for sons as caregivers of aging parents. At worst, this chapter's findings of a precipitous drop in the willingness of sons to co-reside with elder parents when a sister can demand and secure equal inheritance rights provides support for parental fears of abandonment in old age.

Land and gender scholar Prem Chowdhry predicts that the reshaping of familial roles is occurring, but that it is tied to profound conflict and upheaval centered in women's natal families:

> *As of one year ago, I am now seeing women demanding inheritance. [There is fierce social resistance, but] land can be valued at 1 crore Rupees for an acre. So women know that money is there, and they are asking for their inheritance as a result.... Things are also changing because of the "ghar jamai" – the husband who moves in with his wife and her parents, and "takes over." This used to be looked down upon. The earlier view was that the [ancestral] land belongs to the patrilineal line. Women would be silent. Now others only get girl's land by being nice to the girl.*[30]

In sum, this chapter's investigation suggests that land inheritance reform significantly destabilizes familial organization. Resistance by sons, who become increasingly unwilling to care for parents in the face of daughters' anticipated

---

[28] Personal interview with R. R. on January 7, 2017, at AV College, Hyderabad, AP.
[29] Table A.9.32, Column 3.
[30] Personal interview with Prem Chowdhry on January 29, 2014 in her Delhi residence.

inheritance rights, is pervasive and tenacious. The intensity of sons' resistance is compounded by the fact that daughters are unable to assume the role of caregivers for aging parents postreform. Thus, they cannot assuage parental fears of abandonment in old age that result from sons' diminished shares of inheritance. This suggests that, at least in the short term, institutional innovations may dismantle rather than improve the ability of individual women and their natal families to renegotiate slow-moving norms around parental care, in particular, care constrained by marriage arrangements.

Women's political empowerment in local government through reservations may increase the capacity of daughters entering marriage negotiations with gender-equal property rights to support parental welfare by selecting closer marriages in generations to come. If so, this would provide tentative hope for the long-term ability of reform to shift parental behavior toward more equitable inheritance distribution, while generating more sustainable, responsive forms of familial organization.

However, a daughter's new rights do not yet provide robust enough leverage for daughters to renegotiate marriage arrangements with natal and marital families such that they can frictionlessly replace sons as traditional care providers for aging parents. Current results suggest we should anticipate resistance in other dimensions of familial organization following enforcement of gender-equal inheritance. In the next chapter, I investigate a brutal form of backlash: sex selection against daughters.

7

Representation and Violence

Gender Equality and Sex Selection

There is hardly a more compelling indicator of gender inequality in India than its unnaturally male-biased population sex ratio, an important driver of which is the desire to have sons rather than daughters.[1] This chapter poses a crucial question about the relationship between women's political agency and its impact on foundational equality. Do quotas mandating women's political representation destabilize norms through what may simultaneously appear as productive and destructive processes? In particular, can female gatekeepers unsettle social norms enough to foment backlash that precludes future generations of daughters? To answer this, I examine a form of resistance with permanent consequences: sex selection to prevent daughters' birth.

What I examine here is the extent to which diminishing sons' traditionally stronger economic and political position alters preferences for male over female offspring. Chapters 5 and 6 presented evidence that quotas expanding female political representation motivate the claiming and enforcement of gender-equal rights to property, with significant consequences for intrahousehold distribution of resources (land and monetary dowry) as well as responsibilities (care of aging parents). Extrapolating from that evidence, is it not possible that the time-honored preference for sons will be affected by such a potent upheaval?

The remainder of the chapter studies the balance of sons and daughters to which a mother gives birth to causally identify whether quotas mandating

---

[1] Much of the motivation for this chapter derives from joint work with Sonia Bhalotra and Sanchari Roy. For details, see Bhalotra et al. (2018). Son preference has a long history in India. Male-biased sex ratios were documented since the first census in 1871. Possible explanations for this phenomenon include that parents live with sons in their old age, Hindu rituals require that the son lights the parent's funeral pyre, and primogeniture. See Bhalotra and Cochrane (2010) for additional analysis.

female gatekeepers – with the power to catalyze enforcement of substantive economic rights for women – decisively shift parental behavior to inhibit equality, by exacerbating son preferences, or to increase equality, by diminishing these traditional preferences.

Given that equal inheritance rights are a critical component of women's overall empowerment, I expect the credible potential for their enforcement, aided by female political representatives, to upset existing norms about gender equality. I explore the extent to which women's political representation provokes resistance in an as-yet unexplored domain: female feticide that eliminates any notion of women's equality by preventing female births altogether. What do we know about the prevalence of such violent discrimination, and the ability of female representation to affect bias in preferences and behavior?

7.1 SEX SELECTION AND INDIAN SOCIAL INSTITUTIONS

Sen (1990) initially defined the phenomenon of "missing women," that is: females that could could potentially be alive but are not due to the systemic undervaluing of their sex. In India today, 63 million women are estimated to be "missing."[2] This phenomenon occurs in large part because parents have manipulated the ratio of surviving girls to boys after birth by strategic fertility stopping behavior[3] and various forms of neglect, including reducing the duration of breastfeeding and investing less in immunization and nutrition for daughters relative to sons.[4]

In addition, the widespread availability of prenatal sex detection technology increases parental tendency to manipulate the sex ratio prenatally by committing sex-selective abortion or female feticide.[5] Bhalotra and Cochrane (2010) estimate that as many as 0.48 million girls were selectively aborted annually during 1995–2005, which is more than the number of girls born in the United Kingdom each year. In contrast to the more subtle and less ascertainable procedures of neglect, feticide is a conscious and staged act and thus provides a powerful measure of parental preferences for bearing sons rather than daughters.

India's population sex ratio has been unnaturally skewed in favor of men since the first recorded census. This is widely regarded as reflective of women's lower social value, which translates into relative neglect throughout life. As a result, women have relatively higher mortality rates relative to men.[6] While India's all-age female- to-male mortality ratio is not increasing, male bias in the sex ratio at birth has risen significantly since the late 1980s. This points to sex-selective abortion as the source of India's unbalanced sex ratio.

---

[2] Government of India, Ministry of Finance (2018). [3] Arnold, Choe, and Roy (1998); Bhalotra and van Soest (2008). [4] Osters (2009); Jayachandran and Kuziemko (2011).
[5] Jha, Kumar, and Dhingra (2006); Bhalotra and Cochrane (2010). [6] Miller (1981); Sen (1990).

The 2011 census shows no tendency toward reversal.[7] Indeed, the recent national escalation in the ratio of male-to-female live births represents an explosive increase in the conduct of female feticide associated with the availability of prenatal sex-detection technology.[8] Today, the combination of transportable ultrasound machines and greater individual mobility allows nearly every Indian citizen to access prenatal sex scans with minimal effort despite their illegality.[9] As a result, this potential form of resistance to daughters is both physically accessible and cheap enough for most families to employ.

Evidence documents the relationship between increasing women's rights to valuable resources – such as property inheritance – and heightened sex selection in favor of sons. Bhalotra et al. (2018) find that exposure to gender-equalizing inheritance reform increases son-biased sex selection in Indian families with access to ultrasound technology where the existing familial structure magnifies son preferences.[10] Additionally, Rosenblum (2015) finds state-level evidence of increasingly male-biased sex ratios following India's gender-equalizing land inheritance reform. In China, Almond, Li, and Zhang (2017) find that rural land reform significantly increased sex selection in favor of sons, accounting for one-half of all sex selection between 1978–86, translating into roughly one million missing women.

The broader literature suggests the relationship between women's economic empowerment and social value remains conflicted. Powerful evidence from China's post-Mao reforms suggests that we should also expect sex selection to decline as women's income, measured as a share of the total household income, increases.[11] In light of such evidence, one might predict a positive impact from land inheritance reform that redistributes material resources – including income from property – away from men, toward women. Similarly, in Ecuador, Hidrobo, Peterman and Heise (2016) find that targeted cash, voucher, or food transfers to women decrease their likelihood of experiencing intimate partner violence – again suggesting higher social status for women in the presence of greater material resources. In contrast, in Bangladesh, Heath (2014) identifies a

---

7 Intriguingly, this is despite survey data indicating a decline over this period in explicitly stated son preference. The Demographic and Health Surveys query women of reproductive age about their desired fertility. Contra demographic data, both women's desired total number of children and their desired ratio of sons to daughters are declining (Bhalotra et al., 2018).

8 The first imports of ultrasound scanners are recorded in the mid-1980s, associated with India's first attempt at import liberalization. As of the mid-1990s, relaxation of industrial licensing requirements created a sharp increase in availability, which led to domestic production of scanners (Bhalotra and Cochrane, 2010).

9 India's Pre-Conception and Pre-Natal Diagnostic Techniques Act of 1994 banned prenatal sex determination with an aim to prevent the use of ultrasound machines to conduct sex selective abortions. However, families and doctors employ a myriad practices to do exactly this (Bhalotra et al., 2018).

10 Specifically, families with first-born daughters are more likely to practice sex selection in favor of sons, conditional on access to ultrasound technology and exposure to gender-equalizing reform.

11 Qian (2008).

positive relationship between women's work and their experience of domestic violence. Notably, she finds violence is directed against women with the least bargaining power: those with low levels of education or who entered marriage at an early age. This provides support for my gatekeeper theory's focus not only on what resources women possess but also the bargaining power they can harness to determine resource distribution across multiple domains.

When considering the impact of female political representation independent of economic impact, there is good reason to expect a positive, significant relationship between political empowerment and women's social value. As Chapter 2 theorizes and Chapter 5 documents, there is also significant evidence supporting the positive impact of reservations on women's political participation and parental aspirations for the next generation of women.[12] If this relationship dominates, we should expect exposure to female gatekeepers – through reservations – to increase the proportion of daughters born, rather than increasing sex selection in favor of sons.

However, existing literature has yet to study the effect of political representation on sex selection *as a direct response to increased enforcement of economic rights by female representatives,* here for women's property inheritance rights. This chapter enables a more precise estimation of whether female political representation's ability to increase women's access to land inheritance rights actually improves or reduces gender equality amongst future generations.

7.2 HYPOTHESES

In this chapter, I investigate whether the ability of female gatekeepers to enforce gender equal property rights minimizes or magnifies the historic preference of Indian parents for bearing sons rather than daughters. I am interested in the degree to which political representation alters parental decisions about family formation when individual daughters can claim substantial rights to land inheritance at par with sons – rights aimed at equalizing the value of children. Does enforcement of women's legal rights by female representatives encourage behavioral change? If so, do families deviate from or reinforce traditional norms that devalue daughters?

Given the findings in Chapters 5 and 6 that enforcement of women's inheritance rights by female gatekeepers results in multifaceted resistance, including: one, attempts by sons to impede inheritance by their sisters; two, fathers punishing daughters for "dishonorable" marriages; and, three, sons renouncing care for aging parents, I expect reservations will exacerbate parental preferences for sons. In particular, I predict parents in households eligible for gender-equal land inheritance will increase their use of sex selection to prevent bearing daughters who may threaten traditional patrilineal familial

[12] See in particular Chattopadhyay and Duflo (2004b), Duflo and Topalova (2004), and Beaman et al. (2009).

control over resources by demanding substantial land inheritance. If so, I expect parental motivation to practice sex selection to be highest where female *Pradhans* enable enforcement of gender-equal rights.

In contrast, and in line with the assertions of "gatekeeper theory," I expect parental resistance to diminish as daughters become more able to negotiate welfare-enhancing redistribution of resources across multiple domains. Here, I define groups of women with respect to fertility profiles. I begin by considering all women's behavior, and next analyze two subsets of women: those who have likely completed their fertility choices (aged 36 years or greater at the time of the survey) versus women who have yet to complete their childbearing years (aged less than 36 when surveyed). One could consider this subsample analysis simply a measure of the generation-specific impact of female gatekeepers. However, the choice of a threshold value that coincides with the end of fertility (for three-quarters of the sample) also enables us to separately analyze two discrete types of responses to the local presence of an as-if exogenously mandated female gatekeeper, whose variation is as good as random within each subsample. The first group of women, who have nearly all completed fertility decisions, provides a conclusive estimate of female gatekeepers' impact on familial composition for this subset of families.[13] The second group of women, with incomplete fertility choices, help estimate the dynamic decision making about familial composition within a set of households that are still negotiating a response to women's proximate political influence. Here, the impact of female gatekeepers is more immediate but also the quantum of their net influence is less certain.[14]

This chapter's analysis of parental willingness to bear daughters provides the sharpest measure of how gender-equalizing political and economic reforms alter gender equality in its most basic form: women's survival. I expect that exposure to real, credible enforcement of gender-equal inheritance rights by female gatekeepers will decrease parental support for son-biased sex selection for the subsample of women amongst whom we can observe dynamic responses to the presence of female gatekeepers. For this set of women, I predict that bias toward sons will decline alongside parental exposure to gatekeepers with the ability to facilitate integrative bargaining solutions for women entering

---

[13] This implies fully realized preferences for sons and daughters. Thus, parents in this subsample have made a fundamental gender-specific investment in children: deciding the extent to which they practice sex selection.

[14] If this subset of mothers are more likely to bear additional children, analysis of their behavior may underestimate their willingness to use sex selection. This should be particularly true if parents planning to bear multiple children are unlikely to employ sex selection for the first-born child, as India's 2017–18 Economic Survey finds (Government of India, Ministry of Finance, 2018, figure 8a). Notably, Table A.9.42 suggests these concerns about incomplete fertility are unlikely to dominate the second generation: the mean number of children for the second generation of mothers – 2.30 – roughly aligns with India's 2011 census – whereby 54 percent of women note having two or less children in families, with a mean of 2.69 children per married women (including older mothers).

marriage negotiations with substantial inheritance rights to secure new distributions of welfare-enhancing resources.

7.3 DATA AND IDENTIFICATION STRATEGY

I employ the same core methodology here as presented in Chapter 5 to identify the causal effect of as-if randomly applied reservations for female elected heads of local government. I also use the same variations introduced in Chapter 6 to capture the impact of descriptive political representation that enables individuals to claim fundamental economic rights with respect to ongoing fertility decisions amongst the broadest set of individuals possible (those with living and deceased parents).[15] Here, I study behavioral change for two sets of outcomes: the balance of daughters and sons to which a mother gives birth, and their rates of child mortality for all children, as well as for women, men, and women relative to men.

First, I examine whether representation changes *the balance of daughters and sons to which a mother gives birth*, comparing mothers who are eligible versus ineligible for equal property rights. This captures the impact of representation that enables enforcement of substantive (versus symbolic) economic rights on women's behavior as mothers. Analysis follows the format of Equations 6.1 and 6.2.[16] As in Chapter 6, I code exposure to reservations as based on whether or not a the father of a given woman is alive at the first year his village implements reservations to measure decision making by *living parents*. Here, the dependent variable of interest, y_{ihst}, denotes the proportion of female births to mother i living in household h, in state s, born in year t. I code the proportion of daughters as $G/(G + B)$ where G is the number of girl children and B is the number of boy children born to a given mother. I next estimate the effect of female representation – conditional on gender-equal rights – on the balance of daughters and sons that mothers give birth to. I measure a given woman's eligibility for reform using the same procedure as for reservations: based on whether or not her father is alive at the time his state legislates gender equal inheritance rights for daughters. Here, regression analysis takes the form of Equation 6.2.

Last, I capture the impact of female political representation on total *child survival rates*. This enables me to assess whether, in light of sex selection

---

[15] The sample includes all respondents to the 2006/9 round of the REDS conducted by the NCAER who are born between 1956, when women gained symbolic property rights, and the year their state equalized their property rights, culminating in the national mandate for gender-equal inheritance as of 2005 (1976–2005). I focus on the group of "target" women who reform was intended to benefit: those with landowning parents who are subject to Hindu law. I study three samples: the full sample, a subsample excluding women residing in states that use biased reservation implementation mechanisms, and a subsample also excluding late quota implementers.

[16] See Chapter 6 for the full specifications.

measured above, those children born – particular daughters – are more "wanted" and hence more likely to survive. Indeed, work by Anukriti, Bhalotra, and Tam (2016) shows that following widespread access to ultrasound technology enabling sex selection, the gender gap in postneonatal (child) mortality between families prone to employ sex selection[17] and those less likely to do so[18] is completely eliminated. We may expect to see this trend magnified in places where women – as mothers – have greater political representation (vis-à-vis reservations), particularly where such authority enables female constituents to enforce substantial, gender-equal rights to property inheritance.

I consider four separate measures of child survival.[19] The first studies child mortality rates, coded as M_c/T_c, or the proportion of a given mother's children who do not survive the initial (7–9) years of life. Here, M_c represents the number of children born as of 1999 a mother reports have died by the time she is surveyed (2006–9); T_c is the total number of children a mother reports she has given birth to between 1999 and the survey. The second and third measures present a reverse picture of survival: coding the proportion of surviving daughters and surviving sons born since 1999 out of the total number of daughters or sons born as of 1999 to a given mother ((Ds_i/Db_i) and (Ss_i/Sb_i), respectively, for a given mother, i). The final measure presents the rate at which daughters survive childhood relative to that of sons. To avoid bias due to exclusion of families with only one gender (either daughters or sons), I calculate this ratio as equal to daughters' child survival rate plus ϵ divided by sons' child survival rate plus ϵ ($(((Ds_i/Db_i)+\epsilon)/((Ss_i/Sb_i)+\epsilon))$.[20] In each case, regression analysis takes the same form as it does for the prior analysis of sex selection (using the form of Equations 6.1 and 6.2).

I begin by analyzing all mothers, and then subdivide my sample into two sets of mothers, where the first includes those aged at least 36 years (by which point three-quarters of women in my sample have borne their last child) and less than 70 years (thus born after the first colonial legislation legalizing women's lifetime access to inheritance, in 1937) at the time of the survey. The second set of mothers comprises those aged less than 36 years at the time of the survey (below the top age quartile at which women complete childbearing), and therefore still engaged in negotiations about whether or not to bear more children. The second sample likely undertook their fertility decisions after the national implementation of reservations. When considering this subsample from a generational perspective, the second sample suggests the potential to capture the longer-term ("second-generation") impact of representation on

---

[17] That is, families with a first-born daughter.   [18] That is, families with a first-born son.

[19] These numbers are reported only for women residing in the household surveyed, and thus cannot draw from the entirety of life experiences within the household head's complete, extended family.

[20] I set the value of ϵ equal to 0.01 in these calculations, but results are consistent for a range of values.

individual behavior (versus the shorter "first-generation" impact in the first sample). I expect that members of the second sample will accordingly be more likely to consider daughters as agents with the potential to renegotiate entitlements for the improvement of overall familial welfare.[21]

How do these subsets of mothers map onto women's ability to strike integrative bargaining solutions, as presented in the prior two empirical chapters?[22] In India, the average maternal age at the birth of a first child has held steady at 20 years for several decades.[23] As a result, we can expect the first subset of mothers – the youngest of whom began their second decade of life in 1990–3 – to have begun bearing children prior to the national implementation of reservations for female gatekeepers. With this in mind, this set of mothers is more likely to have made decisions about bearing children without being able to leverage female elected leaders to negotiate inherited property rights – particularly not through broad choice bracketing that allows integrative bargaining solutions that benefit collective, familial welfare – relative to the second subset. As a result, I expect resistance to female representation will be concentrated in the first set of mothers.

In contrast, the second set of mothers comprises women still in their childbearing years. They should be more likely to benefit from female gatekeepers to secure gender-equal property rights in ways that support their entire family. These women should also be more able to incorporate this knowledge into their ongoing, strategic investment in the sex composition of their children. I predict any resistance will be attenuated in the second, younger set of women in light of their experiencing – and at the very least observing – the ability of daughters to harness political voice in the service of redistributing material rights to enhance familial welfare. Accordingly, I begin by estimating the impact of treatment by reservations based on each mother's ratio of daughters to total children.

7.4 ANALYSIS

7.4.1 Impact of Female Representation on Sex Selection

Do parents value daughters differently after exposure to female elected representatives that make women's political voice and influence more salient in daily life? Perhaps, if the presence of a female gatekeeper heightens parental

---

[21] Table A.9.42 provides descriptive statistics for all women, as well as for each subsample.

[22] This chapter does not directly analyze women's bargaining power using whether they are entering or have exited marriage negotiations at the time of reform because the sample of women entering such decision-making processes with effective bargaining power (aged less than 20 at reform) and children is extremely small: 937 women in the "target" sample from landholding, Hindu households, and only 647 who reside in states that implement reservations in an as-if random and timely manner. Within this sample, there is inadequate variation in eligibility for gender-equalizing inheritance reform and reservations to capture the impact of representation conditional on individual eligibility for inheritance reform.

[23] For details, see Shrinivasan (2011).

awareness of women's agency that translates into greater respect and esteem for daughters – possibly through enhanced parental aspirations for a daughter's career prospects,[24] which, in turn, translate into increased expectations that daughters will contribute to the natal household's social status and material well-being. If this is true, the balance of children mothers bear should tip toward gender equality (i.e., greater proportions of daughters) following exposure to female *Pradhans*.

In contrast, if the presence of female gatekeepers magnifies parental concerns about the dissolution of traditional norms and escalating demands for nontraditional resource entitlements (for which Chapter 6 provides strong evidence), we should see resistance. In this case, the balance of children mothers report should tip farther away from gender equality (i.e., smaller proportions of daughters).

Indeed, I find clear evidence of backlash to female representation: mothers have proportionately fewer daughters where female representatives can facilitate enforcement of their substantive inheritance rights (Table 7.1). Figure 7.2 graphs the net effect of exposure to reservations on the proportion of daughters born for the full sample, compared to that for the first versus second subset of mothers. For the full set of mothers, reservations diminish the proportion of daughters-to-total children by 8–11 percentage points, significant at the 99.9 percent confidence level for all specifications (Table 7.1, Panel A, Columns 1–4).

To make this effect concrete, note that in landholding, Hindu families, mothers whose fathers pass away prior to reservations with only notional inheritance rights bear a nearly equal proportion of daughters (48.4 percent). In contrast, there is a significant drop of 11 percentage points in this ratio where female representatives enable enforcement of a mother's land inheritance rights (whether notional or substantial). This results in a greater imbalance in the proportion of daughters mothers bear (37.4 percent of all children).[25] To put the effect of female representation in perspective, it is the rough equivalent of moving from the Indian state of Kerala's 2011 sex ratio (964:1,000 women to men) to India's union territory of Daman and Diu (616:1,000 women to men).

Why would female representatives negatively affect parental willingness to bear daughters? My field research suggested that concerns by parents about being cared for in old age undergird this result (as explained and verified in Chapter 6). Specifically, parents fear that a daughter's demands for inheritance – aided and abetted by female *Pradhans* – will upset their implicit social contract with sons, whose agreement to provide parental support is encouraged and rewarded by patrilineal inheritance. A daughter's demand for *gender equal* inheritance substantially lessens these rewards for a son, which Chapter 6 finds uniformly diminishes the willingness of sons to provide essential care for elder parents. As the prior chapter showed, virilocal marriage norms are not

---

[24] As Beaman et al. (2009) find.
[25] Note the baseline effect is calculated for all mothers from Hindu landholding families in states that used random or as-if random criteria for implemented village-level women's reservations.

TABLE 7.1. *Representation's Impact on Sex Ratios*

	(1) Target b/se	(2) Target b/se	(3) Target-NR b/se	(4) Target-NR-Late b/se
Panel A: All respondents				
Father dies postreservations	−0.08***	−0.11***	−0.11***	−0.10***
	(0.02)	(0.02)	(0.02)	(0.02)
Controls	No	Yes	Yes	Yes
State FE	Yes	Yes	Yes	Yes
Cohort FE	Yes	Yes	Yes	Yes
State trends	Yes	Yes	Yes	Yes
Adj. R-sq	0.02	0.03	0.03	0.03
N	7,629	7,629	6,809	6,547
Panel B: Respondents aged 36–69				
Father dies postreservations	−0.08***	−0.10***	−0.10***	−0.09***
	(0.02)	(0.02)	(0.02)	(0.02)
Controls	No	Yes	Yes	Yes
State FE	Yes	Yes	Yes	Yes
Cohort FE	Yes	Yes	Yes	Yes
State trends	Yes	Yes	Yes	Yes
Adj. R-sq	0.02	0.05	0.04	0.04
N	4,895	4,895	4,327	4,161
Panel C: Respondents younger than 36				
Father dies postreservations	−0.12	−0.22*	−0.19+	−0.19
	(0.08)	(0.10)	(0.11)	(0.12)
Controls	No	Yes	Yes	Yes
State FE	Yes	Yes	Yes	Yes
Cohort FE	Yes	Yes	Yes	Yes
State trends	Yes	Yes	Yes	Yes
Adj. R-sq	0.02	0.02	0.02	0.02
N	2,734	2,734	2,482	2,386

+ $p < 0.10$, * $p < 0.05$, ** $p < 0.01$, *** $p < 0.001$

Note: Robust standard errors, clustered at the village level, are in parentheses. Panel A sample includes all mothers in the dataset who are 69 years old or younger. Panel B sample includes only mothers aged 36–69. Panel C sample includes only mothers younger than 36 years old. The dependent variable is the number of girls born to the mother divided by the total number of her children (G/G+B). Treatment by reservations is applied if an individual's father is alive or has passed away by the time of reservations in the village. "Target" includes landed, Hindu mothers only. Column (3) excludes mothers living in states that do not assign reservations for female *pradhans* randomly (AP, Himachal Pradesh, Kerala, Tamil Nadu). Column (4) excludes nonrandom implementers of reservations and the two states to implement women's reservations over 10 years after constitutional amendments: Bihar (2006) and Jharkhand (2010). Controls include caste status, a binary indicator for Western Indian states, and the number of male and female siblings.
Source: REDS 2006/9, NCAER.

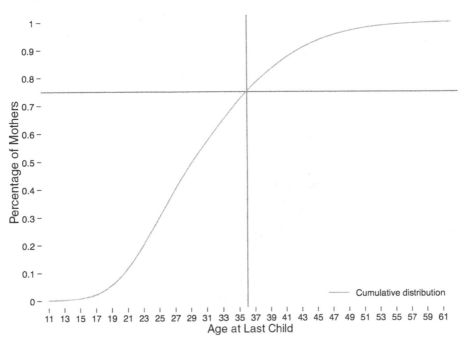

FIGURE 7.1. Cumulative Distribution of Mothers' Age at Last Child

Source: NCAER Rural Economic and Demographic Survey, 2006/9. The sample includes all mothers in REDS 2006/9 round

yet flexible enough to enable a married daughter's relocation to her natal home to substitute for her brother as a traditional caregiver. In addition, the analysis presented here suggests that parental reluctance to bear daughters transcends a mother's exposure to gender-equal inheritance rights. Taken together, these results suggest that resistance by mothers and sons to female representation enabling enforcement of women's economic rights occurs independent of the scope of the rights being conferred.

Notably, the impact of female representation is consistent across the full sample and first subsample of mothers (those aged 36 to 69 years at the survey, Table 7.1, Panel B, Columns 1–4). As noted earlier, I expect my measurement to be most precise for this first cohort of mothers, at least three-quarters of whom have completed bearing children (Figure 7.1). For these women, exposure to female elected heads of local government reduces the proportion of daughters they bear by 8–10 percentage points, significant at the 99.9 percent confidence level across all specifications.

I interpret this as the initial effect of increasing women's political means and authority to enforce their economic rights. This first generation of mothers exposed to female gatekeepers are unlikely to have observed women striking integrative bargaining solutions, agreeing to redistribute traditional resources and responsibility across multiple domains at the time of marriage negotiations (i.e., strategically employing "broad choice bracketing"). They are therefore most likely to experience resistance to women's substantive inheritance rights at close range, either as individuals demanding these rights, or as a sister, sister-in-law, or peer of a woman who is punished by her family for claiming them.

This fits with the reflections of the Haryana-based professor of political science, Gilles Verniers, who observes that backlash is the predominant immediate response to quotas mandating women's political emergence. In his words: *"There is violence against women who vote, but mostly there is [a] high level of resistance towards reservations."*[26]

In contrast, amongst the second cohort of mothers, exposure to reservations has a much weaker relationship to sex selection. Here, in Panel C of Table 7.1, the negative impact of female gatekeepers on a mother's willingness to bear daughters is of larger magnitude (19–22 percentage points), but the statistical significance of these results is weak after excluding nonrandom implementers of reservations. Indeed, significance disappears entirely upon exclusion of the states that were most reluctant to implement these quotas (Table 7.1, Panel C, Columns 3–4). Figure 7.2 illustrates the net effect of female representation on the proportion of daughters and sons mothers give birth to, for each relevant group of mothers.

A conservative interpretation of these results would suggest that while the broad trend is one of backlash to female political representation, it is too soon to analyze female representation's impact on the second set of mothers, who have yet to achieve their desired number and gender balance of children. A more pessimistic reading would find that even these mothers who have observed at close range the potential for integrative bargaining solutions that female gatekeepers can catalyze have internalized backlash to gender-equalizing reforms. In fact, sex selection's magnitude may have increased from the first to the second cohort of women, perhaps because they associate female representation with fear of losing substantial ancestral land to a daughter.

As Chapters 5 and 6 demonstrate, the power of female representatives to successfully enforce a daughter's inheritance rights is a double-edged sword: it is a source of efficacy that destabilizes traditional norms, which often exacerbates conflict within families. As a result, the presence of female representation may increase parental reluctance to give birth to daughters increasingly able to provoke strife within the family and to win such clashes at the expense of traditional familial stability and support.

These findings suggest we should not expect straightforward acceptance of either female political representatives or their capacity to enforce women's economic rights in either the short or medium term. However, it is too early to precisely quantify the scope of long-term resistance. As society becomes more inured to and comfortable with the presence of women in positions of power

---

[26] Personal interview on January 12, 2017, afternoon in Delhi, India.

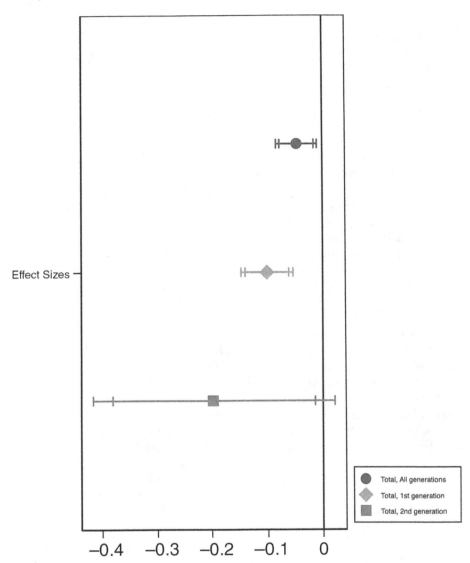

FIGURE 7.2. Representation and Reform's Impact on Sex Ratios: Net Effects

Source: NCAER Rural Economic and Demographic Survey, 2006/9. The sample includes landed, Hindu mothers. It excludes women whose fathers reside in states that do not assign reservations randomly (Andhra Pradesh [AP], Himachal Pradesh, Kerala, and Tamil Nadu). The total effect of reservations for the given group is calculated using the following formula: $\delta' + \delta'' + \delta'''$ from Equation 6.2

and the public and private good that can accrue from the equitable distribution of rights, we may see a gradual, collective turn toward recognizing and valuing women, as Chapter 6 suggests daughters are increasingly willing and able to contribute financially to parents' long-term well-being (Figure 6.4).

7.4.2 Representation, Rights, and Sex Selection

This analysis raises a second question: Do reservations exert a counterbalance against son preference amongst women who are themselves eligible for gender-equal inheritance, such that their ability to inherit, and financial autonomy, bolsters the value of daughters as new sources of familial support? To answer this question, I examine whether the ability of female representatives to help women secure rights decreases the likelihood that these women, as mothers, will conduct female foeticide.

One can imagine two alternative channels through which reservations motivate parental responses to inheritance reform. In the best case scenario, these newly empowered women re envision possibilities for their daughters – both as sources of economic support for the family and as *positive* reflections of the family's social status. Here, women's enhanced economic worth makes their demands more acceptable.

In the worst-case scenario, reservations may be seen as vehicles for daughters to "steal" substantial ancestral land from the natal family without upholding the reciprocal obligation to care for elder parents (as Chapters 5 and 6 suggest holds in the present). If so, women who are themselves eligible for gender-equal inheritance may see these rights as an extreme threat to securing the care from sons essential for their long-term welfare. If most mothers consider female representatives' enforcement of gender-equal inheritance rights as destructive, I expect reservations to significantly increase resistance to bear daughters. If so, the result will be an increase in female foeticide amongst women who are eligible for inheritance reform and exposed to reservations.

I examine the extent to which either of these channels – positive or negative – explains sex selection by mothers eligible for reform with reservation-driven access to female representatives across the two generations of mothers in NCAER's 2006/9 round of the REDS.

Do female representatives able to enforce women's substantive inheritance rights reduce sex selection biased against daughters? For the full sample and the first generation of mothers, the answer is no. Notably, once we analyze the impact of female political representation alongside the varied scope of women's inheritance rights (notional versus substantive), neither variable (representation nor the quantum of rights) singly or jointly changes patterns of sex selection in favor of sons at the margins, either for all mothers or for the first cohort of mothers surveyed (Table 7.2, Panels A–B). In fact, this is an improvement relative to the negative, significant impact of female representation alone on the proportion of daughters mothers bear (Table 7.1). However, as Figure 7.3's

TABLE 7.2. *Representation and Reform's Impact on Sex Ratios*

	(1) Target b/se	(2) Target b/se	(3) Target-NR b/se	(4) Target-NR-Late b/se
Panel A: All respondents				
Father dies postreservations	−0.06	−0.05	−0.07	−0.06
	(0.06)	(0.05)	(0.06)	(0.06)
Father died postreform	0.05	0.05	−0.02	−0.01
	(0.06)	(0.06)	(0.08)	(0.08)
Father died postreform	−0.06	−0.10	−0.03	−0.03
and postreservations	(0.08)	(0.08)	(0.10)	(0.10)
Controls	No	Yes	Yes	Yes
State FE	Yes	Yes	Yes	Yes
Cohort FE	Yes	Yes	Yes	Yes
State trends	Yes	Yes	Yes	Yes
Adj. R-sq	0.02	0.03	0.03	0.03
N	7,629	7,629	6,809	6,547
Panel B: Respondents aged 36–69				
Father dies postreservations	−0.04	−0.04	−0.06	−0.05
	(0.05)	(0.05)	(0.06)	(0.06)
Father died postreform	0.06	0.05	0.01	0.02
	(0.06)	(0.06)	(0.08)	(0.08)
Father died postreform	−0.08	−0.11	−0.06	−0.06
and postreservations	(0.08)	(0.08)	(0.09)	(0.09)
Controls	No	Yes	Yes	Yes
State FE	Yes	Yes	Yes	Yes
Cohort FE	Yes	Yes	Yes	Yes
State trends	Yes	Yes	Yes	Yes
Adj. R-sq	0.02	0.05	0.04	0.04
N	4,895	4,895	4,327	4,161
Panel C: Respondents younger than 36				
Father dies postreservations	−0.57***	−0.52***	−0.50***	−0.51***
	(0.10)	(0.10)	(0.10)	(0.11)
Father died postreform	−0.09	0.05	−0.39[+]	−0.40[+]
	(0.20)	(0.21)	(0.23)	(0.24)
Father died postreform	0.53**	0.26	0.69**	0.70**
and postreservations	(0.20)	(0.22)	(0.23)	(0.23)
Controls	No	Yes	Yes	Yes
State FE	Yes	Yes	Yes	Yes
Cohort FE	Yes	Yes	Yes	Yes
State trends	Yes	Yes	Yes	Yes
Adj. R-sq	0.02	0.02	0.01	0.02
N	2,734	2,734	2,482	2,386

[+] $p < 0.10$, * $p < 0.05$, ** $p < 0.01$, *** $p < 0.001$

Note: Robust standard errors, clustered at the village level, are in parentheses. Panel A sample includes all mothers in the dataset who are 69 years old or younger. Panel B sample includes only mothers aged 36–69. Panel C sample includes only mothers younger than 36 years old. The dependent variable is the number of girls born to the mother divided by the total number of her children (G/G+B). Treatment by reservations is applied if an individual's father is alive by the time of reservations in the village. "Target" includes landed, Hindu mothers only. Column (3) excludes mothers living in states that do not assign reservations for female *pradhans* randomly (AP, Himachal Pradesh, Kerala, Tamil Nadu). Column (4) excludes nonrandom implementers of reservations and the two states to implement women's reservations over 10 years after constitutional amendments: Bihar (2006) and Jharkhand (2010). Controls include caste status, wealth status, a binary indicator for Western Indian states, and the number of male and female siblings.

Source: REDS 2006/9, NCAER.

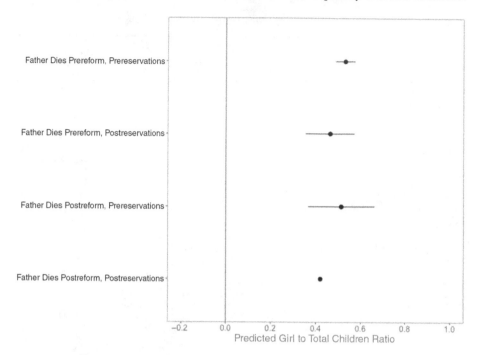

FIGURE 7.3. Representation's Impact: Ratio of Daughters to Total Children, Predicted Values

Source: NCAER Rural Economic and Demographic Survey, 2006/9. The sample includes all mothers from Hindu, landholding families. It excludes women whose fathers reside in states that do not assign reservations randomly (AP, Himachal Pradesh, Kerala, and Tamil Nadu). Each point on the graph represents the predicted value of the ratio of daughters to total children for individuals within the given group, based on regression analysis using Equation 6.2's format. Hatch marks represent 95 percent confidence intervals

predicted ratios of girls-to-total children born indicate, we see a slight decline in the ratio (by 4.7 percentage points) for mothers with access to female gate-keepers and gender-equal inheritance rights, relative to women with neither.[27]

These results highlight the striking, unintended consequences of women's political empowerment that enables their claims to fundamental economic rights on parental decisions about familial composition. Such decisions often began at the dawn of reforms providing women with substantial economic rights, which for many women, arrived prior to changes in female political

---

[27] For the first cohort of mothers exposed to female gatekeepers, the proportion of daughters born drops by 10.1 percentage points (Figure A.9.12). Note that predictions use regression analysis in the form of Equation 6.2, with the sample of mothers who are reform's targets – those from Hindu landed families – in states that use random or as-if random selection methods to implement village-level women's reservations, e.g. Table 7.2, Column 5. Net effects are significant at the 95 percent confidence interval for both the full sample and the first-generation mothers.

representation. Indeed, amongst the first generation of mothers, on average, the first birth occurs in 1977 and last in 1987: at least six years before implementation of the constitutional mandate for female political representation (Table A.9.42). Thus, the best hope for female representatives to alter parental willingness to support daughters may lie with a second, younger set of women. To explore this promise, I analyze the second cohort of mothers in NCAER's REDS 2006/9 sample.

Amongst the second set of mothers still negotiating fertility choices, exposure to female representatives significantly increases the marginal propensity of women eligible for gender-equal inheritance to bear daughters (Table 7.2, Panel C). The best-specified regressions identify an increase in the proportion of daughters born to mothers with access to female gatekeepers and substantial economic rights by 69–70 percentage points, significant at the 99 percent confidence level (Table 7.2, Panel C, Columns 3–4). In this generation, the net effect of eligibility for gender-equal inheritance rights – in the presence of reservations for female *Pradhans* – is to increase the proportion of daughters born by 30 percentage points. These improvements in the willingness of eligible mothers to bear daughters are offset by significant drops in the balance of daughters amongst *ineligible* mothers with access to female representatives: by 50–57 percentage points (significant at the 99.9 confidence level, Table 7.2, Panel C).[28]

In sum, exposure to female gatekeepers seems to encourage the youngest cohort of mothers with gender-equal economic rights to increase the value they place on daughters at the margins. However, the combination of access to female political leaders – who can enforce equal economic rights – has yet to translate into a significant, positive impact, such that mothers decisively grant daughters a chance of surviving to birth equal to that of sons (Figure 9.13). This tendency may reverse in the future, particularly given the diminishing marginal propensity of mothers with female gatekeepers and substantive economic rights to practice sex selection in favor of sons. As subsequent generations of women more fully participate in familial and societal decision making, esteem for daughters may indeed grow as they come to be viewed as favorably as sons.

7.4.3 Representation, Rights, and Child Survival

But what about living daughters? Can female representation increase the value families place on daughters who survive parental decisions about sex selection? In other words, do female gatekeepers encourage parents to support those daughters who are born? To begin I ask: Does the presence of female

---

[28] Given the weakly significant marginal impact of eligibility for gender-equal inheritance rights, the net impact of a mother's access to female gatekeepers and substantial inheritance rights, relative to women with neither, is a slight decrease in her proportion of daughters, which declines by 19.7 percentage points, significant at the 90 percent confidence interval. These figures are calculated for the sample of mothers from Hindu, landholding families who reside in states that implement reservations using random or as-if random formulas.

TABLE 7.3. *Representation's Impact on Child Mortality*

	(1) Target b/se	(2) Target b/se	(3) Target-NR b/se	(4) Target-NR-Late b/se
Panel A				
Father dies postreservations	0.03	−0.04	−0.05	−0.04
	(0.04)	(0.06)	(0.06)	(0.06)
Controls	No	Yes	Yes	Yes
State FE	Yes	Yes	Yes	Yes
Cohort FE	Yes	Yes	Yes	Yes
State trends	Yes	Yes	Yes	Yes
Adj. R-sq	0.05	0.05	0.04	0.02
N	2,547	2,547	2,318	2,199
Panel B				
Father dies postreservations	−0.16**	−0.13+	−0.16+	−0.15+
	(0.06)	(0.07)	(0.08)	(0.09)
Father died postreform	−0.04	−0.00	−0.03	0.09
	(0.06)	(0.05)	(0.11)	(0.06)
Father died postreform	0.23**	0.10	0.15	0.04
and postreservations	(0.08)	(0.08)	(0.13)	(0.11)
Controls	No	Yes	Yes	Yes
State FE	Yes	Yes	Yes	Yes
Cohort FE	Yes	Yes	Yes	Yes
State trends	Yes	Yes	Yes	Yes
Adj. R-sq	0.05	0.05	0.04	0.02
N	2,547	2,547	2,318	2,199

+ $p < 0.10$, * $p < 0.05$, ** $p < 0.01$, *** $p < 0.001$

Note: Robust standard errors, clustered at the village level, are in parentheses. The sample includes all mothers in the dataset. The dependent variable is a measure of "mortality" where the numerator is the sum of the number of children who died from disease and the number of miscarriages, and the denominator is the sum of the number of daughters and sons born since 1999. Treatment by reservations is applied if an individual's father is alive by the time of reservations in the village. "Target" includes landed, Hindu mothers only. Column (3) excludes mothers living in states that do not assign reservations for female *pradhans* randomly (AP, Himachal Pradesh, Kerala, Tamil Nadu). Column (4) excludes nonrandom implementers of reservations and the two states to implement women's reservations over 10 years after constitutional amendments: Bihar (2006) and Jharkhand (2010). Controls include caste status, wealth status, a binary indicator for Western Indian states, and the number of male and female siblings.
Source: REDS 2006, NCAER.

gatekeepers decrease child mortality *as a whole?* Table 7.3 presents regression results and Figure 7.4 graphs the predicted impact of exposure to reservations, in the presence versus the absence of gender-equal inheritance rights, on rates of child mortality.

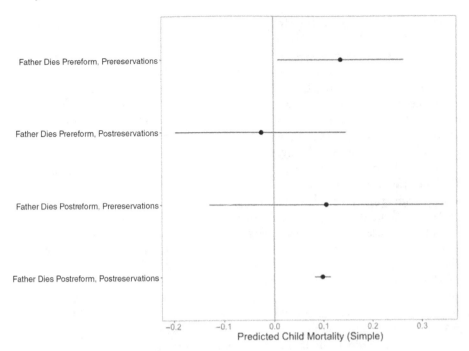

FIGURE 7.4. Representation's Impact: Child Mortality, Predicted Values

Source: NCAER Rural Economic and Demographic Survey, 2006/9. The sample includes landed, Hindu mothers. It excludes women whose fathers reside in states that do not assign reservations randomly (AP, Himachal Pradesh, Kerala, and Tamil Nadu). Each point on the graph represents the predicted values of child mortality for individuals belonging to the given group, with analysis using Equation 6.2's format. Hatch marks represent 95 percent confidence intervals

From Table 7.3 Panel A, we see that, on average, exposure to female *Pradhans* alone has no impact on child mortality. However, once we account for variation in the scope of women's inheritance rights, a more nuanced relationship between representation and child survival emerges. The presence of female gatekeepers consistently, significantly reduces rates of child mortality amongst women with notional, symbolic inheritance rights, by 13–16 percentage points, significant at the 90–99 percent confidence intervals (Table 7.3 Panel B, Columns 1–4). In contrast, for women with gender-equal rights, exposure to female gatekeepers does not further diminish child mortality.[29] Altogether, this suggests female representation can markedly improve the likelihood that both sons and daughters will survive early childhood – but this effect is clearest amongst mothers for whom female *Pradhan*-led enforcement of property rights

[29] In fact, these women have slightly higher child mortality rates, although this impact is not statistically significant after controlling for characteristics of mothers and their families (Table 7.3, Panel B, Column 1 versus 2–4, respectively).

requires parents to provide only symbolic inheritance entitlements, which likely do not spur conflict within natal families.

How does female representation – conditional on the scope of women's economic rights – affect survival rates of daughters relative to those of sons? First, considering the rates at which daughters survive early childhood, there is little evidence of a statistically robust relationship between female representation as a means to enforce women's inheritance rights and daughters' survival. At most there is limited evidence that, absent access to a female gatekeeper, a mother's eligibility for gender-equal inheritance rights makes her daughters less likely to survive childhood (Table A.9.43, Panel A, Columns 3 and 5).[30] When assessing the net effect of reservations and reform on survival rates of daughters, they are not statistically significant.

What about the responsiveness of survival rates for sons to female representation? Here, female gatekeepers have a consistently significant, positive effect across specifications (Table A.9.43, Panel B, Columns 1–5, significant at the 90–95 percent confidence intervals). For the sample of sons from Hindu, landholding families in states that implement reservations as-if randomly – where mothers are ineligible for gender-equal inheritance, the presence of a female *Pradhan* increases the likelihood sons will survive early childhood from 76 to 100 percent.[31] Thus, it appears that sons are the greatest beneficiaries of the relative reductions in early childhood mortality, evident in Table 7.3's analysis, whereas rates do not perceptibly shift for daughters.

Finally, what can we learn from directly comparing early childhood survival rates between daughters and sons? Table A.9.44 confirms the patterns evident from each gender-specific analysis of mortality: variation is most clearly driven by the impact of female *Pradhans* on mothers ineligible for equal property inheritance – for whom the probability that daughters will survive early childhood drops, relative to sons, by 29.6–34.5 percentage points. On net, this essentially moves daughters from a greater probability of survival, in line with global patterns, to a slightly lower probability of survival than sons.[32] These results suggest that rather than diminishing traditional preferences for

---

[30] While the negative impact of inheritance reform is consistent across specifications, it is significant in only two of five specifications, and even then at the lowest threshold for statistical significance (the 90 percent confidence interval).

[31] Net effects calculated from the regression specification presented in Table 9.43, Panel B, Column 4. Indeed, for mothers eligible for equal land inheritance, although the marginal impact of reservations is statistically insignificant, their net impact remains positive and statistically significant. For the same sample used to calcuate such effects in the preceding text, the net effect of reservations postreform is to increase sons' survival rate by 36.5 percentage points, with a t-score of 2.37.

[32] Net effects calculated from the regression specification presented in Table 9.44, Panel B, Column 4. For the control group in this sample, the mean relative survival rate of daughters is 31.95. The net impact of reservations amongst mothers ineligible for reform is to diminish daughters' relative survival rate by 31.16, to 0.79, with a t-statistic of −2.42.

sons, exposure to female gatekeepers increases parental willingness to invest in sons over daughters, both using sex selection prior to birth and additional, subsequent support throughout early childhood.

7.5 DISCUSSION

Overall, this analysis provides decisive evidence that backlash immediately follows quota-mandated female representation that enables enforcement of women's substantial inheritance rights. Does the extent of backlash vary alongside the value of social status, as proposed in Chapter 2 and observed for the prior two chapters? To analyze this question, I return to analysis of behavioral variation alongside the distribution of landownership within villages, captured as village-level Gini coefficients (built and explained in Chapter 5).

Female infanticide increases significantly in response to quotas for female gatekeepers across all levels of inequality (Table A.9.45, Panels A–C). However, there does appear to be a dampening of resistance at the highest levels of inequality, where women's demands for gender-equal inheritance may not be credible and hence not merit backlash.[33] When considering the relationship between female gatekeepers as facilitators of gender-equal inheritance and female infanticide, the only statistically significant relationship measured occurs at moderate levels of inequality.[34] Given the limited statistical significance of this analysis (for one out of four specifications), these findings provide only weak evidence in favor of my proposed hypothesis: that resistance will be greatest at moderate levels of inequality, where inequality is neither too high to inhibit credible threats by daughters for inheritance rights on par with sons, nor too low to make waiting for longer-term behavioral change a credible, cheaper alternative to political action.

Overall, this analysis provides at most suggestive evidence in favor of a relationship between the value of social status – using the proxy of landholding inequality – and resistance. To the extent we can make any conclusions, it would be that high levels of inequality do appear to consistently limit the scope of resistance. If such inequality is indeed associated with the value of social status, the good news is that inequality – and the associated value of social reputation – limits backlash. The bad news is that economic inequality also limits opportunities for shifting to a more egalitarian equilibrium that could benefit everyone, as Bardhan (2005), Huber (2017), and my gatekeeper theory suggest.

33 Levels of statistical confidence for the decline in female sex ratios spurred by female representation are consistently lower in villages with the greatest inequality, relative to other villages (Table A.9.45, Panel C versus A–B).
34 For the well-specified case of mothers in states that apply reservations randomly or as-if randomly, the presence of quotas for female gatekeepers reduces sex ratios amongst mothers *eligible* for substantial inheritance by 27 percentage points, significant at the 90 percent confidence level (9.46, Panel B, Column 3).

7.6 CONCLUSION

This chapter presents a significant body of evidence on a brutal form of resistance to women's political representation that enables enforcement of economic rights: increased sex selection (female infanticide). As Figure 7.2 indicates, exposure to female gatekeepers lowers the proportion of daughters mothers bear by 5–20 percentage points. This supports the hypothesis that while representation motivates women to demand and secure enforcement of their rights (Chapter 5), it also incites realistic fears amongst parents of daughters' demands for substantive inheritance, with great potential to destabilize norms about a son's provision of care to aging parents (Chapter 6).

There is some limited room for optimism about the ability of new political representation that expands opportunities for women to claim gender-equal economic rights to shift behavior amongst the youngest cohorts of mothers exposed to both changes (female-led political institutions and substantive economic rights). For this younger group, the public, political empowerment of women through reservations that enable the private advancement of women through intrahousehold negotiations of substantial inheritance rights may occur early enough in their process of familial formation to enable them, as mothers, to observe how other women harness these forms of bargaining power to benefit the entire natal family. Such experiences may cause them to reassess traditional preferences for sons. Indeed, at the margin, this group of women appear slightly more inclined to value a daughter's agency to renegotiate economic resources and seek out innovative, complementary forms of support for parents as they age. One example of such assistance is the financial support women with female political representatives appear increasingly inclined to provide parents (in Chapter 6).

However, there is very little evidence that reservations decisively shift parental attitudes away from preferential investments in sons, in favor of investments in daughters. If anything, the preceding analysis suggests a slight shift in favor of bearing and raising healthy sons. This is the paradox of gender-equalizing reform, which holds for all but the youngest cohort of mothers. For the youngest group, the positive marginal effect of reservations pushes the generally negative net joint impact (of representation and eligibility for gender-equal rights) just below conventional levels of statistical significance.

What explains the impact of female representation on sex selection and the traditional preference for sons over daughters? The prior chapters addressed this question in terms of the effect of female gatekeepers – who make enforcement of gender-equalizing economic reform real and credible – on the structure of family obligation. Notably, familial obligation is defined by a resilient social norm: virilocal marriage, where a bride leaves her natal family to join her husband's household. In much of India, this protocol is the organizing principle around which economic and social obligations are dictated. The welfare and investment of parents and sons are linked in mutual support over the long term, whereas investment in daughters is considered *paraya dhan,* watering a neighbor's garden, as their welfare and support are contingent on the approval of their marital rather than natal family. In this context, inheritance reform's requirement that parents expend valuable resources "watering the neighbor's garden" may be perceived as a substantial drop in traditional parental investment in a son's welfare, thereby diminishing such men's incentive to care for parents.

In the long run, if daughters can leverage female *Pradhans* to conduct ever-broader bargaining over the distribution of economic rights and familial obligations at the time (or before) they enter marriage negotiations, the integrative bargaining solutions they reach may be powerful enough evidence of gender equality's benefits to shift parental preferences away from what is still currently an enduring son bias. In contrast, if the widespread backlash that we now observe to female representation extends across multiple generations with limited ability to reconceive daughters' responsibility for familial welfare, this suggests a steep, uphill battle for achieving gender equality.

In sum, this chapter suggests that political representation enabling women to claim crucial economic rights to inherit property is not sufficient on its own to bring about meaningful or benign change. Without collateral alteration of social norms that prohibit such change, destructive backlash may be channeled into future generations of children.

8

Conclusion

> The afflicted world in which we live is characterized by deeply unequal sharing
> of the burden of adversities between women and men. Gender inequality exists in
> most parts of the world, from Japan to Morocco, from Uzbekistan to the United
> States of America.... An enhancement of women's active agency can, in many
> circumstances, contribute substantially to the lives of all people – men as well as
> women, children as well as adults.
>
> —Amartya Sen (2001b)

The struggle for gender equality has mobilized global campaigns around
reforming political, economic, and social institutions. One solution to political
inequality – quotas for women in politics – has been widely employed and
frequently vilified.

In this book, I answer three crucial, unresolved questions about the impact of
quotas for women's political representation. First, can electoral quotas improve
women's overall welfare beyond the political sphere? Second, if so, through
what mechanisms do they achieve this? Third, if the impact of quotas varies,
under what conditions do they enhance versus diminish women's well-being?
My analysis provides the first work to causally identify the effect of female
political representation across multiple domains: economic, social, and the intimate political terrain of the household. My focus is India, which mandated an
unprecedented entry of women into local politics. This analysis has important
implications for other countries searching for persuasive instruments to expand
gender equality.

The remainder of this conclusion begins with a summary of my results. I then
reflect on how the theory I have developed here travels to other countries. Next,
I address how my theory and findings contribute to broader scholarship. Finally,

I consider what gaps in our understanding remain, and how we can improve policy and scholarship going forward.

8.1 WHY TUNNEL VISION IS BLINDING: CONNECTING POLITICAL AND ECONOMIC INEQUALITY

Attempts to tackle gender inequality often focus exclusively on either women's economic empowerment or political equality. Statistical evidence is stark in each domain, and the link between these arenas is widely presumed but poorly understood. Economically, gender imbalances are clear in property titles: women own approximately 15 percent of the world's property. This translates into gender-imbalanced opportunities for advancement: the majority of people in poverty (60 percent) and without basic education (two-thirds of illiterates) are also women.[1] Inequality is most severe in the developing world, where approximately 100 million women are "missing," that is are either never born or succumb to early death due to neglect, gender biases in health care, and female infanticide.[2] As if those disparities were not appalling enough, the social norms that encourage lower investments in women – from conception to old age – also have critical consequences for socioeconomic development, limiting demands for investment in child and maternal health, education, and broader public goods.[3]

Disparate value for women versus men is also evident in politics. In January, 2019, at most 10 percent of countries have a female head of state or government (11 and 10, respectively, of 195 countries).[4] While the causes of inequality in political and economic domains are complex, the consequences are clear: inequality in either domain magnifies its entrenchment in the other (Duflo, 2012).

Quotas for women's political representation have gained global acceptance in the two decades following the UN Fourth World Conference on Women in Beijing, in September 1995 (Krook, 2009, 3). The resulting national declarations advocated state-based measures to assure women's equal access to and participation in power structures (United Nations, 1995). Prior to the 1970s, only five countries had adopted quota measures; now more than 100 countries have legislated them (Bush, 2011, 103).

Unsurprisingly, much of the extant work focuses on understanding how this revolution occurred, and its impact to date on women's actual political representation and voice. A growing accumulation of evidence suggests that

---

[1] Doss (2014); Jalal (2015); UNFPA (2015). [2] Sen (2001b); Duflo (2012).

[3] Dollar, Fisman, and Gatti (2001); United Nations (2005); Miller (2008); Lindberg et al. (2011); Duflo (2012); World Bank (2012).

[4] According to UN Women (2019), whose calculation is based on information provided by Permanent Missions to the United Nations. They note that some leaders hold both positions.

quotas increase women's presence in and influence on political deliberations,[5] with significant effects on the distribution of public goods and women's status.[6] However, such changes do not always make everyone in the community better off.[7]

I find evidence that quotas can improve women's economic well-being through a specific mechanism: their ability to spur enforcement of women's rights to inherit property. However, there is a catch. The impact of female political representation varies based on a crucial moderating force: whether or not eligible women gain access to these representatives "at the right time." In India, the crucial time is when women come of age and begin considering marriage arrangements between their natal families and those of potential husbands. These negotiations are critical because in the presence of reform and female representatives to enforce it, they enable a bride to trade traditional inheritance—monetary dowry, given to marital families rather than to women – for land inheritance. When females hold "gatekeeper" positions of elected authority, they catalyze change in how women engage power within the state and the household, enabling "integrative bargaining solutions," where everyone in a woman's family benefits from gender-equal property inheritance.

In fact, I find that quotas increase these women's welfare across other domains as well. Exchanging dowry for property lowers the risk that marital families will attempt to extort additional money from the bride's natal family in the future. In addition, we see greater female solidarity such that mothers are more likely to support a daughter's autonomy in selecting her marriage partner. We also see lower female infanticide. Finally, there is tentative evidence that women who inherit property may be more able and willing to assist in the care of aging parents, over the long term.

Yet, women who have completed marriage negotiations by the time they access female representatives are unable to strike these mutually beneficial bargains, in particular because monetary dowries were likely already paid on their behalf. Quotas diminish these women's welfare, decreasing access to property inheritance and thus increasing reliance on dowry, with its associated vulnerabilities. Overall, this results in weaker familial ties. As parents, these women are more willing to punish a daughter's autonomous marriage decisions, and more likely to conduct female infanticide. This is the paradox of gender-equalizing laws in India: success can initiate severe backlash, with a particularly grim cost for future generations.

Resistance to political enforcement of women's new economic rights is real and conspicuous across contemporary India. Where daughters have rights to ancestral property, sons renounce their preeminent familial duty to care for

[5] Jones (1997); Phillips (1998); Krook (2009); Bush (2011); Karpowitz, Mendelberg, and Shaker (2012).
[6] Ghatak and Ghatak (2002); Chattopadhyay and Duflo (2004b); Beaman et al. (2012); Clayton and Zetterberg (2018).
[7] Duflo and Topalova (2004); Bardhan and Mookherjee (2010); Htun (2016).

elder parents. Even daughters who enjoy substantial inheritance rights are unable to fill this gap in support. In addition, while women who possess the bargaining power to secure real and credible inheritance rights are less likely to conduct female infanticide at the margin, relative to women without bargaining power – suggesting a long-term trend toward lower levels of female infanticide, they still bear fewer daughters. This means that while attitudes toward daughters are improving – that is, we see the slope of sex selection diminishing over time – as of now, these women still internalize resistance to female economic empowerment and commit female infanticide.

What explains such behavior? My gatekeeper theory of female representation identifies the importance of social as well as material determinants of familial responses to female elected representatives. While representatives' enforcement of women's economic rights has the potential to improve the well-being of all family members – not just daughters with new rights – the opportunity for such improvements may not be the dominant factor in a family's decision to resist or comply with reform. Social status also influences familial choices. Where concerns about status dominate, as long as female gatekeepers' commitment to enforce a daughter's rights are in doubt, families will maintain status at the expense of mandated, gender-equal land inheritance. Where high levels of socioeconomic inequality make social identity both more weighty in daily life and more risky to lose, I expect uncertainty about reform's enforcement to encourage resistance independent of material benefits families anticipate from compliance.

8.2 APPLICATIONS

Does gatekeeper theory, with its associated predictions about backlash, scale beyond India? I argue yes, with one caveat. While my work provides maximum analytic leverage by combining qualitative and quantitative research, this strength has geographic limitations. I combine intensive, within-village, qualitative research in a single Indian state – Andhra Pradesh (AP) – with more limited qualitative research in four other states (one in southern, one in western, and two in northern India) to enable cross-state comparisons "nested" within a statistical analysis of more than 100,000 individuals in 17 major Indian states.[8] However, throughout, I hold the national structure of political institutions constant. Looking beyond India, it would be difficult to replicate the rigor of this preceding analysis. Rather, I suggest the following comparisons as an opening to what I hope is a larger discussion about when political representation enables global, long-term economic empowerment with agency to bargain for meaningful social change that overcomes short-term resistance.

Given that the core of this book focuses on whether quotas mandating women's political representation provide a path to enforcement of new

---

[8] As recommended by Lieberman (2005, 435), and employed by Singh (2016, 18).

economic rights, I now ask the same question of a larger set of countries and economic rights. Table 8.1 summarizes four cases – two within Europe and two within Africa – where quotas remain the relevant political tool, but the outcome of interest changes. In the first comparison, reforms are intended to increase women's labor force participation in Eastern and Western Europe (increasing parental leave in the Former USSR and Sweden). In the second, reforms aim to formalize land rights in Africa (privatization in Tanzania and tenure regularization in Rwanda). In each case, I consider how the institutional structure of quotas and reform interact – enabling or inhibiting women to strike integrative bargaining solutions – and whether or not women's well-being improves.

In brief, Table 8.1's typology indicates that where quotas for women are effective, gender-equalizing reforms are enforced with significant impact on welfare. However, the nature of this impact varies with the ability of reform to promote mutually beneficial trade-offs of valuable resources. Two additional nuances emerge: quotas can be meaningful in multiple domains, in the bureaucracy as well as the polity, and, where multiple reforms occur, the sequence of implementation matters.

8.2.1 (Labor Force) Integration as Empowerment

Women's integration into the labor force was once expected to be an immediate consequence of economic progress. After Boserup (1970) provided striking evidence that economic development may constrain rather than empower women's labor participation, more careful investigation of this relationship ensued. Consensus emerged around the existence of a "U"-shaped curve in women's labor force participation: initial economic development pushed paid work from piecework inside the home into factories. This lowered women's overall participation. Even as women's levels of education improved alongside subsequent development, social norms frequently constrained their workforce engagement (Goldin, 1994; Mammen and Paxson, 2000). However, ever-higher levels of educational achievement eventually propelled women back into the workforce (Goldin, 1994).

Today, action to reduce gender-specific barriers to education, mobility, and employment opportunities is considered integral to women's advancement and broader economic development (Duflo, 2012; Kabeer, 2012). This, as Folbre (2020, 14–17) explains, is due in part to the evolution of capitalism in tandem with the welfare state. In countries where workers had sufficient bargaining power to establish at least minimal institutional rights early in the Industrial Revolution, the state invested significantly in citizen "welfare," that is, social safety nets to support citizens early and late in life, and through transitions between unemployment and employment (ibid.). However, support for "welfare state" policies has been steadily diminishing alongside increasing migration and capital mobility, which reduce the incentives for

TABLE 8.1. *Explaining Reforms for Gender Equality's Impact across Countries*

Country	Political Quotas for Women	Reform	Intended Beneficiary	Narrow-Broad Choice Bracketing	Enforcement Quality	Outcome
Former Eastern bloc countries	Yes (parliamentary, symbolic)	Parental leave (within the framework of gender-equality promotion)	Women/mothers	Narrow	Well-enforced	Double burden on women's time; backlash to gender equality
Sweden	Yes (voluntary party quotas, substantive)	Parental leave (within the framework of gender-equality promotion)	Women/mothers	Broad	Well-enforced	Increased male participation in childrearing, high support for gender equality
Tanzania	Yes (national and local reserved seats, superficial)	Land privatization	All farmers (with gender-equal provisions)	NA	Weak enforcement	Women lose traditional protections without new rights being enforced
Rwanda	Yes (national and local, w/ women-only seats, substantive)	Land tenure regularization	All farmers, with emphasis on protecting women's rights to land	NA	Well-enforced	Women's landownership and knowledge of their rights increase
India	Yes (local, substantive)	Gender-equalizing property inheritance reform	Women/daughters	Narrow/Broad	Varied enforcement	Benefits women entering marriage markets w/ rights and representation; backlash if already exited marriage markets

states to subsidize a national workforce (Folbre, 2020, 241). This matters because, as Iversen and Rosenbluth (2006) explain, larger welfare states enable women to overcome disadvantages they suffer in balancing the fulfillment of traditional domestic roles with competition in labor markets that value specific skills that require years of professional investment and training – including in Japan and much of Western Europe. As welfare states shrink dramatically, families bear an increasing portion of the costs of care. Women have responded by lowering fertility. In some nations, this drop in childbearing has been great enough to spur public and private action (Folbre, 2020).

One such set of policies to incentivize women's labor force participation without sacrificing population growth is state-subsidized parental leave. Whether or not such policies increase women's economic agency depends on the ability of both parents to negotiate trade-offs across at least two domains: paid and unpaid (childrearing) work. I predict paid parental leave will facilitate welfare-maximizing negotiations across partners and domains ("broad choice bracketing") when they provide financial incentives for both partners, rather than just one, to access substantial parental leave that they invest in raising children.

To test this hypothesis, I compare neighboring states that made significant investments in parental leave as a means of increasing women's labor force participation: the former Communist, Eastern Bloc countries known as the Union of Soviet Socialist Republics (USSR) and Sweden. Both states were forerunners in legislating parental leave: 1920 in the USSR and 1937 in Sweden. The form and aim of these policies was initially similar, which makes their subsequent divergences all the more striking.

8.2.1.1 *Enforcement's Peril: Parental Leave in Russia*
The former USSR carried out one of the most pronounced efforts to increase women's labor force involvement through Communist rule. Ensuring women's full economic participation was a high priority for Communist state governments, which considered female exclusion from the workforce a major source of oppression (Molyneux, 1990, 25). Policy reform began with the 1920 Congress of the Comintern's resolutions on women's paid employment, motherhood, and liberalization of laws on marriage and the family (Pascall and Manning, 2000, 242, 245). Many states guaranteed extended leaves of absence for mothers, restricted working hours for pregnant and nursing women, and free health care (Lobodzinska, 1995, 7, c.f. Pascall and Manning, 2000, 245).

Comparable parental leave policies persist in contemporary Russia: mothers are entitled to 18 weeks of fully paid leave (10 weeks prior to birth and 8 weeks after), followed by up to 70 weeks of partially paid leave and another 78 weeks of unpaid leave. In contrast, fathers' rights are limited to unpaid leave, which may extend up to 78 weeks (Motiejunaite and Kravchenko, 2008, 41).

The balance of financial incentives in both historical Soviet and contemporary Russian parental leave policies clearly prioritizes subsidized parental leave for women over men. This imbalance limits opportunities for mutually-beneficial trade-offs between mothers and fathers that might encourage shared engagement in childrearing. Unsurprisingly, Communist policy has historically promoted gendered parental leave as a tool for *selectively* reinforcing traditional social roles. As a result, women assumed a "double burden" as workers and mothers (Pop-Eleches and Tucker, 2017).

Concurrent with economic policies supporting women's labor force participation, Soviet Communism employed extensive, albeit symbolic, quotas for women's political representation in parliamentary bodies. The impact of these quotas was blunted by the fact that, numerically speaking, women continued to occupy few key positions in the Communist Party. Leadership remained dominated by men (Pop-Eleches and Tucker, 2017). In Pascall and Manning's (2000, 258) analysis, women's quotas were ineffective because *"parliaments themselves were weak, with decision-making dominated by the Communist Party where women never had more than 5 percent representation."*

Additionally, promotion of gender equality by the strong central state pre-empted local action. This dominance, with a male political cadre unconcerned with women's substantial political representation at the helm, ensured that local political participation remained symbolic.

Parental leave policies were effective at achieving their primary goal: promoting women's labor force integration. This was in large part due to the central state's capacity and the priority it placed on achieving full economic participation by all citizens. Throughout Eastern Europe, Pascall and Manning (2000, 245) document that women occupied half of the labor force by 1980, as compared to 32 percent of labor in Western Europe. Yet, in the former Soviet states, women's domestic investment in unpaid labor doubled that of men's (ibid.). This is because incentives have been consistently low for status quo beneficiaries, men, to trade off lucrative and socially valued paid work for parenting. Thus, the nature of parental leave policies in the USSR and contemporary Russia have ensured that child rearing remains nonremunerative and socially stigmatized as "women's work."

While Soviet and contemporary Russian policies have increased women's ability to secure economic resources through formal employment, they have reduced women's support in other domains. Families once dependent on women's labor force participation now express the strongest views against women's economic participation as detrimental to familial welfare (Motiejunaite and Kravchenko, 2008; Pop-Eleches and Tucker, 2017).

Such responses parallel the unintended consequences of reforms aimed at increasing women's labor force participation in the contemporary member states of the Organization for Economic Cooperation and Development (OECD). In particular, Iversen and Rosenbluth (2011) find that professions that attempt to limit working hours to reduce burdens for women raising families promote fewer women to top positions. Women are expected to interrupt careers to bear and raise children, making new laws vehicles for employer expectations that women will act as mothers first. Here, employers become less likely to hire and promote women because they assume women will be less likely to "commit" to careers over families. Instead, it is only where women are able to work extraordinarily long hours – signaling their career commitment – that they are promoted to top positions (ibid.). In sum, Russia and the former USSR illustrate backlash to gender-equalizing economic reform that is the result of well-enforced policies promoting narrow bargains between women and men.

8.2.1.2 Enforcement's Promise: Parental Leave in Sweden

Sweden, with its close proximity to the former Soviet Union, represents an intriguing comparison. The state introduced parental leave policies as of 1937. As in the Soviet Union, these policies focused on maternity leave as a means to promote women's economic integration (Motiejunaite and Kravchenko, 2008, 41). Sweden incrementally increased women's pay and access to managerial positions in the labor market, albeit with a gender gap in pay remaining in Sweden as in Russia and worldwide (Haas and Hwang, 2008, 90). While this starting point looks similar, the structure of Sweden's policies diverged significantly from those of the USSR and Russia in the ensuing decades.

In 1974, Sweden became the first country in the world to offer parental leave incentives to fathers as a form of "double emancipation" (Haas and Hwang, 2008, 89). According to the then prime minister Olof Palme:

The demand for equality ... involves changes not only in the conditions of women but also in the conditions of men. One purpose of such changes is to give women an increased opportunity for gainful employment and to give men an increased responsibility for care of the children.[9]

Here, policy makers acknowledged the need to make trade-offs across the domains of paid labor and unpaid "care of the children" attractive to all.

Other analysts focus on father-directed incentives as essential precursors to gender-equal labor force participation. As Ferrarini (2003, 34) explains:

one official motive for the reform was to achieve gender equality. The inclusion of both parents in the care of the baby was ... thought to redress within-family imbalances in the distribution of unpaid care work, and to increase possibilities for more equal gendered labor market participation.[10]

Since 2002, each Swedish parent has been allocated 240 days of leave, with up to 80 percent of salary paid by the state for 81 percent of those days. Additionally, 60 days are reserved for each parent's sole use: two "pappa months" and two "mamma months" (Haas and Hwang, 2008, 89).[11]

---

[9] Palme (1972), c.f. Baude (1979, 151) in Haas and Hwang (2008, 88).
[10] Cited from Haas and Rostgaard (2011, 179).
[11] A maximum annual income applies to state-subsidized pay: US $27,804 as of 2006 (ibid.).

The distinction between Sweden and Russia's policies lies in incentives to status quo beneficiaries of formal paid labor, men, to trade off such work for the unpaid, informal care of children within the home. In Sweden, the state works hard to boost men's financial motivation to enter the traditionally unpaid, female domain of childrearing.

Why were these parental leave policies structured so differently? According to Haas and Rostgaard (2011, 178), women's political engagement in grass-roots organizations and national politics was significant around the time that Sweden's parental leave policies were drafted. Specifically, participation began to rise in the 1970s, just prior to passage of relevant legislation (Dahlerup and Freidenvall, 2005, 27).

In Sweden, quotas are implemented voluntarily by parties, and were initi-ated, in the 1980s, in Dahlerup and Freidenvall's (ibid.) analysis, as "a critical act by a large minority of women to consolidate women's representation and make way for more elected women." Quotas thus appear to be one component of a self-reinforcing cycle, where relatively high initial levels of female political participation in Sweden's grassroots and national politics enabled them to successfully advocate for quotas as a means of further expanding women's political voice and economic agency.

Unsurprisingly, Sweden also evidences high levels of policy enforcement. The exceptionally high commitment to gender equity within Scandinavian countries notwithstanding, Sweden emerges as the leader in efforts to publicize parental leave inducements for men.[12] This appears to result in more frequent use: claims by fathers for leave have doubled in the recent past, approaching full take-up following the implementation of reservations for two "pappa months."[13] Thus, Swedish women have achieved high levels of formal economic participation[14] alongside relatively equitable distribution of child-raising duties.[15] A growing consensus supports this ecosystem of new norms, such that gender-equal parenting responsibilities are considered important and welfare enhancing for families.[16] It is plausible that Sweden's female elected "gatekeepers" at least partially explain the relative ease of cultivating a supportive system smoothing the way for women's economic empowerment in the example of Sweden, as opposed to the backlash to similar policies in the former Soviet Union.

How well does this argument travel globally? There is reason to believe that women's participation in local government positively impacts their empower-ment in the domain of labor force integration more broadly. Indeed, Figure 8.1

[12] Klinth (2002), c.f. Haas and Rostgaard (2011, 190).
[13] According to Haas and Hwang (2008), only 51 percent of fathers took parental leave as of 1993, prior to the double "pappa month" policy's implementation, whereas 90 percent of fathers made use of parental leave by 1998, post policy implementation.
[14] Seventy-nine percent of women work as compared to 84 percent of men aged 20–64 by 2004 according to Haas and Hwang (2008, 90).
[15] Swedish mothers report they are responsible for 52 percent of such duties, according to a 2003 survey of 195 mothers and 178 fathers (Haas and Hwang, 2008, 92).
[16] Ibid. Motiejunaite and Kravchenko (2008).

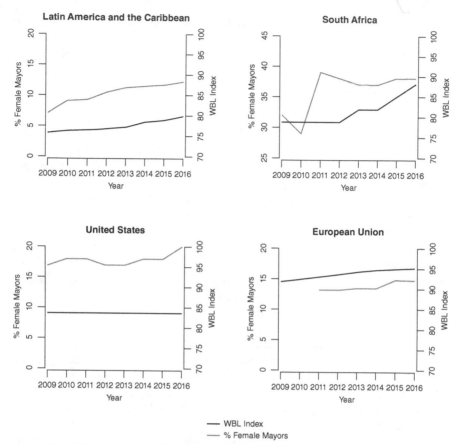

FIGURE 8.1. Women in Local Governance and Economic Rights by Region

Note: I compile the "Women in Business and Law" (WBL) index from the World Bank (2019a). The country-specific index measures the degree to which legal statutes differentially constrain women's economic decisions on a scale ranging from 0 (complete discrimination) to 100 (complete equality). This is calculated as the unweighted average of eight indexes, each comprising 4–5 binary indicators of equality: physical mobility, legal codes on hiring, pay, marriage, childbirth (including paid maternity and paternity leave), access to credit (as well as business and contract registration), asset management (including inheritance rights), and pensions. I compile the percentage of female mayors from country-specific sources: the Center for American Women and Politics data on the US Conference of Mayors (Holman, 2017), European Institute for Gender Equality (2019), Economic Commission for Latin America and the Caribbean (2019), and Statistics South Africa (2016). The US data includes mayors of cities with a population of more than 30,000 citizens. For Latin America and the Caribbean, the data refers to mayors, intendants, prefects, and municipal presidents. For the European Union, the data includes mayors and other council leaders. While mayors are the main focus, in cases in which the position of mayor is ceremonial, the leader of the council is counted instead of the mayor. For South Africa, the data includes full-time mayors of metropolitan, district, and local municipalities. The Latin America and the Caribbean region comprises: Argentina, Belize, Bolivia, Brazil, Chile, Colombia, Costa Rica, Dominica, Ecuador, El Salvador, Guatemala, Honduras, Jamaica, Mexico, Nicaragua, Panama, Paraguay, Peru, Puerto Rico, Republica Dominicana, Suriname, Trinidad and Tobago, and Uruguay. The European Union includes data from all 28 member countries.

indicates that across many regions in the developing and developed world throughout the past decade, women's increasing inclusion is positively correlated with growing levels of economic rights. These rights enable economic agency across the most fraught social transitions in their lives: marriage, childbirth, and retirement from paid work in old age. The relationship between female representation in local politics and breadth of support for negotiating economic rights in the domain of the family is particularly strong where quotas exist: in South Africa.[17] Figure 8.2 finds the same relationship for India. In contrast, the United States, with its aversion to "affirmative action" on women's behalf, stands out as the exceptional case without any relationship between contemporary levels of women's local political representation (which rise and fall in this period) and the scope of women's economic rights, which remain more limited than those of women in either South Africa or member states of the European Union throughout the last decade.[18] I interpret this pattern as evidence of the opportunity quotas present to catalyze change across countries in both the developed and the developing world.

8.2.2 Redrawing Boundaries: Land Tenure Reform

The neighboring East African states of Tanzania and Rwanda share precolonial institutions of communal land tenure where women enjoyed only limited, indirect access to land rights, which were primarily held by males. The subsequent divergence in the political trajectories of these two neighbors presents a relevant comparison of how political institutions may influence the scope, enforcement, and effectiveness of policies formalizing women's land tenure. Notably, both sets of reforms emphasize joint tenure by husbands and wives. As a result, these policies can be seen as a more moderate step toward women's independent landownership relative to India's reforms at the heart of this book. Investigating them allows us to observe the effectiveness of quotas at facilitating women's land rights when conflicts with men, as status quo beneficiaries, are relatively muted.

8.2.2.1 *Quotas' Impotence: Tanzanian Land Tenure Reform*
In Tanzania, the Arusha Declaration of 1967 heralded a new policy of African socialism, with nationalization of land and compulsory resettlement or "villagization" into "Ujamaa Villages." This was accompanied by land reallocation

---

[17] Since 1998 parties are required to seek to ensure that women constitute 50 percent of the party list, with even distribution (International Institute for Democracy and Electoral Assistance, 2019a).

[18] In the European Union, 28 percent of the member states have subnational quotas for women and 61 percent of the member states have voluntary party quotas, while 56 percent of the countries have subnational quotas for women and 40 percent have voluntary party quotas in Latin America and the Caribbean (International Institute for Democracy and Electoral Assistance, 2019a).

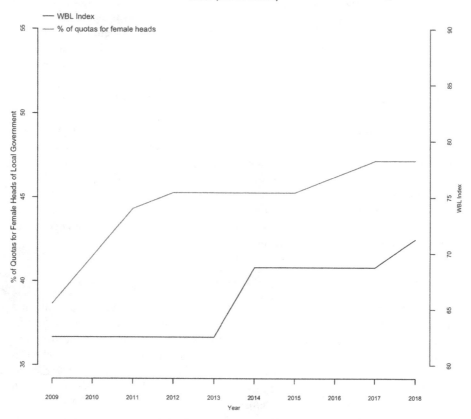

FIGURE 8.2. Women in Local Governance and Economic Rights in India

Note: I compile the "Women in Business and Law" (WBL) index from the World Bank (2019a). See Figure 8.1 for a detailed explanation of the index. "% of quotas for female heads of local government" refers to the average percentage of heads of local government reserved exclusively for women in a given year, across the 18 states included in REDS 2006/09 dataset. For sources, refer to Table 5.1.

to household heads, who were usually male.[19] "Villagization" occurred on a massive scale, initiating the resettlement of "millions of peasants and pastoralists," and leading to subsequent conflicts over land titles between the former and new occupants of these villages.

Land titling programs, which village councils began as of 1982, were unable to progress in the face of long-standing claims by prior occupants. The

---

[19] Land reallocation to each household head or "kaya" occurred following the Villages and Ujamaa Villages (Registration, Designation, Administration) Act, No. 21 of 1975. This had a particularly detrimental impact on women's access to land in matrilineal societies, where land titles became vested exclusively in men. See Tumaini (Silaa, 2001, 5), c.f. Benschop (2002, 100).

result was a revamped government attempt at large-scale land tenure reforms known as the National Land Policy (NLP) as of 1995. The NLP aimed to promote "equitable distribution of, and access to land by all citizens," while giving equal weight to customary and formal, statutory rights of occupancy (Benschop, 2002, 106). Yet there was a rub: the NLP acknowledged that "[u]nder customary law, women generally have inferior land rights to men, and their access to land is indirect and insecure" (NLP, Section 4.2.5, c.f. Benschop [2002, 107]).

Beginning in 1996, women's groups, mainly organized under the National Women's Forum or "Baraza la Wanawake la Taifa," collectively lobbied to influence the Land Act. The state's scant commitment to listening was clear when it suspended their activities as of February 1997. At this point, the Tanzanian Women Lawyers' Association campaigned to raise women's awareness of and voice in land rights legislation (ibid., 108). Simultaneously, the Tanzanian state moved forward politically using a series of quotas beginning with 15 percent of seats in national parliament reserved for women as of 1995. This expanded to 30 percent in 2005.[20] Women also gained representation locally, through quotas mandating their presence as no less than one-third of each district council and one quarter of each village council as of 2000 (Benschop, 2002, 106).

It would appear that women's mobilization across economic and political domains influenced policy. The Land Act of 1999 made a clear commitment to gender equity, affirming "[t]he right of every woman to acquire, hold, use, and deal with, land shall to the same extent and subject to the same restrictions be treated as a right of any man" (Section 3.2, c.f. Benschop 2002, 110). Yet, while action by women led to reform, the persistence of custom in the legal canon limits the state's commitment to enforcing gender equal land policy.

In addition, local politics suggest a tension between gender-egalitarian representation and traditional, inegalitarian authority. Women's representation in village councils is particularly significant given they are the body with primary responsibility for allocating and managing village property on behalf of residents. However, such allocation is contingent on prior approval by the village assembly, akin to India's *Gram Sabha,* in which all adult residents are entitled to participate (ibid., 105). In practice, men still dominate these assemblies. The result is considerable constraints on women's power.

Taken together, Tanzania's tenure reform appears to be ineffective, translating into low public awareness of women's rights with continued application of customary, male-dominated land entitlements, and ineffective advocacy for women's legal rights through the village councils meant to empower them (Benschop, 2002). The limits of quotas and their resultant capacity to bolster

[20] See the Gender Quotas Database by the International Institute for Democracy and Electoral Assistance (International IDEA) at www.idea.int/data-tools/data/gender-quotas. Details for Tanzania are available at www.idea.int/data-tools/data/gender-quotas/country-view/291/35 (accessed on December 31, 2019).

enforcement of land tenure reform are clear. Despite gender equal formal rights, just 16 percent of Tanzania's land area is held solely by women, whereas 44 percent of men are sole owners.[21]

8.2.2.2 *Quotas' Influence: Rwandan Land Tenure Reform*

Rwanda, however, illustrates the opportunity of quotas to effectively integrate women within the local state, including its legislative, administrative and bureaucratic institutions. Here, women's political representation has translated into enforcement of economic rights, as well as the effective development and documentation of such rights.

Let me begin with the caveat that Rwanda's political history is neither typical nor desirable to replicate. In 1994, extremist members of the Hutu ethnic majority conducted genocide against the Tutsi minority, killing 800,000 individuals in one hundred days. This amounted to nearly 10 percent of the country's population, with violence committed mainly by men against other men.[22] In addition, civic leaders were targeted for violence at particularly high rates. For example, Bennett (2014) notes that only 20 out of more than 780 (predominantly male) judges survived. Genocide led to a population that was 70 percent female. It also created a political power vacuum that women worked quickly to fill (ibid.).

Whereas women had held 10 to 15 percent of seats in Parliament prior to 1994, this changed, in part due to quotas for women at all levels of government mandated as of the early 2000s (Bennett, 2014). These reservations included cell, sector, and district-level positions in local elections.[23] As in a number of other sub-Saharan African countries with legacies of conflict, national women's movements were active agents of change, successfully advocating for their inclusion in the process of crafting a new constitution and accompanying legislation.[24]

Currently, 30 percent of seats at all levels of government are reserved for female candidates, to be elected exclusively by women.[25] Yet females compete in unreserved seats as well. In the first round of parliamentary elections with quotas (2003), women's representation rose from 23 to 49 percent. Subsequent elections have seen a consistent shift in the balance of seats in favor of women, to 56 percent as of 2008, 64 percent in 2013, and 61 percent in 2018.[26]

This political metamorphosis has caused a seismic advancement of women's rights. Female representatives are responsible for a staggering number of reforms to benefit women, including property rights expansion, prevention and punishment of gender-based violence, and the promotion of labor force integration (Bennett, 2014). In addition to advancing legislation, women have changed the face of the state's local bureaucracy. This is clearest in the case of

---

[21] Food and Agricultural Organization's Gender and Land Database 2010.   [22] Bennett (2014).
[23] Burnet (2008); Burnet (2011); Guariso, Ingelaere, and Verpoorten (2018, 1366).
[24] Bauer (2012); Tripp (2015); Guariso, Ingelaere, and Verpoorten (2018, 1362).
[25] Bennett (2014).   [26] UN Agencies in Rwanda (2013); Kagire (2018).

Land Tenure Regularization programs, where women make up 40 percent of para-surveyors and 70 percent of field managers.[27]

To be sure, Rwanda's adjudication of land rights has been greatly affected by genocide. Targeted killings on such a large scale created a geographic void, leading to significant abandonment of property that returning refugees subsequently re-occupied. The government's initial policy post-1994 was to request families share plots of land. This frequently led to confusion about demarcation.[28] In an attempt to formalize property rights and reduce the potential for ongoing conflict, the state began a land tenure regularization process in 2008 with the explicit goal of clarifying land titles. Between 2009 and 2013, para-surveyors and field managers registered 10.3 million parcels, with only 11,800 plots still disputed.[29]

Importantly, gender-equal distribution of land was one of the primary goals of the regularization program. However, as in Tanzania's tenure reform, official policy dictated land registration in the names of all family members, typically the husband, wife, and children, for maximum access to land rights.[30] While enforcement varied across Rwanda and Tanzania, the similar requirement for joint registration with spouses as coholders likely moderated distributive conflicts across genders in both cases, relative to reforms seeking sole ownership for women.

Overall, Rwanda's Land Tenure Regularization program was remarkably successful in granting *married* women official land titles. Today, the distribution of landownership by gender is close to parity: women own 54 percent of land either singly or jointly, while men own 55 percent of land in a similar fashion. In fact, women are slightly more likely to have sole ownership of land: out of the 19 percent of land not jointly held, women own 11 percent independently, men 6 percent.[31]

According to independent program assessments, political, administrative, and monitoring support by the state were crucial to the land tenure formalization's success, particularly for women's ability to benefit from formal land titles.[32] State assistance was particularly effective at the local bureaucratic and political levels, where quotas mandated women's representation.

Yet, while quotas have transformed the composition of elected bodies, there is still reason for skepticism about Rwanda's democracy. The country is ruled with a heavy hand by President Paul Kagame and rated by Freedom House as "not free," with weak assurances of voice and accountability for citizens according to the World Bank.[33] In the context of such authoritarianism, critics rightfully question the motivation of quotas as potentially problematic if they are used as means of precluding, rather than strengthening, alternative

[27] Gillingham and Buckle (2014, 11). [28] Jones-Casey, Dick, and Bizoza (2014).
[29] Gillingham and Buckle (2014, 12).
[30] Receipt of the resulting certificates carried with it a legal requirement that all landholders must consent to any subsequent land sale. For details, see ibid., 6.
[31] Ibid. [32] Ibid., 14. [33] Guariso, Ingelaere, and Verpoorten (2018, 1366).

sources of political power (ibid.). While this brief presentation cannot delve into the rationale behind Rwanda's political reforms, it does suggest that independent of motive, quotas for women can be dynamic tools for building self-reinforcing political, legislative, and administrative systems that expand gender-equal access to economic resources at every stage.

8.3 CONTRIBUTION TO SCHOLARSHIP

My findings contribute to our understanding of three important phenomena: how quotas change the relationship between citizens and their families, citizens and their communities, and citizens and the state, looked at through the prism of bargaining power; mechanisms that push the impact of reform toward increasing either social equality or resistance; and the necessity of studying how evolving social norms, political institutions, and economic rights can converge to achieve greater equality. I address each contribution in turn.

8.3.1 Making the State Relevant for Citizens: Are Quotas the Solution?

Throughout this book, my focus has been on theorizing and testing the ability of quotas to spur enforcement of reform that is central to women's economic, social, and political power both in India and globally: gender-equal rights to ancestral property. This represents a hard test of the benefits and efficacy of descriptive representation, given the value and scarcity of land. Property ownership has been the backbone of individual political inclusion, social status, and economic capacity across the world, as well as a catalyst for modern political institutions.[34] As a result, property rights are notoriously difficult to redistribute.[35] By increasing women's ability to demand and realize rights to ancestral land, quotas give women a platform for claiming resources and for furthering their political agency. This may mean articulating distinct preferences over the investment of valuable resources inside the household, in land markets or the village polity, and in larger public and private communities.

My theory on the impact of quotas as creating female heads of local government who spur enforcement complements a growing body of research that identifies quotas as encouraging a host of crucial political behaviors, including the quality of group deliberation,[36] the inclusion of socially stigmatized groups,[37] and accountability.[38] However, prior research considers the impact

[34] North and Thomas (1973); Braudel (1982); Tilly (1989); Acemoglu, Johnson, and Robinson (2002); Stasavage (2003); Greif (2006).
[35] Herring (1983); Binswanger, Deininger, and Gershon (1995); Besley and Burgess (2002); Albertus (2015).
[36] Mansbridge (1999a); Ban, Jha, and Rao (2012).
[37] Lawless (2004); Krook (2009); Jensenius and Verniers (2017).
[38] Goetz and Hassim (2003); Chattopadhyay and Duflo (2004b); Dahlerup and Freidenvall (2005).

of quotas almost exclusively within the political domain. My work allows us to rethink quotas as giving birth to a new form of agency that leverages descriptive political representation – that is, representation by people "like me" – to lead to substantive representation that extends beyond politics, expanding access to economic and social power for members of groups traditionally excluded from both domains.

A small, well-designed body of research identifies complementary mechanisms by which quotas expand notions of agency amongst members of represented groups by transforming their relationship with the state. These scholars use the case of India's quotas for another socially disadvantaged group: those formerly excluded from the caste system (untouchables or Dalits), now known as Scheduled Castes (SCs). Chauchard (2014) finds evidence that quotas help group members secure basic legal protection to participate in social and political spaces. Jensenius and Verniers (2017) identify the benefits of quotas for the small political elite who enter political office as the representatives of disadvantaged groups. Even if the "masses" do not benefit personally, the very presence of these representatives makes electoral politics more diverse. In addition, work by Beaman et al. (2009, 2012) finds that reservations for female heads of local government raise parental aspirations for daughters, which improve their subsequent educational attainment.

Distinctions between India's quotas for women versus for Scheduled Castes and Tribes (SCs and STs) present a fruitful avenue for further scholarship. There is significant evidence that quotas for women alter the distribution of economic resources.[39] However, SC and ST quotas have little or no impact on the receipt of public goods by group members.[40] One explanation as to why rests on the ability of quotas to spur mobilization by the groups they empower.

Women's high potential for mobilization as a voter group may present a greater opportunity and reward for politicians to cultivate as autonomous sources of electoral support. Indeed, it may be relatively cheaper to organize women than others whom political parties already directly target – such as male members of SCs and STs. The investigation of women's local electoral behavior in my theory chapter suggests that with experience as elected representatives, women not only pull ahead of men in terms of reelection probabilities (Table 2.1) but also in their ability to mobilize voters, male and female (Table 9.2 and Figure 2.1). With time, reservations may instigate broader coalitions in favor of improving women's welfare *as a component of broader strategies for improving collective welfare*. In contrast, given that the quantum of SC/ST quotas is fixed to the (small) proportion of the local population these groups constitute, this encourages SC/ST representatives to mobilize larger, multicaste coalitions less centered around advancing SC/ST interests.[41]

[39] Chattopadhyay and Duflo (2004b); Duflo and Topalova (2004); Beaman et al. (2012).
[40] Dunning and Nilekani (2013); Jensenius and Verniers (2017).
[41] Jensenius and Verniers (2017). In REDS 2006/9, the local percentage of the population identified as SC/ST ranges between roughly 10 to 29 percent of state populations.

If voter mobilization is a necessary prerequisite to state responsiveness, should we expect individuals *at the intersection of multiple forms of disadvantage* – gender and caste, class, sexuality, or race, for example – to use quotas differently, either to redistribute or concentrate access to political power? In particular, are elected representatives who face multiple forms of stigma more effective at reducing socio–economic inequality? Clots-Figueras (2011) presents evidence that state-level female legislators in seats reserved for members of SCs and STs are significantly more likely than other female legislators to promote laws that increase investments in health, education, and support for women. I return to what we can learn from studying intersectional identities in subsequent sections.

Finally, does the impact of quotas on gender-equal land inheritance enforcement travel across substantive domains and locations? Evidence supports this. In India, for example, Iyer et al. (2012) find confirmation that quotas improve women's ability to enforce sanctions against violence. Specifically, women are more likely to report crimes against them and to be more satisfied with police responsiveness to their reports where quotas mandate local female representation. The next section explores the relationship between representation and resistance beyond the prism of India's quotas for women.

8.3.2 Who's Afraid of Backlash? Is Reform Always Worthwhile?

There are many reasons to be cautious about "radical" reforms such as quotas. In Germany, Jochen Bittner (2019) argues against the option of quotas to achieve a gender balance in its national legislatures, asking if it is *"worth weakening another hard-fought accomplishment, the right to free electoral choice?"*[42]

This suggests the first of three ways in which quotas may cause backlash: simply due to their structure.

By mandating floors for representation of a certain group (whether women, racial minorities, or underrepresented castes or classes), quotas may be seen as invalidating elections as signals of popular preferences. If so, quotas may weaken trust in electoral representation *writ large*. In the United States, the past two decades have seen a surge of efforts using similar rhetoric to oppose quotas (affirmative action) in government contracting and higher education. Opponents suggest such measures are either unnecessary, having "outgrown their intended benefits to a small percentage of the U.S. population," or destructive of diversity given a "growing perception among whites that the deck has been stacked against them" (Hayden, 2010).

How convinced should we be by these concerns? Krook (2016, 271) categorizes such arguments as supporting "false universalism" given the explicit exclusion of women and minorities from core classical and modern theories of

[42] Bittner (2019).

politics. As feminist political theorists make clear, supposedly neutral concepts like "citizen" and "civic participation" have traditionally been bounded as male-only domains (Okin, 1979; Young et al., 1985; Pateman, 1988). For Okin,

it is impossible to "include women, formerly minor characters, as major ones within the political drama without challenging basic and age-old assumptions about the family, its traditional sex roles, and its relation to the wider world of political society."[43]

The silence of slaves as well as women in "classical" democracies such as Athens casts doubt upon common assumptions about democracy as an egalitarian institution.[44] Acknowledgment that political institutions were not built to be inclusive has a clear implication: universal representation likely requires institutional rewiring.

Indeed, experimental research by Clayton, O'Brien, and Piscopo (2019) in the United States finds that where decision-making bodies include significant female representation, both the processes and outcomes they reach are considered more legitimate than in groups dominated by men. Thus, the true challenge to democracy may be (white) male overrepresentation rather than attempts to expand minority inclusion (Murray, 2014; Besley et al. 2017).

Yet theoretical arguments about the justification, or lack thereof, for quotas miss a second, fundamental source of backlash: the "zero-sum" nature of mandating representation for excluded groups, which reduces seats for traditionally dominant groups (Baldez, 2006). This may explain why, according to Krook (2016, 269) "resistance – not compliance – appears to be the standard with regard to quota implementation." As a result, quotas often trigger "survival tactics" ranging from overt violence to more subtle efforts to diminish or sideline those empowered by quotas (Cockburn 1991; Mansbridge and Shames 2008; Gallagher and Parrott 2011; Krook 2016, 272).

In India, Bhalotra, Clots-Figueras, and Iyer (2017) find that greater representation of minority groups – including women and Muslims – affects the structure of political competition, reducing the field of minority candidates as potential competitors in future elections. This behavior, which can be construed as internalized backlash, appears to be most pronounced in states and political parties with entrenched gender bias. The reticence to compete may also be a direct result of the physical violence perpetrated against many women and members of other vulnerable groups in politics as a "demonstration of [male] power and superiority and to reinforce traditional structures challenged by women leaders" (Majumdar, 2014).

These outcomes are not inevitable. Yet, widespread willingness by Indian political parties to support male politicians with criminal records suggests a lack of concern. In India, 45 percent of female politicians have faced physical violence, kidnapping, killing, verbal abuse, and threats (Center for Social Research and UN Women, 2014). Female politicians from marginalized communities

43 Okin (1979, 286), c.f. Krook (2016, 271).   44 For example, see Beard (2017).

confront even higher levels of hostility (Majumdar, 2014). Therefore, it is not surprising that 60 percent of Indian women "do not enter politics due to fear of violence" (ibid.). Additionally, multiple forms of disadvantage magnify the obstacles. As Asha Kotwal, general secretary of the All India Dalit Women Rights Forum, explains, "Dalit women face greater barriers because they are seen to be rising above their caste. Where there is greater assertion, there is greater violence" (ibid.).

Backlash need not be physical to be effective. Gangadharan et al. (2016) use experimental games to identify the underlying challenges that female leaders face in rural Bihar, India. They find high levels of initial mistrust of female leadership. Specifically, men are much less likely than women to contribute to the public good when the leader in the experiment is a woman. This behavior, which they call *male backlash,* is much more likely to occur when quotas mandate a female elected head of the local government.

Those threatened by quotas attempt to reduce the legitimacy of individuals who come to power in a variety of ways. The most popular arguments frequently cast new entrants as "unfit" for one of two reasons. It is easiest to argue that they are not conforming to traditional roles (e.g., altruistic, motherly, "communal" women versus assertive, powerful men, as per Eagly and Karau, 2002; Okimoto and Brescoll, 2010). This explains the "double bind" women frequently bear to succeed in politics, which requires they demonstrate their capacity as mothers *and* as public representatives (Teele, Kalla, and Rosenbluth, 2018). However, even when women successfully perform stereotypical gender roles, they frequently face another critique: that they are simply proxies for husbands (Franceschet and Piscopo, 2008, 418; Krook, 2009).

Yet, existing studies on resistance to representation offer a few notes of optimism. First, descriptive representation may also *inhibit* backlash that would otherwise occur. For example, in the United States, Preuhs (2007) finds that greater descriptive representation of Latino minorities actually *mitigates* the tendency for backlash against growing minority populations – reduced per capita spending on public welfare – as the percentage minorities grows in a given constituency. Haider-Markel (2007) finds similar results from political representation by openly lesbian, gay, bisexual, and transgender (LGBT) individuals. While anti-LGBT legislation rises following descriptive representation – which may proxy for greater visibility of LGBT groups – backlash is outweighed by the positive advocacy of LGBT legislators.

A second cause for optimism comes from India. Gangadharan et al. (2016) find that male bias against women lessens with prolonged exposure to female elected leaders. They argue that quotas may help change entrenched social norms against minority groups with repeated exposure to them in positions of power. Indeed, Afridi, Iversen, and Sharan (2013) propose that quotas for women will be beneficial for communities only in the long term, once new leaders have adequate opportunities to learn optimal forms of governance through repeated experimentation (and failure).

What can we conclude about the benefits of quotas? Stepping beyond political quotas, the potential for economic quotas to expand women's access to labor market opportunities is clear. Labor force participation has positive implications for women's ability to delay marriage and childbearing[45] and for improving women's intrahousehold bargaining power.[46] However, similar to what we have learned about political quotas, a growing body of research suggests that whether (externally induced) employment opportunity leads to backlash or empowerment depends on women's levels of bargaining power within their households. In particular, women who initially possess low levels of bargaining power are generally found to be more vulnerable to domestic violence upon gaining economic opportunities.[47] Overall, these analyses suggest that paying attention to the bargaining power of individuals around the time they gain significant new resources – be they political, economic, or social – is a crucial factor in minimizing potential backlash to interventions meant to right power imbalances.

8.3.3 Bargaining Away Power?

Let's return to the classic *Exit, Voice, and Loyalty,* by Albert Hirschman. In it, Hirschman (1970, 41) argues that voice – as the prototypical political act – is meaningful only if an individual expects to be able to "marshal some influence or bargaining power." As a result, the use of voice is not a simple, binary decision about whether to speak or remain silent, but rather "an *art* constantly evolving in new directions" (ibid., 43).

If amassing and deploying bargaining power is an art rather than a fundamental, universal component of citizenship, we require far more theory development and policy analysis to learn how this art evolves in the service of citizen empowerment. "Of Rule and Revenue," by Margaret Levi (1988) gives us a crucial starting point. Here, she develops a sweeping theory about when state rulers should choose predatory versus productive systems of taxation, based on the relative bargaining power a ruler possesses. For Levi, bargaining power provides a *top-down constraint* to the type of revenue production system a ruler can impose on citizens. I look at the problem of governance from the opposite direction, *from the bottom up.*

My "gatekeeper theory" suggests important spaces where this art is honed and deployed. Specifically, female heads of elected government facilitate bargaining over political and economic rights *within households* as well as *between households and the state,* enabling often-silent younger, female members to effectively demand rights at moments when commitments about the distribution of multiple, core household assets are being made. For the daughters

---

45 Singh and Samara (1996); Jensen (2012).
46 Dharmalingam and Philip Morgan (1996); Rahman and Rao (2004); Anderson and Eswaran (2009); Majlesi (2012).
47 Tauchen, Witte, and Long (1991); Rao (1997); Eswaran and Malhotra (2011).

at the center of India's gender-equal property inheritance reforms, marriage negotiations are the most opportune time for asserting claims to their portion of the family's ancestral property. Yet, what are other examples of optimal spaces for bargaining? Who are the bargaining parties? When is the critical time to raise one's voice? It is to these questions that I now turn.

I consider the political economy of bargaining power at three levels. First, at the individual level: bargaining over individual, familial, or intrafamilial rights and resources. Second, at the societal level: bargaining by groups with their members, or across members of different, distinct social groups, here to set agendas about who is most deserving of rights and resources and how distribution should proceed. Third, at the state level: collective mobilization of individuals to negotiate changes within or across states.

8.3.3.1 *Wait, Do You Mean Me?*

Individual bargaining power flourishes at moments where structural fissures occur in social, economic, or political institutions present opportunities for individuals to effectively deploy power – regardless of their position in social, economic, and political hierarchies – by negotiating across various dimensions. To think about what this means, we will return to the domain of household formation.

We have already examined the importance of marriage negotiations, but structural breaches also occur around the time of a mother's first pregnancy, when the household decides what resources will be devoted to the care of the forthcoming child, at what times, by whom. As the feminist economist Nancy Folbre (2020, 98–101) explains,

"processes of human and social reproduction entail distinctive forms of work and significant intergenerational transfers that take place within families and communities as well as in firms and markets." Indeed, "a lower-bound estimate of the replacement cost of non-market work in the U.S. in 2010, including time devoted to the supervision of young children, amounts to about 44% of conventionally-measured Gross Domestic Product."[48]

Thus, not only is childbirth an important moment for determining distribution of consequential resources, it is also a time when conflict occurs over *how much* to invest in care, and *who* will bear these costs in *what way*: specializing entirely in care, or integrating care behavior into multidimensional life courses.[49] At this juncture, politics can shift the bargaining power of mothers – who typically bear the greatest weight for investments in the care of a new child – by increasing the

[48] Estimate according to Folbre and Suh, "Valuing Unpaid Child Care," c.f. Folbre (2020, 101).
[49] It is worth noting that many sociologists and demographers implicitly believe the later distribution is possible, arguing that "reproduction serves the entire body politic" but that the structure of decision making about who will occupy this role "is influenced by social institutions that shape transfers of income and labor time based on gender, age, and sexuality" (Folbre, 2020, 110). See Ryder (1973a, 77); Caldwell (1982).

incentives for contributions by other members of the family and the state, which can provide infrastructure that reduces the risks of childbirth and supports child care.

Indeed, Bhalotra and Clots-Figueras (2014) find that where political gate-keepers – here again, elected heads of local government in India – are present, they improve both the village-level health infrastructure and the provision of information about the importance of public and private services for newborn care. As a result, female leaders improve the likelihood that youth in the locales they represent will survive childhood. Child mortality drops by 2.1 percentage points (a 33 percent reduction) following a 10 percentage point increase in female representation. When a female leader is present for *the birth of the first child,* Bhalotra and Clots-Figueras (2014) find an even more dramatic decline of child mortality, suggesting that female political representation may have the most marked impact when present at the clearest structural break in familial formation – when a household shifts its primary investment from the care of adults to the care of children (Folbre, 2020, 119).

Evidence also exists as to the importance of employing individual bargaining power across economic domains: in particular, human capital development and subsequent labor force integration. Here, it is useful to think about how politics can affect bargaining power in adolescence – when families are making dynamic decisions about how much to invest in a given child's human capital (and future labor opportunities). Consider two cases: the positive example of India's quotas for female heads of local government and the negative case of Afghanistan under the Taliban.

Beaman et al. (2012) find that exposure to female gatekeepers raises parental aspirations for their children, in particular for daughters. This makes daughters potential contributors to long-term familial welfare rather than simply dependents, increasing their bargaining power. The greater a child's expected ability to contribute to – and be rewarded by – the labor market, the higher the long-term gains a parent is likely to anticipate from investment in the given child's skills. If aspirations for a daughter's successful integration into the labor force are low, parents might expect higher returns to investment in a son's human capital. This makes them more likely to regard investment in the daughter's education in a narrow, one-dimensional bargaining context: any resources they invest in her represent a net loss, that is, resources they can no longer invest in sons.

Now consider Afghanistan. Here, Noury and Speciale (2016) find that for individuals of school age, one additional year of exposure to the religious fundamentalism practiced by the *Taliban* government – which virtually eliminated much of women's bargaining power by prohibiting them from labor force participation and public life – led to a decline in the probability that women would complete basic education by 2 percentage points, with a 0.2 percentage point decline in the probability of employment outside the household (a decrease of 12 percent).

The challenge that regressive political regimes such as the Taliban pose for enabling effective bargaining by vulnerable citizens substantiate a broader discourse about the importance of bringing men (and more broadly, the majority of the world's states that rely on male political networks to select and support leaders) "on board" to achieve gender equity.[50]

Policy assessments are clear on the necessity of men's inclusion for gender equality, but rarely provide precise ways to initiate collaboration. In Connell's (2005, 1802) words: *"Men and boys are thus in significant ways gatekeepers for gender equality. Whether they are willing to open the gates for major reforms is an important strategic question."*

Connell's analysis reminds us that effective bargaining requires engagement by *all* parties – those seeking empowerment and those who benefit from the status quo distribution of power. This suggests we should expect political gatekeepers to influence individuals differently, depending on a person's capacity to deploy bargaining power.

8.3.3.2 Cooperation for Who? Group Dynamics.

Most of the investigation in this book has focused on the microlevel dynamics of bargaining, that is within households. But negotiation is just as dynamic at the group level. To explain, let me sketch out how an alternative to the state – the Communists who initiated Vietnam's revolution–effectively encouraged peasants to employ "broad choice bracketing," which led elites to redistribute property rights. Similar strategies worked in Costa Rica, but not in Guatemala and Colombia.

Popkin (1979) studies the willingness of Vietnam's rural peasants to rebel against an exploitative political order. This is relevant because the bargaining he considers is explicitly political. Here, the presence of a *alternative* to the state – the Communist Party – enabled local bargaining between peasants and the party, as well as between peasants and the state. In Popkin's view, the Communist Viet Minh convinced a critical mass of peasants to support revolution by framing it as part of a simultaneous, interconnected set of decisions about *both* individual political action and property rights. They did so by making land redistribution the immediate consequence of participation in revolution, such that both the Party and peasants benefited. *"After land was redistributed and rents reduced in Cochinchina, peasants commonly went out of their way to warn Viet Minh cadres that French soldiers or agents were in the area ..."*[51]

The Viet Minh relaxed Communist proscriptions against private property to shift bargaining over participation in a costly, violent revolution away from a narrow, one-dimensional space (to conduct violence or not) to a two-dimensional space where support now ensured increased economic security

---

[50] Cockburn (1991); Connell (2005).
[51] From Popkin (1979, 257), cited in Acemoglu and Robinson (2005, 126–7).

in the immediate future. Here, refusal to support violence also had a cost: blocking access to new property rights. The Viet Minh's ability to wield political authority – by amassing a monopoly over the use of force – was essential to making these multidimensional bargains credible. Their political presence in rural villages *at a time when peasants faced extreme subsistence threats* made multidimensional bargaining not only plausible but also made bargaining a matter of survival.

A second case concerns elites in former Spanish colonies. Nugent and Robinson (2010) track historical patterns of growth across pairs of ex-colonies where the economy is centered on coffee. These include high-growth Costa Rica and Colombia, versus low-growth El Salvador and Guatemala. Like the Viet Minh, elites gained the support of agriculturalists by linking political decisions (about elite support) to property rights in Costa Rica and Colombia. The result was that each nation passed a version of the United States 1862 Homestead Act, which enabled small-scale coffee producers to accrue rights in exchange for supporting the elites who achieved national power in these politically competitive environments.

In contrast, elites in El Salvador and Guatemala maintained decisive military control over national territory. Given this monopoly over violence, elites had no need to shift away from strategies of narrow choice bracketing (about which elite to support politically) to broad choice bracketing that would require distributing valuable rights to coffee-producing peasants. As a result, political bargains enhanced collective welfare in Costa Rica and Colombia but not in El Salvador or Guatemala.

8.3.3.3 Break It Up! Bargaining with the State.
Thus far, we have considered states as secondary actors. However, bargaining is also essential to states. One of the most explosive contemporary issues concerns the integration of refugees within Europe. Could "broad choice bracketing" empower European states to support more holistic responses to the ongoing global migration crisis? If so, could these countries improve the welfare of existing citizens and those seeking refuge?

In 2015, 1,015,078 individuals sought shelter in Europe. This represented a staggering increase from 60,000 in 2010, and even from 2014, which saw an influx of 280,000.[52] Many of them were fleeing combinations of conflict and poverty; in particular, in Syria, Afghanistan, and Iraq (Eurostat).[53] This crisis highlights the challenges of achieving integrative bargaining solutions where inequality is most extreme. Narrow choice bracketing clearly dominates in many European Union member country debates. Citizens from Germany to

---

[52] See Landau, Kihato, and Postel (2018).

[53] 2018 Eurostat database, "Asylum applications (non-EU) in the EU-28 Member States (2008–2018)." Available at https://ec.europa.eu/eurostat/statistics-explained/index.php/Asylum_statistics#Citizenship_of_first-time_applicants:_largest_shares_from_Syria.2C_Afghanistan_and_Iraq (accessed on December 31, 2019).

Greece are increasingly focused on the material and social "price" of migrant inclusion for relatively homogeneous European welfare states rather than its benefits.

State policies currently physically isolate asylum seekers, which, in turn narrows the popular imagination about the benefits to refugee integration. A growing body of research, including Scacco and Warren's (2018) analysis of Nigeria's Urban Youth Vocational Training (for Christian and Muslim men in riot-prone Kaduna), points to positive social contact as a tool for reducing discrimination between groups with antagonistic cultural identities. Yet, many state policies isolate those seeking asylum from the general host state population. Their places of residence are physically separate. Lengthy bureaucratic processes for economic integration prevent asylum seekers from making formal contributions to economic communities until long after their arrival. The frontiers of "welcome centers" are pushed as far away as possible, to locations with minimal resources to guarantee fair consideration of asylum claims.[54]

If state policy makers and citizens employed broad rather than narrow choice bracketing strategies, an interlinked, simultaneous consideration of options might help make the benefits of physical, economic, and cultural isolation pale in comparison to the rewards for integration, and its associated ability to encourage economic flourishing. As Germany's Joschka Fischer (2015) writes:

As European populations age and shrink, the continent urgently needs immigration. Yet many in Europe strongly oppose immigration, because it also means social change.... Europe's labor force must grow, which is just one reason why Europeans should stop treating migrants as a threat and start viewing them as an opportunity.[55]

The problem is not only a dearth of multidimensional decision making, but also the absence of a voice – due in large part to a lack of fundamental human rights – for those who bear the largest share of costs: displaced persons, "non-citizens" who either live in a country without the effective capacity to protect them, or who are asking for help on the doorstep of states that refuse to recognize their presence (Castles, 2011).[56] The magnitude of tragedy is amplified by a vicious circle: inequality in state-provided protection of citizens narrows incentives by more privileged states to integrate asylum seekers to the extent required to build consensus around welfare-enhancing strategies.

---

[54] Landau (2018).   [55] Accessed online, February 7, 2019.

[56] Of course, some of the worst offenders are outside Europe: Australia, whose policy of refugee "deterrence" forces asylum seekers into indefinite residence within immigration detention centers in the South Pacific, on the islands of Manus and Nauru. Conditions are abysmal, leading the Australian Medical Association to declare them in a state of "humanitarian emergency" (Isaacs, 2018). In addition, the US "Travel Ban" essentially prohibiting any arrivals by asylum seekers from majority Muslim countries, with associated cuts in the maximum allowable number of refugees from a multidecade mean of roughly 95,000–30,000 is responsible for dismantling the infrastructure required to care for all refugees (Cunningham, 2018).

The takeaway about bargaining power is that both the timing of political interventions and the manner in which they encourage or preclude multidimensional bargaining are critical for individuals, groups, and states attempting to design and implement global policy. Medical, demographic, and education research focuses on moments in the life cycle when individuals have the greatest leverage to renegotiate norms and behaviors, such as early childhood or adolescence (Adams, Salazar, and Lundgren, 2013; Bhalotra and Venkataramani, 2015). Yet, political scientists rarely consider how political institutions affect individual agency in social and economic domains at critical junctures.

To the extent that the existing literature accounts for bargaining power, it largely does so by considering how bargaining resolves the tension between elites and the citizens they are mandated to serve. Relevant examples of the power of citizen–elite bargaining include the expansion of the state's infrastructure for taxation to capture gains from trade in ancient Rome, medieval and Renaissance England and France, late-eighteenth-century Britain, and Australia post–World War II (Levi, 1988). In addition, we see parallels in land reform occurring in contemporary South Asia (Herring, 1983). Twentieth-century attempts at authoritarian state planning in Russia, Brazil, and Tanzania are also relevant (Scott, 1998), as is the expansion of social protection in the United States (Skocpol, 1992), and state-led economic growth in the "newly industrializing countries" of South Korea, Brazil, India (for Evans, 1995), and Nigeria (for Kohli, 2004), and in the "latecomers" to industrialization (Amsden, 2001). Bargaining power is also crucial to understanding how bureaucrats implement digital technology in contemporary India (Bussell, 2012a).

The larger implication of my findings is that political economy scholarship must engage more fully with the necessity of leveraging interconnected social, economic, and political institutions to increase the agency of vulnerable groups. This brings me to a third and final research agenda: advancing our knowledge about how shifts from inegalitarian to egalitarian social norms can be fomented.

8.3.4 Can Equality Travel?

I situate my work at the center of three contrasting theories. One set argues that political and social institutions are so intertwined that social change cannot be studied separately from revolutionary breaks in political regimes. Another set argues that inegalitarian social norms are so sticky that externally formulated, global policies are the only path to ensuring the dissemination of egalitarian social norms. Sitting between these two poles is a theory positing that internally-driven, progressive change is possible if levels of socioeconomic equality are not too high to preclude credible commitments by citizens to revolt. I will explain each theory, and situate my contribution within this third body of thought.

One set of political economy scholars considers social institutions so fundamentally bound up with institutions of political power that change cannot be independently identified in either. In the language of North et al. (2009, xii): change can only occur when a given society shifts from a hierarchical "natural state" with centralized political control to an egalitarian "open access order" where "entry into economic and political organizations is open to all citizens." A simultaneous shift in economics and politics is required to move institutions from hierarchical to egalitarian organization. Similarly, Platteau (2000b) argues that political institutions are intimately bound up with widespread support for social institutions that dictate trust. In these accounts, the shift from hierarchical to egalitarian political and social institutions is important but difficult to predict. For Platteau (2000b, 36): *"To admit that moral norms have a role to play in [political and] economic development is an embarrassing statement because nobody really knows how to make the right kind of norms emerge."*

There is merit to these theories, which identify the complexity of attempts to alter foundational norms around the distribution of power. However, they suggest little optimism for attempts to build and test theory about how the state can promote socio-economic equality.

A second school of thought has a clear answer. Finnemore and Sikkink (1998) develop a theory of norm cascades that identifies international norms such as human rights as originating with global leaders and institutions. These actors broadcast the symbolic and substantive importance of equality to global audiences. Once a small set of influential actors – norm entrepreneurs – convince a "critical mass of states" to adopt these norms, other states imitate them to gain prestige and material resources. The end result is that new norms – in particular for their study, norms about human rights – become "the standard of appropriateness" across all states, which leads to the passage and enforcement of domestic reform.[57] Theory on the diffusion of gender quotas relies on this core mechanism to pinpoint the Fourth World Conference on Women in Beijing, hosted by the United Nations in 1995, as the catalyst for women's political inclusion.[58]

Yet, even after passing social reform, significant variation in norms persists within countries. This variation as our point of departure suggests the need to study domestic political institutions as relevant for influencing individual behavior. A growing political economy literature does exactly this, arguing that political institutions can nudge behavior toward greater equality when existing levels of inequality are neither too high to preclude credible commitments by subordinate groups, nor too low to make investments in less costly, informal changes more attractive.

Pranab Bardhan (2005) argues that distributive conflicts are key constraints to institutional change. In particular, gross disparities between local elites and those with few social and economic resources create no incentives for elites to relinquish goods or power. Thus, high levels of socioeconomic inequality

<hr/>

[57] Finnemore and Sikkink (1998, 895).   [58] Tripp and Kang (2008); Krook (2009); Bush (2011).

may make the state an inhospitable source of reform. In these cases, the most powerful political individuals are likely to be drawn from elites locked in distributive conflicts that preclude collective action with "the weaker sections of society" in any domain. Yet, where state policies begin to redistribute economic power, this may open the door to building political coalitions committed to furthering socioeconomic equality.

Acemoglu and Robinson (2005) propose a formal theory of democratization, arguing that we should see an inverted U-shaped relationship between equality and one form of institutional change: democratization. They point to the de facto political power of nonelites as crucial. Where citizens pose a credible threat of revolution or significant social unrest that would damage the economic and social interests of the elites who control de jure political power, citizens possess adequate de facto power to successfully demand democratization. This occurs when inequality is neither too high nor too low.

I make similar predictions about the extent of resistance to female gatekeepers' enforcement of gender-equalizing land inheritance reforms across India. To further address how microlevel inequality is related to the enforcement of women's property rights within Indian states, consider Table 8.2. Here, I draw from multiple historical archives and contemporary databases to map gender- and caste-based variation in social, economic, and political inequality over time. I ground this in the comparisons of social development across Indian states conducted by Singh (2016). The state-level sample includes her primary cases: Kerala and Tamil Nadu (in southern India) and Rajashtan and Uttar Pradesh (in northern India). I also include the other three that legislated gender-equalizing inheritance reforms before the central government: AP and Karnataka (in the south) and Maharashtra (in the west), and add two more states to round out the geographic focus: Gujarat (in the west) and West Bengal (in the east). These states provide a rough map of India's vast and varied geography, including regions at the upper and lower ends of gender-egalitarian cultures (the south and east versus the north, respectively), material flourishing (the west and south versus the north and east, respectively), and political reform (where the western state of Maharashtra and the northern state of Rajasthan are particularly notable for movements to mobilize women around political quotas). The final two columns compare statistics for India as a whole to those for the world, as data permits.

Moderate levels of socioeconomic inequality do appear to predict women's ability to secure land inheritance. Politically, the states where women are most likely to inherit land are those with below-average rates of women's historical political representation.[59] These trends hold true for contemporary India. In the 2017 State Legislative Assembly elections, women represented only 3 percent of Members of Legislative Assemblies (MLAs) in Karnataka, and

---

[59] Karnataka elected zero female Members of Parliament in 1957, and Maharashtra only 2 percent (versus a national average of 5 percent).

7 percent in Maharashtra (versus 9 percent nationally). Economically, states where women are most likely to inherit enjoy moderate levels of landholding per capita.[60] While rural inequality in these states hovers around the national mean (0.24),[61] it is offset by above-average attempts to redistribute agricultural land.[62] Finally, considering women's marginal landholdings,[63] we see that those who are traditionally most socially vulnerable – members of SCs and STs – own percentages of land that are roughly equal to their representation in the broader population.[64] Overall, these state-level patterns of female land inheritance and inequality confirm the broader political economy literature's focus on moderate inequality as a precursor to change.

8.4 CODA

As we come to the end of our journey into the process of building equality in India, let us return to the question with which we began. Are electoral quotas a "fast track" to women's political empowerment or do they bear the hallmarks of early modern statecraft described by James Scott (1998, 3–6) as a direct path to "the great human tragedies of the twentieth century"? This concern is relevant because quotas are in fact a development project where powerful government planners seek to recast society using a "modern" template of scientific and technical progress that extols the virtues of equality.

Many thoughtful studies on the evolution and contemporary scope of quotas raise questions about whether laws promoting "historical leaps in women's representation" overnight can produce the lasting empowerment

---

[60] Individuals own about half an acre on average (0.57 acres in Karnataka; 0.51 in Maharashtra in 2000–01. These levels are above the national average (0.38 acres) but significantly below the large landholdings in sparsely populated Rajasthan (0.92 acres). Considering landholdings alongside the statewide national domestic product per capita (in 2011–12 Indian rupees), these states appear above average in terms of economic well-being: with the highest and fourth highest levels: 90,263 and 99,173, respectively, relative to a national average of 63,492.

[61] Inequality is slightly above average in Maharashtra (0.27).

[62] Specifically, Maharashtra distributed 77 percent of land declared "surplus" by 1996. Such action was higher than the national mean of 66 percent, but still lower than the maximum for the sample: 83 percent in Tamil Nadu.

[63] I focus on marginal landholding as this the one (size-based) category of landholding where women represent a significant proportion of owners.

[64] Twenty percent in Karnataka, equal to the 1981 SC/ST population proportion, and 14 percent in Maharashtra, slightly below the 1981 population proportion of 16 percent. In both states, SC/ST female landholdings are more representative than the national average (where SC/ST women were 24 percent of the 1981 population, but own only 21 percent of female marginal landholdings).

that took decades to establish in Denmark, Norway, and Sweden (Dahlerup and Freidenvall, 2005, 27). Recent work from the United States finds troubling evidence that women's presence in decision-making bodies increases the perceived legitimacy of policies restricting women's rights, particularly amongst men (Clayton, O'Brien, and Piscopo, 2019). If this is true more broadly, quotas that pull women into office in advance of social norms may serve to reinforce dominant hierarchies rather than enabling female agents of change.

But what if pessimism blinds us to the revolutionary power of a woman poised to act at the helm of a village, district, or state's elected government? My research in rural villages across India suggests that where electoral quotas reserve seats for women in meaningful positions, as heads of local government, these women can and do transform the state into an effective tool for enforcing economic rights. This influence is a double-edged sword, which increases economic resources and social value for some women, while others lose agency. Whether or not these ladders to greater levels of female political representation benefit women depends on when a given individual gains access to female representatives.

The challenge, this book suggests, is to acknowledge the influence that socially disadvantaged groups (here women) wield thanks to political quotas and the resistance that such "gender shocks" can inspire. Taking redistribution of power seriously leads to an important insight: local political institutions can productively engage with social norms to bring about progressive, egalitarian change at critical junctures where multiple paths are possible. However, this is hard and dangerous work.

In India, these moments are most clear around marriage, when women and their families determine the division of property inheritance, monetary dowry and future responsibilities for care of elder parents. Such points of opening may vary across geography, culture, and time, but they exist in every society. By identifying and paying close attention to these windows of opportunity, we foster mutually beneficial agreements within families in the service of incremental social progress.

The warning for lawmakers is that attempts to redistribute power to vulnerable groups can harm not only present but also future groups. This paradoxical result is likely when reformers ignore the simple fact that claiming valuable rights and resources requires substantial bargaining power. Absent such power, members of vulnerable groups are at a disadvantage in the zero-sum negotiations that typically occur around rights. Laws are most likely to promote equality when they empower beneficiaries to deploy the art of bargaining in the service of redistribution.

TABLE 8.2. *Variation in Gender Equality: Select Indian States and the World*

CATEGORIES	Southern India					North, West, and East India				All India	World
	AP	KA	KL	MH	TN	UP	RJ	GJ	WB		
SOCIAL											
Historical Status											
1931 Sex Ratio of First Born (Females per 1,000 Males)	882	967	862	808	882	–	–	699	730	–	–
1891–1931 Matrilineal Groups (% Population)	–	0.15	0.56	–	0.09	–	–	–	–	–	–
Inheritance and Related Norms											
Inherited Land (% Women)	0.02	0.09	0.05	0.09	0.02	0.03	0.05	0.04	0.05	0.05	0.05–0.20
2004–8 Dowry Paid in Cash (Rs.)	13,783	24,765	74,013	19,403	35,274	40,649	25,052	66,962	19,987	33,947	–
2004–5 Women's Age at Marriage	15.90	17.70	20.90	18.10	18.80	16.10	15.80	18.20	17.50	17.40	24.26
Literacy Rates											
2011 Female Literacy Rates	0.59	0.68	0.92	0.76	0.73	0.57	0.52	0.70	0.71	0.65	0.81
2011 Literacy Rates (Gender Gap)	0.79	0.83	0.96	0.86	0.85	0.74	0.66	0.81	0.86	0.80	0.91
Sex Ratio											
2001 0–6 Child Sex Ratio (Females per 1,000 Males)	961	946	960	913	942	916	909	883	960	927	952
2004–5 Elder Care; Expecting to Live with Sons (% Total)	0.86	0.83	0.75	0.86	0.71	0.93	0.95	0.83	0.71	0.85	–
Expecting to Live with Daughters (% Total)	0.16	0.14	0.36	0.05	0.13	0.09	0.01	0.09	0.13	0.09	–

POLITICAL											
1957 Elections											
Women MPs (% MPs)	0.07	0.00	0.00	0.02	0.03	0.00	0.02	0.08	0.05		—
1984 Elections											
Upper Caste MPs (% MPs)	0.07	0.11	0.05	0.68	0.05	—	0.32	0.31	0.59	0.31	—
Shudra MPs (% MPs)	0.10	0.61	0.40	0.04	0.56	—	0.32	0.34	—	0.29	—
SC/ST MPs (% MPs)	0.23	0.18	0.10	0.15	0.20	—	0.28	0.27	0.26	0.24[a]	—
1985 Administrative Officers											
Female Officers (% Total)	0.05	0.09	0.06	0.06	0.07	0.09	0.09	0.06	0.08		—
2014 Elections											
Female Voter Turnout (% Female Electors)	0.74	0.66	0.58	0.74	0.57	0.61	0.60	0.82	0.66		0.59
Voter Turnout (Gender Gap)	1	0.96	1	1	0.97	0.95	0.89	1	0.98		0.98
2017 Legislative Assembly											
Women MLAs (% MLAs)	0.11	0.03	0.06	0.09	0.1	0.14	0.09	0.14	0.09		0.22
ECONOMIC											
Women's Historical Status											
1987–8 Earnings (Gender Gap)	0.69	0.71	0.74	0.66	0.63	0.77	0.94	0.98	0.90	0.75	—
1993–4 Earnings (Gender Gap)	0.71	0.74	0.69	0.62	0.6	0.77	0.82	0.96	0.82	0.71	—
Women's Current Status											
2011 Female Labor Force Participation	0.36	0.32	0.18	0.31	0.32	0.17	0.35	0.23	0.18	0.26	0.39
2011 Labor Force Participation (Gender Gap)	0.56	0.38	0.42	0.49	0.50	0.49	0.49	0.34	0.31	0.37	0.67
2011–12											
Statewise NDP per Capita (Rs.)	69,000	90,263	97,912	99,173	92,984	32,002	57,192	87,481	63,492		719,538

(continued)

TABLE 8.2. (continued)

CATEGORIES	Southern India					North, West, and East India				All India	World
	AP	KA	KL	MH	TN	UP	RJ	GJ	WB		
SOCIOECONOMIC INEQUALITY											
Land Redistribution as of 1996											
Surplus Distributed (% Area)	0.71	0.42	0.47	0.77	0.83	0.69	0.75	0.58	0.76	0.66	–
SC/ST Beneficiaries (% Area)	0.60	0.64	0.47	0.47	0.39	0.68	0.42	0.84	0.57	0.50	–
[T]Gender, Caste, and Landholding											
2000–1 Female Marginal Land (% All Area)	0.05	0.02	0.11	0.02	0.06	0.02	0.00	0.01	0.01	0.02	–
2000–1 SC/ST Female Marginal Land (% Female Marginal Area)	0.17	0.20	0.07	0.14	0.12	0.00	0.33	0.17	0.36	0.21	–
1981 SC/ST Population (% Total)	0.21	0.20	0.11	0.16	0.19	0.21	0.29	0.21	0.28	0.24[b]	–
2000s Rural Inequality											
2000–1 Landholdings per Capita (Acres)	0.47	0.57	0.11	0.51	0.27	0.27	0.92	0.47	0.16	0.38	0.56
2004–5 Rural Gini Coefficient	0.24	0.23	0.29	0.27	0.26	0.23	0.20	0.25	0.24	0.24	0.42

Note: The following state abbreviations are used: Andhra Pradesh (AP), Karnataka (KA), Kerala (KL), Maharashtra (MH), Tamil Nadu (TN), Uttar Pradesh (UP), Rajasthan (RJ), Gujarat (GJ), West Bengal (WB). For "Historical Status – 1931 Sex Ratio of First Born" (AP) and (TN) refer to Madras, (KA) refers to Mysore, (KL) refers to Travancore, (MH) refers to Bombay, (GJ) refers to Baroda, (WB) refers to Bengal. For "Historical Status – 1891–1931 Matrilineal Groups" (KA) refers to Mysore and Coorg in 1931, (KL) refers to Travancore in 1891, (TN) refers to Madras in 1931. For "1957 Elections – Women MPs", (KA) refers to Mysore state, (MH) and (GJ) refer to Bombay state, and (TN) refers to Madras State.

[a] Figures show average across states reported in Frankel and Rao (1989).

[b] Excludes Assam, Jammu, and Kashmir.

Note: Explanation and Sources for Table 8.2

1. "Gender Gap" values are calculated as a ratio of female values over male values, where 1 is perfect equality and 0 is perfect inequality (World Economic Forum, 2018).
2. SC refers to Scheduled Caste and ST refers to Scheduled Tribes.
3. Within "Historical Status" "Sex Ratio of First Born" (females first born per 1,000 males first born) and the population for "Matrilineal Groups" are compiled from Stuart 1893 and Hutton 1933.
4. "Inherited Land" refers to the percentage of Hindu women born post-1956 and pre-nationwide land inheritance reform, from landholding families who inherited any land; data pertaining to India and Indian states is compiled from the Rural Economic and Demographic Survey, 2006–09 round, while "World Value" refers to women's landownership, retrieved from the Council on Foreign Relations Stone (2018). "Dowry Paid in Cash" is given for women whose marriage year is 2004 or later, data is compiled from the Rural Economic and Demographic Survey, 2006–09 round. For "Women's Age at Marriage," data pertaining to India and Indian states is accessed from the India Human Development Survey, 2004–05 (Desai et al., 2010), while "World Value" is calculated as the average of women's age at first marriage for 124 countries, for the year 2002 (Encyclopedia of the Nations, 2019).
5. "Female Literacy Rates" for India and Indian States were accessed from the Population Census of India 2011, while "World Value" refers to figure accessed from the UNESCO Institute for Statistics (2019a), for the year 2011. "Literacy Rates (Gender Gap)" is calculated as a ratio of female literacy rate over male literacy rate.
6. "0–6 Child Sex Ratio" is compiled from the 2001 Population Census of India, while "World Value" refers to sex ratio at birth (Central Intelligence Agency, 2001).
7. Figures for "2004–05 Elder Care" are compiled from India Human Development Survey, 2004–05 (Desai et al., 2010).
8. "1957 Elections" refer to the 1957 Lok Sabha Elections; "1957 Elections – Women MPs" is compiled from Singer (2007, 74).
9. "1984 Elections" refer to the 1984 General Elections of the Lok Sabha, where not otherwise noted. Figures for the Caste Composition of States for the 1984 General Elections of the Lok Sabha are compiled from Frankel and Rao (1989).
10. Figures on the "1985 Administrative Officers – Female Officers" refers to the distribution of female officers of the Indian Administrative Service, compiled from Frankel and Rao (1989).
11. "2014 Elections – Female Voter Turnout" is compiled from the Election Commission (2014). "2014 Elections – Voter Turnout (Gender Gap)" refers to the ratio of female voter turnout over male voter turnout in 2014, where 1 is perfect equality and 0 is perfect inequality.
12. "2017 Legislative Assembly – Women MLAs" refers to the distribution of female MLAs in 2017, compiled from *The Wire* (Jamil and Anmolam, 2017).

13. Within "Women's Historical Status," "Earnings (Gender Gap)" is calculated as the ratio between Female Average Earnings (Rs./Day) over Male Average Earnings (Rs./Day) in rural households, where 1 is perfect equality and 0 is perfect inequality. Data is compiled from the Rural Development Statistics 2002–03 (National Institute of Rural Development, 2019).

14. Within "Women's Current Status" "Female Labor Force Participation" for India is compiled from the National Sample Survey Office of the Ministry of Statistics and Programme Implementation of India 2017, while "World Values" for the same year are compiled using ILO data (2011), retrieved from the World Bank 2019a. "Labor Force Participation (Gender Gap)" – refers to the ratio between Female and Male Labor Force Participation in 2011, where 1 is perfect equality and 0 is perfect inequality.

15. For "Statewise NDP per Capita," NDP refers to Net Domestic Product. Figures were accessed from the Government of Punjab, Economic and Statistical Organization (2019), "World Figure" refers to GDP per capita, accessed from the World Bank (2018), using current US$ data and converted to INR using the 52-week average of the INR-USD exchange rate, as found on Bloomberg on January 8, 2019.

16. "1996 Land Redistribution" refers to the Implementation of Land Ceiling Laws (as of 1996), compiled from Mohanty (2001). "Surplus Distributed" refers to percentage of area distributed to area declared surplus possession. "SC/ST Beneficiaries" refers to the beneficiaries of said distribution.

17. Within "Gender, Caste, and Landholding," "Female Marginal Land," and "SC/ST Female Marginal Land" refer to landholdings held by members of the respective group in 2000–01, compiled from the Agricultural Census of 2000–01 Government of India (2019). Landholdings refer to "Operational Landholding," which "constitutes of all land that was used wholly or partly for agricultural production and was operated (directed/managed) by one household member alone or with assistance of others, without regard to title, size or location." "Marginal" refers to landholdings of 1 hectare or less (Ministry of Statistics & Programme Implementation [2013]). Figures relating to the "1981 SC/ST Population" figures are compiled from Mohanty (2001).

18. The "2004–05 Rural Gini Coefficient" figures are compiled from the Planning Commission (2010), accessed from Goel and Birla (2013), while "World Value" refers to global Gini coefficient of late 2000s, including Urban and Rural, accessed from Seguino et al. (2013). The Gini coefficient "measures the extent to which the distribution of income among individuals or households within a country deviates from a perfectly equal distribution. A value of 0 represents perfect equality and a value of 1 represents perfect inequality" (ibid.).

19. "Landholdings," as referenced within "Socioeconomic Inequality" for "Landholdings per Capita," refers to Operational Landholding, which "constitutes of all land that was used wholly or partly for agricultural production and was operated (directed/managed) by one household member alone or with assistance of others, without regard to title, size or location" (Ministry of Statistics & Programme Implementation 2013, from Government of India 2019).

9

Data Appendix

9.1 CHAPTER 2: DATA APPENDIX

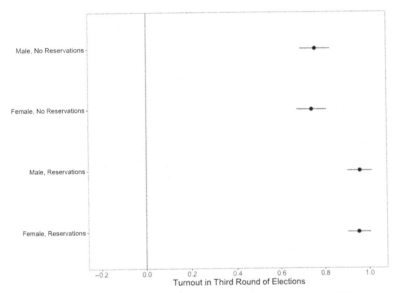

FIGURE 9.1. Differential Impact of Two Consecutive Reservations for Women on Voter Turnout, Third *Panchayat* Elections, Predicted Values

Source: NCAER Rural Economic and Demographic Survey, 2006/9. The sample includes all individuals for whom there are records of voting in *Gram Panchayat* elections within constituencies for which there is information about reservations. Each point on the graph represents the predicted values of turnout for individuals belonging to the given group. "Reservation" refers to whether the *Pradhan* seat was reserved for a female candidate in the second and third rounds of elections. Predictions are based on OLS regression analysis that includes fixed effects for the year of elections (table A.9.2, Panel B, Column 2). Lines represent 95 percent confidence intervals

TABLE 9.1. *Differential Impact of Reservations on Women's Turnout in* Panchayat *Elections*

	(1) All b/se	(2) All b/se	(3) All b/se	(4) All-NR-Late b/se
Panel A: First Election				
Female	−0.03*	−0.03*	−0.01[+]	−0.01
	(0.01)	(0.01)	(0.01)	(0.01)
Reservation	0.05	0.03	−0.01	−0.01
	(0.04)	(0.04)	(0.03)	(0.03)
Female * Reservation	0.03[+]	0.03[+]	0.02	0.02
	(0.02)	(0.02)	(0.01)	(0.02)
State FE	No	No	Yes	Yes
Election Year FE	No	Yes	Yes	Yes
Adj. R-sq	0.00	0.03	0.20	0.07
N	17,069	17,069	17,069	13,768
Panel B: Second Election				
Female	−0.02**	−0.02**	−0.01*	−0.01
	(0.01)	(0.01)	(0.01)	(0.01)
Reservation	−0.03	−0.04	−0.06	−0.10*
	(0.06)	(0.05)	(0.04)	(0.05)
Female * Reservation	−0.03	−0.03	0.00	0.00
	(0.03)	(0.03)	(0.01)	(0.01)
State FE	No	No	Yes	Yes
Election Year FE	No	Yes	Yes	Yes
Adj. R-sq	0.00	0.03	0.26	0.15
N	19,285	19,285	19,285	13,996
Panel C: Third Election				
Female	−0.03*	−0.03*	−0.01**	−0.02***
	(0.01)	(0.01)	(0.00)	(0.01)
Reservation	0.04	0.03	0.01	0.02
	(0.04)	(0.04)	(0.03)	(0.03)
Female * Reservation	0.01	0.01	−0.00	0.01
	(0.02)	(0.02)	(0.01)	(0.01)
State FE	No	No	Yes	Yes
Election Year FE	No	Yes	Yes	Yes
Adj. R-sq	0.00	0.03	0.44	0.30
N	19,867	19,867	19,867	14,336

[+] $p < 0.10$, * $p < 0.05$, ** $p < 0.01$, *** $p < 0.001$

Note: Robust standard errors, clustered at the village level, are in parentheses. The sample includes all individuals for whom there are records of voting in constituencies with information on reservations in the dataset. The dependent variable is a binary indicator whether an individual voted in the first, second, or third round of elections, as specified in the Panel titles. "Reservation" refers to whether the *pradhan* seat was reserved for a female candidate in the election period specified in the Panel title. Column 4 excludes states that do not assign reservations for female *pradhans* randomly (Andhra Pradesh, Himachal Pradesh, Kerala, Tamil Nadu) as well as the two states to implement women's reservations over 10 years after constitutional amendments: Bihar (2006) and Jharkhand (2010).

TABLE 9.2. *Differential Impact of Consecutive Reservations on Women's Turnout in* Panchayat *Elections*

	(1) All b/se	(2) All b/se	(3) All b/se	(4) All-NR-Late b/se
Panel A: Two Consecutive Reservations in Second Round of Elections				
Female	−0.02**	−0.02**	−0.02**	−0.02+
	(0.01)	(0.01)	(0.01)	(0.01)
Reservation	0.16***	0.17**	0.04+	0.04+
	(0.03)	(0.05)	(0.02)	(0.02)
Female * Reservation	0.03+	0.03+	0.03	0.03
	(0.02)	(0.02)	(0.02)	(0.02)
State FE	No	No	Yes	Yes
Election Year FE	No	Yes	Yes	Yes
Adj. R-sq	0.01	0.03	0.24	0.11
N	11,516	11,516	11,516	7,660
Panel B: Two Consecutive Reservations in Third Round of Elections				
Female	−0.02*	−0.02*	−0.01*	−0.03***
	(0.01)	(0.01)	(0.01)	(0.01)
Reservation	0.20***	0.20***	0.04	0.08
	(0.04)	(0.05)	(0.04)	(0.05)
Female * Reservation	0.01	0.01	0.01	0.01
	(0.01)	(0.01)	(0.01)	(0.02)
State FE	No	No	Yes	Yes
Election Year FE	No	Yes	Yes	Yes
Adj. R-sq	0.02	0.04	0.46	0.33
N	10,535	10,535	10,535	6,490

+ $p < 0.10$, * $p < 0.05$, ** $p < 0.01$, *** $p < 0.001$

Note: Robust standard errors, clustered at the village level, are in parentheses. The sample includes all individuals for whom there are records of voting in constituencies with information on reservations in the dataset. The dependent variable is a binary indicator whether an individual voted in the second or third round of elections, as specified in the Panel titles. In Panel A, "Reservation" takes a value of 1 if the *pradhan* seat was reserved for a female candidate in the first and second rounds of elections and takes a value of 0 if it was not reserved in either of the two elections. In Panel B, "Reservation" takes a value of 1 if the *pradhan* seat was reserved for a female candidate in the second and third rounds of elections and takes a value of 0 if it was not reserved in either of the two elections. Column 4 excludes states that do not assign reservations for female *pradhans* randomly (Andhra Pradesh, Himachal Pradesh, Kerala, Tamil Nadu) as well as the two states to implement women's reservations over 10 years after constitutional amendments: Bihar (2006) and Jharkhand (2010).

9.2 CHAPTER 5: DATA APPENDIX

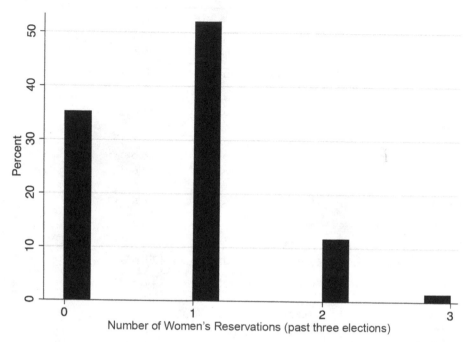

FIGURE 9.2. Village-level Distribution of Reservations for Female *Pradhans*
Source: NCAER Rural Economic and Demographic Survey, 2006/8

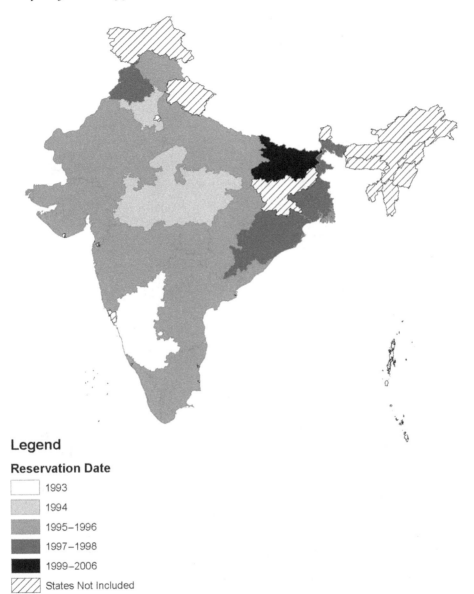

Legend

Reservation Date

- ☐ 1993
- ☐ 1994
- ☐ 1995–1996
- ■ 1997–1998
- ■ 1999–2006
- ▨ States Not Included

FIGURE 9.3. Indian States by Implementation Date of Women's Reservations

Note: Figure is based on villages included in NCAER's Rural Economic and Demographic Survey, 2006/8.

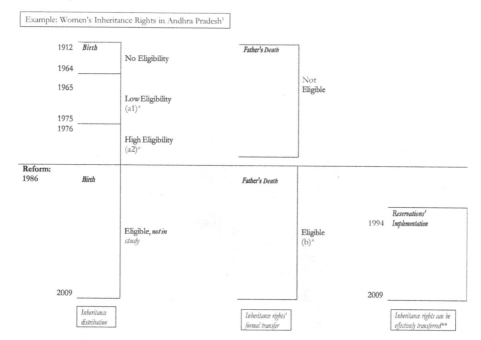

Example: Women's Inheritance Rights in Andhra Pradesh[1]

*A woman receives gender equal inheritance rights if she is eligible under both conditions (a) and (b).
** A woman is able to effectively transfer formal land inheritance rights where reservations for female heads of local government (*pradhans*) have been in place before/at the time of the patriarch's death.
[1] States amended the HSA in varied years, beginning with Kerala in 1976, followed by Andhra Pradesh in 1986, Tamil Nadu in 1989, and Maharashtra and Karnataka in 1994. As of 2005, a national amendment applied reform to all states, making all Indian citizens subject to Hindu Law (Hindus, Buddhists, Jains, and Sikhs) with fathers who die post-2005 without wills eligible for gender equal inheritance rights.

FIGURE 9.4. Coding Strategy: Treatment by Women's Reservations and Eligibility for Gender-Equal Inheritance Rights

Note to Figure A.9.4: Application of Hindu Succession Amendment Act

Inheritance or "succession" is an item that forms a part of the "Concurrent List" (i.e. List-III [Seventh Schedule]) of the Indian constitution, thereby granting both states and the central government the right to legislate on it. In addition, inheritance is subject to "personal law," dictated by the faith of each citizen. Here, I focus on Hindu personal law, which in fact applies to Buddhists, Jains, Sikhs, and Parsees as well as Hindus.

One of Independent India's first legislative acts was to pass the Hindu Succession Act of 1956 (hereafter HSA). This reform provided unbalanced inheritance rights to daughters as compared with sons. Each daughter whose father died after reform's passage received a notional share of her father's land, equal to a portion of the share that a son inherits when his Hindu father dies intestate. Sons became members of the *coparcenary* upon birth and received their own independent share of ancestral property. At this time, the

Note to Figure A.9.4, (Continued)

coparcenary included three generations of *all-male* descendants, each of whom received a direct right upon birth to an independent share of the joint family property. Upon the death of his father, a son received his (indirect) share of the father's property alongside his own independent (or direct) share. Additionally, sons could demand partition of the joint family property while daughters could not. In contrast, a daughter's share was generally small enough to be purely symbolic, as it was derived exclusively from her *father's* share in the joint family property, as separate from each other Hindu male coparcener's independent share. Unlike sons, daughters never received an independent (or direct) share of the joint family property *upon birth*, as did their brothers, or at any point later in life. Roy (2015) notes that a daughter's "notional" portion of her father's share in the joint family property was determined on a per capita basis, calculated according to the hypothetical partitioning of a given Hindu Joint Family property, as if partition had taken place just before paternal death.

To provide a more concrete example, Chowdhry (2008) explains the relative gender imbalance of inheritance shares in a minimal family arrangement, which is the most generous to daughters. She considers a family comprised of three members: a father, a son, and a daughter. Following the father's death post-HSA, the son inherits a three-fourth share – including one-half by "virtue of right by birth" that is, as a member of the coparcenary and "one-fourth by succession under the Act – while the daughter gets only one-fourth" (ibid., xvii). For daughters, inheritance granted them circumscribed access to a *limited estate,* which meant that while they could enjoy profits from the family property during their lives, they were not allowed to alienate (sell) their share, unlike brothers.

Following state-level amendments of the HSA, eligible daughters gained a share of her joint family property, which was exactly equivalent to that of sons in the same family. Different states amended the HSA in different years. Andhra Pradesh, Tamil Nadu, Karnataka, Kerala, and Maharashtra each enacted inheritance reform between the years of 1976 and 1994 (i.e. 1976, 1986, 1989, 1994, and 1994, respectively). Thereafter, in 2005, the national government enacted legislation that would be applicable in all Indian states. The text of reform is nearly identical across states. The major exception is Kerala, which abolished the Hindu Joint Family as an entity rather than amending the HSA, but still shares the Hindu Succession Amendment Act's (HSAA's) goal of establishing gender-equal inheritance rights. The primary change legislated by the HSAA was to deem daughters members of the *coparcenary*, each of whom are each entitled to an independent share in the Hindu Joint Family property upon birth. The HSAA also made it possible for daughters to alienate their share, demand partition of Hindu Joint Family property, and become the *karta* (manager) of the joint family property.

Legend

Proportion of Individuals in Reserved Villages

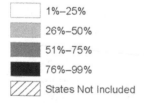

- 1%–25%
- 26%–50%
- 51%–75%
- 76%–99%
- States Not Included

FIGURE 9.5. Indian States by Proportion of Individuals in Ever Reserved Villages

Source: Figure is based on villages included in NCAER's Rural Economic and Demographic Survey, 2006/8

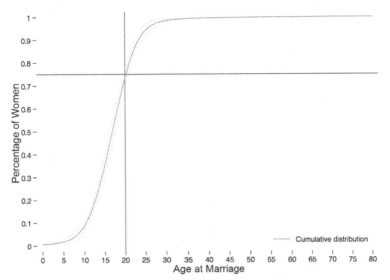

FIGURE 9.6. Cumulative Distribution of Marriage Age for Women

Source: NCAER Rural Economic and Demographic Survey, 2006/8. The sample includes all women with marriage and birth years recorded in REDS. The x-axis represents marriage age. The y-axis represents the cumulative probability of a woman marrying at that age. Each point on the graph represents the cumulative probability of marriage at a certain age

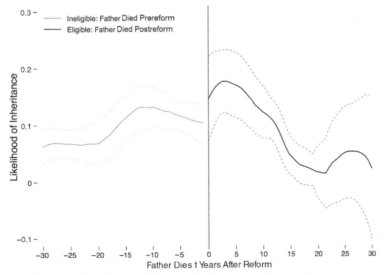

FIGURE 9.7. Impact of Reform on Women's Inheritance: Raw Data

Source: Data from NCAER REDS, 2006/9. The sample includes women born into landed, Hindu families after 1956 HSA, but before state-specific HSAA. The x-axis represents when an individual's father passed away relative to the introduction of reform in the relevant state. The y-axis represents the probability of inheritance. Each point on the graph represents the average probability of inheritance for individuals whose fathers passed away *t* years after reform's legislation in their state

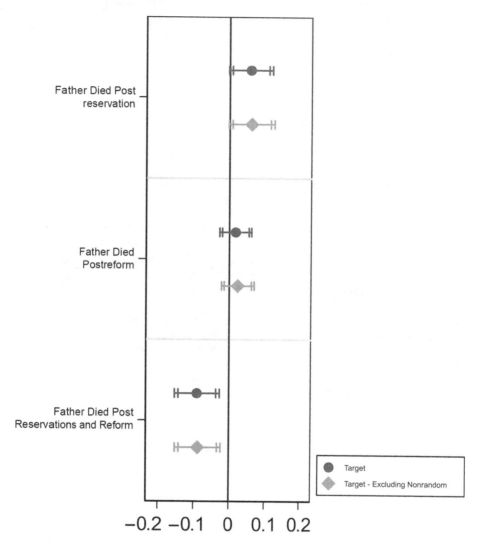

FIGURE 9.8. Impact of Reform and Reservations on Women's Inheritance: Coefficient Sizes

Source: Data from NCAER REDS 2006/9. Analysis from Table 5.5, Columns 2–3

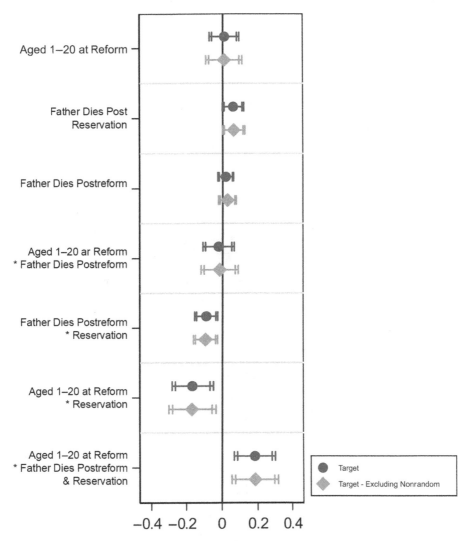

FIGURE 9.9. Impact of Reform, Reservations, and Marriage Markets on Women's Inheritance: Coefficient Sizes

Sources: Data from NCAER REDS, 2006/9, analysis from Table 5.5, Columns 6–7

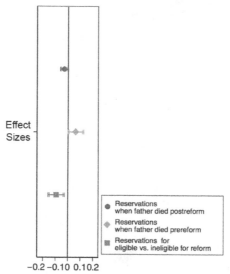

a) Women entering marriage markets at reform.

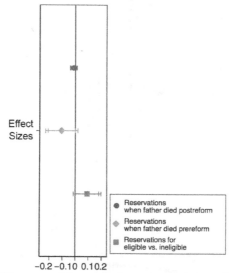

b) Women exiting marriage markets at reform.

FIGURE 9.10. Comparison of Net Effects for Table 5.5: Reservations' Impact on Daughters' Inheritance in Presence vs. Absence of Reservations

Source: NCAER Rural Economic and Demographic Survey, 2006/8. The sample includes women born into landed, Hindu families after 1956 HSA, but before state-specific HSAA. It excludes women born in states that do not assign reservations randomly (Andhra Pradesh, Himachal Pradesh, Kerala, and Tamil Nadu). For Figure A.9.10a, the net effect of reform prereservations is calculated using the following formula: $\delta' + \theta''$, the net effect of reform postreservations is calculated by $\delta' + \delta''' + \theta'' + \delta''''$, their difference is given by $\delta''' + \delta''''$ from Equation 5.2. For Figure A.9.10b, the net effect of reform prereservations is given by δ', the net effect of reform postreservations is $\delta' + \delta'''$

Note: Coding Procedure for Table 5.2: Women's Reservations

To compile this table, I consulted each state's *Panchayati Raj* Act, *Panchayat* Election Rules, Department of Rural Development and *Panchayat Raj*, according to document availability. I also utilize invaluable secondary analysis by Mishra (2003), Chattopadhyay and Duflo (2004), Paul (2006), Nilekani (2010), Ghosh et al. (2011), and Shankar (2016). Three facets of the data presented in this table are worth noting.

First, variation in the timing of State Panchayat Act's passage, from 1993 to 2001, and the subsequent timing of each state's first *Panchayat* elections, which start in 1994 and end in 2010. While most states implemented initial elections and reservations within two years of constitutional amendments' passage, two states took more than five years to implement the amendments. In Bihar, the 14-year gap between the Panchayat Act's passage in 1993 and elections in 2006 is due to legal challenges. For Jharkhand, state reorganization explains the nine-year gap between the Panchayat Act's ratification in 2001 and the first round of elections in 2010.

Second, states had discretion over how to implement reservations' rotation. Nearly half of states with available documentation (6 of 14) randomly select female *pradhans* through draw of lots or in alphabetic (*panchayat*) or numeric (legislative assemblies' arbitrary numeric code) order. Another quarter (4) utilize as-if random methods to assign reservations, mainly based on population size to determine reservation status. Thus, most states select *pradhan*'s reservation status using a random or as-if random mechanism. The remaining quarter of states use a potentially non-random selection mechanism: the proportion of women in the population. If the proportion of women in a village's population is an indicator of preexisting norms about women's value, this selection criteria could bias the sample of villages receiving reservations earlier to the subset with norms that particularly value women. This might be true if villages with norms promoting women are less likely to contain households that limit female births using the illegal but widespread practice of sex selection. This suggests two methods of identifying appropriate samples for analysis: first, excluding states with nonrandom selection of reservation status, and second, excluding both states with nonrandom selection mechanisms and late-implementing states. Both methods lead to highly comparable "control" villages, where women's reservations have yet to be implemented, and "treatment" villages where women's reservations have already been implemented.

Third and finally, rotation of women's reservations mainly occurs every five-year electoral cycle. Three exceptions exist: the Indian states of Bihar, Punjab, and Tamil Nadu. Two of these exceptions – Bihar and Tamil Nadu – are already excluded from tests that study states that are timely-implementers using as-if random selection mechanisms only. As a result, variation in reservations' rotation period is unlikely to introduce bias into analysis. However, the impact of reservations' varied rotation mechanisms is a worthy topic for future research.

TABLE 9.3. *Descriptive Statistics: Villages without vs. with Reservations*

	(1) All Villages Mean	(2) With Reservations Mean	(3) Without Reservations Mean	(4) Difference of Means Difference (t-score)
District population, 1991 census	280,805.24	283,301.58	285,668.90	2,367.32 (0.08)
% women in the subdistrict (*tehsil*) population, 1991 census	0.51	0.53	0.48	−0.05 (−1.99)
Village population: first *panchayat* period	4,870.86	4,700.90	5,275.92	575.01 (0.62)
Number of *panchayat* members: first *panchayat*	12.15	12.31	11.80	−0.51 (−0.80)
% SC *panchayat* members: first *panchayat* period	0.21	0.22	0.19	−0.04 (−1.44)
% ST *panchayat* members: first *panchayat* period	0.10	0.10	0.10	−0.01 (−0.17)
% OBC *panchayat* members: first *panchayat* period	0.37	0.39	0.31	−0.08 (−1.63)
% Hindu in village population currently	0.87	0.87	0.87	−0.01 (−0.17)
% Muslims in village population currently	0.07	0.06	0.08	0.01 (0.62)
% SCs in village population currently	0.05	0.05	0.04	−0.01 (−1.02)
% STs in village population currently	0.08	0.06	0.11	0.04 (1.42)
% OBCs in village population currently	0.09	0.08	0.13	0.05 (1.82)
% own < 2 acres of land in village population currently	0.26	0.27	0.26	−0.01 (−0.44)
% own land in village population currently	0.47	0.48	0.45	−0.04 (−1.11)
Average price: unirrigated land currently (Rs.)	103,740.33	113,642.86	90,859.38	−22,783.48 (−1.03)
Average price: residential land currently (Rs.)	417,181.82	432,931.30	406,238.10	−26,693.20 (−0.36)
% villages experienced drought, 1999	0.19	0.17	0.23	0.06 (1.06)
% villages experienced flood, 1999	0.16	0.14	0.21	0.07 (1.28)
% villages experienced pests, 1999	0.15	0.15	0.13	−0.02 (−0.38)
Number of villages	240	151	82	

Source: Rural Economic and Demographic Survey, 2006. Village level means are provided.
Column (4) displays beta coefficients, *t* statistics are in parentheses.

TABLE 9.4. *Reservation's Impact on* Pradhan's *Gender*

	(1) All	(2) All	(3) All-NR	(4) All-NR-Late
Pradhan seat is reserved	0.89***	0.90***	0.92***	0.92***
for women	(0.02)	(0.02)	(0.02)	(0.02)
Adj. R-sq	0.75	0.76	0.82	0.81
N	699	673	520	505

$^+ p < 0.10,$ $^* p < 0.05,$ $^{**} p < 0.01,$ $^{***} p < 0.001$

Note: Robust standard errors in parentheses. Observations correspond to a village in a particular election cycle. The dependent variable is a binary indicator of whether the *Pradhan* is female. "All" includes all villages in the dataset. Columns (2)–(4) include election cycles post-1993 when reservations for women were implemented. "All-NR" excludes villages from states that do not assign reservations for female *pradhans* randomly (Andhra Pradesh, Himachal Pradesh, Kerala, Tamil Nadu). "All-NR-Late" excludes nonrandom implementers of reservations and villages from the two states to implement women's reservations over 10 years after constitutional amendments: Bihar (2006) and Jharkhand (2010).

TABLE 9.5. *Impact of Father's Death Postreservations on* Pradhan's *Gender at Father's Death*

	(1) All	(2) All	(3) All	(4) All	(5) All-NR	(6) All-NR-Late
Father died	0.59***	0.59***	0.59***	0.60***	0.61***	0.61***
postreservations	(0.04)	(0.04)	(0.04)	(0.04)	(0.04)	(0.04)
Controls	No	No	Yes	Yes	Yes	Yes
State FE	No	No	No	Yes	Yes	Yes
Birth year FE	No	No	No	Yes	Yes	Yes
State trends	No	No	No	Yes	Yes	Yes
Adj. R-sq	0.40	0.40	0.40	0.44	0.45	0.45
N	12,457	12,285	12,285	12,285	10,086	10,006

$^+ p < 0.10,$ $^* p < 0.05,$ $^{**} p < 0.01,$ $^{***} p < 0.001$

Note: Robust standard errors in parentheses. The dependent variable is a binary indicator of whether the *Pradhan* is female at the time of father's death. "All" includes all individuals in the dataset. Columns (2)–(6) include individuals whose father died post-1993 when reservations for women were implemented. "All-NR" excludes individuals from states that do not assign reservations for female *pradhans* randomly (Andhra Pradesh, Himachal Pradesh, Kerala, Tamil Nadu). "All-NR-Late" excludes nonrandom implementers of reservations and individuals from the two states to implement women's reservations over 10 years after constitutional amendments: Bihar (2006) and Jharkhand (2010). Controls include caste status, total number of children, total number of female and male children, wealth status, and binary indicator for Western Indian states.
Source: REDS 2006, NCAER.

TABLE 9.6. *Descriptive Statistics, Individuals*

	All	Women	Men
Subject to Hindu law (Hindu, Jain, Sikh, Buddhist)	0.92	0.92	0.92
	(0.27)	(0.27)	(0.27)
Inherit land?	0.13	0.04	0.24
	(0.34)	(0.19)	(0.43)
Total land inherited	0.43	0.14	0.74
	(1.85)	(1.18)	(2.33)
Age (years)	30.65	30.79	30.51
	(12.78)	(12.36)	(13.21)
Education (years completed)	6.43	5.50	7.29
	(4.51)	(4.36)	(4.47)
Siblings: proportion of sisters	0.38	0.41	0.35
	(0.23)	(0.23)	(0.23)
Father: secondary or more education	0.36	0.37	0.36
	(0.48)	(0.48)	(0.48)
Mother: secondary or more education	0.13	0.13	0.13
	(0.34)	(0.34)	(0.34)
Parents = top 20% landholders (15 acres+)	0.21	0.21	0.21
	(0.40)	(0.41)	(0.40)
Patriarch's land (acres)	6.75	6.88	6.62
	(16.43)	(17.78)	(14.86)
Scheduled Caste	0.18	0.18	0.19
	(0.39)	(0.39)	(0.39)
Scheduled Tribe	0.10	0.10	0.10
	(0.29)	(0.30)	(0.29)
Other Backward Caste	0.26	0.25	0.27
	(0.44)	(0.43)	(0.44)
Muslim	0.07	0.07	0.07
	(0.26)	(0.25)	(0.26)
Total number of children (household head)	3.87	3.95	3.79
	(2.03)	(2.05)	(2.00)
Western states (Gujarat, Maharashtra)	0.13	0.12	0.13
	(0.33)	(0.33)	(0.34)
Wealthy: Head's parents own 8 acres or more	0.25	0.26	0.25
	(0.44)	(0.44)	(0.43)
Patriarch: number of daughters	2.08	2.22	1.92
	(1.51)	(1.55)	(1.45)
Patriarch: number of sons	3.04	2.91	3.18
	(1.50)	(1.46)	(1.52)
Observations	61,569	31,729	29,840

Source: Rural Economic and Demographic Survey, 2006. The sample includes men and women born post-HSA and pre-HSAA in their states. Standard deviations are in parantheses.

TABLE 9.7. *Reservations' and Reform's Impact on Women's Inheritance and Dowry, Logit Model*

	(1) Inheritance Target-NR	(2) Inheritance Target-NR	(3) Dowry Target-NR
Father died postreservations	0.70*	0.70*	−0.22
	(0.28)	(0.27)	(0.22)
Father died postreform	0.45+	0.43	−1.76***
	(0.26)	(0.27)	(0.23)
Father died postreform and postreservations	−1.55***	−1.53***	0.43
	(0.42)	(0.42)	(0.29)
Age < 20 at reform		−0.00	2.29**
		(0.50)	(0.76)
Age < 20 at reform * Father died postreform		0.25	−1.57*
		(0.47)	(0.75)
Age < 20 at reform * Father died postreservations		−7.82***	11.53***
		(1.91)	(0.86)
Aged < 20 at reform * Father died postreform and postreservations		7.65***	−11.93***
		(1.95)	(0.89)
Controls	Yes	Yes	Yes
State FE	Yes	Yes	Yes
Birth year FE	Yes	Yes	Yes
State trends	Yes	Yes	Yes
Pseudo R^2	0.21	0.21	0.76
N	8,932	8,932	9,670

+ $p < 0.10$, * $p < 0.05$, ** $p < 0.01$, *** $p < 0.001$

Note: Robust standard errors, clustered at the village level, are in parentheses. The dependent variable in Columns (1)–(2) a binary indicator of whether or not women inherit. In Column (3), the dependent variable is a binary indicator of whether or not women receive dowry. "Target-NR" includes landed, Hindu women who were born post-1956 HSA, but prior to state-specific amendments. Additionally, women living in states that do not assign reservations for female *pradhans* randomly (Andhra Pradesh, Himachal Pradesh, Kerala, Tamil Nadu) are excluded. Controls include caste status, total number of female and male children of the household head, wealth status, and a binary indicator for Western Indian states.

Source: REDS 2006, NCAER.

TABLE 9.8. *Reservation's Impact on Women's Likelihood of Inheritance, Logit Model*

	(1) All	(2) All	(3) Matched	(4) Target	(5) Target-NR	(6) Target-NR-Late
Father died postreservations	0.51+	0.48+	0.47	0.68*	0.70*	0.71*
	(0.29)	(0.29)	(0.53)	(0.27)	(0.28)	(0.28)
Father died postreform	−0.62**	0.24	−0.01	0.36	0.45+	0.49+
	(0.21)	(0.22)	(0.27)	(0.25)	(0.26)	(0.26)
Father died postreform and postreservations	−1.70***	−1.34***	−1.32*	−1.49***	−1.55***	−1.59***
	(0.40)	(0.39)	(0.64)	(0.40)	(0.42)	(0.42)
Controls	No	Yes	Yes	Yes	Yes	Yes
State FE	Yes	Yes	Yes	Yes	Yes	Yes
Birth year FE	Yes	Yes	Yes	Yes	Yes	Yes
State trends	Yes	Yes	Yes	Yes	Yes	Yes
Pseudo R^2	0.12	0.17	0.17	0.20	0.21	0.21
Observations	15,197	15,197	8,453	9,993	8,932	8,575

$+ p < 0.10$, $* p < 0.05$, $** p < 0.01$, $*** p < 0.001$

Note: Robust standard errors clustered at the village level in parentheses. The dependent variable is a binary indicator of whether or not women inherit. "All" includes all women born post-1956 HSA and prestate HSAA. "Matched" uses the genetically matched subset of women. "Target" in Columns (4)–(6) includes only landed, Hindu women born post-1956 HSA and pre-HSAA. "Target-NR" excludes states that do not assign reservations for female *pradhans* randomly (Andhra Pradesh, Himachal Pradesh, Kerala, and Tamil Nadu). "Target-NR-Late" excludes nonrandom implementers of reservations and the two states to implement women's reservations over 10 years after constitutional amendments: Bihar (2006) and Jharkhand (2010). "Matched" refers to the sample of genetically matched individuals. Controls include caste status, total number of children, total number of female and male children, wealth status, and binary indicator for Western India.

Source: NCAER REDS 2006/9.

TABLE 9.9. *Reservation's Impact on Women's Area of Inheritance (Acres)*

	(1) Target	(2) Target	(3) Target-NR	(4) Target-NR-Late
Father died postreservations	0.06	0.08+	0.09*	0.09*
	(0.05)	(0.04)	(0.05)	(0.05)
Father died postreform	−0.08	−0.09	0.02	0.02
	(0.07)	(0.10)	(0.03)	(0.03)
Father died postreform and postreservations	−0.02	−0.04	−0.09	−0.10
	(0.08)	(0.07)	(0.06)	(0.06)
Controls	No	Yes	Yes	Yes
State FE	Yes	Yes	Yes	Yes
Birth year FE	Yes	Yes	Yes	Yes
State trends	Yes	Yes	Yes	Yes
Adj. R-sq	0.01	0.01	0.01	0.01
N	11,826	11,826	10,698	10,259

+ $p < 0.10$, * $p < 0.05$, ** $p < 0.01$, *** $p < 0.001$

Note: Robust standard errors clustered at the village level in parentheses. The dependent variable is the land area that women inherit, in acres. "Target" includes only landed, Hindu women born post-1956 HSA and pre-HSAA. "Target-NR" excludes states that do not assign reservations for female *pradhans* randomly (Andhra Pradesh, Himachal Pradesh, Kerala, and Tamil Nadu). "Target-NR-Late" excludes nonrandom implementers of reservations and the two states to implement women's reservations over 10 years after constitutional amendments: Bihar (2006) and Jharkhand (2010). Controls include caste status, total number of children, total female children and male children, wealth status, and binary indicator for Western India.

Source: NCAER REDS 2006/9.

TABLE 9.10. *Reservations' Dynamic Impact on Women's Inheritance, Logit Model*

	(1) All	(2) All	(3) Matched	(4) Target	(5) Target-NR	(6) Target-NR-Late
Age < 20 at reform	−0.33	−0.25	−0.32	0.13	−0.00	−0.05
	(0.45)	(0.45)	(0.62)	(0.48)	(0.50)	(0.50)
Father died postreservations	0.51+	0.49+	0.49	0.69*	0.70*	0.70*
	(0.29)	(0.29)	(0.53)	(0.27)	(0.27)	(0.28)
Father died postreform	−0.64**	0.24	0.01	0.35	0.43	0.47+
	(0.23)	(0.24)	(0.31)	(0.26)	(0.27)	(0.27)
Father died postreform and postreservations	−1.67***	−1.34***	−1.34*	−1.47***	−1.53***	−1.56***
	(0.42)	(0.40)	(0.65)	(0.41)	(0.42)	(0.43)
Age < 20 at reform * Father died postreservations	0.20	0.05	−0.20	−0.04	0.25	0.24
	(0.54)	(0.49)	(0.67)	(0.51)	(0.47)	(0.47)
Age < 20 at reform * Father died postreform postreservations	−10.71***	−11.06***	−12.03***	−7.96***	−7.82***	−9.32***
	(1.65)	(1.50)	(2.27)	(1.90)	(1.91)	(1.92)
Age < 20 at reform * Father died postreform and postreservations	10.53***	11.04***	12.03***	7.78***	7.65***	9.14***
	(1.80)	(1.63)	(2.41)	(1.95)	(1.95)	(1.97)
Controls	No	Yes	Yes	Yes	Yes	Yes
State FE	Yes	Yes	Yes	Yes	Yes	Yes
Birth year FE	Yes	Yes	Yes	Yes	Yes	Yes
State trends	Yes	Yes	Yes	Yes	Yes	Yes
Pseudo R^2	0.12	0.17	0.17	0.20	0.21	0.21
Observations	15,197	15,197	8,453	9,993	8,932	8,575

+ $p < 0.10$, * $p < 0.05$, ** $p < 0.01$, *** $p < 0.001$

Note: Robust standard errors clustered at the village level in parentheses. The dependent variable is a binary indicator of whether or not women inherit. "All" includes all women born post-1956 HSA and prestate HSAA. "Matched" uses the genetically matched subset of women. "Target" includes only landed, Hindu women. "Target-NR" excludes states that do not assign reservations for female *pradhans* randomly (Andhra Pradesh, Himachal Pradesh, Kerala, Tamil Nadu). "Target-NR-Late" excludes nonrandom implementers of reservations and the two states to implement women's reservations over 10 years after constitutional amendments: Bihar (2006) and Jharkhand (2010). "Matched" refers to the genetically matched subsample. Controls include caste status, total number of children, total number of female and male children, wealth status, and binary indicator for Western Indian states.

Source: NCAER REDS 2006/9.

TABLE 9.11. *Reservation's and Inheritance's Impact on Women's Participation in Latest Gram Sabha, Logit Model*

	(1) Target	(2) Target	(3) Matched	(4) Target-NR	(5) Target-NR-Late
Last *Gram Sabha*: attended? (%)					
Female	−2.33***	−1.70***	−1.58***	−1.64***	−1.63***
	(0.20)	(0.19)	(0.17)	(0.22)	(0.22)
Latest *pradhan* seat reserved for woman	−0.20	−0.23	−0.09	−0.28	−0.30
	(0.19)	(0.19)	(0.32)	(0.21)	(0.21)
Female * Reservations	0.20	0.25	0.39	0.16	0.18
	(0.38)	(0.37)	(0.39)	(0.43)	(0.43)
Controls	No	Yes	Yes	Yes	Yes
State FE	Yes	Yes	Yes	Yes	Yes
Birth year FE	Yes	Yes	Yes	Yes	Yes
Pseudo R^2	0.3346	0.3538	0.3315	0.3320	0.3325
N	15,309	15,309	13,332	13,419	13,196

Standard errors in parentheses
+ $p < 0.10$, * $p < 0.05$, ** $p < 0.01$, *** $p < 0.001$

TABLE 9.12. *Reservations' Dynamic Impact on Women's Dowry, Logit Model*

	(1) All	(2) All	(3) Matched	(4) Target	(5) Target-NR	(6) Target-NR-Late
Age < 20 at reform	0.37	0.39	0.21	0.71	2.29**	2.23**
	(0.38)	(0.46)	(0.50)	(0.64)	(0.76)	(0.78)
Father died postreservations	0.23	0.12	−0.12	−0.02	−0.22	−0.20
	(0.22)	(0.23)	(0.29)	(0.26)	(0.22)	(0.23)
Father died postreform	−3.73***	−1.49***	−1.32***	−1.66***	−1.76***	−1.77***
	(0.15)	(0.19)	(0.22)	(0.21)	(0.23)	(0.25)
Father died postreform and postreservations	−0.78**	−0.08	−0.24	0.27	0.43	0.44
	(0.26)	(0.29)	(0.36)	(0.30)	(0.29)	(0.30)
Age < 20 at reform * Father died postreform	0.04	0.53	0.84+	0.48	−1.57*	−1.61*
	(0.40)	(0.49)	(0.49)	(0.75)	(0.75)	(0.77)
Age < 20 at reform * Father died postreservations	13.20***	12.83***	10.52***	12.21***	11.53***	11.75***
	(0.52)	(0.72)	(0.80)	(0.88)	(0.86)	(0.89)
Age < 20 at reform * Father died postreform and postreservations	−13.93***	−13.98***	−11.50***	−13.20***	−11.93***	−12.17***
	(0.57)	(0.75)	(0.84)	(0.96)	(0.89)	(0.91)
Controls	No	Yes	Yes	Yes	Yes	Yes
State FE	Yes	Yes	Yes	Yes	Yes	Yes
Cohort FE	Yes	Yes	Yes	Yes	Yes	Yes
State trends	Yes	Yes	Yes	Yes	Yes	Yes
Pseudo R^2	0.444	0.744	0.760	0.739	0.760	0.761
N	16,446	16,446	9,092	10,768	9,670	9,288

+ $p < 0.10$, * $p < 0.05$, ** $p < 0.01$, *** $p < 0.001$

Note: Robust standard errors clustered at the village level in parentheses. The dependent variable is a binary indicator of whether or not women receive dowry from their families. "All" includes all women born post-1956 HSA and prestate HSAA. "Target" includes only landed, Hindu women. "Target-NR" excludes states that do not assign reservations for female *pradhans* randomly (Andhra Pradesh, Himachal Pradesh, Kerala, Tamil Nadu). "Target-NR-Late" excludes nonrandom implementers of reservations and the two states to implement women's reservations over 10 years after constitutional amendments: Bihar (2006) and Jharkhand (2010). "Matched" refers to the genetically matched subsample. Controls include caste status, total number of children, total number of female and male children, wealth status, and a binary indicator for Western Indian states. *Source:* NCAER REDS 2006/9.

TABLE 9.13. *Reservation's Impact on Women's Inheritance, Excluding Sisters without Brothers*

	(1) Target	(2) Target	(3) Target-NR	(4) Target-NR-Late	(5) Target	(6) Target	(7) Target-NR	(8) Target-NR-Late
Father died postreservations	0.06+ (0.03)	0.07* (0.03)	0.07* (0.03)	0.07* (0.03)	0.06 (0.03)	0.06* (0.03)	0.07* (0.03)	0.07* (0.03)
Father died postreform	0.07* (0.03)	0.07* (0.03)	0.08* (0.03)	0.08* (0.04)	0.10* (0.04)	0.10* (0.04)	0.11* (0.05)	0.11* (0.05)
Father died postreform and postreservations	-0.14** (0.04)	-0.14*** (0.04)	-0.15** (0.05)	-0.15** (0.05)	-0.19*** (0.06)	-0.19*** (0.06)	-0.20** (0.06)	-0.21** (0.06)
Age < 20 at reform					0.04 (0.04)	0.04 (0.04)	0.03 (0.05)	0.03 (0.05)
Age < 20 at reform * Father died postreform					-0.08 (0.06)	-0.08 (0.05)	-0.06 (0.07)	-0.06 (0.07)
Age < 20 at reform * Father died postreservations					-0.07 (0.04)	-0.12** (0.04)	-0.10* (0.04)	-0.10* (0.04)
Age < 20 at reform * Father died postreform and postreservations					0.19** (0.06)	0.23*** (0.06)	0.23** (0.07)	0.23** (0.07)
Controls	No	Yes	Yes	Yes	No	Yes	Yes	Yes
State FE	Yes	Yes	Yes	Yes	Yes	Yes	Yes	Yes
Birth year FE	Yes	Yes	Yes	Yes	Yes	Yes	Yes	Yes
State trends	Yes	Yes	Yes	Yes	Yes	Yes	Yes	Yes
Adj. R-sq	0.05	0.06	0.06	0.06	0.05	0.06	0.06	0.06
N	5,505	5,505	4,933	4,729	5,505	5,505	4,933	4,729

+ $p < 0.10$, * $p < 0.05$, ** $p < 0.01$, *** $p < 0.001$

Note: Robust standard errors clustered at the village level in parentheses. The dependent variable is a binary indicator of whether or not women inherit. The sample is limited to women with male siblings. "Target" includes only landed, Hindu women who were born post-1956 HSA, but prior to their state-specific HSAA's passage. "Target-NR" excludes states that do not assign reservations for female *pradhans* randomly (Andhra Pradesh, Himachal Pradesh, Kerala, Tamil Nadu). "Target-NR-Late" excludes nonrandom implementers of reservations and the two states to implement women's reservations over 10 years after constitutional amendments: Bihar (2006) and Jharkhand (2010). Controls include caste status, total number of children, total female children and male children, wealth status, and binary indicator for Western Indian states.

Source: NCAER REDS 2006/9.

TABLE 9.14. *Reservation's Impact on Women's Likelihood of Inheritance, OLS*

	(1) All	(2) All	(3) Matched
Father died postreservations	0.03	0.03	0.03
	(0.02)	(0.02)	(0.05)
Father died postreform	−0.04***	0.00	−0.01
	(0.01)	(0.01)	(0.02)
Father died postreform and postreservations	−0.06*	−0.05*	−0.05
	(0.02)	(0.02)	(0.04)
Controls	No	Yes	Yes
State FE	Yes	Yes	Yes
Birth year FE	Yes	Yes	Yes
State trends	Yes	Yes	Yes
Adj. R-sq	0.04	0.05	0.05
N	17,737	17,737	9,672

$^+ p < 0.10, ^* p < 0.05, ^{**} p < 0.01, ^{***} p < 0.001$

Note: Robust standard errors clustered at the village level in parentheses. The dependent variable is a binary indicator of whether or not women inherit. "All" includes all women born post-1956 HSA and prestate HSAA. "Matched" uses the genetically matched subset of women. Controls include caste status, total number of children, total female children and male children, wealth status, and binary indicator for Western Indian states.
Source: NCAER REDS 2006/9.

TABLE 9.15. *Placebo Test: Reservation's Impact on Women's Likelihood of Inheritance*

	(1) All	(2) All	(3) Matched	(4) Target	(5) Target-NR	(6) Target-NR-Late
Father died post-1984	0.02	0.01	0.02	0.01	0.01	0.01
	(0.02)	(0.02)	(0.02)	(0.02)	(0.02)	(0.02)
Father died postreform	−0.00	0.01	0.02	0.21^{+}	−0.00	−0.00
	(0.04)	(0.04)	(0.06)	(0.12)	(0.02)	(0.02)
Father died postreform and 1984	−0.06	−0.03	−0.05	-0.22^{+}	0.00	0.00
	(0.04)	(0.04)	(0.06)	(0.12)	(.)	(.)
Controls	No	Yes	Yes	Yes	Yes	Yes
State FE	Yes	Yes	Yes	Yes	Yes	Yes
Birth year FE	Yes	Yes	Yes	Yes	Yes	Yes
State trends	Yes	Yes	Yes	Yes	Yes	Yes
Adj. R-sq	0.04	0.05	0.05	0.07	0.08	0.08
N	17,727	17,727	9,662	11,818	10,693	10,254

$+ p < 0.10, * p < 0.05, ** p < 0.01, *** p < 0.001$

Note: Robust standard errors clustered at the village level in parentheses. The dependent variable is a binary indicator of whether or not women inherit. The main independent variable is whether father dies in or after 1984, 10 years before the introduction of women's reservations. "All" includes all women born post-1956 HSA and prestate HSAA. "Matched" uses the genetically matched subset of women. "Target" includes only landed, Hindu women born post-1956 HSA and pre-HSAA. "Target-NR" excludes states that do not assign reservations for female *pradhans* randomly (Andhra Pradesh, Himachal Pradesh, Kerala, and Tamil Nadu). "Target-NR-Late" excludes nonrandom implementers of reservations and the two states to implement women's reservations over 10 years after constitutional amendments: Bihar (2006) and Jharkhand (2010). Additionally, Columns (7)–(9) exclude women with fathers whose death year is unknown. "Matched" refers to the genetically matched subsample. Controls include caste status, total number of children, total female children and male children, wealth status, and binary indicator for Western India.
Source: NCAER REDS 2006/9.

TABLE 9.16. *Reservations' Dynamic Impact on Women's Inheritance and Dowry*

	(1) Inherit All	(2) Inherit All	(3) Inherit Matched	(4) Dowry All	(5) Dowry All	(6) Dowry Matched
Aged < 20 at reform	-0.01 (0.03)	-0.01 (0.03)	-0.02 (0.04)	-0.03 (0.03)	0.01 (0.02)	0.00 (0.02)
Father died postreservations	0.03 (0.02)	0.03 (0.02)	0.03 (0.05)	0.04+ (0.02)	0.01 (0.02)	-0.01 (0.02)
Father died postreform	-0.04*** (0.01)	0.00 (0.02)	-0.01 (0.02)	-0.66*** (0.02)	-0.17*** (0.02)	-0.14*** (0.02)
Father died postreform and postreservations	-0.06* (0.03)	-0.06* (0.02)	-0.06 (0.05)	-0.12*** (0.03)	-0.01 (0.02)	-0.01 (0.03)
Age < 20 at reform * Father died postreform	0.00 (0.03)	-0.00 (0.03)	-0.00 (0.04)	0.10* (0.04)	0.04+ (0.02)	0.04 (0.03)
Age < 20 at reform * Father died postreservations	-0.08* (0.03)	-0.09** (0.03)	-0.09+ (0.05)	0.27*** (0.04)	0.08* (0.03)	0.07+ (0.04)
Age < 20 at reform * Father died postreform and postreservations	0.09* (0.04)	0.11** (0.04)	0.11+ (0.06)	-0.32*** (0.05)	-0.12*** (0.03)	-0.09* (0.04)
Controls	No	Yes	Yes	No	Yes	Yes
State FE	Yes	Yes	Yes	Yes	Yes	Yes
Birth year FE	Yes	Yes	Yes	Yes	Yes	Yes
State trends	Yes	Yes	Yes	Yes	Yes	Yes
Adj. R-sq	0.04	0.06	0.05	0.53	0.78	0.79
N	17,737	17,737	9,672	17,737	17,737	9,672

+ $p < 0.10$, * $p < 0.05$, ** $p < 0.01$, *** $p < 0.001$

Note: Robust standard errors clustered at the village level in parentheses. The dependent variable in Columns (1)–(3) is a binary indicator of whether or not women inherit. In Columns (4)–(6) the dependent variable is a binary indicator of whether or not women receive dowry from their families. "All" includes all women born post-1956 HSA and prestate HSAA. "Matched" uses the genetically matched subset of women. Controls include caste status, total number of children, total female children and male children, wealth status, and binary indicator for Western Indian states.

Source: NCAER REDS 2006/9.

TABLE 9.17. *Placebo Test: Reservations' Dynamic Impact on Women's Inheritance*

	(1) All	(2) All	(3) Matched	(4) Target	(5) Target-NR	(6) Target-NR-Late
Age < 20 at reform	-0.02	-0.01	-0.01	0.01	-0.02	-0.02
	(0.03)	(0.03)	(0.05)	(0.05)	(0.06)	(0.06)
Father died in 1984	0.01	0.01	0.02	0.01	0.01	0.00
	(0.02)	(0.02)	(0.02)	(0.02)	(0.02)	(0.02)
Father died postreform	0.01	0.01	-0.00	0.20^{+}	-0.00	-0.00
	(0.04)	(0.05)	(0.07)	(0.11)	(0.02)	(0.02)
Father died postreform and 1984	-0.07	-0.03	-0.03	-0.21^{+}	0.00	0.00
	(0.04)	(0.05)	(0.07)	(0.11)	(.)	(.)
Age < 20 at reform * Father died postreform	0.00	0.01	0.02	0.00	0.00	0.01
	(.)	(0.03)	(0.04)	(.)	(0.06)	(0.06)
Age < 20 at reform * Father died post-1984	0.00	-0.01	-0.02	-0.02	0.02	0.02
	(0.04)	(0.04)	(0.05)	(0.06)	(0.06)	(0.06)
Age < 20 at reform * Father died post-reform and 1984	0.02	0.00	0.00	0.01	0.00	0.00
	(0.03)	(.)	(.)	(0.05)	(.)	(.)
Controls	No	Yes	Yes	Yes	Yes	Yes
State FE	Yes	Yes	Yes	Yes	Yes	Yes
Birth year FE	Yes	Yes	Yes	Yes	Yes	Yes
State trends	Yes	Yes	Yes	Yes	Yes	Yes
Adj. R-sq	0.04	0.05	0.05	0.07	0.08	0.08
N	17,727	17,727	9,662	11,818	10,693	10,254

$+ p < 0.10, * p < 0.05, ** p < 0.01, *** p < 0.001$

Note: Robust standard errors clustered at the village level in parentheses. The dependent variable is a binary indicator of whether or not women inherit. The main independent variable is whether father dies in or after 1984, 10 years before the introduction of women's reservations. "All" includes all women born post-1956 HSA and prestate HSAA. "Matched" uses the genetically matched subset of women. "Target" includes only landed, Hindu women born post-1956 HSA and pre-HSAA. "Target-NR" excludes states that do not assign reservations for female pradhans randomly (Andhra Pradesh, Himachal Pradesh, Kerala, and Tamil Nadu). "Target-NR-Late" excludes nonrandom implementers of reservations and the two states to implement women's reservations over 10 years after constitutional amendments: Bihar (2006) and Jharkhand (2010). Additionally, Columns (7)–(9) exclude women with fathers whose death year is unknown. Controls include caste status, total number of children, total female children and male children, wealth status, and binary indicator for Western India.
Source: NCAER REDS 2006/9.

TABLE 9.18. *Reservations' and Reform's Impact on Inheritance and Dowry, Placebo Test with Reservations as of 1984*

	(1) Inheritance Target-NR	(2) Inheritance Target-NR	(3) Area Target-NR	(4) Dowry Target-NR	(5) Violence Target-NR
Father died post-1984	0.01	0.01	−0.18	0.06**	0.02
	(0.02)	(0.02)	(0.92)	(0.02)	(0.05)
Father died postreform	−0.00	−0.00	0.63	−0.20***	−0.01
	(0.02)	(0.02)	(1.44)	(0.02)	(0.07)
Father died postreform and 1984	0.00	0.00	0.00	0.00	0.00
	(.)	(.)	(.)	(.)	(.)
Aged < 20 at reform		−0.02		0.09+	−0.20*
		(0.06)		(0.05)	(0.03)
Aged < 20 at reform * Father died postreform		0.00		−0.02	0.23*
		(0.06)		(0.01)	(0.10)
Aged < 20 at reform * Father died post-1984		0.02		−0.05	−0.04
		(0.06)		(0.05)	(0.07)
Aged < 20 at reform * Father died postreform and 1984		0.00		0.00	0.00
		(.)		(.)	(.)
Controls	Yes	Yes	Yes	Yes	Yes
State FE	Yes	Yes	Yes	Yes	Yes
Birth year FE	Yes	Yes	Yes	Yes	Yes
State trends	Yes	Yes	Yes	Yes	Yes
Adj. R-sq	0.08	0.08	0.49	0.80	0.09
N	10,693	11,376	124	11,376	10,693

+ $p < 0.10$, * $p < 0.05$, ** $p < 0.01$, *** $p < 0.001$

Note: Robust standard errors, clustered at the village level, are in parentheses. The dependent variable in Columns (1)–(2) a binary indicator of whether or not women inherit. In Column (3), the dependent variable is the area of land women receive in acres. In Column (4) the dependent variable is a binary indicator of whether or not women receive dowry. "Target-NR" includes landed, Hindu women who were born post-1956 HSA, but prior to state-specific amendments. Additionally, women living in states that do not assign reservations for female *pradhans* randomly (Andhra Pradesh, Himachal Pradesh, Kerala, Tamil Nadu) are excluded. Controls include caste status, total number of female and male children of the household head, wealth status, and a binary indicator for Western Indian states.

Source: REDS 2006, NCAER.

TABLE 9.19. *Descriptive Statistics: Women's Mean Probability of Land Inheritance Conditional on Village Rate of Women's* Gram Sabha *Participation, Currently Reserved Villages*

	(1) Individual Observations Mean Pr(Inherit)	(2) Village Observations Mean Pr(Inherit)
Above Average Participation	0.047	0.050
Average – Below Average Participation	0.028	0.026
Total (in currently reserved villages)	0.030	0.029
Observations	16,147	71

Source: Rural Economic and Demographic Survey, 2006/9. Village-level means are calculated by assessing all women's participation in the most recent *Gram Sabha* conducted in each village currently reserved for a female *Pradhan*. Women's "average" participation at the village level is calculated slightly differently for each specification. Column 1 calculates the average of all village-level averages using the entire population of women in REDS 2006/9 sample of currently reserved villages. Here, 9.7 percent of women participated in the latest *Gram Sabha* meeting, on average. Column 2 collapses observations by villages, such that women's "average" participation is calculated over the total number of villages currently reserved for a female *Pradhan*. Using this method, 11.1 percent of women participated in the most recent *Gram Sabha* meeting, on average. The correlation of "above average" participation with women's inheritance is positive in both cases: 0.109 for individual-level observations (Column 1) and 0.164 for village-level observations (Column 2).

TABLE 9.20. *Representation's Impact on Women's Inheritance, Variation by Village-Level Gini Coefficient*

	(1) Target b/se	(2) Target b/se	(3) Target-NR b/se	(4) Target-NR-Late b/se
Panel A: First Tercile of Gini Coefficients (most equal)				
Father died postreservations	0.06	0.06	0.06	0.06
	(0.06)	(0.06)	(0.06)	(0.06)
Father died postreform	−0.04+	0.06+	0.06	0.06
	(0.02)	(0.03)	(0.03)	(0.04)
Father died postreform and postreservations	−0.12+	−0.10+	−0.10+	−0.10
	(0.06)	(0.06)	(0.06)	(0.06)
Controls	No	Yes	Yes	Yes
State FE	Yes	Yes	Yes	Yes
Birth year FE	Yes	Yes	Yes	Yes
State trends	Yes	Yes	Yes	Yes
Adj. R-sq	0.08	0.13	0.13	0.13
N	5,385	5,385	5,185	4,969
Panel B: Second Tercile of Gini Coefficients				
Father died postreservations	0.07+	0.07+	0.08+	0.08+
	(0.04)	(0.04)	(0.04)	(0.04)
Father died postreform	−0.05**	−0.02	−0.02	−0.02
	(0.02)	(0.02)	(0.03)	(0.03)
Father died postreform and postreservations	−0.08*	−0.08+	−0.09*	−0.09*
	(0.04)	(0.04)	(0.04)	(0.04)
Controls	No	Yes	Yes	Yes
State FE	Yes	Yes	Yes	Yes
Birth year FE	Yes	Yes	Yes	Yes
State trends	Yes	Yes	Yes	Yes
Adj. R-sq	0.05	0.06	0.07	0.07
N	4,166	4,166	3,762	3,660

Panel C: Third Tercile of Gini Coefficients (least equal)

Father died postreservations	−0.02	−0.02	−0.01	−0.02
	(0.06)	(0.06)	(0.06)	(0.06)
Father died postreform	−0.07**	−0.04	−0.02	−0.02
	(0.02)	(0.02)	(0.03)	(0.03)
Father died postreform and postreservations	0.03	0.04	0.05	0.05
	(0.06)	(0.06)	(0.06)	(0.06)
Controls	No	Yes	Yes	Yes
State FE	Yes	Yes	Yes	Yes
Birth year FE	Yes	Yes	Yes	Yes
State trends	Yes	Yes	Yes	Yes
Adj. R-sq	0.04	0.06	0.07	0.07
N	2,275	2,275	1,751	1,630

$+ p < 0.10, * p < 0.05, ** p < 0.01, *** p < 0.001$

Note: Robust standard errors clustered at the village level in parentheses. The dependent variable is a binary indicator of whether or not women inherit. Panel titles specify the villages to which individuals belong, based on terciles of intravillage landownership Gini coefficient. Panel A shows results for villages with a land Gini coefficient larger than or equal to 0.2101 and less than or equal to 0.4782 (most equal tercile). Panel B shows villages with Gini coefficients larger than 0.4784 and less than or equal to 0.6076 (moderately equal tercile). Panel C shows villages with Gini coefficients larger than 0.6096 (least equal tercile). "Target" includes only landed, Hindu women who were born post-1956 HSA, but prior to their state-specific HSAA's passage. "Target-NR" excludes states that do not assign reservations for female *pradhans* randomly (Andhra Pradesh, Himachal Pradesh, Kerala, Tamil Nadu). "Target-NR-Late" excludes nonrandom implementers of reservations and the two states to implement women's reservations over 10 years after constitutional amendments: Bihar (2006) and Jharkhand (2010). Controls include caste status, total number of children, total female children and male children, wealth status, and binary indicator for Western Indian states.

Source: REDS 2006/9, NCAER.

TABLE 9.21. *Representation's Impact on Women's Participation in Latest Gram Sabha and Willingness to Conduct Violence vs. Daughter's Marital Choice, Variation by Village-Level Gini Coefficient*

	(1) Attendance Target b/se	(2) Attendance Target b/se	(3) Attendance Target-NR b/se	(4) Attendance Target-NR-late b/se	(5) Violence Target b/se	(6) Violence Target b/se	(7) Violence Target-NR b/se	(8) Violence Target-NR-Late b/se
Panel A: First Tercile of Gini Coefficients (most equal)								
Female	-0.27***	-0.18***	-0.16***	-0.16***	-0.07***	-0.08***	-0.07**	-0.07**
	(0.03)	(0.03)	(0.03)	(0.03)	(0.02)	(0.02)	(0.02)	(0.02)
Latest *pradhan* seat reserved for woman	-0.06	-0.06	-0.06	-0.06	0.04	0.03	0.04	0.04
	(0.04)	(0.04)	(0.04)	(0.04)	(0.05)	(0.05)	(0.05)	(0.05)
Female * Reservations	0.06	0.06	0.05	0.05	-0.06*	-0.05+	-0.07*	-0.07*
	(0.05)	(0.05)	(0.05)	(0.05)	(0.03)	(0.03)	(0.03)	(0.03)
Controls	No	Yes	Yes	Yes	No	Yes	Yes	Yes
Adj. R-sq	0.33	0.36	0.35	0.35	0.04	0.04	0.04	0.04
N	6,589	6,589	6,249	6,249	5,231	5,231	5,014	5,014
Panel B: Second Tercile of Gini Coefficients								
Female	-0.26***	-0.18***	-0.17***	-0.17***	-0.07***	-0.08***	-0.09***	-0.09***
	(0.03)	(0.02)	(0.02)	(0.02)	(0.02)	(0.02)	(0.02)	(0.02)
Latest *pradhan* seat reserved for woman	-0.03	-0.03	-0.04	-0.04	0.00	0.02	0.02	0.03
	(0.06)	(0.06)	(0.07)	(0.07)	(0.05)	(0.05)	(0.05)	(0.05)
Female * Reservations	0.08+	0.08+	0.08+	0.08+	0.02	0.01	0.02	0.03
	(0.04)	(0.04)	(0.05)	(0.05)	(0.04)	(0.04)	(0.04)	(0.04)
Controls	No	Yes	Yes	Yes	No	Yes	Yes	Yes
Adj. R-sq	0.30	0.32	0.24	0.25	0.03	0.04	0.04	0.04
N	5,663	5,663	5,000	4,862	4,021	4,021	3,596	3,510

Panel C: Third Tercile of Gini Coefficients (least equal)

Female	−0.31***	−0.23***	−0.16***	−0.16***	−0.05*	−0.05+	−0.06+	−0.05
	(0.04)	(0.04)	(0.04)	(0.04)	(0.02)	(0.03)	(0.03)	(0.03)
Latest *pradhan* seat reserved for woman	−0.07+	−0.07+	−0.03	−0.03	0.10	0.10	0.10	0.11
	(0.04)	(0.04)	(0.04)	(0.04)	(0.07)	(0.07)	(0.08)	(0.08)
Female * Reservations	0.11+	0.11+	0.04	0.04	−0.10+	−0.10+	−0.10	−0.10
	(0.06)	(0.06)	(0.06)	(0.06)	(0.06)	(0.06)	(0.07)	(0.07)
Controls	No	Yes	Yes	Yes	No	Yes	Yes	Yes
Adj. R-sq	0.37	0.39	0.31	0.31	0.04	0.04	0.04	0.04
N	3,109	3,109	2,209	2,123	2,103	2,103	1,577	1,523

$+ \; p < 0.10, \; * \; p < 0.05, \; ** \; p < 0.01, \; *** \; p < 0.001$

Note: Robust standard errors clustered at the village level in parentheses. For Columns (1)–(4), the dependent variable is a binary indicator of whether or not individuals attended the latest *Gram Sabha*. For Columns (5)–(8), the dependent variable is a binary indicator of a respondent's response willingness to engage in violence in response to the following hypothetical scenario: your daughter has eloped with a person who belongs to a family whom you do not approve. Would you involve in violence with that family? For maximum relevance, analysis is restricted to the current *Pradhan*. Panel titles specify the villages to which individuals belong, based on terciles of intravillage landownership Gini coefficient. Panel A shows results for villages with a land Gini coefficient larger than or equal to 0.2101 and less than or equal to 0.4782 (most equal tercile). Panel B shows villages with Gini coefficients larger than 0.4784 and less than or equal to 0.6076 (moderately equal tercile). Panel C shows villages with Gini coefficients larger than 0.6096 (least equal tercile). "Target" includes all adult (aged 18 or older) residents of landed, Hindu households born prior to the time their state legislated the HSAA. "Target-NR" excludes states that do not assign reservations for female *pradhans* randomly (Andhra Pradesh, Himachal Pradesh, Kerala, Tamil Nadu). "Target-NR-Late" excludes nonrandom implementers of reservations and the two states to implement women's reservations over 10 years after constitutional amendments: Bihar (2006) and Jharkhand (2010). Controls include caste status, wealth status, total number of children, total female children and male children, wealth status, and a binary indicator for Western Indian states.

Source: REDS 2006/9, NCAER.

TABLE 9.22. *Representation's Impact on Women's Inheritance, Variation by Caste*

	(1) Target b/se	(2) Target b/se	(3) Target-NR b/se	(4) Target-NR-Late b/se
Panel A: SC				
Father died postreservations	−0.13*	−0.12*	−0.12+	−0.12+
	(0.05)	(0.06)	(0.07)	(0.07)
Father died postreform	0.06	0.06	0.04	0.04
	(0.07)	(0.07)	(0.07)	(0.07)
Father died postreform and postreservations	0.04	0.03	0.05	0.05
	(0.09)	(0.09)	(0.10)	(0.10)
Controls	No	Yes	Yes	Yes
State FE	Yes	Yes	Yes	Yes
Birth year FE	Yes	Yes	Yes	Yes
State trends	Yes	Yes	Yes	Yes
Adj. R-sq	0.07	0.07	0.07	0.08
N	540	540	488	474
Panel B: OBC				
Father died postreservations	0.07	0.08	0.08+	0.08+
	(0.05)	(0.05)	(0.05)	(0.05)
Father died postreform	0.05	0.05	0.07	0.08
	(0.04)	(0.04)	(0.05)	(0.05)
Father died postreform and postreservations	−0.13*	−0.13*	−0.17*	−0.17*
	(0.06)	(0.06)	(0.07)	(0.07)
Controls	No	Yes	Yes	Yes
State FE	Yes	Yes	Yes	Yes

Birth year FE	Yes	Yes	Yes	Yes
State trends	Yes	Yes	Yes	Yes
Adj. R-sq	0.04	0.05	0.04	0.04
N	2,343	2,343	2,045	1,964
Panel C: OC				
Father died postreservations	0.09*	0.09*	0.10*	0.10*
	(0.04)	(0.04)	(0.05)	(0.05)
Father died postreform	0.07	0.07	0.08	0.08
	(0.05)	(0.05)	(0.06)	(0.06)
Father died postreform and postreservations	−0.21**	−0.21**	−0.24**	−0.24**
	(0.07)	(0.07)	(0.08)	(0.08)
Controls	No	Yes	Yes	Yes
State FE	Yes	Yes	Yes	Yes
Birth year FE	Yes	Yes	Yes	Yes
State trends	Yes	Yes	Yes	Yes
Adj. R-sq	0.06	0.06	0.06	0.06
N	1,649	1,649	1,411	1,380

+ $p < 0.10$, * $p < 0.05$, ** $p < 0.01$, *** $p < 0.001$

Note: Robust standard errors clustered at the village level in parentheses. The dependent variable is a binary indicator of whether or not women inherit. SC refers to individuals who are members of scheduled castes. OBC refers to individuals who are members of Other Backward Classes. OC refers to individuals who are members of Forward Castes. "Target" includes only landed, Hindu women who were born post-1956 HSA, but prior to their state-specific HSAA's passage. "Target-NR" excludes states that do not assign reservations for female *pradhans* randomly (Andhra Pradesh, Himachal Pradesh, Kerala, Tamil Nadu). "Target-NR-Late" excludes nonrandom implementers of reservations and the two states to implement women's reservations over 10 years after constitutional amendments: Bihar (2006) and Jharkhand (2010). Controls include caste status, total number of children, total female children and male children, wealth status, and binary indicator for Western Indian states.

Source: REDS 2006/9, NCAER.

TABLE 9.23. *Representation's Impact on Women's Inheritance, Variation by Parental Landholdings*

	(1) Target b/se	(2) Target b/se	(3) Target-NR b/se	(4) Target-NR-Late b/se
Panel A: First and Second Quartile of Landowners (smallest)				
Father died postreservations	0.08	0.08	0.11	0.11
	(0.06)	(0.06)	(0.07)	(0.07)
Father died postreform	−0.04*	−0.01	−0.01	−0.01
	(0.02)	(0.02)	(0.03)	(0.03)
Father died postreform and postreservations	−0.10+	−0.10	−0.12+	−0.12+
	(0.06)	(0.06)	(0.07)	(0.07)
Controls	No	Yes	Yes	Yes
State FE	Yes	Yes	Yes	Yes
Birth year FE	Yes	Yes	Yes	Yes
State trends	Yes	Yes	Yes	Yes
Adj. R-sq	0.06	0.07	0.08	0.08
N	3,343	3,343	2,734	2,561
Panel B: Third Quartile of Landowners				
Father died postreservations	−0.00	0.00	−0.00	−0.01
	(0.04)	(0.04)	(0.04)	(0.04)
Father died postreform	−0.05*	0.03	0.04	0.03
	(0.02)	(0.03)	(0.04)	(0.04)
Father died postreform and postreservations	−0.03	−0.03	−0.02	−0.01
	(0.04)	(0.04)	(0.04)	(0.04)
Controls	No	Yes	Yes	Yes
State FE	Yes	Yes	Yes	Yes
Birth year FE	Yes	Yes	Yes	Yes
State trends	Yes	Yes	Yes	Yes
Adj. R-sq	0.05	0.09	0.10	0.10
N	4,496	4,496	4,119	3,934

Panel C: Fourth Quartile of Landowners (largest)

Father died postreservations	0.11*	0.11*	0.11*	0.12*
	(0.05)	(0.05)	(0.05)	(0.05)
Father died postreform	−0.04+	0.04	0.05	0.06
	(0.02)	(0.04)	(0.04)	(0.04)
Father died postreform and postreservations	−0.15**	−0.14**	−0.15**	−0.15**
	(0.05)	(0.05)	(0.05)	(0.05)
Controls	No	Yes	Yes	Yes
State FE	Yes	Yes	Yes	Yes
Birth year FE	Yes	Yes	Yes	Yes
State trends	Yes	Yes	Yes	Yes
Adj. R-sq	0.05	0.08	0.09	0.09
N	3,987	3,987	3,845	3,764

$+ p < 0.10, * p < 0.05, ** p < 0.01, *** p < 0.001$

Note: Robust standard errors clustered at the village level in parentheses. The dependent variable is a binary indicator of whether or not women inherit. Landownership refers to the amount of land owned by the patriarch (in acres). The first and second quartile of landownership refers to individuals owning less than 2.5 acres of land. The third quartile of landownership refers to individuals owning between 2.5 and 8 acres of land. The fourth quartile refers to individuals owning more than eight acres of land. "Target" includes only landed, Hindu women who were born post-1956 HSA, but prior to their state-specific HSAA's passage. "Target-NR" excludes states that do not assign reservations for female *pradhans* randomly (Andhra Pradesh, Himachal Pradesh, Kerala, Tamil Nadu). "Target-NR-Late" excludes nonrandom implementers of reservations and the two states to implement women's reservations over 10 years after constitutional amendments: Bihar (2006) and Jharkhand (2010). Controls include caste status, total number of children, total female children and male children, wealth status, and binary indicator for Western Indian states.

Source: REDS 2006/9, NCAER.

9.3 CHAPTER 6: DATA APPENDIX

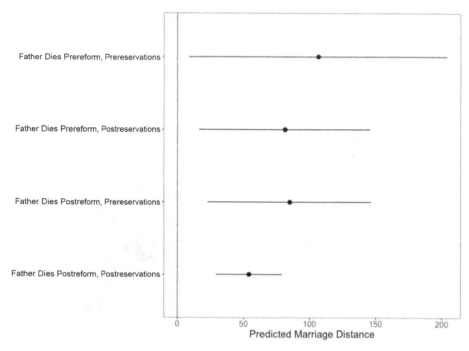

FIGURE 9.11. Reservations' and Reform's Impact on Daughters' Marriage Distance: Predicted Values

Source: NCAER Rural Economic and Demographic Survey, 2006/9. The sample includes all married daughters aged 18 or older, born post-1956 HSA, with at least one living parent. Each point on the graph represents the predicted values of marriage distance for individuals belonging to the given group, with analysis using Equation 6.2's format. Hatch marks represent 95 percent confidence intervals

TABLE 9.24. *Descriptive Statistics, Individuals*

	(1) All *mean/sd*	(2) Women *mean/sd*	(3) Men *mean/sd*
Subject to Hindu law	0.92	0.92	0.92
(Hindu, Jain, Sikh, Buddhist)	(0.26)	(0.27)	(0.26)
Adult child co-residing	0.21	0.03	0.34
with parent(s)	(0.40)	(0.18)	(0.48)
Distance between natal	69.92	78.98	54.35
and marital village	(536.58)	(732.00)	(156.34)
Age (years)	34.57	33.58	35.89
	(9.18)	(9.25)	(8.74)
Education (years completed)	8.16	7.74	8.25
	(4.14)	(3.55)	(4.42)
Siblings: proportion sisters	0.37	0.41	0.34
	(0.25)	(0.24)	(0.25)
Father: secondary or more	0.36	0.36	0.35
education (%)	(0.48)	(0.48)	(0.48)
Mother: secondary or more	0.14	0.13	0.15
education (%)	(0.35)	(0.34)	(0.35)
Scheduled Caste	0.19	0.18	0.19
	(0.39)	(0.39)	(0.39)
Scheduled Tribe	0.09	0.10	0.09
	(0.29)	(0.30)	(0.28)
Other Backward Caste	0.38	0.46	0.32
	(0.48)	(0.50)	(0.47)
Muslim	0.06	0.06	0.06
	(0.24)	(0.24)	(0.24)
Head: total no. children	3.63	3.90	3.51
	(1.90)	(1.89)	(1.88)
Western states (Gujarat,	0.14	0.12	0.14
Maharashtra)	(0.34)	(0.33)	(0.35)
Wealthy: Head's parents own	0.23	0.23	0.23
8 acres or more	(0.42)	(0.42)	(0.42)
Patriarch: number of daughters	1.83	2.02	1.68
	(1.42)	(1.40)	(1.41)
Patriarch: number of sons	2.79	2.74	2.83
	(1.42)	(1.44)	(1.41)
Observations	6,575	2,797	3,481

Source: Rural Economics and Demographic Survey, 2006/9. "All" includes all married individuals, who are the first-born child amongst their siblings, aged 18 or older, born post-1956 HSA, with at least one living parent. The "male" sample includes married sons, first-born in their families, aged 18 or older, born post-1956 HSA, with at least one living parent and one sister. The "female" sample includes married daughters, first-born in their families, aged 18 or older, born post-1956 HSA, with at least one living parent. Standard deviations are in parentheses.

TABLE 9.25. *Descriptive Statistics, Main Dependent and Independent Variables*

	(1) All mean/sd	(2) Women mean/sd	(3) Men mean/sd
Adult child in co-residence with parent(s)	0.21 (0.40)	0.03 (0.18)	0.34 (0.48)
Distance between natal and marital village	69.92 (536.58)	78.98 (732.00)	54.35 (156.34)
Father died postreform	0.91 (0.29)	0.93 (0.26)	0.89 (0.31)
Father dies postreservations	0.89 (0.31)	0.91 (0.28)	0.87 (0.34)
Father died postreform and postreservations	0.88 (0.33)	0.90 (0.30)	0.85 (0.36)
Aged < 20 at reform		0.26 (0.44)	
Sister aged < 20 at reform			0.47 (0.50)
Observations	6,575	2,797	3,481

Source: Rural Economics and Demographic Survey, 2006/9. The sample presented here is the basis for all co-residence analysis. "All" includes all married individuals, who are the first-born child amongst their siblings, aged 18 or older, born post-1956 HSA, with at least one living parent. The "male" sample includes married sons, first-born in their families, aged 18 or older, born post-1956 HSA, with at least one living parent and at least one daughter in the family. The "female" sample includes married daughters, first-born in their families, aged 18 or older, born post-1956 HSA, with at least one living parent. Standard deviations are in parentheses.

TABLE 9.26. *Impact of Birth Order on Children's Co-residence with Parents*

	(1) Target b/se	(2) Target b/se	(3) Target-NR b/se	(4) Target-NR-Late b/se
Panel A: Impact of Birth Order on Son's Care for Parents				
Birth order excl. twins (all children)	−0.04***	0.00	0.00	0.00
acc. to case ID	(0.00)	(0.00)	(0.00)	(0.00)
State fixed effects	Yes	Yes	Yes	Yes
Cohort fixed effects	Yes	Yes	Yes	Yes
State-specific trends	Yes	Yes	Yes	Yes
Controls	No	Yes	Yes	Yes
Adj. R-sq	0.13	0.59	0.59	0.59
N	8,741	8,741	7,807	7,482
Panel B: Impact of Birth Order on Daughter's Care for Parents				
Birth order excl. twins (all children)	−0.00**	−0.00	−0.00	−0.00
acc. to caseid	(0.00)	(0.00)	(0.00)	(0.00)
Controls	No	Yes	Yes	Yes
State fixed effects	Yes	Yes	Yes	Yes
Cohort fixed effects	Yes	Yes	Yes	Yes
State-specific trends	Yes	Yes	Yes	Yes
Adj. R-sq	0.12	0.66	0.65	0.66
N	8,316	8,316	7,425	7,173

+ $p < 0.10$, * $p < 0.05$, ** $p < 0.01$, *** $p < 0.001$

Note: Robust standard errors, clustered at the village level, are in parentheses. The Panel A sample includes all married sons aged 18 or older, born post-1956 HSA, with at least one living parent and one sister. Panel B sample includes all married daughters aged 18 or older, born post-1956 HSA, with at least one living parent. The dependent variable is a binary indicator of whether a given individual co-resides with a parent. The independent variable is a measure of the order in which a given individual was born to a family, ranging from 1 (first-born) to 15, excluding twins. "Target" refers individuals from Hindu, landholding families. Column (3) excludes individuals living in states that do not assign reservations for female *pradhans* randomly (Andhra Pradesh, Himachal Pradesh, Kerala, Tamil Nadu). Column (4) excludes nonrandom implementers of reservations and the two states to implement women's reservations over 10 years after constitutional amendments: Bihar (2006) and Jharkhand (2010). Controls include caste status, total number of female and male children of the household head, wealth status, and a binary indicator for Western Indian states.
Source: REDS 2006/9, NCAER.

TABLE 9.27. *Representation's Impact on First-Born Son's Care for Parents, Logit Model*

	(1) Target b/se	(2) Target b/se	(3) Matched Sample b/se	(4) Target-NR b/se	(5) Target-NR-Late b/se
Panel A					
Adult child co-resides with parent(s)					
Father dies postreservations	−0.35+	−1.93***	−1.54***	−1.96***	−1.91***
	(0.19)	(0.25)	(0.25)	(0.27)	(0.27)
Controls	No	Yes	Yes	Yes	Yes
State fixed effects	Yes	Yes	Yes	Yes	Yes
Cohort fixed effects	Yes	Yes	Yes	Yes	Yes
State-specific trends	Yes	Yes	Yes	Yes	Yes
Pseudo R-sq	0.16	0.60	0.62	0.60	0.59
N	2,127	2,127	1,934	1,878	1,797
Panel B					
Adult child co-resides with parent(s)					
Father dies postreservations	−0.00	0.49	1.23+	0.58	0.58
	(0.39)	(0.49)	(0.74)	(0.51)	(0.51)
Father died postreform	−0.14	−0.14	−0.12	0.12	0.05
	(0.39)	(0.40)	(0.39)	(0.45)	(0.46)
Father died postreform and postreservations	−0.25	−2.53***	−2.79***	−2.88***	−2.77***
	(0.52)	(0.61)	(0.81)	(0.68)	(0.69)
Controls	No	Yes	Yes	Yes	Yes
State fixed effects	Yes	Yes	Yes	Yes	Yes
Cohort fixed effects	Yes	Yes	Yes	Yes	Yes
State-specific trends	Yes	Yes	Yes	Yes	Yes
Pseudo R-sq	0.16	0.61	0.62	0.61	0.61
N	2,127	2,127	1,934	1,878	1,797

+ $p < 0.10$, * $p < 0.05$, ** $p < 0.01$, *** $p < 0.001$

Note: Robust standard errors, clustered at the village level, are in parentheses. The sample includes all married sons, who are the first-born child amongst their siblings, aged 18 or older, born post-1956 HSA, with at least one living parent and at least one sister. The dependent variable is a binary indicator of whether a given married, adult son co-resides with a parent. Treatment by reservations is coded as 1 if one's father was alive at the time reservations were implemented in the village. "Target" refers to individuals from Hindu, landholding families. Column (3) includes the full sample of genetically-matched individuals following Sekhon and Titiunik's (sekhon2012natural) replication study. Column (4) excludes sons living in states that do not assign reservations for female *pradhans* randomly (Andhra Pradesh, Himachal Pradesh, Kerala, Tamil Nadu). Column (5) excludes nonrandom implementers of reservations and the two states to implement women's reservations over 10 years after constitutional amendments: Bihar (2006) and Jharkhand (2010). Controls include caste status, total number of female and male children of the household head, wealth status, and a binary indicator for Western Indian states.

Source: REDS 2006/9, NCAER.

TABLE 9.28. *Representation's Impact on First-Born Son's Co-residence with Parents, Sister Entering Marriage Markets*

	(1) Target b/se	(2) Target b/se	(3) Matched Sample b/se	(4) Target-NR b/se	(5) Target-NR-Late b/se
Panel A: Sister Entering Marriage Market					
Father dies	0.11	0.23	0.29	0.28	0.28
postreservations	(0.31)	(0.27)	(0.36)	(0.27)	(0.28)
Father died postreform	−0.08	−0.11	−0.05	0.06	0.06
	(0.12)	(0.11)	(0.10)	(0.15)	(0.15)
Father died postreform	−0.13	−0.50+	−0.43	−0.67*	−0.67*
and postreservations	(0.32)	(0.28)	(0.37)	(0.30)	(0.30)
State fixed effects	Yes	Yes	Yes	Yes	Yes
Cohort fixed effects	Yes	Yes	Yes	Yes	Yes
State-specific trends	Yes	Yes	Yes	Yes	Yes
Controls	No	Yes	Yes	Yes	Yes
Adj. R-sq	0.14	0.66	0.66	0.66	0.66
N	964	964	1,048	786	755
Panel B: Sister Exiting Marriage Market					
Father dies	0.03	0.07	0.07	0.07	0.07
postreservations	(0.09)	(0.09)	(0.14)	(0.09)	(0.09)
Father died postreform	0.02	−0.03	0.04	−0.01	−0.04
	(0.08)	(0.08)	(0.07)	(0.08)	(0.08)
Father died postreform	−0.11	−0.27*	−0.28+	−0.30*	−0.27*
and postreservations	(0.11)	(0.11)	(0.16)	(0.12)	(0.12)
State fixed effects	Yes	Yes	Yes	Yes	Yes
Cohort fixed effects	Yes	Yes	Yes	Yes	Yes
State-specific trends	Yes	Yes	Yes	Yes	Yes
Controls	No	Yes	Yes	Yes	Yes
Adj. R-sq	0.17	0.61	0.63	0.61	0.61
N	1,186	1,186	904	1,113	1,060

+ $p < 0.10$, * $p < 0.05$, ** $p < 0.01$, *** $p < 0.001$
Note: Robust standard errors, clustered at the village level, are in parentheses. The sample includes all married sons, who are the first-born child amongst their siblings, aged 18 or older, born post-1956 HSA, with at least one living parent and at least one sister. The dependent variable is a binary indicator of whether a given married, adult son co-resides with a parent. Treatment by reservations is coded as 1 if one's father was alive at the time reservations were implemented in the village. "Target" refers to individuals from Hindu, landholding families. Column (3) includes the full sample of geneticallymatched individuals. Column (4) excludes sons living in states that do not assign reservations for female *pradhans* randomly (Andhra Pradesh, Himachal Pradesh, Kerala, Tamil Nadu). Column (5) excludes nonrandom implementers of reservations and the two states to implement women's reservations over 10 years after constitutional amendments: Bihar (2006) and Jharkhand (2010). Controls include caste status, total number of female and male children of the household head, wealth status, and a binary indicator for Western Indian states.
Source: REDS 2006/9, NCAER.

TABLE 9.29. *Representation's Impact on First-Born Son's Co-residence with Parents*

	(1) Target b/se	(2) Target b/se	(3) Matched Sample b/se	(4) Target-NR b/se	(5) Target-NR-Late b/se
Father dies postreservations	0.00 (0.09)	0.08 (0.09)	0.08 (0.14)	0.09 (0.09)	0.08 (0.09)
Father died postreform	−0.00 (0.08)	−0.03 (0.08)	0.02 (0.07)	−0.01 (0.08)	−0.04 (0.08)
Father died postreform and postreservations	−0.07 (0.11)	−0.28* (0.11)	−0.28+ (0.15)	−0.31** (0.11)	−0.28* (0.12)
Sister aged < 20 at reform	0.12 (0.08)	0.17* (0.08)	0.05 (0.09)	0.12 (0.08)	0.12 (0.09)
Sister aged < 20 at reform * Father died postreform	−0.09 (0.13)	−0.10 (0.13)	−0.10 (0.12)	0.05 (0.15)	0.08 (0.15)
Sister aged < 20 at reform * Father died postreservations	0.14 (0.26)	0.14 (0.30)	0.19 (0.39)	0.18 (0.30)	0.19 (0.31)
Sister aged < 20 at reform * Father died postreform and postreservations	−0.11 (0.29)	−0.18 (0.32)	−0.12 (0.40)	−0.33 (0.33)	−0.36 (0.33)
Controls	No	Yes	Yes	Yes	Yes
State FE	Yes	Yes	Yes	Yes	Yes
Birth year FE	Yes	Yes	Yes	Yes	Yes
State trends	Yes	Yes	Yes	Yes	Yes
Adj. R-sq	0.17	0.64	0.65	0.64	0.64
N	2,150	2,150	1,953	1,899	1,815

+ p < 0.10, * p < 0.05, ** p < 0.01, *** p < 0.001

Note: Robust standard errors, clustered at the village level, are in parentheses. The sample includes all married sons, who are the first-born child amongst their siblings, aged 18 or older, born post-1956 HSA, with at least one living parent and one sister. The dependent variable is a binary indicator of whether a given married, adult son co-resides with a parent. Treatment by reservations is coded as 1 if one's father was alive at the time reservations were implemented in the village. Column (3) includes the full sample of geneticallymatched individuals. "Target" refers to individuals from Hindu, landholding families. Column (4) excludes sons living in states that do not assign reservations for female *pradhans* randomly (Andhra Pradesh, Himachal Pradesh, Kerala, Tamil Nadu). Column (5) excludes nonrandom implementers of reservations and the two states to implement women's reservations over 10 years after constitutional amendments: Bihar (2006) and Jharkhand (2010). Controls include caste status, wealth status, total number of female and male children of the household head, wealth status, and a binary indicator for Western Indian states.

Source: REDS 2006/9, NCAER.

TABLE 9.30. *Representation's Impact on First-Born Daughter's Co-residence with Parents*

	(1) Target b/se	(2) Target b/se	(3) Matched Sample b/se	(4) Target-NR b/se	(5) Target-NR-Late b/se
Panel A					
Father dies postreservations	−0.02	−0.03+	−0.01	−0.01	−0.01
	(0.02)	(0.01)	(0.01)	(0.01)	(0.01)
Controls	No	Yes	Yes	Yes	Yes
State fixed effects	Yes	Yes	Yes	Yes	Yes
Cohort fixed effects	Yes	Yes	Yes	Yes	Yes
State-specific trends	Yes	Yes	Yes	Yes	Yes
Adj. R-sq	0.15	0.81	0.86	0.79	0.78
N	1,774	1,774	1,594	1,563	1,500
Panel B					
Father dies postreservations	−0.00	0.01	−0.01	0.03	0.03
	(0.04)	(0.04)	(0.01)	(0.04)	(0.04)
Father died postreform	−0.00	0.01	0.01	0.00	0.00
	(0.03)	(0.02)	(0.02)	(0.01)	(0.01)
Father died postreform and postreservations	−0.01	−0.05	−0.01	−0.04	−0.04
	(0.05)	(0.05)	(0.02)	(0.04)	(0.04)
Controls	No	Yes	Yes	Yes	Yes
State fixed effects	Yes	Yes	Yes	Yes	Yes
Cohort fixed effects	Yes	Yes	Yes	Yes	Yes
State-specific trends	Yes	Yes	Yes	Yes	Yes
Adj. R-sq	0.15	0.81	0.86	0.79	0.78
N	1,774	1,774	1,594	1,563	1,500

+ $p < 0.10$, * $p < 0.05$, ** $p < 0.01$, *** $p < 0.001$

Note: Robust standard errors, clustered at the village level, are in parentheses. The sample includes all married daughters, who are the first-born child amongst their siblings, aged 18 or older, born post-1956 HSA, with at least one living parent. The dependent variable is a binary indicator of whether a given daughter co-resides with a parent. Treatment by reservations is coded as 1 if one's father was alive at the time reservations were implemented in the village. "Target" refers to individuals from Hindu, landholding families. Column (3) includes the full sample of genetically matched individuals. Column (4) excludes daughters living in states that do not assign reservations for female *pradhans* randomly (Andhra Pradesh, Himachal Pradesh, Kerala, Tamil Nadu). Column (5) excludes nonrandom implementers of reservations and the two states to implement women's reservations over 10 years after constitutional amendments: Bihar (2006) and Jharkhand (2010). Controls include caste status, total number of female and male children of the household head, wealth status, and a binary indicator for Western Indian states.

Source: REDS 2006/9, NCAER.

TABLE 9.31. *Representation's Impact on Daughter's Marriage Distance (km)*

	(1) Target b/se	(2) Target b/se	(3) Matched Sample b/se	(4) Target-NR b/se	(5) Target-NR-Late b/se
Panel A: Daughter Entering Marriage Market					
Father dies	14.35	−2.06	43.05	−8.06	−8.49
postreservations	(15.85)	(24.72)	(30.58)	(8.46)	(8.55)
Father died postreform	77.16	73.62	56.70	7.91	8.38
	(64.87)	(68.20)	(43.60)	(11.33)	(11.25)
Father died postreform	−64.27	−29.66	−43.80	8.94	9.34
and postreservations	(65.41)	(76.48)	(36.01)	(13.53)	(13.58)
Controls	No	Yes	Yes	Yes	Yes
State FE	Yes	Yes	Yes	Yes	Yes
Cohort FE	Yes	Yes	Yes	Yes	Yes
State trends	Yes	Yes	Yes	Yes	Yes
Adj. R-sq	0.03	0.03	0.00	0.04	0.01
N	2,108	2,108	3,088	1,429	1,393
Panel B: Daughter Exiting Marriage Market					
Father dies	−10.01	−13.90*	1.88	−14.78*	−12.95
postreservations	(7.48)	(8.24)	(7.70)	(8.36)	(8.52)
Father died postreform	−2.20	−7.93	−8.34	−22.87	−21.36
	(12.74)	(13.76)	(11.18)	(14.25)	(14.81)
Father died postreform	10.07	25.07	24.59	36.86**	35.82*
and postreservations	(13.03)	(16.84)	(19.68)	(17.52)	(18.15)
Controls	No	Yes	Yes	Yes	Yes
State FE	Yes	Yes	Yes	Yes	Yes
Cohort FE	Yes	Yes	Yes	Yes	Yes
State trends	Yes	Yes	Yes	Yes	Yes
Adj. R-sq	0.02	0.02	0.02	0.02	0.02
N	10,770	10,770	8,093	10,078	9,691

$+ p < 0.10, * p < 0.05, ** p < 0.01, *** p < 0.001$

Note: Robust standard errors, clustered at the village level, are in parentheses. The sample includes all married daughters aged 18 or older, born post-1956 HSA. The dependent variable is a measure of how many kilometers away a woman's married home is located from her natal home. Treatment by reservations is coded as 1 if one's father was alive at the time reservations were implemented in the village. "Target" refers to individuals from Hindu, landholding families. Column (3) includes the full sample of geneticallymatched individuals. Column (4) excludes daughters living in states that do not assign reservations for female *pradhans* randomly (Andhra Pradesh, Himachal Pradesh, Kerala, Tamil Nadu). Column (5) excludes nonrandom implementers of reservations and the two states to implement women's reservations over 10 years after constitutional amendments: Bihar (2006) and Jharkhand (2010). Controls include caste status, total number of female and male children of the household head, wealth status, and a binary indicator for Western Indian states.
Source: REDS 2006/9, NCAER.

TABLE 9.32. *Representation and Bargaining Power's Impact on Marriage Distance (km)*

	(1) Target b/se	(2) Target b/se	(3) Matched Sample b/se	(4) Target-NR b/se	(5) Target-NR-Late b/se
Father dies postreservations	−9.96 (7.51)	−13.12 (8.31)	1.35 (8.56)	−14.66* (8.19)	−12.75 (8.34)
Father died postreform	−1.22 (12.93)	−6.12 (13.62)	−11.81 (16.09)	−22.57 (13.98)	−21.13 (14.52)
Father died postreform and postreservations	9.11 (13.18)	24.88 (16.13)	30.93 (24.22)	36.34*** (16.99)	35.32** (17.59)
Aged < 20 at reform	−40.43** (19.72)	−35.98* (20.54)	−77.76 (58.06)	0.36 (11.88)	2.14 (12.29)
Aged < 20 at reform * Father died postreform	75.73 (69.59)	77.74 (69.65)	61.87 (40.62)	27.62 (19.89)	25.50 (20.43)
Aged < 20 at reform * Father died postreservations	15.00 (16.08)	16.60 (19.69)	55.83 (46.17)	6.91 (16.75)	2.89 (16.18)
Aged < 20 at reform * Father died postreform and postreservations	−65.14 (70.76)	−71.76 (71.40)	−89.88* (49.38)	−29.32 (28.20)	−25.82 (28.47)
Controls	No	Yes	Yes	Yes	Yes
State FE	Yes	Yes	Yes	Yes	Yes
Cohort FE	Yes	Yes	Yes	Yes	Yes
State trends	Yes	Yes	Yes	Yes	Yes
Adj. R-sq	0.02	0.02	0.01	0.02	0.02
N	12,878	12,878	11,181	11,507	11,084

$+ p < 0.10,$ $* p < 0.05,$ $** p < 0.01,$ $*** p < 0.001$

Note: Robust standard errors, clustered at the village level, are in parentheses. The sample includes all married daughters aged 18 or older, born post-1956 HSA. The dependent variable is a measure of how many kilometers away a woman married home is located from her natal home. Treatment by reservations is coded as 1 if one's father was alive at the time reservations were implemented in the village. "Target" refers to individuals from Hindu, landholding families. Column (3) includes the full sample of geneticallymatched individuals. Column (4) excludes daughters living in states that do not assign reservations for female *pradhans* randomly (Andhra Pradesh, Himachal Pradesh, Kerala, Tamil Nadu). Column (5) excludes nonrandom implementers of reservations and the two states to implement women's reservations over 10 years after constitutional amendments: Bihar (2006) and Jharkhand (2010). Controls include caste status, total number of female and male children of the household head, wealth status, and a binary indicator for Western Indian states.

Source: REDS 2006/9, NCAER.

TABLE 9.33. *Representation's Impact on Daughter's Planned Support for Parents*

	(1) Target b/se	(2) Target b/se	(3) Matched Sample b/se	(4) Target-NR b/se	(5) Target- NR-Late b/se
Panel A					
Father dies	0.41***	0.24*	0.01	0.26*	0.24
postreservations	(0.09)	(0.14)	(0.17)	(0.15)	(0.16)
Controls	No	Yes	Yes	Yes	Yes
State FE	Yes	Yes	Yes	Yes	Yes
Cohort FE	Yes	Yes	Yes	Yes	Yes
State trends	Yes	Yes	Yes	Yes	Yes
Adj. R-sq	0.04	0.04	0.06	0.04	0.04
N	5,554	5,554	4,993	5,000	4,809
Panel B					
Father dies	0.43 **	0.42*	−0.02	0.42*	0.42*
postreservations	(0.21)	(0.21)	(0.38)	(0.22)	(0.22)
Father died postreform	0.20	0.20	0.12	−0.00	0.00
	(0.18)	(0.18)	(0.17)	(0.26)	(0.26)
Father died postreform	−0.19	−0.38	−0.05	−0.21	−0.25
and postreservations	(0.26)	(0.30)	(0.40)	(0.36)	(0.37)
Controls	No	Yes	Yes	Yes	Yes
State FE	Yes	Yes	Yes	Yes	Yes
Cohort FE	Yes	Yes	Yes	Yes	Yes
State trends	Yes	Yes	Yes	Yes	Yes
Adj. R-sq	0.04	0.04	0.06	0.04	0.04
N	5,554	5,554	4,993	5,000	4,809

$^+ p < 0.10,$ $^* p < 0.05,$ $^{**} p < 0.01,$ $^{***} p < 0.001$

Note: Robust standard errors, clustered at the village level, are in parentheses. The sample includes all married daughters aged 18 or older, born post-1956 HSA. The dependent variable is a response to the survey question: If your parents are alive, what methods will you use to support them? Responses have been coded and ordered based on increasing financial cost born by the individual: 0 – Will not be able to support; 1 – Old age home; 2 – Ask them to live within the same household; 3 – Take an extra job, depend on husband for financial assistance, use savings. Treatment by reservations is coded as 1 if one's father was alive at the time reservations were implemented in the village. "Target" refers to individuals from Hindu, landholding families. Column (3) includes the full sample of geneticallymatched individuals. Column (4) excludes daughters living in states that do not assign reservations for female *pradhans* randomly (Andhra Pradesh, Himachal Pradesh, Kerala, Tamil Nadu). Column (5) excludes nonrandom implementers of reservations and the two states to implement women's reservations over 10 years after constitutional amendments: Bihar (2006) and Jharkhand (2010). Controls include caste status, total number of female and male children of the household head, wealth status, and a binary indicator for Western Indian states.
Source: REDS 2006/9, NCAER.

TABLE 9.34. *Representation's Impact on Daughter's Planned Support for Parents; Alternate Coding*

	(1) Target *b/se*	(2) Target *b/se*	(3) Matched Sample *b/se*	(4) Target-NR *b/se*	(5) Target- NR-Late *b/se*
Panel A					
Father dies	0.41***	0.28*	−0.05	0.34**	0.29*
postreservations	(0.11)	(0.15)	(0.17)	(0.16)	(0.17)
Controls	No	Yes	Yes	Yes	Yes
State FE	Yes	Yes	Yes	Yes	Yes
Cohort FE	Yes	Yes	Yes	Yes	Yes
State trends	Yes	Yes	Yes	Yes	Yes
Adj. R-sq	0.04	0.04	0.07	0.04	0.04
N	5,554	5,554	4,993	5,000	4,809
Panel B					
Father dies	0.70***	0.68***	0.31	0.70***	0.68***
postreservations	(0.21)	(0.21)	(0.39)	(0.21)	(0.22)
Father died postreform	0.22	0.23	0.03	0.06	0.04
	(0.22)	(0.21)	(0.21)	(0.29)	(0.29)
Father died postreform	−0.47	−0.68**	−0.42	−0.53	−0.55
and postreservations	(0.28)	(0.32)	(0.43)	(0.38)	(0.38)
Controls	No	Yes	Yes	Yes	Yes
State FE	Yes	Yes	Yes	Yes	Yes
Cohort FE	Yes	Yes	Yes	Yes	Yes
State trends	Yes	Yes	Yes	Yes	Yes
Adj. R-sq	0.04	0.04	0.07	0.04	0.04
N	5,554	5,554	4,993	5,000	4,809

$^+ p < 0.10, {}^* p < 0.05, {}^{**} p < 0.01, {}^{***} p < 0.001$

Note: Robust standard errors, clustered at the village level, are in parentheses. The sample includes all married daughters aged 18 or older, born post-1956 HSA. The dependent variable is a response to the survey question: If your parents are alive, what methods will you use to support them? Responses have been coded and ordered based on increasing financial cost born by the individual: 0 – Will not be able to support; 1 – Ask them to live within the same household; 2 – Old age home; 3 – Take an extra job, depend on husband for financial assistance, use savings. Treatment by reservations is coded as 1 if one's father was alive at the time reservations were implemented in the village. "Target" refers to individuals from Hindu, landholding families. Column (3) includes the full sample of geneticallymatched individuals. Column (4) excludes daughters living in states that do not assign reservations for female *pradhans* randomly (Andhra Pradesh, Himachal Pradesh, Kerala, Tamil Nadu). Column (5) excludes nonrandom implementers of reservations and the two states to implement women's reservations over 10 years after constitutional amendments: Bihar (2006) and Jharkhand (2010). Controls include caste status, total number of female and male children of the household head, wealth status, and a binary indicator for Western Indian states.

Source: REDS 2006/9, NCAER.

TABLE 9.35. *Representation's Impact on First-Born Son's Co-residence with Parents, Variation by Parental Landholdings*

	(1) Target b/se	(2) Target b/se	(3) Matched Sample b/se	(4) Target-NR b/se	(5) Target-NR-Late b/se
Panel A: First and Second Quartile of Landowners					
Father dies postreservations	−0.13	−0.11	−0.04	−0.10	−0.09
	(0.12)	(0.10)	(0.11)	(0.11)	(0.11)
Father died postreform	−0.03	−0.04	−0.04	0.06	0.10
	(0.11)	(0.09)	(0.07)	(0.11)	(0.11)
Father died postreform and postreservations	0.06	−0.11	−0.08	−0.23	−0.25+
	(0.15)	(0.12)	(0.12)	(0.15)	(0.15)
State fixed effects	Yes	Yes	Yes	Yes	Yes
Cohort fixed effects	Yes	Yes	Yes	Yes	Yes
State-specific trends	Yes	Yes	Yes	Yes	Yes
Controls	No	Yes	Yes	Yes	Yes
Adj. R-sq	0.12	0.49	0.59	0.49	0.49
N	622	622	1,004	491	457
Panel B: Third Quartile of Landowners					
Father dies postreservations	0.12	0.19	0.46*	0.19	0.17
	(0.13)	(0.14)	(0.22)	(0.13)	(0.13)
Father died postreform	−0.02	0.00	−0.04	0.03	−0.02
	(0.12)	(0.13)	(0.12)	(0.13)	(0.13)
Father died postreform and postreservations	−0.19	−0.44*	−0.66**	−0.47**	−0.41*
	(0.16)	(0.18)	(0.24)	(0.18)	(0.18)
State fixed effects	Yes	Yes	Yes	Yes	Yes
Cohort fixed effects	Yes	Yes	Yes	Yes	Yes
State-specific trends	Yes	Yes	Yes	Yes	Yes
Controls	No	Yes	Yes	Yes	Yes
Adj. R-sq	0.23	0.70	0.72	0.68	0.68
N	828	828	498	742	705

Panel C: Fourth Quartile of Landowners

	(1)	(2)	(3)	(4)	(5)
Father dies postreservations	0.15	0.38	−0.25+	0.40	0.40
	(0.26)	(0.27)	(0.13)	(0.27)	(0.27)
Father died postreform	−0.15	−0.07	0.05	−0.09	−0.09
	(0.14)	(0.13)	(0.16)	(0.13)	(0.13)
Father died postreform and postreservations	−0.05	−0.58+	0.00	−0.57+	−0.58+
	(0.29)	(0.30)	(.)	(0.29)	(0.30)
State fixed effects	Yes	Yes	Yes	Yes	Yes
Cohort fixed effects	Yes	Yes	Yes	Yes	Yes
State-specific trends	Yes	Yes	Yes	Yes	Yes
Controls	No	Yes	Yes	Yes	Yes
Adj. R-sq	0.20	0.72	0.75	0.71	0.71
N	700	700	450	666	653

+ $p < 0.10$, * $p < 0.05$, ** $p < 0.01$, *** $p < 0.001$

Note: Robust standard errors, clustered at the village level, are in parentheses. The sample includes all married sons, who are the first-born child amongst their siblings, aged 18 or older, born post-1956 HSA, with at least one living parent and at least one daughter in the family. The dependent variable is a binary indicator of whether a given married, adult son co-resides with a parent. Treatment by reservations is coded as 1 if one's father was alive at the time reservations were implemented in the village. Landownership refers to the amount of land owned by the patriarch (in acres). The first and second quartile of landownership refers to individuals owning less than 2.5 acres of land. The third quartile of land ownership refers to individuals owning between 2.5 and 8 acres of land. The fourth quartile refers to individuals owning more than eight acres of land. "Target" refers to individuals from Hindu, landholding families. Column (3) includes the full sample of geneticallymatched individuals. Column (4) excludes sons living in states that do not assign reservations for female *pradhans* randomly (Andhra Pradesh, Himachal Pradesh, Kerala, Tamil Nadu). Column (5) excludes nonrandom implementers of reservations and the two states to implement women's reservations over 10 years after constitutional amendments: Bihar (2006) and Jharkhand (2010). Controls include caste status, total number of female and male children of the household head, wealth status, and a binary indicator for Western Indian states.
Source: REDS 2006/9, NCAER.

TABLE 9.36. *Representation's Impact on First-Born Son's Co-residence with Parents, Variation by Caste*

	(1) Target b/se	(2) Target b/se	(3) Matched Sample b/se	(4) Target-NR b/se	(5) Target-NR-Late b/se
Panel A: Scheduled Castes					
Father dies postreservations	-0.03	-0.01	-0.25	-0.07	-0.07
	(0.22)	(0.23)	(0.18)	(0.21)	(0.21)
Father died postreform	0.25	0.30	-0.02	0.33+	0.33+
	(0.21)	(0.20)	(0.16)	(0.19)	(0.19)
Father died postreform and postreservations	-0.50+	-0.54+	0.11	-0.58*	-0.58*
	(0.28)	(0.28)	(0.21)	(0.26)	(0.26)
State fixed effects	Yes	Yes	Yes	Yes	Yes
Cohort fixed effects	Yes	Yes	Yes	Yes	Yes
State-specific trends	Yes	Yes	Yes	Yes	Yes
Controls	No	Yes	Yes	Yes	Yes
Adj. R-sq	0.15	0.14	0.05	0.20	0.20
N	175	175	222	157	157
Panel B: OBC					
Father dies postreservations	0.08	0.08	0.37+	0.08	0.08
	(0.12)	(0.12)	(0.19)	(0.12)	(0.12)
Father died postreform	0.01	0.03	0.08	0.14	0.14
	(0.11)	(0.11)	(0.10)	(0.14)	(0.15)
Father died postreform and postreservations	-0.39*	-0.37*	-0.58**	-0.48**	-0.47*
	(0.16)	(0.15)	(0.21)	(0.18)	(0.19)
State fixed effects	Yes	Yes	Yes	Yes	Yes
Cohort fixed effects	Yes	Yes	Yes	Yes	Yes
State-specific trends	Yes	Yes	Yes	Yes	Yes
Controls	No	Yes	Yes	Yes	Yes
Adj. R-sq	0.19	0.22	0.15	0.22	0.22
N	667	667	605	578	541

Panel C: OC

	(1)	(2)	(3)	(4)	(5)
Father dies postreservations	0.15	0.14	0.33	0.23	0.21
	(0.19)	(0.19)	(0.43)	(0.20)	(0.19)
Father died postreform	−0.02	−0.04	−0.10	−0.06	−0.07
	(0.10)	(0.10)	(0.10)	(0.11)	(0.11)
Father died postreform and postreservations	−0.39*	−0.35+	−0.51	−0.39+	−0.39+
	(0.19)	(0.19)	(0.44)	(0.21)	(0.21)
State fixed effects	Yes	Yes	Yes	Yes	Yes
Cohort fixed effects	Yes	Yes	Yes	Yes	Yes
State-specific trends	Yes	Yes	Yes	Yes	Yes
Controls	No	Yes	Yes	Yes	Yes
Adj. R-sq	0.17	0.19	0.13	0.20	0.18
N	409	409	371	336	330

+ $p < 0.10$, * $p < 0.05$, ** $p < 0.01$, *** $p < 0.001$

Note: Robust standard errors, clustered at the village level, are in parentheses. The sample includes all married, who are the first-born child amongst their siblings, aged 18 or older, born post-1956 HSA, with at least one living parent and one sister. The dependent variable is a binary indicator of whether a given married, adult son co-resides with a parent. Treatment by reservations is coded as 1 if one's father was alive at the time reservations were implemented in the village. Scheduled Castes refers to individuals who are members of Scheduled Castes. OBC refers to individuals who are members of Other Backward Classes. OC refers to individuals who are members of Forward Castes. "Target" refers to individuals from Hindu, landholding families. Column (3) includes the full sample of geneticallymatched individuals. Column (4) excludes sons living in states that do not assign reservations for female *pradhans* randomly (Andhra Pradesh, Himachal Pradesh, Kerala, Tamil Nadu). Column (5) excludes nonrandom implementers of reservations and the two states to implement women's reservations over 10 years after constitutional amendments: Bihar (2006) and Jharkhand (2010). Controls include caste status, total number of female and male children of the household head, wealth status, and a binary indicator for Western Indian states.
Source: REDS 2006/9, NCAER.

TABLE 9.37. *Representation's Impact on Daughter's Marriage Distance (km), Variation by Parental Landholdings*

	(1) Target b/se	(2) Target b/se	(3) Matched Sample b/se	(4) Target-NR b/se	(5) Target-NR-Late b/se
Panel A: First and Second Quartile of Landowners					
Father dies postreservations	−1.14 (10.64)	−3.84 (10.17)	0.84 (20.96)	−9.05 (9.22)	−3.94 (8.67)
Father died postreform	27.66* (14.91)	25.24* (14.83)	−4.42 (27.92)	−7.94 (9.36)	−3.62 (8.69)
Father died postreform and postreservations	−10.39 (15.22)	8.61 (18.78)	36.08 (42.38)	39.59** (19.25)	36.54* (21.10)
Controls	No	Yes	Yes	Yes	Yes
State FE	Yes	Yes	Yes	Yes	Yes
Cohort FE	Yes	Yes	Yes	Yes	Yes
State trends	Yes	Yes	Yes	Yes	Yes
Adj. R-sq	0.01	0.02	0.01	0.02	0.02
N	3,711	3,711	5,557	2,973	2,796
Panel B: Third Quartile of Landowners					
Father dies postreservations	−1.60 (11.34)	−5.10 (11.73)	−5.52 (16.01)	−4.02 (11.24)	−2.86 (11.55)
Father died postreform	59.31 (58.10)	59.18 (59.29)	65.35 (60.25)	−1.28 (15.53)	−0.33 (15.94)
Father died postreform and postreservations	−62.55 (58.55)	−53.58 (60.86)	−52.91 (53.94)	0.15 (16.65)	−1.19 (16.96)
Controls	No	Yes	Yes	Yes	Yes
State FE	Yes	Yes	Yes	Yes	Yes
Cohort FE	Yes	Yes	Yes	Yes	Yes
State trends	Yes	Yes	Yes	Yes	Yes
Adj. R-sq	0.03	0.03	0.03	0.02	0.02
N	4,987	4,987	3,080	4,524	4,344

Panel C: Fourth Quartile of landowners

Father dies postreservations	−22.51	−27.45	10.67	−32.36	−32.35
	(21.48)	(22.62)	(14.70)	(22.75)	(23.14)
Father died postreform	−33.39	−40.87	−25.37	−48.50	−48.36
	(28.83)	(30.43)	(21.49)	(31.95)	(32.39)
Father died postreform and postreservations	44.58	58.96*	29.04	65.95**	66.17**
	(29.45)	(30.35)	(27.04)	(31.23)	(31.53)
Controls	No	Yes	Yes	Yes	Yes
State FE	Yes	Yes	Yes	Yes	Yes
Cohort FE	Yes	Yes	Yes	Yes	Yes
State trends	Yes	Yes	Yes	Yes	Yes
Adj. R-sq	0.03	0.03	0.05	0.02	0.02
N	4,180	4,180	2,544	4,010	3,944

+ $p < 0.10$, * $p < 0.05$, ** $p < 0.01$, *** $p < 0.001$

Note: Robust standard errors, clustered at the village level, are in parentheses. The sample includes all married daughters aged 18 or older, born post-1956 HSA. The dependent variable is a measure of how many kilometers away from her natal home a woman's married home is located. Treatment by reservations is coded as 1 if one's father was alive at the time reservations were implemented in the village. Landownership refers to the amount of land owned by the patriarch (in acres). The first and second quartile of landownership refers to individuals owning less than 2.5 acres of land. The third quartile of landownership refers to individuals owning between 2.5 and 8 acres of land. The fourth quartile refers to individuals owning more than eight acres of land. "Target" refers to individuals from Hindu, landholding families. Column (3) includes the full sample of geneticallymatched individuals. Column (4) excludes daughters living in states that do not assign reservations for female *pradhans* randomly (Andhra Pradesh, Himachal Pradesh, Kerala, Tamil Nadu). Column (5) excludes nonrandom implementers of reservations and the two states to implement women's reservations over 10 years after constitutional amendments: Bihar (2006) and Jharkhand (2010). Controls include caste status, total number of female and male children of the household head, wealth status, and a binary indicator for Western Indian states.

Source: REDS 2006/9, NCAER.

TABLE 9.38. *Reservations' Impact on Marriage Distance (km), Variation by Caste*

	(1) Target b/se	(2) Target b/se	(3) Matched Sample b/se	(4) Target-NR b/se	(5) Target-NR-Late b/se
Panel A: Scheduled Castes					
Father dies postreservations	−13.23 (9.69)	−13.07 (10.31)	−6.32 (10.66)	−19.70 (12.03)	−21.02* (11.19)
Father died postreform	−27.81 (21.92)	−28.25 (22.31)	−29.79 (20.10)	−2.39 (10.50)	3.66 (8.89)
Father died postreform and postreservations	52.73** (22.99)	55.58** (25.02)	36.54* (20.54)	29.05* (16.64)	28.94* (15.52)
Controls	No	Yes	Yes	Yes	Yes
State FE	Yes	Yes	Yes	Yes	Yes
Cohort FE	Yes	Yes	Yes	Yes	Yes
State trends	Yes	Yes	Yes	Yes	Yes
Adj. R-sq	0.17	0.17	0.00	−0.01	−0.01
N	1,084	1,084	1,113	958	939
Panel B: OBC					
Father dies postreservations	2.73 (7.07)	4.16 (8.14)	5.64 (17.49)	2.51 (6.52)	5.57 (5.82)
Father died postreform	39.56 (34.44)	39.01 (34.27)	47.55 (31.56)	−5.77 (9.71)	−1.81 (9.27)
Father died postreform and postreservations	−35.56 (35.18)	−40.40 (36.63)	−40.68 (25.73)	3.50 (11.42)	−0.94 (10.93)
Controls	No	Yes	Yes	Yes	Yes
State FE	Yes	Yes	Yes	Yes	Yes
Cohort FE	Yes	Yes	Yes	Yes	Yes
State trends	Yes	Yes	Yes	Yes	Yes
Adj. R-sq	0.02	0.03	0.00	0.01	0.01
N	4,575	4,575	3,605	4,116	3,966

Panel C: OC

Father dies postreservations	−6.22	−7.14	17.54	−20.57	−19.96
	(26.07)	(26.50)	(46.43)	(31.09)	(31.67)
Father died postreform	−34.05	−34.18	−71.93	−32.73	−31.88
	(36.85)	(37.04)	(52.79)	(37.21)	(37.30)
Father died postreform and postreservations	59.27*	59.45*	88.37	55.89	55.37
	(35.44)	(33.98)	(81.04)	(37.29)	(36.82)
Controls	No	Yes	Yes	Yes	Yes
State FE	Yes	Yes	Yes	Yes	Yes
Cohort FE	Yes	Yes	Yes	Yes	Yes
State trends	Yes	Yes	Yes	Yes	Yes
Adj. R-sq	0.03	0.03	0.03	0.03	0.03
N	3,230	3,230	2,441	2,796	2,734

Note: Robust standard errors, clustered at the village level, are in parentheses. The sample includes all married daughters aged 18 or older, born post-1956 HSA. The dependent variable is a measure of how many kilometers away from her natal home a woman's married home is located. Treatment by reservations is coded as 1 if one's father was alive at the time reservations were implemented in the village. "Scheduled Castes" refers to individuals who are members of scheduled castes. OBC refers to individuals who are members of Other Backward Classes. OC refers to individuals who are members of Forward Castes. "Target" refers to individuals from Hindu, landholding families. Column (3) includes the full sample of geneticallymatched individuals. Column (4) excludes daughters living in states that do not assign reservations for female *pradhans* randomly (Andhra Pradesh, Himachal Pradesh, Kerala, Tamil Nadu). Column (5) excludes nonrandom implementers of reservations and the two states to implement women's reservations over 10 years after constitutional amendments: Bihar (2006) and Jharkhand (2010). Controls include caste status, total number of female and male children of the household head, wealth status, and a binary indicator for Western Indian states.
Source: REDS 2006, NCAER.

TABLE 9.39. *Representation's Impact on First-Born Son's Co-residence Parents, Variation by Village-Level Gini Coefficients*

	(1) Target b/se	(2) Target b/se	(3) Target-NR b/se	(4) Target-NR-Late b/se
Panel A: First Tercile of Gini Coefficients (most equal)				
Father dies postreservations	−0.07	−0.26***	−0.25***	−0.25***
	(0.05)	(0.04)	(0.05)	(0.05)
Controls	No	Yes	Yes	Yes
State fixed effects	Yes	Yes	Yes	Yes
Cohort fixed effects	Yes	Yes	Yes	Yes
State-specific trends	Yes	Yes	Yes	Yes
Adj. R-sq	0.19	0.65	0.65	0.65
N	1,005	1,005	955	920
Panel B: Second Tercile of Gini Coefficients				
Father dies postreservations	−0.04	−0.17**	−0.22**	−0.22**
	(0.06)	(0.06)	(0.07)	(0.07)
Controls	No	Yes	Yes	Yes
State fixed effects	Yes	Yes	Yes	Yes
Cohort fixed effects	Yes	Yes	Yes	Yes
State-specific trends	Yes	Yes	Yes	Yes
Adj. R-sq	0.16	0.62	0.63	0.62
N	728	728	645	619

Panel C: Third Tercile of Gini Coefficients (least equal)

Father dies postreservations	-0.06	-0.23**	-0.21*	-0.21+
	(0.09)	(0.07)	(0.10)	(0.11)
Controls	No	Yes	Yes	Yes
State fixed effects	Yes	Yes	Yes	Yes
Cohort fixed effects	Yes	Yes	Yes	Yes
State-specific trends	Yes	Yes	Yes	Yes
Adj. R-sq	0.15	0.64	0.62	0.62
N	417	417	299	276

+ $p < 0.10$, * $p < 0.05$, ** $p < 0.01$, *** $p < 0.001$

Note: Robust standard errors, clustered at the village level, are in parentheses. The sample includes all married sons, who are the first-born child amongst their siblings, aged 18 or older, born post-1956 HSA, with at least one living parent and one sister. The dependent variable is a binary indicator of whether a given married, adult son co-resides with a parent. Treatment by reservations is coded as 1 if one's father was alive at the time reservations were implemented in the village. Panel titles specify the villages to which individuals belong, based on terciles of intravillage land ownership Gini coefficient. Panel A shows results for villages with a land Gini coefficient larger than or equal to 0.2101 and less than or equal to 0.4782 (most equal tercile). Panel B shows villages with Gini coefficients larger than 0.4784 and less than or equal to 0.6076 (moderately equal tercile). Panel C shows villages with Gini coeffients larger than 0.6096 (least equal tercile). "Target" refers to individuals from Hindu, landholding families. Column (3) excludes sons living in states that do not assign reservations for female *pradhans* randomly (Andhra Pradesh, Himachal Pradesh, Kerala, Tamil Nadu). Column (4) excludes nonrandom implementers of reservations and the two states to implement women's reservations over 10 years after constitutional amendments: Bihar (2006) and Jharkhand (2010). Controls include caste status, total number of female and male children of the household head, wealth status, and a binary indicator for Western Indian states.

TABLE 9.40. *Representation and Reform's Impact on First-Born Son's Co-residence Parents, Variation by Village-Level Gini Coefficients*

	(1) Target b/se	(2) Target b/se	(3) Target-NR b/se	(4) Target-NR-Late b/se
Panel A: First Tercile (most equal)				
Father dies postreservations	0.01	0.07	0.09	0.08
	(0.12)	(0.13)	(0.13)	(0.13)
Father died postreform	0.01	0.01	0.06	0.04
	(0.10)	(0.09)	(0.10)	(0.11)
Father died postreform and postreservations	−0.09	−0.35*	−0.39*	−0.37*
	(0.14)	(0.15)	(0.16)	(0.16)
Controls	No	Yes	Yes	Yes
State fixed effects	Yes	Yes	Yes	Yes
Cohort fixed effects	Yes	Yes	Yes	Yes
State-specific trends	Yes	Yes	Yes	Yes
Adj. R-sq	0.19	0.65	0.66	0.66
N	1,005	1,005	955	920
Panel B: Second Tercile				
Father dies postreservations	−0.05	0.09	0.12	0.12
	(0.12)	(0.12)	(0.12)	(0.12)
Father died postreform	−0.14	−0.16	0.02	0.02
	(0.13)	(0.11)	(0.12)	(0.12)
Father died postreform and postreservations	0.12	−0.16	−0.39*	−0.40*
	(0.17)	(0.14)	(0.15)	(0.15)
Controls	No	Yes	Yes	Yes
State fixed effects	Yes	Yes	Yes	Yes
Cohort fixed effects	Yes	Yes	Yes	Yes
State-specific trends	Yes	Yes	Yes	Yes
Adj. R-sq	0.16	0.63	0.64	0.63
N	728	728	645	619

Panel C: Third Tercile (least equal)

	(1)	(2)	(3)	(4)
Father dies postreservations	−0.07	−0.00	−0.01	−0.02
	(0.35)	(0.32)	(0.32)	(0.32)
Father died postreform	0.15	0.08	−0.04	0.01
	(0.18)	(0.15)	(0.22)	(0.22)
Father died postreform and postreservations	−0.10	−0.29	−0.17	−0.21
	(0.38)	(0.33)	(0.37)	(0.36)
Controls	No	Yes	Yes	Yes
State fixed effects	Yes	Yes	Yes	Yes
Cohort fixed effects	Yes	Yes	Yes	Yes
State-specific trends	Yes	Yes	Yes	Yes
Adj. R-sq	0.14	0.64	0.62	0.62
N	417	417	299	276

+ $p < 0.10$, * $p < 0.05$, ** $p < 0.01$, *** $p < 0.001$

Note: Robust standard errors, clustered at the village level, are in parentheses. The sample includes all married sons, who are the first-born child amongst their siblings, aged 18 or older, born post-1956 HSA, with at least one living parent and one sister. The dependent variable is a binary indicator of whether a given married, adult son co-resides with a parent. Treatment by reservations is coded as 1 if one's father was alive at the time reservations were implemented in the village. Panel titles specify the villages to which individuals belong, based on terciles of intravillage landownership Gini coefficient. Panel A shows results for villages with a land Gini coefficient larger than or equal to 0.2101 and less than or equal to 0.4782 (most equal tercile). Panel B shows villages with Gini coefficient larger than 0.4784 and less than or equal to 0.6076 (moderately equal tercile). Panel C shows villages with Gini coefficients larger than 0.6096 (least equal tercile). "Target" refers to individuals from Hindu, landholding families. Column (3) excludes sons living in states that do not assign reservations for female *pradhans* randomly (Andhra Pradesh, Himachal Pradesh, Kerala, Tamil Nadu). Column (4) excludes nonrandom implementers of reservations and the two states to implement women's reservations over 10 years after constitutional amendments: Bihar (2006) and Jharkhand (2010). Controls include caste status, total number of female and male children of the household head, wealth status, and a binary indicator for Western Indian states.

TABLE 9.41. *Representation's Impact on Daughter's Marriage Distance (km), Variation by Village-Level Gini Coefficients*

	(1) Target b/se	(2) Target b/se	(3) Target-NR b/se	(4) Target-NR-Late b/se
Panel A: First Tercile of Gini Coefficients (most equal)				
Father dies postreservations	10.14**	13.31**	12.20**	12.91**
	(4.80)	(5.12)	(5.45)	(5.63)
Controls	No	Yes	Yes	Yes
State FE	Yes	Yes	Yes	Yes
Cohort FE	Yes	Yes	Yes	Yes
State trends	Yes	Yes	Yes	Yes
Adj. R-sq	0.01	0.01	0.01	0.01
N	5,868	5,868	5,611	5,403
Panel B: Second Tercile of Gini Coefficients				
Father dies postreservations	−13.14	−10.91	−1.47	−1.08
	(13.77)	(13.24)	(4.52)	(4.60)
Controls	No	Yes	Yes	Yes
State FE	Yes	Yes	Yes	Yes
Cohort FE	Yes	Yes	Yes	Yes
State trends	Yes	Yes	Yes	Yes
Adj. R-sq	0.04	0.04	0.00	0.01
N	4,445	4,445	3,990	3,895

Panel C: Third Tercile of Gini Coefficients (least equal)

Father dies postreservations	−19.50	10.98	−16.70	−6.89
	(31.38)	(41.62)	(55.58)	(60.28)
Controls	No	Yes	Yes	Yes
State FE	Yes	Yes	Yes	Yes
Cohort FE	Yes	Yes	Yes	Yes
State trends	Yes	Yes	Yes	Yes
Adj. R-sq	0.01	0.01	0.01	0.02
N	2,565	2,565	1,906	1,786

+ $p < 0.10$, * $p < 0.05$, ** $p < 0.01$, *** $p < 0.001$

Note: Robust standard errors, clustered at the village level, are in parentheses. The sample includes all married daughters aged 18 or older, born post-1956 HSA. The dependent variable is a measure of how many kilometers away a woman's married home is located from her natal home. Treatment by reservations is coded as 1 if one's father was alive at the time reservations were implemented in the village. Panel titles specify the villages to which individuals belong, based on terciles of intravillage land ownership Gini coefficient. Panel A shows results for individuals who live in villages with a land Gini coefficient larger than or equal to 0.2101 and less than or equal to 0.4782 (most equal tercile). Panel B shows results for individuals who live in villages with Gini coefficients larger than 0.4784 and less than or equal to 0.6076 (moderately equal tercile). Panel C shows results for individuals who live in villages with Gini coefficients larger than 0.6096 (least equal tercile). "Target" refers to individuals from Hindu, landholding families. Column (3) excludes daughters living in states that do not assign reservations for female *pradhans* randomly (Andhra Pradesh, Himachal Pradesh, Kerala, Tamil Nadu). Column (4) excludes nonrandom implementers of reservations and the two states to implement women's reservations over 10 years after constitutional amendments: Bihar (2006) and Jharkhand (2010). Controls include caste status, wealth status, total number of female and male children of the household head, wealth status, and a binary indicator for Western Indian states.

Source: REDS 2006/9, NCAER.

9.4 CHAPTER 7: DATA APPENDIX

TABLE 9.42. *Descriptive Statistics: Sex Ratio Samples*

	(1) All Mothers	(2) First Generation Mothers	(3) Second Generation Mothers
Resides in early reformer states	0.291	0.300	0.276
	(0.454)	(0.458)	(0.447)
Age (years)	43.00	51.29	28.17
	(13.83)	(9.639)	(4.969)
Father died postreform	0.954	0.933	0.993
	(0.209)	(0.251)	(0.0831)
Father dies postreservations	0.953	0.931	0.992
	(0.212)	(0.253)	(0.0894)
Father died postreform	0.948	0.924	0.992
and postreservations	(0.222)	(0.266)	(0.0914)
Total number of children	3.255	3.791	2.296
	(1.834)	(1.877)	(1.281)
Marriage year	1976.3	1972.1	1993.0
	(13.04)	(10.78)	(5.700)
Marriage age	15.85	15.84	15.90
	(4.774)	(4.868)	(4.388)
Birth year of first child	1984.6	1977.4	1997.5
	(14.62)	(11.13)	(10.67)
Birth year of last child	1992	1986.5	2001.9
	(11.56)	(9.615)	(7.377)
Age at first child	19.89	20.90	18.09
	(8.027)	(5.903)	(10.60)
Age at last child	27.30	29.99	22.48
	(8.169)	(6.893)	(8.058)
Scheduled Caste	0.127	0.128	0.125
	(0.333)	(0.334)	(0.330)
Scheduled Tribe	0.109	0.105	0.114
	(0.311)	(0.307)	(0.318)
Wealthy (top 20%)	0.367	0.360	0.380
	(0.482)	(0.480)	(0.485)
Western states (Gujarat	0.153	0.154	0.151
& Maharashtra)	(0.360)	(0.361)	(0.359)
Patriarch: number of daughters	1.943	1.956	1.918
	(1.468)	(1.471)	(1.461)
Patriarch: number of sons	2.852	2.847	2.860
	(1.419)	(1.415)	(1.426)
Observations	7,629	4,895	2,734

Source: Rural Economics and Demographic Survey, 2006/9. "All mothers" includes all mothers of age 69 or less, from Hindu, landholding families. "First generation mothers" includes all mothers of age 36–69, from Hindu, landholding families. "Second generation mothers" includes all mothers of age younger than 36 years old, from Hindu, landholding families. Standard deviations are in parentheses.

TABLE 9.43. *Representation's Impact on Children's Rate of Survival*

	(1) Target b/se	(2) Target b/se	(3) Matched Sample b/se	(4) Target-NR b/se	(5) Target-NR-Late b/se
Panel A: Daughters' Rate of Survival					
Father dies postreservations	0.19 (0.17)	0.06 (0.18)	0.01 (0.06)	0.08 (0.23)	−0.11 (0.22)
Father died postreform	−0.08 (0.17)	−0.19 (0.18)	−0.13[+] (0.08)	−0.14 (0.23)	−0.31[+] (0.17)
Father died postreform and postreservations	−0.10 (0.22)	0.01 (0.25)	0.00 (.)	−0.07 (0.32)	0.26 (0.26)
Controls	No	Yes	Yes	Yes	Yes
State FE	Yes	Yes	Yes	Yes	Yes
Cohort FE	Yes	Yes	Yes	Yes	Yes
State trends	Yes	Yes	Yes	Yes	Yes
Adj. R-sq	0.26	0.26	0.36	0.17	0.18
N	1,474	1,474	1,279	1,354	1,280
Panel B: Sons' Rate of Survival					
Father dies postreservations	0.29[*] (0.13)	0.31[*] (0.14)	0.41[+] (0.23)	0.28[+] (0.14)	0.34[*] (0.16)
Father died postreform	0.00 (0.11)	−0.01 (0.12)	−0.13 (0.11)	−0.17 (0.17)	−0.07 (0.19)
Father died postreform and postreservations	−0.13 (0.14)	−0.02 (0.16)	−0.47[+] (0.27)	0.09 (0.21)	−0.02 (0.22)
Controls	No	Yes	Yes	Yes	Yes
State FE	Yes	Yes	Yes	Yes	Yes
Cohort FE	Yes	Yes	Yes	Yes	Yes
State trends	Yes	Yes	Yes	Yes	Yes
Adj. R-sq	0.26	0.26	0.39	0.16	0.17
N	1,757	1,757	1,544	1,582	1,497

[+] $p < 0.10$, [*] $p < 0.05$, [**] $p < 0.01$, [***] $p < 0.001$

Note: Robust standard errors, clustered at the village level, are in parentheses. The sample includes includes all mothers in the dataset. The dependent variable for Panel A is a measure of "survival rate" where the numerator is the the number of living daughters born since 1999, and the denominator is the number of daughters born since 1999. The dependent variable for Panel B is a measure of "survival rate" where the numerator is the the number of living sons born since 1999, and the denominator is the number of sons born since 1999. Treatment by reservations is applied if an individual's father is alive by the time of reservations in the village. "Target" includes landed, Hindu mothers only. Column (3) includes the full sample of genetically matched individuals. Column (4) excludes mothers living in states that do not assign reservations for female *pradhans* randomly (Andhra Pradesh, Himachal Pradesh, Kerala, Tamil Nadu). Column (5) excludes nonrandom implementers of reservations and the two states to implement women's reservations over 10 years after constitutional amendments: Bihar (2006) and Jharkhand (2010). Controls include caste status, wealth status, a binary indicator for Western Indian states, and the number of male and female siblings.

Source: REDS 2006/9, NCAER.

TABLE 9.44. *Representation's Impact on Daughter's Relative Rate of Survival*

	(1) Target b/se	(2) Target b/se	(3) Matched Sample b/se	(4) Target-NR b/se	(5) Target- NR-Late b/se
Panel A					
Father dies	−5.38	−9.15	−20.95*	−12.48	−18.13
postreservations	(8.35)	(10.61)	(9.27)	(11.44)	(11.97)
Controls	No	Yes	Yes	Yes	Yes
State FE	Yes	Yes	Yes	Yes	Yes
Cohort FE	Yes	Yes	Yes	Yes	Yes
State trends	Yes	Yes	Yes	Yes	Yes
Adj. R-sq	0.03	0.04	0.01	0.03	0.02
N	2,547	2,547	2,198	2,318	2,199
Panel B					
Father dies	−34.51**	−29.56*	−55.79	−31.16*	−34.11*
postreservations	(12.63)	(11.84)	(37.70)	(12.88)	(14.40)
Father died postreform	1.31	−5.23	4.36	4.46	−1.34
	(23.21)	(20.81)	(15.29)	(31.05)	(34.47)
Father died postreform	28.17	27.81	32.65	17.09	19.73
and postreservations	(24.67)	(23.49)	(43.49)	(32.91)	(36.27)
Controls	No	Yes	Yes	Yes	Yes
State FE	Yes	Yes	Yes	Yes	Yes
Cohort FE	Yes	Yes	Yes	Yes	Yes
State trends	Yes	Yes	Yes	Yes	Yes
Adj. R-sq	0.03	0.04	0.01	0.02	0.02
N	2,547	2,547	2,198	2,318	2,199

[+] $p < 0.10$, * $p < 0.05$, ** $p < 0.01$, *** $p < 0.001$

Note: Robust standard errors, clustered at the village level, are in parentheses. The sample includes all mothers in the dataset with at least one child (either son or daughter). The dependent variable is a measure of "survival rate" where the numerator is the rate of survival of daughters born since 1999 (number of living daughters born since 1999 over the number of daughters born since 1999), and the denominator is the rate of survival of sons born since 1999 (number of living sons born since 1999 over number of sons born since 1999). To avoid division by 0 for mothers with no sons, we transform the variable by adding ϵ (where $\epsilon = 0.01$) to both the resulting daughter survival ratio (nominator) and son survival ratio (denominator). Treatment by reservations is applied if an individual's father is alive by the time of reservations in the village. "Target" includes landed, Hindu mothers only. Column (3) includes the full sample of genetically matched individuals. Columns (4) excludes mothers living in states that do not assign reservations for female *pradhans* randomly (Andhra Pradesh, Himachal Pradesh, Kerala, Tamil Nadu). Columns (5) excludes nonrandom implementers of reservations and the two states to implement women's reservations over 10 years after constitutional amendments: Bihar (2006) and Jharkhand (2010). Controls include caste status, wealth status, a binary indicator for Western Indian states, and the number of male and female siblings.
Source: REDS 2006, NCAER.

TABLE 9.45. *Representation's Impact on Sex Ratios, Variation by Village-Level Land Gini Coefficient (Terciles)*

	(1) Target b/se	(2) Target b/se	(3) Target-NR b/se	(4) Target-NR-Late b/se
Panel A: First Tercile of Land Gini Coefficient				
Father dies postreservations	-0.07*	-0.10***	-0.10***	-0.09**
	(0.03)	(0.03)	(0.03)	(0.03)
Controls	No	Yes	Yes	Yes
State FE	Yes	Yes	Yes	Yes
Cohort FE	Yes	Yes	Yes	Yes
State trends	Yes	Yes	Yes	Yes
Adj. R-sq	0.02	0.04	0.04	0.04
N	3,459	3,459	3,320	3,212
Panel B: Second Tercile of Land Gini Coefficient				
Father dies postreservations	-0.11**	-0.14***	-0.13**	-0.12**
	(0.04)	(0.04)	(0.04)	(0.04)
Controls	No	Yes	Yes	Yes
State FE	Yes	Yes	Yes	Yes
Cohort FE	Yes	Yes	Yes	Yes
State trends	Yes	Yes	Yes	Yes
Adj. R-sq	0.03	0.03	0.03	0.02
N	2,652	2,652	2,365	2,291

(continued)

TABLE 9.45. *(continued)*

Panel C: Third Tercile of Land Gini Coefficient

	(1) Target b/se	(2) Target b/se	(3) Target-NR b/se	(4) Target-NR-Late b/se
Father dies postreservations	-0.06+	-0.10*	-0.10*	-0.08+
	(0.04)	(0.04)	(0.04)	(0.04)
Controls	No	Yes	Yes	Yes
State FE	Yes	Yes	Yes	Yes
Cohort FE	Yes	Yes	Yes	Yes
State trends	Yes	Yes	Yes	Yes
Adj. R-sq	0.04	0.04	0.03	0.04
N	1,518	1,518	1,124	1,044

+ $p < 0.10$, * $p < 0.05$, ** $p < 0.01$, *** $p < 0.001$

Note: Robust standard errors, clustered at the village level, are in parentheses. The sample includes all mothers in the dataset who are 69 years old or younger. Panel titles specify the villages to which individuals belong, based on terciles of intravillage landownership Gini coefficient. Panel A shows results for mothers who live in villages with a land Gini coefficient larger than or equal to 0.2101 and less than or equal to 0.4782 (most equal tercile). Panel B shows results for mothers who live in villages with Gini coefficients larger than 0.4784 and less than or equal to 0.6076 (moderately equal tercile). Panel C shows mothers who live in villages with Gini coefficients larger than 0.6096 (least equal tercile). The dependent variable is the number of girls born to the mother divided by the total number of her children (G/G+B). Treatment by reservations is applied if an individual's father is alive by the time of reservations in the village. "Target" includes landed, Hindu mothers only. Column (3) excludes mothers living in states that do not assign reservations for *female pradhans* randomly (Andhra Pradesh, Himachal Pradesh, Kerala, Tamil Nadu). Column (4) excludes nonrandom implementers of reservations and the two states to implement women's reservations over 10 years after constitutional amendments: Bihar (2006) and Jharkhand (2010). Controls include caste status, wealth status, a binary indicator for Western Indian states, and the number of male and female siblings.
Source: REDS 2006/9, NCAER.

TABLE 9.46. *Representation and Reform's Impact on Sex Ratios, Variation by Village-Level Gini Coefficients*

	(1) Target b/se	(2) Target b/se	(3) Target-NR b/se	(4) Target-NR-Late b/se
Panel A: First Tercile of Gini Coefficients (most equal)				
Father dies postreservations	−0.06	−0.04	−0.04	−0.03
	(0.08)	(0.07)	(0.08)	(0.08)
Father died postreform	−0.03	−0.03	−0.01	−0.00
	(0.09)	(0.08)	(0.08)	(0.08)
Father died postreform and postreservations	0.02	−0.03	−0.06	−0.06
	(0.12)	(0.10)	(0.11)	(0.11)
Controls	No	Yes	Yes	Yes
State FE	Yes	Yes	Yes	Yes
Cohort FE	Yes	Yes	Yes	Yes
State trends	Yes	Yes	Yes	Yes
Adj. R-sq	0.02	0.04	0.04	0.04
N	3,459	3,459	3,320	3,212
Panel B: Second Tercile of Gini Coefficients				
Father dies postreservations	−0.08	−0.09	−0.11	−0.11
	(0.08)	(0.08)	(0.08)	(0.08)
Father died postreform	0.22	0.23	−0.00	−0.01
	(0.15)	(0.14)	(0.28)	(0.28)
Father died postreform and postreservations	−0.23	−0.27[+]	−0.02	−0.01
	(0.16)	(0.16)	(0.29)	(0.29)
Controls	No	Yes	Yes	Yes
State FE	Yes	Yes	Yes	Yes
Cohort FE	Yes	Yes	Yes	Yes
State trends	Yes	Yes	Yes	Yes
Adj. R-sq	0.03	0.04	0.02	0.02
N	2,652	2,652	2,365	2,291

(continued)

TABLE 9.46. (continued)

	(1) Target b/se	(2) Target b/se	(3) Target-NR b/se	(4) Target-NR-Late b/se
Panel C: Third Tercile of Gini Coefficients (least equal)				
Father dies postreservations	−0.03 (0.16)	−0.00 (0.17)	−0.04 (0.17)	−0.00 (0.17)
Father died postreform	0.06 (0.09)	0.05 (0.09)	−0.07 (0.07)	−0.05 (0.08)
Father died postreform and postreservations	−0.08 (0.18)	−0.14 (0.20)	0.01 (0.18)	−0.03 (0.18)
Controls	No	Yes	Yes	Yes
State FE	Yes	Yes	Yes	Yes
Cohort FE	Yes	Yes	Yes	Yes
State trends	Yes	Yes	Yes	Yes
Adj. R-sq	0.04	0.04	0.03	0.04
N	1,518	1,518	1,124	1,044

+ $p < 0.10$, * $p < 0.05$, ** $p < 0.01$, *** $p < 0.001$

Note: Robust standard errors, clustered at the village level, are in parentheses. The sample includes all mothers in the dataset who are 69 years old or younger. Panel titles specify the villages to which individuals belong, based on terciles of intravillage landownership Gini coefficient. Panel A shows results for mothers who live in villages with a land Gini coefficient larger than or equal to 0.2101 and less than or equal to 0.4782 (first tercile). Panel B shows results for mothers who live in villages with Gini coefficients larger than 0.4784 and less than or equal to 0.6076 (second tercile). Panel C shows mothers who live in villages with Gini coefficients larger than 0.6096 (third tercile). The dependent variable is the number of girls born to the mother divided by the total number of her children (G/G+B). Treatment by reservations is applied if an individual's father is alive by the time of reservations in the village. "Target" includes landed, Hindu mothers only. Column (3) excludes mothers living in states that do not assign reservations for female *pradhans* randomly (Andhra Pradesh, Himachal Pradesh, Kerala, Tamil Nadu). Column (4) excludes nonrandom implementers of reservations and the two states to implement women's reservations over 10 years after constitutional amendments: Bihar (2006) and Jharkhand (2010). Controls include caste status, wealth status, a binary indicator for Western Indian states, and the number of male and female siblings.
Source: REDS 2006/9, NCAER.

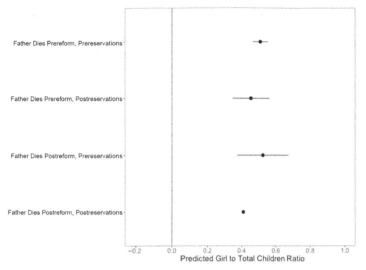

FIGURE 9.12. Representation's Impact on Daughters: Total Children, First Generation: Predicted Values

Source: NCAER Rural Economic and Demographic Survey, 2006/9. The sample includes mothers aged 36–69, from Hindu, landholding families. It excludes women whose fathers reside in states that do not assign reservations randomly (Andhra Pradesh, Himachal Pradesh, Kerala, and Tamil Nadu). Each point on the graph represents the predicted value of the ratio of daughters to total children for individuals within the given group, based on regression analysis using Equation 6.2's format. Hatch marks represent 95 percent confidence intervals

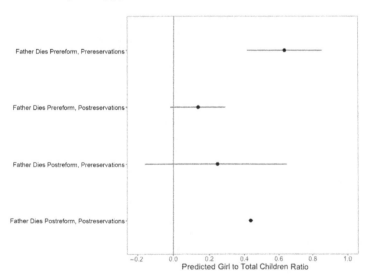

FIGURE 9.13. Representation's Impact on Daughters: Total Children, Second Generation: Predicted Values

Source: NCAER Rural Economic and Demographic Survey, 2006/9. The sample includes mothers younger than 36 years old, from Hindu, landholding families. It excludes women whose fathers reside in states that do not assign reservations randomly (Andhra Pradesh, Himachal Pradesh, Kerala, and Tamil Nadu). Each point on the graph represents the predicted value of the ratio of daughters to total children for individuals within the given group, based on regression analysis using Equation 6.2's format. Hatch marks represent 95 percent confidence intervals

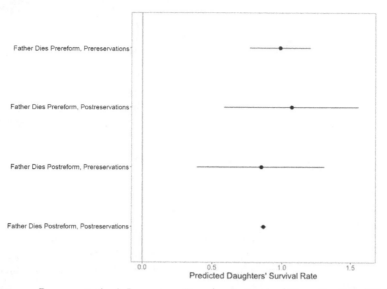

FIGURE 9.14. Representation's Impact on Daughter's Survival Rate: Predicted Values

Source: NCAER Rural Economic and Demographic Survey, 2006/9. The sample includes landed, Hindu mothers. It excludes women whose fathers reside in states that do not assign reservations randomly (Andhra Pradesh, Himachal Pradesh, Kerala, and Tamil Nadu). Each point on the graph represents the predicted values of daughter's survival rate for individuals belonging to the given group, with analysis using Equation 6.2's format. Hatch marks represent 95 percent confidence intervals

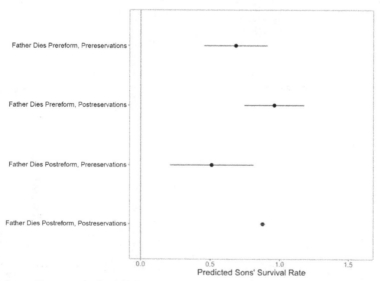

FIGURE 9.15. Representation's Impact on Son's Survival Rate: Predicted Values

Source: NCAER Rural Economic and Demographic Survey, 2006/9. The sample includes landed, Hindu mothers. It excludes women whose fathers reside in states that do not assign reservations randomly (Andhra Pradesh, Himachal Pradesh, Kerala, and Tamil Nadu). Each point on the graph represents the predicted values of son's survival rate for individuals belonging to the given group, with analysis using Equation 6.2's format. Hatch marks represent 95 percent confidence intervals

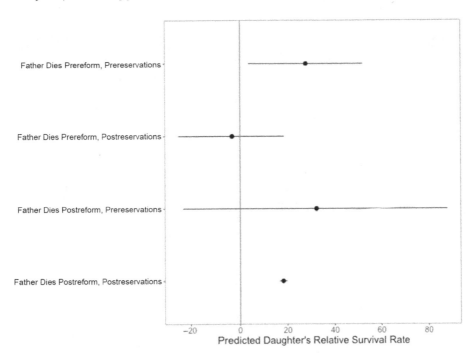

FIGURE 9.16. Representation's Impact on Daughter's Relative Survival Rate: Predicted Values

Source: NCAER Rural Economic and Demographic Survey, 2006/9. The sample includes all mothers with at least one child (either son or daughter). Each point on the graph represents the predicted values of daughter's relative survival rate for individuals belonging to the given group, with analysis using Equation 6.2's format. Hatch marks represent 95 percent confidence intervals

Bibliography

Abrevaya, J. (2009). "Are There Missing Girls in the United States? Evidence from Birth Data." *American Economic Journal: Applied Economics* 1(2), 1–34.

Acemoglu, D., and J. A. Robinson (2005). *Economic Origins of Dictatorship and Democracy*. Cambridge: Cambridge University Press.

(2008). "Persistence of Power, Elites, and Institutions." *American Economic Review* 98(1), 267–93.

(2013). *Why Nations Fail: The Origins of Power, Prosperity, and Poverty*. New York: Crown Business.

Acemoglu, D., S. Johnson, and J. A. Robinson (2001). "The Colonial Origins of Comparative Development: An Empirical Investigation." *American Economic Review* 91(5), 1369–1401.

"Reversal of Fortune: Geography and Institutions in the Making of the Modern World Income Distribution." *The Quarterly Journal of Economics* 117(4), 1231–94.

Acemoglu, D., S. Johnson, P. Querubin, and J. A. Robinson (2008). "When Does Policy Reform Work? The Case of Central Bank Independence." *Brookings Papers on Economic Activity* 1, 351–418.

Adams, M. K., E. Salazar, and R. Lundgren (2013). "Tell Them You Are Planning for the Future: Gender Norms and Family Planning among Adolescents in Northern Uganda." *International Journal of Gynecology and Obstetrics* 123, 7–10.

Afridi, F., V. Iversen, and M. R. Sharan (2013). "Women Political Leaders, Corruption and Learning: Evidence from a Large Public Program in India." IZA Discussion Paper 7212.

Agarwal, B. (1994). *A Field of One's Own: Gender and Land Rights in South Asia*. Cambridge: Cambridge University Press.

"'Bargaining' and Gender Relations: Within and beyond the Household." *Feminist Economics* 3(1), 1–51.

Agarwal, B., et al. (1983). *Mechanization in Indian Agriculture: An Analytical Study Based on the Punjab*. New Delhi: Allied Publishers Pvt. Ltd.

Agnes, F. (2000). *Law and Gender Inequality: The Politics of Women's Rights in India*. New Delhi: Oxford University Press.

Aidt, T. S., and B. Dallal (2008). "Female Voting Power: The Contribution of Women's Suffrage to the Growth of Social Spending in Western Europe (1869–1960)." *Public Choice 134*(3–4), 391–417.

AIWC (1932–3). "All India Women's Conference Annual Reports."

Aiya, V. N. (1875). "Travancore Census Report, 1875." Trevandrum: Travancore Government Press.

Albertus, M. (2015). *Autocracy and Redistribution*. Cambridge: Cambridge University Press.

Aldashev, G., J.-P. Platteau, and Z. Wahhaj (2011). "Legal Reform in the Presence of a Living Custom: An Economic Approach." *Proceedings of the National Academy of Sciences 108*(4), 21320–5.

Aldashev, G., I. Chaara, J.-P. Platteau, and Z. Wahhaj (2012). "Using the Law to Change the Custom." *Journal of Development Economics 97*(2), 182–200.

Alesina, A., P. Giuliano, and N. Nunn (2013). "On the Origins of Gender Roles: Women and the Plough." *The Quarterly Journal of Economics 128*(2), 469–530.

Allendorf, K. (2007). "Do Women's Land Rights Promote Empowerment and Child Health in Nepal?" *World Development 35*(11), 1975–88.

Almond, D., and L. Edlund (2008). "Son-Biased Sex Ratios in the 2000 United States Census." *Proceedings of the National Academy of Sciences 105*(15), 5681–2.

Almond, D., H. Li, and S. Zhang (2017). "Land Reform and Sex Selection in China." Working Paper no. w19153, National Bureau of Economic Research.

Amaral, S. (2014). "Do Improved Property Rights Decrease Violence against Women in India?" Working Paper, Social Science Research Network. https://papers.ssrn.com/sol3/papers.cfm?abstract_id=2504579 (accessed December 28, 2019).

Amaral, S., S. Bandyopadhyay, and R. Sensarma (2015). "Employment Programmes for the Poor and Female Empowerment: The Effect of NREGS on Gender-Based Violence in India." *Journal of Interdisciplinary Economics 27*(2), 199–218.

Ambedkar, B. R. (1979). "The Untouchables and the Pax Britannica." In V. Moon (Ed.), *Dr. Babasaheb Ambedkar: Writings and Speeches*, pp. 75–154. New Delhi: Dr. Ambedkar Foundation.

Ambedkar, B. R., and V. Rodrigues (2002). *The Essential Writings of BR Ambedkar*. Oxford: Oxford University Press.

Ambrus, A., E. Field, and M. Torero (2010). "Muslim Family Law, Prenuptial Agreements, and the Emergence of Dowry in Bangladesh." *The Quarterly Journal of Economics 125*(3), 1349–97.

Amsden, A. H. (2001). *The Rise of the Rest: Challenges to the West from Late-Industrializing Economies*. Oxford: Oxford University Press.

Anandhi, S. (2003). "The Women's Question in the Dravidian Movement c. 1925–48." In A. Rao (Ed.), *Gender and Caste*, pp. 141–63. London: Zed.

Anderson, M. R. (1993). "Islamic Law and the Colonial Encounter in British India." *Institutions and Ideologies: A SOAS South Asia Reader 15*(10), 165.

Anderson, S. (2003). "Why Dowry Payments Declined with Modernization in Europe but Are Rising in India." *Journal of Political Economy 111*(2), 269–310.

(2007). "The Economics of Dowry and Brideprice." *Journal of Economic Perspectives 21*(4), 151–74.

Anderson, S., and C. Bidner (2015). "Property Rights over Marital Transfers." *The Quarterly Journal of Economics 130*(3), 1421–84.

Anderson, S., and M. Eswaran (2009). "What Determines Female Autonomy? Evidence from Bangladesh." *Journal of Development Economics 90*(2), 179–91.

Anderson, S., and G. Genicot (2015). "Suicide and Property Rights in India." *Journal of Development Economics 114*, 64–78.

Anderson, S., et al. (2012). "The Age Distribution of Missing Women in India." *Economic and Political Weekly 47*(47–8), 87–95.

Anderson, T. L., and F. S. McChesney (2003a). *The Economic Approach to Property Rights.* Princeton, NJ: Princeton University Press.

(2003b). *Property Rights: Cooperation,Conflict, and Law.* Princeton, NJ: Princeton University Press.

Andhra Pradesh, State Legislative Assembly (1985). "Debates on the Hindu Succession (Andhra Pradesh Amendment) Bill."

Anoll, A. P. (2018). "What Makes a Good Neighbor? Race, Place, and Norms of Political Participation." *American Political Science Review 112*(3), 1–15.

Antecol, H., K. Bedard, and J. Stearns (2018). "Equal but Inequitable: Who Benefits from Gender-Neutral Tenure Clock Stopping Policies." *American Economic Review 108*(9), 2420–41.

Anukriti, S., and S. Dasgupta (2018). "Marriage Markets in Developing Countries." In Averett, Susan A. L. and S. Hoffman (Eds.), *The Oxford Handbook of Women and the Economy*, pp. 1–27. London: Oxford University Press.

Anukriti, S., S. R. Bhalotra, and H. Tam (2016). "On the Quantity and Quality of Girls: New Evidence on Abortion, Fertility, and Parental Investments." IZA Discussion Paper 10271.

Anukriti, S., S. Kwon, and N. Prakash (2018). "Dowry: Household Responses to Expected Marriage Payments." Working Paper. www2.bc.edu/s-anukriti/ (accessed April 30, 2019).

Arnold, D. (1987). "Touching the Body: Perspectives on the Indian Plague, 1896–1900." In R. Guha and G. C. Spivak (Eds.), *Selected Subaltern Studies*, pp. 87–111. Oxford: Oxford University Press.

Arnold, F., M. K. Choe, and T. K. Roy (1998). "Son Preference, the Family-Building Process and Child Mortality in India." *Population Studies 52*(3), 301–15.

Arunima, G. (1995). "Matriliny and Its Discontents." *India International Centre Quarterly 22*(2/3), 157–67.

Ashraf, N., N. Bau, N. Nunn, and A. Voena (2016). "Bride Price and Female Education." Working Paper 22417, National Bureau of Economic Research.

AsiaNews (2006). "Indian Widows Still Pressured to Throw Themselves on Husbands' Pyres." *AsiaNews*, January 6. www.asianews.it/news-en/Widows-still-pressured-to-throw-themselves-on-husbands 27-pyres-6332.html (accessed on May 23, 2017).

Atkeson, L. R. (2003). "Not All Cues Are Created Equal: The Conditional Impact of Female Candidates on Political Engagement." *Journal of Politics 65*(4), 1040–61.

Atkeson, L. R., and N. Carrillo (2007). "More Is Better: The Influence of Collective Female Descriptive Representation on External Efficacy." *Politics and Gender 3*(01), 79–101.

Awad, I., and U. Natarajan (2018). "Migration Myths and the Global South." *The Cairo Review of Global Affairs.* www.thecairoreview.com/essays/migration-myths-and-the-global-south/ (accessed on February 7, 2019).

Awasthi, P. (2017). "Beaten but Unbowed – Sunanda Sahoo's Silent Struggle." *People's Archive of Rural India.* https://ruralindiaonline.org/articles/beaten-but-unbowed---sunanda-sahoos-silent-struggle (accessed on March 26, 2018).

Ayuko, B., and T. Chopra (2008). "The Illusion of Inclusion: Women's Access to Rights in Northern Kenya." Research Report, World Bank, Nairobi. https://openknowledge .worldbank.org/handle/10986/12787. License: CC BY 3.0 IGO.

Aziz, A. (2000). "Democratic Decentralisation: Experience of Karnataka." *Economic and Political Weekly* 35(39), 3521–6.

Babcock, L., S. Laschever, M. Gelfand, and D. Small (2003). "Nice Girls Don't Ask." *Harvard Business Review* 81(10), 14–16.

Bachrach, P., and M. S. Baratz (1962). "Two Faces of Power." *The American Political Science Review* 56(4), 947–52.

Baden-Powell, B. H. (1882). *A Manual of the Land Revenue Systems and Land Tenures of British India*. Calcutta: Superintendent of Government Printing.

Baines, J. A. (1893). *Census of India, 1891: General Report*. London: Eyre and Spottiswoode for the Indian Government.

Baldez, L. (2006). "The Pros and Cons of Gender Quota Laws: What Happens When You Kick Men Out and Let Women In?" *Politics and Gender* 2(1), 102–9.

Baldwin, K. (2015). *The Paradox of Traditional Chiefs in Democratic Africa*. New York: Cambridge University Press.

Baldwin, K., and J. D. Huber (2010). "Economic versus Cultural Differences: Forms of Ethnic Diversity and Public Goods Provision." *American Political Science Review* 104(4), 644–62.

Ball, A. F. (2006). *Multicultural Strategies for Education and Social Change: Carriers of the Torch in the United States and South Africa*, Volume 25. New York: Teachers College Press.

Ball, C. A. (2006). "The Backlash Thesis and Same-Sex Marriage: Learning from Brown v. Board of Education and Its Aftermath." *William and Mary Bill of Rights Journal* 14(4), 1493–1538.

Ballakrishnen, S. S. (2019). "Just Like Global Firms: Unintended Gender Parity and Speculative Isomorphism in India's Elite Professions." *Law and Society Review* 53(1), 108–40.

Ban, R., and V. Rao (2008). "Tokenism or Agency? The Impact of Women's Reservations on Village Democracies in South India." *Economic Development and Cultural Change* 56(3), 501–30.

Ban, R., S. Jha, and V. Rao (2012). "Who Has Voice in a Deliberative Democracy? Evidence from Transcripts of Village Parliaments in South India." *Journal of Development Economics* 99(2), 428–38.

Banerjee, A., and E. Duflo (2012). *Poor Economics: A Radical Rethinking of the Way to Fight Global Poverty*. New York: PublicAffairs.

Banerjee, A. V., P. J. Gertler, and M. Ghatak (2002). "Empowerment and Efficiency: Tenancy Reform in West Bengal." *Journal of Political Economy* 110(2), 239–80.

Bardhan, P. (2005). *Scarcity, Conflicts, and Cooperation: Essays in the Political and Institutional Economics of Development*. Cambridge, MA: MIT Press.

Bardhan, P., and D. Mookherjee (2000). "Capture and Governance at Local and National Levels." *The American Economic Review* 90(2), 135–9.

    (2010). "Determinants of Redistributive Politics: An Empirical Analysis of Land Reforms in West Bengal, India." *The American Economic Review* 100(4), 1572–1600.

Bardhan, P. K., D. Mookherjee, and M. P. Torrado (2005). "Impact of Political Reservations in West Bengal Local Governments on Anti-Poverty Targeting." Bureau for Research and Economic Analysis of Development. Working Paper no. 104.

(2010). "Impact of Political Reservations in West Bengal Local Governments on Anti-Poverty Targeting." *Journal of Globalization and Development* 1(1), 1–38.

Barnes, T. D., and S. M. Burchard (2013). "Engendering Politics: The Impact of Descriptive Representation on Women's Political Engagement in Sub-Saharan Africa." *Comparative Political Studies* 46(7), 767–90.

Barry, E. (2016). "In India, a Small Band of Women Risk It All for a Chance to Work." *The New York Times*, January 31, 2016. www.nytimes.com/2016/01/31/world/asia/indian-women-labor-work-force.html?_r=0 (accessed February 3, 2017).

Basu, A. M. (1992). *Culture, the Status of Women, and Demographic Behaviour: Illustrated with the Case of India*. Oxford: Clarendon Press.

(2005a). "Women, Political Parties and Social Movements in South Asia." In A. M. Goetz (Ed.), *Governing Women: Women's Political Effectiveness in Contexts of Democratization and Governance Reform*, pp. 87–111. New York: Routledge.

(2005b). "The Demographics of Religious Fundamentalism." In K. Basu and S. Subrahmanyam (Eds.), *Unravelling the Nation: Sectarian Conflict and India's Secular Identity*, pp.129–56. New Delhi: Penguin Books.

Basu, M. (1887). *Hindu Rites and Rituals*. Calcutta: Unknown Publisher.

Basu, N. (2013). "Honour Killings: India's Crying Shame." *Al Jazeera*, November 28, 2013. www.aljazeera.com/indepth/opinion/2013/11/honour-killings-india-crying-shame-20131127105910392176.html (accessed on June 19, 2017).

Baude, A. (1979). *Public Policy and Changing Family Patterns in Sweden 1930–1977*. Beverly Hills, CA: Sage Publications.

Bauer, G. (2012). "Let There Be a Balance: Women in African Parliaments." *Political Studies Review* 10(3), 370–84.

BBC (2018). "Migration to Europe in Charts." *BBC*, September 11. www.bbc.com/news/world-europe-44660699 (accessed on February 7, 2019).

Beaman, L., E. Duflo, R. Pande, and P. Topalova (2012). "Female Leadership Raises Aspirations and Educational Attainment for Girls: A Policy Experiment in India." *Science* 335(6068), 582–6.

Beaman, L., R. Chattopadhyay, E. Duflo, R. Pande, and P. Topalova (2009). "Powerful Women: Female Leadership and Gender Bias." *Quarterly Journal of Economics* 124(4), 1497–1540.

Beaman, L., et al. (2010). "Political Reservation and Substantive Representation: Evidence from Indian Village Councils." In *India Policy Forum*, Volume 7, pp. 159–201. National Council of Applied Economic Research.

Beard, M. (2017). *Women and Power: A Manifesto*. London: Liveright Publishing Corporation, a Division of W. W. Norton and Company.

Becker, G. (1981). *A Treatise on the Family*. Cambridge, MA: Harvard University Press.

Bendor, J. (2010). *Bounded Rationality and Politics*. Berkeley: University of California Press.

Bennett, E. (2014). "Rwanda Strides towards Gender Equality in Government." *Kennedy School Review*. Retrieved from http://harvardkennedyschoolreview.com/rwanda-strides-towards-gender-equality-in-government/ (accessed December 28, 2019).

Benschop, M. (2002). *Rights and Reality: Are Women's Equal Rights to Land, Housing and Property Implemented in East Africa?* Nairobi: UN-HABITAT.

Berry, R. A., et al. (1979). *Agrarian Structure and Productivity in Developing Countries: A Study Prepared for the International Labour Office within the Framework of the World Employment Programme.* Baltimore: Johns Hopkins University Press.

Besley, T. (1995). "Property Rights and Investment Incentives: Theory and Evidence from Ghana." *Journal of Political Economy 103*(5), 903–37.

Besley, T., and R. Burgess (2002). "The Political Economy of Government Responsiveness: Theory and Evidence from India." *Quarterly Journal of Economics 117*(4), 1415–51.

Besley, T., and A. Case (2003). "Political Institutions and Policy Choices: Evidence from the United States." *Journal of Economic Literature 41*(1), 7–73.

Besley, T., and S. Coate (1997). "An Economic Model of Representative Democracy." *Quarterly Journal of Economics 112*(1), 85–114.

(1998). "Sources of Inefficiency in a Representative Democracy: A Dynamic Analysis." *American Economic Review*, 139–56.

Besley, T., R. Pande, and V. Rao (2005). "Participatory Democracy in Action: Survey Evidence from South India." *Journal of the European Economic Association 3*(2–3), 648–657.

Besley, T., O. Folke, T. Persson, and J. Rickne (2017). "Gender Quotas and the Crisis of the Mediocre Man: Theory and Evidence from Sweden." *American Economic Review 107*(8), 2204–42.

Besley, T., R. Pande, L. Rahman, and V. Rao (2004). "The Politics of Public Good Provision: Evidence from Indian Local Governments." *Journal of the European Economic Association 2*(2–3), 416–26.

Bhalotra, S., and I. Clots-Figueras (2014). "Health and the Political Agency of Women." *American Economic Journal: Economic Policy 6*(2), 164–97.

Bhalotra, S., and A. van Soest (2008). "Birth-Spacing, Fertility and Neonatal Mortality in India: Dynamics, Frailty, and Fecundity." *Journal of Econometrics 143*(2), 274–90.

Bhalotra, S., and A. Venkataramani (2015). "Shadows of the Captain of the Men of Death: Early Life Health Interventions, Human Capital Investments, and Institutions." Working Paper, available on SSRN, https://core.ac.uk/download/pdf/74374667.pdf (accessed December 28, 2019).

Bhalotra, S. R., and T. Cochrane (2010). "Where Have All the Young Girls Gone? Identification of Sex Selection in India." IZA Discussion Paper 5381.

Bhalotra, S., R. Brule, and S. Roy (2018). "Women's Inheritance Rights Reform and the Preference for Sons in India." *Journal of Development Economics.* https://doi.org/10.1016/j.jdeveco.2018.08.001 (accessed January 3, 2020).

Bhalotra, S., A. Chakravarty, and S. Gulesci (2018). "The Price of Gold: Dowry and Death in India." CEPR Discussion Paper No. DP12712.

Bhalotra, S., A. Chakravarty, D. Mookherjee, and F. J. Pino (2019). "Property Rights and Gender Bias: Evidence from Land Reform in West Bengal." *American Economic Journal: Applied Economics 11*(2), 205–37.

Bhalotra, S., I. Clots-Figueras, and L. Iyer (2017). "Pathbreakers? Women's Electoral Success and Future Political Participation." *The Economic Journal 128*(613) 1844–78.

Bharadwaj, K. (1974). *Production Conditions in Indian Agriculture: A Study Based on Farm Management Survey.* Cambridge: Cambridge University Press.

Bhavnani, R. R. (2009). "Do Electoral Quotas Work after They Are Withdrawn? Evidence from a Natural Experiment in India." *American Political Science Review 103*(1), 23–35.

Bhavnani, R. R., and G. Nellis (2016). "Can Government-Controlled Media Cause Social Change? Television and Fertility in India." Working Paper. https://faculty .polisci.wisc.edu/bhavnani/wp-content/uploads/2015/09/BhavnaniNellisFertility.pdf. (accessed December 28, 2019)

Bhushan, P. (1978). *The Case That Shook India*. New Delhi: Vikas Publishing House Private.

Binswanger, H. P., K. A. Deininger, and F. Gershon (1995). "Power Distortions Revolt and Reform in Agricultural Land Relations." In D. Rodrik and M. Rosenzweig (Eds.), *Handbook of Development Economics*, Volume 3, pp. 2659–2772. Amsterdam: Elsevier.

Birvaykar, S., and L. Yadav (2011). "Women in Governance." In S. G. Chaudhuri and S. Ghosh (Eds.), *Thus Spoke the Press Vol. 7*, pp. 1–8. New Delhi: The Hunger Project.

Bittner, J. (2019). "Germany Wants More Women in Politics: But Quotas Are a Bad Idea." *New York Times*, February 1. www.nytimes.com/2019/02/01/opinion/ germany-wants-more-women-in-politics-but-quotas-are-a-bad-idea.html (accessed on February 1, 2019).

Bleck, J., and K. Michelitch (2018). "Is Women's Empowerment Associated with Political Knowledge and Opinions? Evidence from Rural Mali." *World Development 106*, 299–323.

Bloch, F., and V. Rao (2002). "Terror as a Bargaining Instruments: A Case Study of Dowry Violence in Rural India." *American Economic Review 92*(4), 1029–43.

Bohlken, A. (2015). *Democratization from Above: The Logic of Local Democracy in the Developing World*. Cambridge: Cambridge University Press.

Bolzendahl, C., and C. Brooks (2007). "Women's Political Representation and Welfare State Spending in 12 Capitalist Democracies." *Social Forces 85*(4), 1509–34.

Boone, C. (2003). *Political Topographies of the African State: Territorial Authority and Institutional Choice*. New York: Cambridge University Press.

Borker, G., J. Eeckhout, N. Luke, S. Minz, K. Munshi, and S. Swaminathan (2017). "Wealth, Marriage and Sex Selection." Working Paper. www.janeeckhout.com/.

Boserup, E. (1970). *The Role of Women in Economic Development*. New York: St. Martin's.

Botticini, M., and A. Siow (2003). "Why Dowries?" *The American Economic Review 93*(4), 1385–98.

Boyce, J. K. (1987). *Agrarian Impasse in Bengal: Institutional Constraints to Technological Change*. Oxford: Oxford University Press.

Braseelle, A.-S., F. Gaspart, and J.-P. Platteau (2002). "Land Tenure Security and Investment Incentives: Puzzling Evidence from Burkina Faso." *Journal of Development Economics 67*(2), 373–418.

Brass, P. R. (1997). *Theft of an Idol: Text and Context in the Representation of Collective Violence*. Princeton, NJ: Princeton University Press.

Braudel, F. (1982). *On History*. Chicago: University of Chicago Press.

Braun, S., and M. Kvasnicka (2013). "Men, Women, and the Ballot: Gender Imbalances and Suffrage Extensions in the United States." *Explorations in Economic History 50*(3), 405–26.

Braunstein, E., and N. Folbre (2001). "To Honor or Obey: The Patriarchy as Residual Claimant." *Feminist Economics 7*(1), 25–54.

Brown, J., K. Ananthpur, and R. Giovarelli (2002). "Women's Access and Rights to Land in Karnataka." Research Report, Rural Development Institute, Seattle, WA.

Browning, M., and R. Subramaniam (1995). "Gender Bias in India: Parental Preferences or Marriage Costs." Mimeograph.

Brulé, R. (2020) "Reform, Representation & Resistance: The Politics of Property Rights' Enforcement." *The Journal of Politics.* https://doi.org/10.1086/708645 (accessed on May 22, 2020).

Brulé, R. and N. Gaikwad (Forthcoming). "Culture, Capital and the Political Economy Gender Gap: Evidence from Meghalaya's Matrilineal Tribes." *The Journal of Politics.*

Buch, N. (2010). *From Oppression to Assertion: Women and Panchayats in India.* New Delhi: Routledge India.

Burnet, J. E. (2008). "Gender Balance and the Meanings of Women in Governance in Post-Genocide Rwanda." *African Affairs* 107(428), 361–86.

    (2011). "Women Have Found Respect: Gender Quotas, Symbolic Representation, and Female Empowerment in Rwanda." *Politics and Gender* 7(3), 303–34.

Burns, N., K. L. Schlozman, and S. Verba (2001). *The Private Roots of Public Action.* Cambridge, MA: Harvard University Press.

Bush, S. S. (2011). "International Politics and the Spread of Quotas for Women in Legislatures." *International Organization* 65(1), 103–37.

Bussell, J. (2012a). *Corruption and Reform in India: Public Services in the Digital Age.* Cambridge: Cambridge University Press.

    (2019). *Clients and Constituents: Political Responsiveness in Patronage Democracies.* Oxford: Oxford University Press.

Caldwell, J. C. (1982). *Theory of Fertility Decline.* London: Academic Press.

Campbell, N. (2001). "Blackstone's Commentaries on the Laws of England." *Canadian Law Libraries* 27(5), 151–2.

Carroll, L. (1989). "Law, Custom and Statutory Social Reform." In J. Krishnamurty (Ed.), *Women in Colonial India: Essays on Survival, Work and the State*, pp. 1–26. Oxford: Oxford University Press.

Castles, S. (2011). "Migration, Crisis, and the Global Labour Market." *Globalizations* 8(3), 311–24.

Census Organization of India (2011). "Census 2011 – Literacy in India." www.census2011.co.in/literacy.php (accessed on January 22, 2019).

Center for American Women and Politics (2019). "Current Numbers." www.cawp.rutgers.edu/current-numbers (accessed on April 22, 2019).

Center for Social Research and UN Women (2014). "Violence against Women in Politics." Research Report, UN Women. www.unwomen.org/-/media/headquarters/attachments/sections/library/publications/2014/violenceagainstwomeninpolitics-report.pdf?la=en&vs=4441.

Central Intelligence Agency (2001). "The CIA World Factbook 2001." www.cia.gov/library/publications/download/download-2001/index.html (accessed on January 22, 2019).

Chakravarti, U. (1993). "Conceptualising Brahmanical Patriarchy in Early India: Gender, Caste, Class and State." *Economic and Political Weekly* 28(14), 582.

    (1998). *Rewriting History: The Life and Times of Pandita Ramabai.* New Delhi: Zubaan Books.

    (2003). *Gendering Caste through a Feminist Lens.* Calcutta: Stree Publications.

Chakravorty, S. (2015). "Why Is India Facing Growing Conflict over Land?" *BBC News*, March 17, 2015. www.bbc.com/news/world-asia-india-31705131 (accessed on March 25, 2017).

Chandra, K. (2004). *Why Ethnic Parties Succeed: Patronage and Ethnic Head Counts in India*. New York: Cambridge University Press.

(2006). "What Is Ethnic Identity and Does It Matter?" *Annual Review of Political Science* 9, 397–424.

Chandran, R. (2016). "Forced by Tradition to Give Up Inheritance, Indian Women Embrace Property Ownership." *Reuters*, November 2. www.reuters.com/article/us-india-landrights-women/forced-by-tradition-to-give-up-inheritance-indian-women-embrace-property-ownership-idUSKBN12X1OZ (accessed on March 20, 2018).

Chatterjee, P. (1990). "The Nationalist Resolution of the Women's Question." In K. Sangari and S. Vaid (Eds.), *Recasting Women: Essays in Indian Colonial History*, pp. 233–53. New Brunswick, NJ: Rutgers University Press.

(1993). *The Nation and Its Fragments: Colonial and Postcolonial Histories*, Volume 11. Princeton, NJ: Princeton University Press.

(1998). *State and Politics in India*. Oxford: Oxford University Press.

Chattopadhyay, R., and E. Duflo (2004a). "Impact of Reservation in Panchayati Raj: Evidence from a Nationwide Randomized Experiment." *Economic and Political Weekly* 39(9), 979–86.

(2004b). "Women as Policy Makers: Evidence from a Randomized Policy Experiment in India." *Econometrica* 72(5), 1409–43.

Chauchard, S. (2014). "Can Descriptive Representation Change Beliefs about a Stigmatized Group? Evidence from Rural India." *American Political Science Review* 108(2), 403–22.

(2017). *Why Representation Matters: The Meaning of Ethnic Quotas in Rural India*. Cambridge: Cambridge University Press.

Chauhan, N. "CBI Confirms Rape Charge against Unnao MLA Kuldeep Singh Sengar." *Times of India*, May 12, 2018. https://timesofindia.indiatimes.com/india/cbi-confirms-rape-charge-against-unnao-mla-kuldeep-singh-sengar/articleshow/64116434.cms (accessed on March 24, 2019).

Chen, M., and J. Drèze (1992). "Widows and Health in Rural North India." *Economic and Political Weekly* 27(43/44), WS81–92.

Chhibber, P. (2002). "Why Are Some Women Politically Active? The Household, Public Space, and Political Participation in India." *International Journal of Comparative Sociology* 43(3–5), 409–29.

Chidambaranar, S. (1983). *Tamilar Thalaivar*. Madras: Periyar Self-Respect Propaganda Organisation.

Chin, A., and N. Prakash (2011). "The Redistributive Effects of Political Reservation for Minorities: Evidence from India." *Journal of Development Economics* 96(2), 265–77.

Chowdhary, N., B. J. Nelson, A. K. Carver, N. J. Johnson, and P. O'Loughlin (1997). "Redefining Politics: Patterns of Women's Political Engagement from a Global Perspective." In B. Nelson and N. Chowdhary (Eds.), *Women and Politics Worldwide*, pp. 3–24. Oxford: Oxford University Press.

Chowdhry, P. (1997). "Enforcing Cultural Codes: Gender and Violence in Northern India." *Economic and Political Weekly* 32(19), 1019–28.

(1998). "Sexuality, Unchastity and Fertility: Economy of Production and Reproduction in Colonial Haryana." In M. A. Chen (Ed.), *Widows in India: Social Neglect and Public Action*, pp. 93–123. New Delhi: Sage Publications.

(2005). "The Crisis of Masculinity in Haryana: The Unmarried, the Unemployed and the Aged." *Economic and Political Weekly* 40(49), 5189–98.

(2008). *Gender Discrimination in Land Ownership: Land Reforms in India.* New Delhi: Sage Publications.

(2012). "Infliction, Acceptance and Resistance: Containing Violence on Women in Rural Haryana." *Economic and Political Weekly* 47(37), 43–59.

Chowdhury, A. (2009). "Microfinance as a Poverty Reduction? A Critical Assessment." Working Papers, United Nations, Department of Economics and Social Affairs.

Chung, W., and M. Das Gupta (2007). "Why Is Son Preference Declining in South Korea? The Role of Development and Public Policy, and the Implications for China and India." Working Paper Series no. 4373, World Bank.

Clayton, A. (2015). "Women's Political Engagement under Quota-Mandated Female Representation: Evidence from a Randomized Policy Experiment." *Comparative Political Studies* 48(3), 333–69.

Clayton, A., and P. Zetterberg (2018). "Quota Shocks: Electoral Gender Quotas and Government Spending Priorities Worldwide." *The Journal of Politics* 80(3), 916–32.

Clayton, A., D. Z. O'Brien, and J. M. Piscopo (2019). "All Male Panels? Representation and Democratic Legitimacy." *American Journal of Political Science* 63(1), 113–29.

Clinton, H. R. (1995). "Remarks to the UN 4th World Conference Women's Plenary Session." *American Rhetoric.* www.americanrhetoric.com/speeches/hillaryclintonbeijingspeech.htm (accessed on May 15, 2017).

Clots-Figueras, I. (2011). "Women in Politics: Evidence from the Indian States." *Journal of Public Economics* 95(7), 664–90.

Coase, R. H. (1937). "The Nature of the Firm." *Economica* 4(16), 386–405.

(1960). "The Problem of Social Cost." *The Journal of Law and Economics* 3(1), 1–44.

Cockburn, C. (1991). *In the Way of Women: Men's Resistance to Sex Equality in Organizations.* Ithaca, NY: ILR Press.

Cohn, B. S. (1996). *Colonialism and Its Forms of Knowledge: The British in India.* Princeton, NJ: Princeton University Press.

Colebrooke, H. (1810). *Two Treatises on the Hindu Law of Inheritance.* Calcutta: A. H. Hubbard.

Coleman, I. (2012). "Are Quotas for Women in Politics a Good Idea?" *The Atlantic,* January 11, 2012. www.theatlantic.com/international/archive/2012/01/are-quotas-for-women-in-politics-a-good-idea/251237/ (accessed on May 24, 2018).

(2013). *Paradise beneath Her Feet: How Women Are Transforming the Middle East.* New York: Random House Incorporated.

Committee, A. M., et al. (1978). "Report of the Committee on Panchayati Raj Institutions." Technical Report, Government of India, Ministry of Agriculture and Irrigation, Department of Rural Development.

Connell, R. W. (2005). "Change among the Gatekeepers: Men, Masculinities, and Gender Equality in the Global Arena." *Signs: Journal of Women in Culture and Society* 30(3), 1801–25.

Cooper, J. (2018). "Does the State Crowd Out Non-State Institutions? A Field Experiment on Community Policing and Gender Inequality in Papua New Guinea." Working Paper. http://jasper-cooper.com/papers/Cooper_CAP.pdf (accessed April 28, 2019).

Corno, L., N. Hildebrandt, and A. Voena (2017). "Age of Marriage, Weather Shocks and the Direction of Marriage Payments." Working Paper 23604, National Bureau of Economic Research.

Cunningham, P. W. (2018). "The Health 202: The Trump Administration's Refugee Policy Is Dismantling the Infrastructure That Cares for Them." *The Washington Post*, December 19. www.washingtonpost.com/news/powerpost/paloma/the-health-202/2018/12/19/the-health-202-the-trump-administration-s-refugee-policy-is-dismantling-the-infrastructures-that-cares-for-them/5c193e8a1b326b2d6629d4e3/?noredirect=on&utm_term=.5a24b84b7c61 (accessed on February 7, 2019).

Cyert, R. M., and J. G. March (1963). *A Behavioral Theory of the Firm*. Englewood Cliffs, NJ: Prentice Hall, Inc.

Dafoe, A., and D. Caughey (2016). "Honor and War: Southern US Presidents and the Effects of Concern for Reputation." *World Politics* 68(2), 341–81.

Dahl, R. (1957). "The Concept of Power." *Behavioral Science* 2(3), 201–15.

Dahlerup, D. (Ed.) (2006). *Women, Quotas and Politics*. Routledge Research in Comparative Politics. New York: Routledge.

Dahlerup, D., and L. Freidenvall (2005). "Quotas as a 'Fast Track' to Equal Representation for Women." *International Feminist Journal of Politics* 7(1), 26–48.

DAKASH (2016). "Access to Justice Survey." http://dakshindia.org/access-to-justice-survey-results/index.html (accessed on November 3, 2016).

Dasgupta, A., K. Gawande, and D. Kapur (2016). "(When) Do Anti-Poverty Programs Reduce Violence? India's Rural Employment Guarantee and Maoist Conflict." *International Organization*. Working Paper from April 22, 2016, https://papers.ssrn.com/sol3/papers.cfm?abstract_id=2495803 (accessed December 28, 2019).

Dasgupta, B., and W. H. Morris-Jones (1975). *Patterns and Trends in Indian Politics: An Ecological Analysis of Aggregate Data on Society and Elections*. New Delhi: Allied Publishers.

Datta, B. (1998a). *And Who Will Make the Chapatis? A Study of All-Women Panchayats in Maharashtra*. Calcutta: Stree Publications.

(1998b). "Conclusion." In B. Datta (Ed.), *And Who Will Make the Chapatis? A Study of All-Women Panchayats in Maharashtra*, pp. 110–35. Calcutta: Stree Publications.

(1998c). "Metikheda." In B. Datta (Ed.), *And Who Will Make the Chapatis? A Study of All-Women Panchayats in Maharashtra*, pp. 74–90. Calcutta: Stree Publications.

Datta, R. (2018). "Eldercare: Demographic Downside." *India Today*, April 26, 2018. www.indiatoday.in/magazine/nation/story/20180507-branded-corporate-elderly-care-old-age-homes-1221657-2018-04-26 (accessed on December 3, 2018).

Deere, C. D., and M. Leon (2003). "The Gender Asset Gap: Land in Latin America." *World Development* 31(6), 925–47.

Deininger, K. A., A. Goyal, and H. Nagarajan (2013). "Women's Inheritance Rights and Intergenerational Transmission of Resources in India." *Journal of Human Resources* 48(1), 114–41.

Deininger, K. A., S. Jin, H. K. Nagarajan, and F. Xia (2015). "Does Female Reservation Affect Long-Term Political Outcomes? Evidence from Rural India." *The Journal of Development Studies* 51(1), 32–49.

Derrett, J. D. M. (1968). *Religion, Law and the State in India*. London: Faber & Faber.

Desai, B. S., A. Dubey, B. Joshi, M. Sen, A. Shariff, and R. D. Vanneman (2010). *Human Development in India: Challenges for a Society in Transition*. Oxford: Oxford University Press.

Desai, S. A. (2010). *Mulla: Hindu Law, 21st Edition*. Nagpur: Lexis Nexis India.

De Soto, H. (2000). *The Mystery of Capital: Why Capitalism Triumphs in the West and Fails Everywhere Else*. New York: Basic books.

Dharmalingam, A., and S. Philip Morgan (1996). "Women's Work, Autonomy, and Birth Control: Evidence from Two South Indian Villages." *Population Studies* 50(2), 187–201.

Diaz-Cayeros, A., F. Estevez, and B. Magaloni (2016). *The Political Logic of Poverty Relief: Electoral Strategies and Social Policy in Mexico*. Cambridge: Cambridge University Press.

Divya, A. (2009). "Why Sati Is Still a Burning Issue." *Times of India*, August 16, 2009. http://timesofindia.indiatimes.com/home/sunday-times/Why-sati-is-still-a-burning-issue/articleshow/4897797.cms (accessed on March 23, 2017).

Dixit, A. K. (2007). *Economics with and without the Law, from Lawlessness and Economics: Alternative Modes of Governance*. Princeton, NJ: Princeton University Press.

Dobston-Hughes, L. (2017). "Malgré la présidence de Trump, les administrations étatiques et municipales peuvent faire avancer les droits des femmes." *Options Politiques*, http://policyoptions.irpp.org/fr/magazines/janvier-2017/what-will-trump-mean-for-gender-equality/ (accessed on June 23, 2017)

Doepke, M., and M. Tertilt (2009). "Women's Liberation: What's in It for Men?" *The Quarterly Journal of Economics* 124(4), 1541–91.

Dollar, D., R. Fisman, and R. Gatti (2001). "Are Women Really the 'Fairer' Sex? Corruption and Women in Government." *Journal of Economic Behavior and Organization* 46(4), 423–9.

Doss, C. (2014). "Women's Landownership: Why We Need to Set the Record Straight." *CGIAR development dialogues*.

Dovi, S. (2002). "Preferable Descriptive Representatives: Will Just Any Woman, Black, or Latino Do?" *American Political Science Review* 96(4), 729–43.

Drazen, A. (2000). "The Political Business Cycle after 25 Years." National Bureau of Economic Research Macroeconomic Annual Paper.

Dubbudu, R. (2015). "The 'Beti' Issue – Declining Child Sex Ratio in India." *Factly*, June 29, 2015. https://factly.in/the-beti-isssue-declining-child-sex-ratio/ (accessed on June 23, 2017).

Duflo, E. (2003). "Grandmothers and Granddaughters: Old-Age Pensions and Intra Household Allocation in South Africa." *The World Bank Economic Review* 17(1), 1–25.

(2012). "Women Empowerment and Economic Development." *Journal of Economic Literature* 50(4), 1051–79.

Duflo, E., and P. Topalova (2004). *Unappreciated Service: Performance, Perceptions, and Women: Leaders in India*. Cambridge, MA: Massachusetts Institute of Technology, Department of Economics.

Duflo, E., and C. Udry (2004). "Intra-Household Resource Allocation in Cote d'Ivoire: Social Norms, Separate Accounts and Consumption Choices." Working Paper no. 10498, National Bureau of Economic Research.

Dunning, T. (2012). *Natural Experiments in the Social Sciences: A Design-Based Approach*. New York: Cambridge University Press.

Dunning, T., and J. Nilekani (2013). "Ethnic Quotas and Political Mobilization: Caste, Parties, and Distribution in Indian Village Councils." *American Political Science Review* 107(1), 35–56.

Eagly, A. H., and S. J. Karau (2002). "Role Congruity Theory of Prejudice toward Female Leaders." *Psychological Review 109*(3), 573.

Easterly, W. (2014). *Tyranny of Experts*. New York: Basic Books.

Economic Commission for Latin America and the Caribbean (2019). "Elected Mayors Who Are Female." http://interwp.cepal.org/sisgen/ConsultaIntegrada.asp?idIndicador=1617&idioma=i (accessed April 18, 2019).

Election Commission (2014). "State-Wise Voter Turnout in General Elections 2014." http://pib.nic.in/newsite/PrintRelease.aspx?relid=105116 (accessed on January 22, 2019).

Electoral Commission of India (2019). "Election History." www.ceo.kerala.gov.in/electionhistory.html (acessed on February 7, 2019).

Ellickson, R. C. (1991). *Order without Law: How Neighbors Settle Disputes*. Cambridge, MA: Harvard University Press.

(2010). *The Household: Informal Order around the Hearth*. Princeton, NJ: Princeton University Press.

Elster, J. (1989). *The Cement of Society: A Survey of Social Order*. New York: Cambridge University Press.

Encyclopedia of the Nations (2019). "Age at First Marriage, Female: Gender Statistics." www.nationsencyclopedia.com/WorldStats/Gender-age-first-marriage-female.html (accessed January 22, 2019).

England, P. (2010). "The Gender Revolution: Uneven and Stalled." *Gender and Society 24*(2), 149–166.

Ensminger, J. (1996). *Making a Market: The Institutional Transformation of an African Society*. New York: Cambridge University Press.

Eswaran, M., and N. Malhotra (2011). "Domestic Violence and Women's Autonomy in Developing Countries: Theory and Evidence." *Canadian Journal of Economics/Revue canadienne d'économique 44*(4), 1222–63.

European Institute for Gender Equality (2019). "Local/Municipals Councils: Mayors or Other Leaders and Members." https://eige.europa.eu/gender-statistics/dgs/indicator/eustrat_prev_eqstrat15_dec_pol__wmid_locpol/metadata (accessed April 18, 2019).

Evans, P. B. (1995). *Embedded Autonomy: States and Industrial Transformation*. Princeton, NJ: Princeton University Press.

(1997). *State-Society Synergy: Government and Social Capital in Development*. Berkeley: University of California.

Fafchamps, M., and A. R. Quisumbing (2007). "Household Formation and Marriage Markets in Rural Areas." *Handbook of Development Economics 4*, 3187–3247.

Faludi, S. (2006). *Backlash: The Undeclared War against American Women*. New York: Three Rivers Press.

Ferrarini, T. (2003). "Parental Leave Institutions in Eighteen Post-War Welfare States." PhD dissertation, Swedish Institute for Social Research.

Field, E. (2007). "Entitled to Work: Urban Property Rights and Labor Supply in Peru." *The Quarterly Journal of Economics 122*(4), 1561–1602.

Fincher, L.H. (2020) "Women Leaders are Doing a Disproportionately Great Job at Handling the Pandemic So Why Aren't There More of Them?" CNN, 16 April, 2020. Accessed on 16 April, 2020 at: https://www.cnn.com/2020/04/14/asia/women-government-leaders-coronavirus-hnk-intl/index.html.

Finnemore, M., and K. Sikkink (1998). "International Norm Dynamics and Political Change." *International Organization 52*(4), 887–917.

Fischer, J. (2015). "Europe's Migration Paralysis." *Project Syndicate*, August 25. www
.project-syndicate.org/commentary/eu-migration-crisis-by-joschka-fischer-2015-08
(accessed February 7, 2019).

Flood, G. D. (1996). *An Introduction to Hinduism.* Cambridge: Cambridge University
Press.

Folbre, N. (1994). *Who Pays for the Kids? Gender and the Structures of Constraint*,
Volume 4. New York: Routledge.

(2009). *Greed, Lust, and Gender: A History of Economic Ideas.* New York: Oxford
University Press.

(2020). *The Rise and Decline of Patriarchal Systems.* Pages refer to submitted
manuscript. New York: Verso Press. Citations from October 8, 2018 manuscript.

Forbes, G. H. (1979). "Women and Modernity: The Issue of Child Marriage in India."
Women's Studies International Quarterly 2(4), 407–19.

(1996). *The New Cambridge History of India: Women in Modern India.* Cambridge:
Cambridge University Press.

Fouka, V. (2016). "Backlash: The Unintended Effects of Language Prohibition in
US Schools after World War I." Working Paper, Stanford University, https://people
.stanford.edu/vfouka/sites/default/files/backlash_december2016.pdf.

(2019). "How Do Immigrants Respond to Discrimination? The Case of Germans in
the US during World War I." *American Political Science Review* 113(2), 405–22.

Fox, R. L., and J. L. Lawless (2014). "Uncovering the Origins of the Gender Gap in
Political Ambition." *American Political Science Review* 108(3), 499–519.

Franceschet, S., and J. M. Piscopo (2008). "Gender Quotas and Women's Substantive
Representation: Lessons from Argentina." *Politics and Gender* 4(3), 393–425.

Franke, R. W., and B. H. Chasin (1994). *Kerala: Radical Reform as Development in an
Indian State.* Oakland, CA: Institute for Food and Development Policy.

Frankel, F., and M. Rao (1989). *Dominance and State Power in Modern India.* Volume
1. Delhi: Oxford University Press.

Frederick, B. (2009). "Are Female House Members Still More Liberal in a Polarized
Era? The Conditional Nature of the Relationship between Descriptive and Substantive
Representation." *Congress and the Presidency* 36(2), 181–202.

Frykenberg, E. (1977). *Land Tenure and Peasant in South Asia.* New Delhi: Orient
Longman.

Gaikwad, N., and G. Nellis (2017). "Do Politicians Discriminate against Internal
Migrants? Evidence from Nationwide Field Experiments in India." *American Journal
of Political Science* 61(2), 456–72.

Galanter, M. (1978a). "Remarks on Family Law and Social Change in India." In
D. Buxbaum (Ed.), *Chinese Family Law in Historical and Comparative Perspective*,
pp. 492–497. Seattle: University of Washington Press.

(1978b). "Who Are the Other Backward Classes? An Introduction to a Constitutional
Puzzle." *Economic and Political Weekly* 13(43–4), 1812–28.

(1981). "Justice in Many Rooms: Courts, Private Ordering, and Indigenous Law." *The
Journal of Legal Pluralism and Unofficial Law* 13(19), 1–47.

(1984). *Competing Inequalities: Law and Backward Classes in India.* Delhi: Oxford
University Press.

Gallagher, K. E., and D. J. Parrott (2011). "What Accounts for Men's Hostile Attitudes
toward Women? The Influence of Hegemonic Male Role Norms and Masculine
Gender Role Stress." *Violence against Women* 17(5), 568–83.

Gangadharan, L., T. Jain, P. Maitra, and J. Vecci (2016). "Social Identity and Governance: The Behavioral Response to Female Leaders." *European Economic Review* 90, 302–25.

Geertz, C. (1973). *The Interpretation of Cultures*. New York: Basic Books.

Gentleman, A. (2006). "Indian Brides Pay a High Price." *The New York TImes*, October 22. www.nytimes.com/2006/10/22/world/asia/22iht-dowry.3246644.html (accessed March 24, 2019).

George, R. (2019). "Gender Norms and Women's Political Participation: Global Trends and Findings on Norm Change." *ALIGN*. www.alignplatform.org/resources/2019/02/gender-norms-and-womens-political-participation-global-trends-and-findings-norm (accessed April 11, 2019).

George, S. M. (2006). "Sex Ratio in India." *The Lancet* 367(9524), 1725.

Ghatak, M., and T. Besley (2010). "Property Rights and Economic Development." In D. Rodrik and M. Rosenzweig (Eds.), *Handbook of Development Economics*, Volume 5, pp. 389–430. Amsterdam: Elsevier.

Ghatak, M., and M. Ghatak (2002). "Recent Reforms in the Panchayat System in West Bengal: Toward Greater Participatory Governance?" *Economic and Political Weekly* 37(1), 45–58.

Ghatak, M., and D. Mookherjee (2014). "Land Acquisition for Industrialization and Compensation of Displaced Farmers." *Journal of Development Economics* 110, 303–12.

Ghatak, M., and S. Roy (2007). "Land Reform and Agricultural Productivity in India: A Review of the Evidence." *Oxford Review of Economic Policy* 23(2), 251–69.

Gillingham, P., and F. Buckle (2014). "Rwanda Land Tenure Regularisation Case Study." Evaluation Report, UK Department of International Development. http://dx.doi.org/10.12774/eod_hd.march2014.gillingham (accessed December 28, 2019).

Girls Count (2016). "Case Study 6: Pasupathi's Efforts in Pullaneri Village: Campaign in Tamil Nadu." *Girls Count*. www.girlscount.in/programmes/campaign-tamilnadu.php (accessed April 26, 2018).

Goel, M., and K. K. P. Birla (2013). "State Level Inequalities in Economic Development." www.indiastat.com/SOCIO_PDF/91/fulltext.pdf (accessed Indiastat, January 22, 2019).

Goetz, A. M., and S. Hassim (Eds.) (2003). *No Shortcuts to Power: African Women in Politics and Policy-Making*. New York: Zed Books.

Goetz, A. M., and R. Jenkins (2018). "Feminist Activism and the Politics of Reform: When and Why Do States Respond to Demands for Gender Equality Policies?" *Development and Change* 49(3), 714–34.

Goldin, C. (1994). "The U-Shaped Female Labor Force Function in Economic Development and Economic History." Working Paper no. 4707, National Bureau of Economic Research.

Goldstein, M., and C. Udry (2008). "The Profits of Power: Land Rights and Agricultural Investment in Ghana." *Journal of Political Economy* 116(6), 981–1022.

Goody, J. (1973). *Polygyny, Economy, and the Role of Women*. Cambridge: Cambridge University Press.

Gottlieb, J. (2016). "Why Might Information Exacerbate the Gender Gap in Civic Participation? Evidence from Mali." *World Development* 86, 95–110.

Gottlieb, J., G. Grossman, and A. Robinson (2018). "Do Men and Women Have Different Policy Preferences in Africa? Determinants and Implications of Gender Gaps in Policy Prioritization." *British Journal of Political Science* 48(3), 611–36.

Gough, E. K. (1956). "Brahman Kinship in a Tamil Village." *American Anthropologist* 58(5), 826–53.

Gough, K. (1961). "Nayar: Central Kerala." In David M. Schneider and Kathleen Gough (Eds.), *Matrilineal Kinship*, 298–384. Berkeley: University of California Press.

——— (1967). "Kerala Politics and the 1965 Elections." *International Journal of Comparative Sociology* 8, 55.

Gould, H. A. (1997). "General Elections, 1996: Karnataka: Decline and Fall of the Congress Machine." *Economic and Political Weekly* 32(37), 2335–49.

Government of India (1892). "Report of the Malabar Marriage Commission." Technical Report, Madras.

——— (1973). "Kerala State Legislature Proceedings of July 11, 1973 on 'The Hindu Marriage (Kerala Amendment) Bill, 1973 and the Kerala Joint Hindu Family System (Abolition) Bill, 1973'."

——— (1975). "Kerala State Legislature Proceedings of August 1, 1975 on 'The Hindu Marriage (Kerala Amendment) Bill, 1973 and the Kerala Joint Hindu Family System (Abolition) Bill, 1975'."

——— (1993). "8th State Legislative Session, Karnataka Legislative Assembly Debates."

——— (2005). "Mahatma Gandhi National Rural Employment Guarantee Act."

——— (2008). *Land Revenue Adminsitration: A Historical Look*. New Delhi: Indian Institute of Dalit Studies.

——— (2011). *Census of India*. New Delhi: Office of the Registrar General.

——— (2019). "Agricultural Census of India." http://agcensus.dacnet.nic.in/ (accessed January 22, 2019).

Government of India, Ministry of Finance (2018). *Economic Survey 2017–2018*. New Delhi: Department of Economic Affairs, Economic Division.

Government of India, Ministry of Law and Justice (2007). "The Maintenance and Welfare of Parents and Senior Citizens Act." http://socialjustice.nic.in/writereaddata/UploadFile/Annexure-X635996104030434742.pdf (accessed April 19, 2019).

Government of India, Ministry of Statistics and Programme Implementation (2013). "Household Ownership and Operational Holdings in India." Technical Report. NSS Report No. 571.

——— (2017). "Women and Men in India – 2017." www.mospi.gov.in/sites/default/files/publication_reports/Womenandmeninindia-2017Mail.pdf (accessed January 22, 2019).

Government of Punjab, Economic and Statistical Organization (2019). "State Wise Data." www.esopb.gov.in/Static/PDF/GSDP/Statewise-Data/StateWiseData.pdf (accessed April 1, 2019).

Government of Sweden (2018). "SEK 1 Billion to Government's First Global Gender Equality Strategy." www.government.se/press-releases/2018/04/sek-1-billion-to-governments-first-global-gender-equality-strategy/ (accessed April 23, 2019).

Gowen, A. (2016). "It's Not Easy for Women to Own Land in India: One Woman Died Fighting for Hers." *The Washington Post*, September 29, 2016. www.washingtonpost.com/world/asia_pacific/its-not-easy-for-women-to-own-land-in-india-one-woman-died-fighting-for-hers/2016/09/29/0e5564f6-654e-11e6-b4d8-33e931b5a26d_story.html (accessed April 23, 2019).

Gravchev, G. (2006). "Hindu Wives Still Burn Themselves Alive When Their Husbands Die." *PravdaReport*. www.pravdareport.com/society/stories/07-06-2006/81664-hindu-0/ (accessed June 28, 2018).

Greif, A. (2006). *Institutions and the Path to the Modern Economy: Lessons from Medieval Trade*. New York: Cambridge University Press.

Grindle, M. S. (2000). *Audacious Reforms: Institutional Invention and Democracy in Latin America*. Baltimore: John Hopkins University Press.

(2007). *Going Local: Decentralization, Democratization, and the Promise of Good Governance*. Princeton, NJ: Princeton University Press.

Guariso, A., B. Ingelaere, and M. Verpoorten (2018). "When Ethnicity Beats Gender: Quotas and Political Representation in Rwanda and Burundi." *Development and Change* 49(6), 1361–91.

Guha, P. (1974). *Towards Equality: Report of the Committee on the Status of Women in India*. Government of India, Ministry of Education and Social Welfare.

Guha, R. (2007). *India after Gandhi: The History of the World's Largest Democracy*. London: Pan Macmillan.

Haas, L., and C. P. Hwang (2008). "The Impact of Taking Parental Leave on Fathers Participation in Childcare and Relationships with Children: Lessons from Sweden." *Community, Work and Family* 11(1), 85–104.

Haas, L., and T. Rostgaard (2011). "Fathers' Rights to Paid Parental Leave in the Nordic Countries: Consequences for the Gendered Division of Leave." *Community, Work and Family* 14(2), 177–95.

Haider-Markel, D. P. (2007). "Representation and Backlash: The Positive and Negative Influence of Descriptive Representation." *Legislative Studies Quarterly* 32(1), 107–33.

Halhed, N. B. (1781). *A Code of Gentoo Laws, or, Ordinations of the Pundits*. London: n.p.

Harris (1996). "Review of Bina Agarwal." *The Economic Journal* 106(436), 708–9.

Hayden, E. (2010). "End Affirmative Action to Avoid White Backlash." *The Atlantic*, August 2. www.theatlantic.com/politics/archive/2010/08/end-affirmative-action-to-avoid-white-backlash/340396/ (accessed March 31, 2019).

Hayes, D., and J. L. Lawless (2015). "A Non-Gendered Lens? Media, Voters and Female Candidates in Contemporary Congressional Elections." *Perspectives on Politics* 13(1), 95–118.

Hayes, D., J. L. Lawless, and G. Baitinger (2014). "Who Cares What They Wear? Media, Gender, and the Influence of Candidate Appearance." *Social Science Quarterly* 95(5), 1194–1212.

Heath, R. (2014). "Women's Access to Labor Market Opportunities, Control of Household Resources, and Domestic Violence: Evidence from Bangladesh." *World Development* 57, 32–46.

Helmke, G., and S. Levitsky (2004). "Informal Institutions and Comparative Politics: A Research Agenda." *Perspectives on Politics* 2(4), 725–40.

Herbst, J. (2000). *States and Power in Africa: Comparative Lessons in Authority and Control*. Princeton, NJ: Princeton University Press.

Herring, R. (1983). *Land to the Tiller: The Political Economy of Land Reform in South Asia*. New Haven, CT: Yale University Press.

Hettne, B. (1978). *The Political Economy of Indirect Rule: Mysore 1881–1947*. London: Curzon Press.

Heyman, G. M. (1996). "Resolving the Contradictions of Addiction." *Behavioral and Brain Sciences* 19(4), 561–74.

Hidrobo, M., and L. Fernald (2013). "Cash Transfers and Domestic Violence." *Journal of Health Economics* 32(1), 304–19.

Hidrobo, M., Peterman, A., and L. Heise (2016). "The Effect of Cash, Vouchers, and Food Transfers on Intimate Partner Violence: Evidence from a Randomized Experiment in Northern Ecuador." *American Economic Journal: Applied Economics* 8(3), 284–303.

Higgins, C. (2018). "The Age of Patriarchy: How an Unfashionable Idea Became a Rallying Cry for Feminism Today." *The Guardian*, June 22. www.theguardian.com/news/2018/jun/22/the-age-of-patriarchy-how-an-unfashionable-idea-became-a-rallying-cry-for-feminism-today (accessed April 23, 2019).

High-Pippert, A., and J. Comer (1998). "Female Empowerment: The Influence of Women Representing Women." *Women and Politics* 19(4), 53–66.

Hirschman, A. O. (1970). *Exit, Voice, and Loyalty: Responses to Decline in Firms, Organizations, and States.* Cambridge, MA: Harvard University Press.

Hirschon, R. *Women and Property – Women as Property.* London: Croom Helm.

Holman, M. R. (2017). "Women in Local Government: What We Know and Where We Go from Here." *State and Local Government Review* 49(4), 285–96.

Hoodfar, H. (1997). *Between Marriage and the Market: Intimate Politics and Survival in Cairo.* Berkeley: University of California Press.

Htun, M. (2016). *Inclusion without Representation in Latin America: Gender Quotas and Ethnic Reservations.* New York: Cambridge University Press.

Htun, M., and L. Weldon (2012). "Sex Equality in Family Law: Historical Legacies, Feminist Activism, and Religious Power in 70 Countries." Washington, DC: World Bank. https://openknowledge.worldbank.org/handle/10986/9204 License: CC BY 3.0 IGO.

Huber, J. D. (2017). *Exclusion by Elections: Inequality, Ethnic Identity, and Democracy.* Cambridge: Cambridge University Press.

Huber, J. D., and P. Suryanarayan (2016). "Ethnic Inequality and the Ethnification of Political Parties: Evidence from India." *World Politics* 68(1), 149–88.

Hutton, J. H. (1933). *Census of India, 1931: India. Report.* Manager of Publications.

Ikegame, A. (2013). *Princely India Re-Imagined: A Historical Anthropology of Mysore from 1799 to the Present.* New York: Routledge.

India Filings (2007). "Indira Gandhi National Old Age Pension Scheme." www.indiafilings.com/learn/indira-gandhi-national-old-age-pension-scheme-ignoaps/ (accessed April 19, 2019).

India Today (1994). "Andhra Pradesh and Karnataka Assembly Polls: Main parties Run Neck and Neck." *India Today*, December 15, 2015. www.indiatoday.in/magazine/cover-story/story/19941215-andhra-pradesh-and-karnataka-assembly-polls-main-parties-run-neck-and-neck-809998-1994-12-15 (accessed January 13, 2019).

Inglehart, R., and P. Norris (2003). *Rising Tide: Gender Equality and Cultural Change around the World.* Cambridge: Cambridge University Press.

International Institute for Democracy and Electoral Assistance (2019a). "Gender Quotas Database." www.idea.int/data-tools/data/gender-quotas/regions-overview (accessed April 21, 2019).

 (2019b). "Gender Quotas Database – Tanzania." www.idea.int/data-tools/data/gender-quotas/country-view/291/35 (accessed January 22, 2019).

International Labour Organization (2019a). "World Development Indicators – Labour Force Participation Rate, Female (% of Female Population Ages 15+)." https://data.worldbank.org/indicator/SL.TLF.CACT.FE.ZS (accessed World Bank DataBank, January 22, 2019).

(2019b). "World Development Indicators – Labour Force Participation Rate, Male (% of Male Population Ages 15+)." https://data.worldbank.org/indicator/SL.TLF.CACT.MA.ZS (accessed World Bank DataBank, January 22, 2019).

Isaacs, M. (2018). "Australia's Draconian Refugee Policy Comes Home to Roost." *Foreign Policy*, November 21. https://foreignpolicy.com/2018/11/21/australias-draconian-refugee-policy-comes-home-to-roost-nauru-manus-island-offshore-detention-scott-morrison-asylum-seekers/ (accessed February 7, 2019).

Iversen, T., and F. Rosenbluth (2006). "The Political Economy of Gender: Explaining Cross-National Variation in the Gender Division of Labor and the Gender Voting Gap." *American Journal of Political Science* 50(1), 1–19.

(2008). "Work and Power: The Connection between Female Labor Force Participation and Female Political Representation." *Annual Review of Political Science* 11, 479–95.

(2010). *Women, Work, and Politics: The Political Economy of Gender Inequality*. New Haven, CT: Yale University Press.

Iyer, L., and A. Mani (2012). "Traveling Agents: Political Change and Bureaucratic Turnover in India." *Review of Economics and Statistics* 94(3), 723–39.

Iyer, L., A. Mani, P. Mishra, and P. Topalova (2012). "The Power of Political Voice: Women's Political Representation and Crime in India." *American Economic Journal: Applied Economics* 4(4), 165–93.

JaagoRe (2014). "5 Women Sarpanch Leaders Showing India the Way Forward." *JaagoRe*. www.jaagore.com/power-of-49/5-women-sarpanch-leaders-showing-india-the-way-forward (accessed March 26, 2018).

Jain, D. (1996). *Panchayat Raj: Women Changing Governance*. New York: UNDP New York.

Jalal, I. (2015). "The Meek Shall Not Inherit the Earth – Gender Equality and Access to Land." *Asian Development Blog*, January 27, 2015. http://blogs.adb.org/blog/meek-shall-not-inherit-earth-gender-equality-and-access-land (accessed April 23, 2019).

Jamil, H., and Anmolam (2017). "Why Aren't We Dealing with the Lack of Women in Indian Politics." *The Wire*, August 2. https://thewire.in/gender/politics-womens-representation (accessed January 22, 2019).

Jayachandran, S. (2015). "The Roots of Gender Inequality in Developing Countries." *Economics* 7(1), 63–88.

Jayachandran, S., and I. Kuziemko (2011). "Why Do Mothers Breastfeed Girls Less Than Boys? Evidence and Implications for Child Health in India." *The Quarterly Journal of Economics* 126(3), 1485–1538.

Jeffrey, R. (1976). *The Decline of Nayar Dominance: Society and Politics in Travancore, 1847–1908*. London: Sussex University Press.

(1993). *Politics, Women and Well-Being: How Kerala Became "a Model."* London: Palgrave Macmillan.

(2004). "Legacies of Matriliny: The Place of Women and the 'Kerala Model.'" *Pacific Affairs* 77(4), 647–64.

(2010). *Media and Modernity: Communications, Women, and the State in India*. Bangalore: Orient Blackswan.

Jensen, R. (2012). "Do Labor Market Opportunities Affect Young Women's Work and Family Decisions? Experimental Evidence from India." *The Quarterly Journal of Economics* 127(2), 753–92.

Jensenius, F. (2015). "Development from Representation? A Study of Quotas for Scheduled Castes in India." *American Economic Journal: Applied Economics* 7(3), 196–220.

(2016). "Competing Inequalities? On the Intersection of Gender and Ethnicity in Candidate Nominations in Indian Elections." *Government and Opposition* 51(3), 440–63.

(2017). *Social Justice through Inclusion: The Consequences of Electoral Quotas in India*. Oxford: Oxford University Press.

Jensenius, F., and G. Verniers (2017). "Studying Indian Politics with Large-Scale Data: Indian Election Data 1961–Today." *Studies in Indian Politics* 5(2), 269–75.

Jha, N. (2014). "The Despicable Persistence of the Dowry in India." *The Daily Beast*, April 8. www.thedailybeast.com/the-despicable-persistence-of-the-dowry-in-india (accessed March 24, 2019).

Jha, P., R. Kumar, and N. Dhingra (2006). "Low Male-to-Female Sex Ratio of Children Born in India: National Survey of 1.1 Million Households." *Lancet* 367(9506), 1727.

John, M. E. (2007). "Women in Power? Gender, Caste and the Politics of Local Urban Governance." *Economic and Political Weekly* 42(9), 3986–93.

(2008). "Reservations and the Women's Movement in Twentieth Century India." In M. Dhanda (Ed.), *Reservations for Women*, pp. 20–58. New Delhi: Women Unlimited, Kali for Women.

Jones, M. P. (1997). "Legislator Gender and Legislator Policy Priorities in the Argentine Chamber of Deputies and the United States House of Representatives." *Policy Studies Journal* 25(4), 613–29.

(1998). "Gender Quotas, Electoral Laws, and the Election of Women: Lessons from the Argentine Provinces." *Comparative Political Studies* 31(1), 3–21.

Jones, W. (2007). *Institutes of Hindu Law, or, the Ordinances of Manu, According to the Gloss of Cullúca, Comprising the Indian System of Duties, Religious, and Civil*. Clark, NJ: The Lawbook Exchange, Ltd.

Jones-Casey, K., L. Dick, and A. Bizoza (2014). "The Gendered Nature of Land and Property Rights in Post-Reform Rwanda." LAND Project Report, Kigali.

Joseph, N. (2001). *Gender Related Problems of Women, Women's Empowerment and Panchayati Raj*. Mumbai: Himalaya Publishing House.

Joshi, S. (1998). "Bitargaon." In B. Datta (Ed.), *And Who Will Make the Chapatis? A Study of All-Women Panchayats in Maharashtra*, pp. 32–62. Calcutta: Stree Publications.

Juluri, V. (2013). *Bollywood Nation: India through Its Cinema*. New Delhi: Penguin Books India.

Kabeer, N. (2012). "Women's Economic Empowerment and Inclusive Growth: Labour Markets and Enterprise Development." Discussion Paper 10, International Development Research Centre.

(2018). "Gender, Livelihood Capabilities and Women's Economic Empowerment: Reviewing Evidence over the Life Course." Technical Report, Gender and Adolescence: Global Evidence.

Kagire, E. (2018). "Number of Women MPs in Rwanda Drops Slightly." *The East African*, September 8. www.theeastafrican.co.ke/news/ea/Number-of-women-MPs-in-Rwanda-drops-slightly/4552908-4750160-0gix9p/index.html (accessed February 7, 2019).

Kahneman, D. (2011). *Thinking, Fast and Slow*. New York: Farrar, Straus and Giroux.

Kahneman, D., and D. Lovallo (1993). "Timid Choices and Bold Forecasts: A Cognitive Perspective on Risk Taking." *Management Science* 39(1), 17–31.

Kahneman, D., and A. Tversky (1979). "Prospect Theory: An Analysis of Decision under Risk." *Econometrica: Journal of the Econometric Society*, 263–91.

Kandiyoti, D. (1988). "Bargaining with Patriarchy." *Gender and Society* 2(3), 274–90.

Kapur, D., K. Gawande, and S. Satyanath (2012). "Renewable Resource Shocks and Conflict in India's Maoist Belt." Center for Global Development.

Karnataka Debates, State Legislative Assembly (1990). "Debates on Hindu Success (Karnataka) Amendment Act, 1990."

Karpowitz, C. F., T. Mendelberg, and L. Shaker (2012). "Gender Inequality in Deliberative Participation." *American Political Science Review* 106(3), 533–47.

Karve, I. (1993). "The Kinship Map of India." In P. Uberoi (Ed.), *Family, Kinship and Marriage in India*, pp. 50–73. New Delhi: Oxford University Press.

Kasara, K. (2013). "Separate and Suspicious: Local Social and Political Context and Ethnic Tolerance in Kenya." *The Journal of Politics* 75(4), 921–36.

Kasara, K., and I. Mares (2017). "Unfinished Business: The Democratization of Electoral Practices in Britain and Germany." *Comparative Political Studies* 50(5), 636–64.

Kaushik, A., and G. Shaktawat (2010). "Women in Panchayati Raj Institutions: A Case Study of Chittorgarh District Council." *Journal of Developing Societies* 26(4), 473–83.

Kevane, M., and L. Gray (1999). "A Woman's Field Is Made At Night: Gendered Land Rights and Norms in Burkina Faso." *Feminist Economics* 5(3), 1–26.

Khan, S. (2017). "Personal Is Political: Prospects for Women's Substantive Representation in Pakistan." Working Paper. www.khansarah.com/research.html (accessed December 28, 2019).

Kishwar, M. (1987). "Toiling without Rights: Ho Women of Singhbhum." *Economic and Political Weekly*, 95–101.

(1994). "Codified Hindu Law: Myth and Reality." *Economic and Political Weekly*, 2145–61.

Klarman, M. J. (1994). "How Brown Changed Race Relations: The Backlash Thesis." *The Journal of American History* 81(1), 81–118.

Klinth, R. (2002). "Göra pappa med barn: Den svenska pappapolitiken 1960–1995 [*Making Dad Pregnant: The Swedish Daddy Politics 1960–1995*]." PhD thesis, Linköping University.

Knight, J. (1992). *Institutions and Social Conflict*. Cambridge: Cambridge University Press.

Kodoth, P. (2002). "Framing Custom, Directing Practices: Authority, Property and Matriliny under Colonial Law in Nineteenth Century Malabar." Technical Report. CDS Working Paper no. 338 Trivandrum: CDS.

Kohli, A. (1982). "The State and Agrarian Policy: Karnataka's Land Reforms: A Model for India?" *Journal of Commonwealth and Comparative Politics* 20(3), 309–28.

(1990). *Democracy and Discontent: India's Growing Crisis of Governability*. Cambridge: Cambridge University Press.

(2004). *State-Directed Development: Political Power and Industrialization in the Global Periphery.* Cambridge: Cambridge University Press.

(2006 [1987]). *The State and Poverty in India: The Politics of Reform.* Cambridge: Cambridge University Press.

Kohli, A., and P. Singh (2013). *Routledge Handbook of Indian Politics.* New York: Routledge.

Kothari, R. (1964). "The Congress System in India." *Asian Survey* 4(12), 1161–73.

Krook, M. L. (2009). *Quotas for Women in Politics: Gender and Candidate Selection Reform Worldwide.* Oxford: Oxford University Press.

(2016). "Contesting Gender Quotas: Dynamics of Resistance." *Politics, Groups, and Identities* 4(2), 268–83.

Krueger, A. O. (1974). "The Political Economy of the Rent-Seeking Society." *The American Economic Review* 64(3), 291–303.

Kruks-Wisner, G. (2011). "Seeking the Local State: Gender, Caste, and the Pursuit of Public Services in Post-Tsunami India." *World Development* 39(7), 1143–54.

(2018). *Claiming the State: Active Citizenship and Social Welfare in Rural India.* New York: Cambridge University Press.

Kudva, N. (2003). "Engineering Elections: The Experiences of Women in Panchayati Raj in Karnataka, India." *International Journal of Politics, Culture, and Society* 16(3), 445–63.

Kulkarni, P. (2017). "Can Religious Norms Undermine Effective Property Rights? Evidence from Inheritance Rights of Widows in Colonial India." *British Journal of Political Science* 47(3), 479–99.

Kumar, A. P. (2016). "Uniform Civil Code: A Heedless Quest?" *Economic and Political Weekly* 51(25), 10–11.

Kumar, R. (1995). "From Chipko to Sati: Contemporary Indian Women's Movement." In A. Basu (Ed.), *The Challenge of Local Feminisms. Women's Movement in Global Perspective*, pp. 58–86. Boulder, CO: Westview Press.

(1999). "From Chipko to Sati: Contemporary Indian Women's Movement." In N. Menon (Ed.), *Gender and Politics in India*, pp. 342–69. New Delhi: Oxford University Press.

Landau, B. L., W. C. Kihato, and H. Postel (2018). "Europe Is Making Its Migration Problem Worse." *Foreign Affairs*, September 5, 2018. www.foreignaffairs.com/articles/africa/2018-09-05/europe-making-its-migration-problem-worse (accessed February 7, 2019).

Landesa (2002). "Women's Secure Rights to Land: Benefits, Barriers and Best Practices." Issue Brief, Rural Development Institute, Seattle.

Larson, C. (2014). "In China, More Girls Are on the Way." *Bloomberg Business*, August 1. www.bloomberg.com/bw/articles/2014-07-31/chinas-girl-births-ratio-improves-as-country-gets-more-educated (accessed June 23, 2017).

Law Commission India (2005). "Property Rights of Women: Proposed Reforms under the Hindu Law – 174th Report." Report, Law Commission India.

Lawless, J. L. (2004). "Politics of Presence? Congresswomen and Symbolic Representation." *Political Research Quarterly* 57(1), 81–99.

Lawry, S., C. Samii, R. Hall, A. Leopold, D. Hornby, and F. Mtero (2016). "The Impact of Land Property Rights Interventions on Investment and Agricultural Productivity in Developing Countries: A Systematic Review." *Journal of Development Effectiveness* 9(1), 1–21.

Levi, M. (1988). *Of Rule and Revenue*. Berkeley: University of California Press.

Libecap, G. D. (1993). *Contracting for Property Rights*. Cambridge: Cambridge University Press.

Lieberman, E. S. (2005). "Nested Analysis as a Mixed-Method Strategy for Cross-National Research." *American Political Science Review* 99, 574–602.

Lindberg, S., V. B. Athreya, R. Vidyasagar, G. Djurfeldt, and A. Rajagopal (2011). "A Silent 'Revolution'? Women's Empowerment in Rural Tamil Nadu." *Economic and Political Weekly* 46(13), 111–20.

Lipton, M. (2009). *Land Reform in Developing Countries: Property Rights and Property Wrongs*. Abingdon, UK: Routledge.

Lipton, M., and R. Longhurst (1989). *New Seeds and Poor People*. London: Unwin Hyman.

Lobodzinska, B. (1995). *Family, Women, and Employment in Central-Eastern Europe*. Barbara Lobodzinska (Ed.). Westport, CT: Greenwood Press.

Locke, J. (1988). *Locke: Two Treatises of Government Student Edition*. Cambridge: Cambridge University Press.

Lok Sabha Secretariat (1947). *Constituent Assembly Debates*. Delhi.

Lowes, S., and N. Nunn (2017). "Bride Price and the Wellbeing of Women." WIDER Working Paper 2017/131.

Lukes, S. (1974). *Power: A Radical View*. London: Macmillan.

Lundberg, S., and R. A. Pollak (1996). "Bargaining and Distribution in Marriage." *The Journal of Economic Perspectives* 10(4), 139–58.

   (2001). "Efficiency in Marriage." *Review of Economics of the Household* 1(3), 153–67.

Mabsout, R., and I. Van Staveren (2010). "Disentangling Bargaining Power from Individual and Household Level to Institutions: Evidence on Women's Position in Ethiopia." *World Development* 38(5), 783–96.

Machiavelli, N. (1957). *Discourse*. Boston: Routledge.

Mackie, G. (1996). "Ending Footbinding and Infibulation: A Convention Account." *American Sociological Review*, 61(6), 999–1017.

Mahal, A., A. Varshney, and S. Taman (2006). "Diffusion of Diagnostic Medical Devices and Policy Implications for India." *International Journal of Technology Assessment in Health Care* 22(2), 184–90.

Maine, H. (1861). *Ancient Law, Its Connection with the Early History of Society, and Its Relation to Modern Ideas*. London: John Murray.

Majlesi, K. (2012). "Labor Market Opportunities and Sex Specific Investment in Children's Human Capital: Evidence from Mexico." Working Paper, Lund University.

Majumdar, S. (2014). "India Politics So Dangerous to Women They Keep Out." *WeNews*, May 16. https://womensenews.org/2014/05/india-politics-so-dangerous-women-they-keep-out/ (accessed May 24, 2018).

Mammen, K., and C. Paxson (2000). "Women's Work and Economic Development." *The Journal of Economic Perspectives* 14(4), 141–64.

Mandela, N. (1994). "State of the Nation Address by President of South Africa, Nelson Mandela." www.gov.za/node/538197 (accessed December 28, 2019).

Mani, L. (1998). *Contentious Traditions: The Debate on Sati in Colonial India*. Berkeley: University of California Press.

Manimala, S. (1983). "Zameen Kenkar? Jote Onkar!-Women's Participation in the Bodhgaya Land Struggle." *Manushi* 14, 2–16.

Manor, J. (1989). "Karnataka: Caste, Class, Dominance and Politics in a Cohesive Society." *Dominance and State Power in Modern India: Decline of a Social Order 1*, 322–61.

Mansbridge, J. (1983). *Beyond Adversary Democracy.* Chicago: University of Chicago Press.

    (1999a). "On the Idea That Participation Makes Better Citizens." *Citizen Competence and Democratic Institutions*, 291–325.

    (1999b). "Should Blacks Represent Blacks and Women Represent Women? A Contingent 'Yes.'" *The Journal of Politics 61*(3), 628–57.

Mansbridge, J., and S. L. Shames (2008). "Toward a Theory of Backlash: Dynamic Resistance and the Central Role of Power." *Politics and Gender 4*(4), 623–34.

Mantena, K. (2010). *Alibis of Empire: Henry Maine and the Ends of Liberal Imperialism.* Princeton, NJ: Princeton University Press.

March, J. G. (1955). "An Introduction to the Theory and Measurement of Influence." *The American Political Science Review 49*(2), 431–51.

Mathew, G. (Ed.) (1984). *Shift in Indian Politics: 1983 Elections in Andhra Pradesh And Karnataka.* New Delhi: Christian Institute for the Study of Religion and Society.

Mayaram, S. (2002). "New Modes of Violence: The Backlash against Women in the Panchayat System." In K. Kapadia (Ed.), *The Violence of Development: The Politics of Identity, Gender and Social Inequalities in India*, pp. 393–424. New Delhi: Zed Books.

McCubbins, M. D., and T. Schwartz (1984). "Congressional Oversight Overlooked: Police Patrols versus Fire Alarms." *American Journal of Political Science 28*(1), 165–79.

McDonald, H., E. Graham-Harrison, and S. Baker (2018). "Ireland Votes by Landslide to Legalise Abortion." *The Guardian*, May 26. www.theguardian.com/world/2018/may/26/ireland-votes-by-landslide-to-legalise-abortion (accessed April 18, 2019).

Mehta, U., R. Billimoria, and U. Thakkar (1981). *Women and Men Voters, the 1977–80 Experiment.* Election Archives.

Mendelberg, T., C. Karpowitz, and N. Goedert (2014). "Does Descriptive Representation Facilitate Women's Distinctive Voice? How Gender Composition and Decision Rules Affect Deliberation." *American Journal of Political Science 58*(2), 291–306.

Mendelberg, T., C. F. Karpowitz, and J. B. Oliphant (2014). "Gender Inequality in Deliberation: Unpacking the Black Box of Interaction." *Perspectives on Politics 12*(1), 18–44.

Menon, A. K. (1984). "Andhra Pradesh CM N.T. Rama Rao Seeks to Give Women Equal Share in Paternal Property." *India Today*, August 15. www.indiatoday.in/magazine/indiascope/story/19840815-andhra-pradesh-cm-n.t.-rama-rao-seeks-to-give-women-equal-share-in-paternal-property-803230-1984-05-31 (accessed January 13, 2019).

Menon, N. (2000). "Elusive 'Woman': Feminism and Women's Reservation Bill." *Economic and Political Weekly 35*(43–44), 3835–44.

Mercier, C. (1989). *Hinduism for Today.* Oxford: Oxford University Press.

Miller, B. D. (1981). *The Endangered Sex: Neglect of Female Children in Rural North India.* Ithaca, NY: Cornell University Press.

Miller, E. J. (1954). "Caste and Territory in Malabar." *American Anthropologist 56*(3), 410–20.

Miller, G. (2008). "Women's Suffrage, Political Responsiveness, and Child Survival in American History." *The Quarterly Journal of Economics 123*(3), 1287–1327.

Mitter, D. N. (1913). *The Position of Women in Hindu Law*, Volume 1. New Delhi: Genesis Publishing Pvt Ltd.

MK, A. (2016). "Veteran Communist Revolutionary DV Rao Remembered." *Counter Currents*, July 15. www.countercurrents.org/2016/07/15/veteran-communist-revoluti onary-dv-rao-remembered (accessed June 27, 2017).

Mohanty, B. B. (2001). "Land Distribution among Scheduled Castes and Tribes." *Economic and Political Weekly 36*(40), 346–62.

Molyneux, M. (1990). "The 'Woman Question' in the Age of Perestroika." *New Left Review 183*, 23–49.

Mooij, J. E. (2003). *Smart Governance? Politics in the Policy Process in Andhra Pradesh, India*. London: Overseas Development Institute.

Morris-Jones, W. H. (1967). "The Indian Congress Party: A Dilemma of Dominance." *Modern Asian Studies 1*(2), 109–32.

Motiejunaite, A., and Z. Kravchenko (2008). "Family Policy, Employment and Gender-Role Attitudes: A Comparative Analysis of Russia and Sweden." *Journal of European Social Policy 18*(1), 38–49.

Mueller, U. (2016). "Lost in Representation? Feminist Identity Economics and Women's Agency in India's Local Governments." *Feminist Economics 22*(1), 158–82.

Mullainathan, S., and E. Shafir (2013). *Scarcity: Why Having Too Little Means So Much*. New York: Macmillan.

Murray, R. (2014). "Quotas for Men: Reframing Gender Quotas as a Means of Improving Representation for All." *American Political Science Review 108*(3), 520–32.

Murthy, K. K., and G. L. Rao (1968). *Political Preferences in Kerala: An Electoral Analysis of the Kerala General Elections, 1957, 1960, 1965 and 1967*. Delhi: Radha Krishna.

Murthy, L. V. B., and D. Sharma (2006). "The Business of Sex Selection: The Ultrasonography Boom." Presented at the Nehru Memorial Museum and Library Workshop on Declining Child Sex Ratio, January 23–4.

Naidu, R. (1984). "Symbolic Imagery Used by the Telugu Desam in Andhra Elections (1983)." In G. Mathew (Ed.), *Shift in Indian Politics: 1983 Elections in Andhra Pradesh and Karnataka*, pp. 129–38. New Delhi: Christian Institute for the Study of Religion and Society.

Nair, J. (1996). *Women and Law in Colonial India: A Social History*. New Delhi: Kali for Women.

(2008a). "'Imperial Reason', National Honour and New Patriarchal Compacts in Early Twentieth-Century India." *History Workshop Journal* (66), 208–26.

(2008b). "The Troubled Relationship of Feminism and History." *Economic and Political Weekly 43*(43), 57–65.

National Institute of Rural Development (2019). "State-wise Average Daily Earnings of Men, Women and Children in Rural Labour Households (agricultural Occupations) In India." www.indiastat.com/table/agriculture-data/2/agricultural-wages/31519/334116/data.aspx (accessed Indiastat, January 22, 2019).

Neumayer, E. (1983). *Prehistoric Indian Rock Paintings*. Oxford: Oxford University Press.

(2013). *The Hindu Family and the Emergence of Modern India: Law, Citizenship and Community*. Cambridge: Cambridge University Press.

Nilekani, J. (2010). "Reservation for Women in Karnataka Gram Panchayats: The Implications of Non-Random Reservation and the Effect of Women Leaders." Senior Honors Thesis, Yale College.

Niranjana, S. (2002). "Exploring Gender Inflections within Panchayati Raj Institutions: Women's Politicization in Andhra Pradesh." In K. Kapadia (Ed.), *The Violence of Development: The Politics of Identity, Gender and Social Inequalities in India*, pp. 352–92. New Delhi: Zed Books.

Nisbett, R., and D. Cohen (1996). *New Directions in Social Psychology. Culture of Honor: The Psychology of Violence in the South*. Boulder, CO: Westview Press.

Nooruddin, I. (2011). *Coalition Politics and Economic Development*. Cambridge: Cambridge University Press.

Norris, P., and M. L. Krook (2009). "One of Us: Multilevel Models Examining the Impact of Descriptive Representation on Civic Engagement." https://papers.ssrn.com/sol3/papers.cfm?abstract_id=1451149 (accessed December 28, 2019).

North, D. C. (1981). *Structure and Change in Economic History*. New York: Norton.
  (1990). *Institutions, Institutional Change and Economic Performance*. Cambridge: Cambridge University Press.

North, D. C., and R. Thomas (1973). *The Rise of the Western World: A New Economic History*. Cambridge: Cambridge University Press.

North, D. C., and B. R. Weingast (1989). "Constitutions and Commitment: The Evolution of Institutions Governing Public Choice in Seventeenth-Century England." *Journal of Economic History* 49(4), 803–32.

North, D. C., et al. (2009). *Violence and Social Orders: A Conceptual Framework for Interpreting Recorded Human History*. Cambridge: Cambridge University Press.

Nossiter, T. J. (1982). *Communism in Kerala: A Study in Political Adaptation*. Berkeley: University of California Press.

Noury, A. G., and B. Speciale (2016). "Social Constraints and Women's Education: Evidence from Afghanistan under Radical Religious Rule." *Journal of Comparative Economics* 44(4), 821–41.

Nugent, J. B., and J. A. Robinson (2010). "Are Factors Endowment Fate?" *Revista de Historia Economica-Journal of Iberian and Latin American Economic History* 28(1), 45–82.

Ober, J. (1998). *Political Dissent in Democratic Athens: Intellectual Critics of Popular Rule*. Princeton, NJ: Princeton University Press.
  (2008). *Democracy and Knowledge: Innovation and Learning in Classical Athens*. Princeton, NJ: Princeton University Press.

O'Hanlon, R. (1985). *Caste, Conflict and Ideology: Mahatma Jotirao Phule and Low Caste Protest in Nineteenth Century Western India*. Cambridge: Cambridge University Press.

Oi, J. C., and S. Goldstein (2018). *Zouping Revisited: Adaptive Governance in a Chinese County*. Stanford, CA: Stanford University Press.

Ojha, A. K. (2017). "Woman Sarpanch in Bihar Settles 20-Year-Old Land Dispute in 6 Days." *Hindustan Times*, June 16. www.hindustantimes.com/india-news/woman-sarpanch-in-bihar-settles-20-year-old-land-dispute-in-6-days/story-9ymqBmIo2JoXcFRcDkkgpO.html (accessed March 26, 2018).

Okimoto, T. G., and V. L. Brescoll (2010). "The Price of Power: Power Seeking and Backlash against Female Politicians." *Personality and Social Psychology Bulletin* 36(7), 923–936.

Okin, S. M. (1979). *Women in Western Political Thought*. Princeton, NJ: Princeton University Press.

Onoma, A. K. (2009). *The Politics of Property Rights Institutions in Africa*. Cambridge: Cambridge University Press.

Osters, E. (2009). "Proximate Sources of Population Sex Imbalance in India." *Demography* 46(2), 325–39.

Oxfam India (2018). "Move over 'Sons of the Soil': Why You Need to Know the Female Farmers That Are Revolutionizing Agriculture in India." www.oxfamindia .org/women-empowerment-india-farmers (accessed April 24, 2019).

Page, L., and R. Pande (2018). "Ending Global Poverty: Why Money Isn't Enough." *Journal of Economic Perspectives* 32(4), 173–200.

Paluck, E. L. (2008). "The Promising Integration of Qualitative Methods and Field Experiments." *Qualitative and Multi-Method Research* 6(2), 23–30.

Panda, P., and B. Agarwal (2005). "Marital Violence, Human Development and Women's Property Status in India." *World Development* 33(5), 823–50.

Pande, M. (2017). "The Invisible Women Farmers." *Indian Express*, June 21. https://indianexpress.com/article/opinion/columns/the-invisible-women-farmers-agriculture-labourer-4714072/ (accessed March 24, 2019).

Pande, R. (2003). "Can Mandated Political Representation Increase Policy Influence for Disadvantaged Minorities? Theory and Evidence from India." *The American Economic Review* 93(4), 1132–51.

Panikkar, K. N. (1992). *Against Lord and State: Religion and Peasant Uprisings in Malabar, 1836–1921*. Oxford: Oxford University Press.

Pardeshi, P. (2003). "The Hindu Code Bill for the Liberation of Women." In A. Rao (Ed.), *Gender and Caste*, pp. 346–62. London: Zed, 346–62.

Parish, P. J. (1989). *Slavery: History and Historians*. New York: Routledge.

Park, J. (2015). "Europe's Migration Crisis." *Council on Foreign Relations*, September 23. www.cfr.org/backgrounder/europes-migration-crisis (accessed on February 7, 2019).

Pascall, G., and N. Manning (2000). "Gender and Social Policy: Comparing Welfare States in Central and Eastern Europe and the Former Soviet Union." *Journal of European Social Policy* 10(3), 240–66.

Patel, V. (1985). "Women's Liberation in India." *New Left Review* 153(1), 75–6.

Pateman, C. (1988). "The Patriarchal Welfare State" In Amy Gutman (Ed.), Democracy and the Welfare State. Princeton, NJ: Princeton University Press, 134–51.

Pathak, N., and A. Raj (2013). "Why India's Youth Are Abandoning Their Elderly Parents." *Gulf News*, January 23. http://gulfnews.com/life-style/general/why-india-s-youth-are-abandoning-their-elderly-parents-1.1136422 (accessed February 18, 2018).

Paxton, P., and M. M. Hughes (2016). *Women, Politics, and Power: A Global Perspective*. Washington, DC: CQ Press.

Persson, T., G. Roland, and G. Tabellini (1997). "Separation of Powers and Political Accountability." *The Quarterly Journal of Economics* 112(4), 1163–1202.

Phillips, A. (1995). *The Politics of Presence*. Oxford: Clarendon Press.

(1998). *Feminism and Politics*. Oxford: Oxford University Press.

Piketty, T. (2014). *Capital in the 21st Century*. Cambridge, MA: Harvard University Press.

Pillai, S. D., and G. S. Ghurye (1976). *Aspects of Changing India: Studies in Honour of Prof. GS Ghurye.* Bombay: Popular Prakashan.

Piscopo, J. M. (2015). "States as Gender Equality Activists: The Evolution of Quota Laws in Latin America." *Latin American Politics and Society* 57(3), 27–49.

Pitkin, H. F. (1967). *The Concept of Representation.* Berkeley: University of California Press.

Platteau, J.-P. (2000a). *Institutions, Social Norms and Economic Development.* New York: Routledge.

(2000b). "Order, the Rule of Law and Moral Norms." Paper prepared for high-level round table on trade and development: Directions for the twenty-first century.

Plutarch (2004). "Plutarch's Lives: Life of Solon." www.gutenberg.org/files/14033/ 14033-h/14033-h.htm (accessed December 28, 2019).

Poleman, H. I. (1934). "The Ritualistic Continuity of Rgveda X. 14–18." *Journal of the American Oriental Society,* 276–8.

Pollak, R. A. (2003). "Gary Becker's Contributions to Family and Household Economics." *Review of Economics of the Household* 1(1–2), 111–41.

Pope Francis (2015). "Pope Francis: Compensation Disparity a 'Pure Scandal.'" *Vatican Radio,* April 29. http://en.radiovaticana.va/news/2015/04/29/pope_francis_ compensation_disparity_a_pure_scandal/1140428 (accessed December 28, 2019).

Pop-Eleches, G., and J. A. Tucker (2017). *Communism's Shadow: Historical Legacies and Contemporary Political Attitudes.* Princeton, NJ: Princeton University Press.

Popkin, S. L. (1979). *The Rational Peasant: The Political Economy of Rural Society in Vietnam.* Berkeley: University of California Press.

Posner, E. A. (2000). "Law and Social Norms: The Case of Tax Compliance." *Virginia Law Review* 86, 1781–1819.

Prasad, M. M. (2014). *Cine-politics.* Chennai: Orient Blackswan.

Press Trust of India (2015). "Proportion of Landless Families Falls to 7.41% in Rural India." *The Economic Times,* December 17. https://economictimes.indiatimes.com/ news/economy/indicators/proportion-of-landless-families-falls-to-7-41-in-rural- india/articleshow/50207604.cms (accessed July 29, 2018).

Preuhs, R. R. (2007). "Descriptive Representation as a Mechanism to Mitigate Policy Backlash: Latino Incorporation and Welfare Policy in the American States." *Political Research Quarterly* 60(2), 277–92.

Prillaman, S. A. (2017). "Strength in Numbers: How Women's Groups Close India's Political Gender Gap." Working Paper. www.soledadprillaman.com/research (accessed December 28, 2019).

Qian, N. (2008). "Missing Women and the Price of Tea in China: The Effect of Sex-specific Earnings on Sex Imbalance." *The Quarterly Journal of Economics* 123(3), 1251–85.

Rachlin, H. (1995). "Self-Control: Beyond Commitment." *Behavioral and Brain Sciences* 18(1), 109–21.

Raghavan, E., and J. Manor (2009). *Broadening and Deepening Democracy: Political Innovation in Karnataka.* New York: Routledge.

Rahman, L., and V. Rao (2004). "The Determinants of Gender Equity in India: Examining Dyson and Moore's Thesis with New Data." *Population and Development Review* 30(2), 239–68.

Rai, P. (2011). "Electoral Participation of Women in India: Key Determinants and Barriers." *Economic and Political Weekly* 46(3), 47–55.

Raj, A., S. N., D. Balaiah, and J. Silverman (2009). "Prevalence of Child Marriage and Its Effect on Fertility and Fertility Control Outcomes of Young Women in India: A Cross-Sectional, Observational Study." *Lancet* 373(9678), 1883–89.

Rajasekhariah, A., P. Jayaramu, and H. Jayraj (1987). "Karnataka Ideology and Politics." *The Indian Journal of Political Science* 48(4), 575–96.

Rajeev, M. (2015). "State View: Rayalaseema in a State of Discontent." *The Hindu*, October 11. www.thehindu.com/news/national/state-view-rayalaseema-in-a-state-of-ddiscontent/article7747573.ece (accessed June 3, 2017).

Rajghatta, C. (1989). "Nobody Saw the Congress (I) Storm That Wiped Janata Dal away in Karnataka." *India Today*, December 15. www.indiatoday.in/magazine/nation/story/19891215-nobody-saw-the-congressi-storm-that-wiped-janata-dal-away-in-karnataka-816943-1989-12-15 (accessed January 13, 2019).

Ramabai, S. P. (1887). *The High Caste Hindu Woman*. Philadelphia: The Jas B. Rodgers Printing Company.

Ramakrishnan, V. (2013). "A Broken Promise: Dowry Violence in India." *John Hopkins Bloomberg School of Public Health Magazine* https://pulitzercenter.org/reporting/broken-promise-dowry-violence-india (accessed December 28, 2019).

Ramesh, A., and B. Ali (2001). *33 1/3% Reservation towards Political Empowerment*. Bangalore: Books for Change.

Rao, A. (2003). *Gender and Caste*. London: Zed.

Rao, B. (2015). "From Proxies to Politicians: Bihar's Female MLAs." *IndiaSpend*, September 26. https://archive.indiaspend.com/cover-story/from-proxies-to-politicians-bihars-female-mlas-10368 (accessed June 26, 2017).

  (2018a). "Tamil Nadu's Women Leaders Live, Work in the Shadow of Violence." *India Spend*, April 21. www.indiaspend.com/cover-story/tamil-nadus-women-leaders-live-work-in-the-shadow-of-violence-95289 (accessed April 26, 2018).

  (2018b). "Why Muthukanni, a Dalit, Had to Build Her Own Panchayat Office." *India Spend*, April 14. www.indiaspend.com/cover-story/why-muthukanni-a-dalit-had-to-build-her-own-panchayat-office-36754 (accessed May 30, 2018).

Rao, N. (2005a). "Questioning Women's Solidarity: The Case of Land Rights, Santal Parganas, Jharkhand, India." *The Journal of Development Studies* 41(3), 353–75.

  (2005b). "Women's Rights to Land and Assets: Experience of Mainstreaming Gender in Development Projects." *Economic and Political Weekly* 40(44–5), 4701–8.

  (2011). "Women's Access to Land: An Asian Perspective." Technical Report, United Nations, Accra. Expert Group Meeting, Enabling Rural Women's Economic Empowerment: Institutions, Opportunities and Participation.

Rao, N., and P. Cagna (2018). "Feminist Mobilization, Claims Making and Policy Change: An Introduction." *Development and Change* 49(3), 708–13.

Rao, V. (1997). "Wife-Beating in Rural South India: A Qualitative and Econometric Analysis." *Social Science and Medicine* 44(8), 1169–80.

Raut, S. (2017). "Remember the Time: This Quirky Scooter Delayed Marriages and Ferried Families." *Moneycontrol*, December 26. www.moneycontrol.com/news/technology/auto/delhi-govt-maruti-to-develop-automated-driving-test-tracks-2469075.html (accessed March 24, 2019).

Ray, M. K. (1981). *Princely States and the Paramount Power, 1858–1876: A Study on the Nature of Political Relationship between the British Government and the Indian State*. New Delhi: Rajesh Publications.

Ray, R. (1999). *Fields of Protest: Women's Movements in India*, Volume 8. Minneapolis: University of Minnesota Press.

Read, D., G. Loewenstein, M. Rabin, G. Keren, and D. Laibson (1999). "Choice Bracketing." In B. Fischhoff (Ed.), *Elicitation of Preferences*, pp. 171–202. Amsterdam: Springer Netherlands.

Reddy, D. N., and A. Patnaik (1993). "Anti-Arrack Agitation of Women in Andhra Pradesh." *Economic and Political Weekly* 28(21), 1059–66.

Reddy, V. R., and R. N. Rao (2003). "Primary Education: Progress and Constraints." *Economic and Political Weekly* 38(12–13), 1242–51.

Rehavi, M. M. (2007). "Sex and Politics: Do Female Legislators Affect State Spending?" Working Paper 78, University of Michigan.

Reingold, B., and J. Harrell (2010). "The Impact of Descriptive Representation on Women's Political Engagement: Does Party Matter?" *Political Research Quarterly* 63(2), 280–94.

Risse, T., and E. Stollenwerk (2018). "Legitimacy in Areas of Limited Statehood." *Annual Review of Political Science* 21, 403–18.

Robins, N. (2017). *The Corporation That Changed the World: How the East India Company Shaped the Modern Multinational*. London: Pluto Press.

Rodrik, D. (1996). "Understanding Economic Policy Reform." *Journal of Economic Literature* 34(1), 9–41.

Rosenberg, T. (2016). "Letting Some of India's Women Own Land." *The New York Times*, March 22. https://opinionator.blogs.nytimes.com/2016/03/22/letting-some-of-indias-women-own-land/ (accessed May 23, 2018).

Rosenblum, D. (2015). "Unintended Consequences of Women's Inheritance Rights on Female Mortality in India." *Economic Development and Cultural Change* 63(2), 223–48.

Rosenzweig, M., and O. Stark (1989). "The Formal and Informal Barriers in the Implementation of the Hindu Succession (Amendment) Act 2005." *Journal of Political Economy* 97(4), 905–26.

Rowbotham, S. (2014 [1974]). *Women, Resistance and Revolution: A History of Women and Revolution in the Modern World*. London: Verso.

Roy, A. (1987). *Paintings of Mahindra Bhusan Gupta*. Calcutta: Birla Academy of Art and Culture.

Roy, K. C., and C. A. Tisdell (2002). "Property Rights in Women's Empowerment in Rural India: A Review." *International Journal of Social Economics* 29(4), 315–34.

Roy, S. (2015). "Empowering Women? Inheritance Rights, Female Education and Dowry Payments in India." *Journal of Development Economics* 114, 233–51.

Roy, T. (2010). "Rethinking the Origins of British India: State Formation and Military-Fiscal Undertakings in an Eighteenth Century World Region." Working Papers no. 142/10, London School of Economics, Department of History.

Rubinstein, A. (1998). *Modeling Bounded Rationality*. Cambridge, MA: MIT Press.

Rubio, G. (2014). "How Love Conquered Marriage: Theory and Evidence on the Disappearance of Arranged Marriages." http://gabrielarubio.bol.ucla.edu/ (accessed December 2, 2018).

Rudman, L. A., and K. Fairchild (2004). "Reactions to Counterstereotypic Behavior: the Role of Backlash in Cultural Stereotype Maintenance." *Journal of Personality and Social Psychology* 87(2), 157.

Rudolph, L. I. (1965). "The Modernity of Tradition: The Democratic Incarnation of Caste in India." *American Political Science Review* 59(4), 988.

Ryder, N. B. (1973). "A New Approach to the Economic Theory of Fertility Behavior: Comment." *Journal of Political Economy* 81(2), S65–9.

Sachs, J. (2005). *The End of Poverty: How We Can Make It Happen in Our Lifetime.* New York: Penguin Books.

Samii, C. (2013). "Perils or Promise of Ethnic Integration? Evidence from a Hard Case in Burundi." *American Political Science Review* 107(3), 558–73.

Sankaran, S. (1996). "Introduction." In B. Yugandhar (Ed.), *Land Reforms in India: Andhra Pradesh – People's Pressure and Administrative Innovations*, pp. 17–27. New Delhi: Sage Publications.

Saradamoni, K. (1982). "Women's Status in Changing Agrarian Relations: A Kerala Experience." *Economic and Political Weekly* 17(5), 155–62.

Sarasvati, R. (2000). *Pandita Ramabai through Her Own Words: Selected Works.* Oxford: Oxford University Press.

Sarkar, S. (1983). *Modern India 1885–1947.* Delhi: Macmillan.

Sarkar, T. (1993). "Rhetoric against Age of Consent-Resisting Colonial Reason and Death of a Child-Wife." *Economic and Political Weekly* 28(36), 1869–78.

(2010). *Hindu Wife, Hindu Nation: Community, Religion, and Cultural Nationalism.* Bloomington: Indiana University Press.

(2010). *Rebels, Wives, Saints: Designing Selves and Nations in Colonial Times.* Calcutta: Seagull Books.

Sathaye, S. (1998). "Vitner." In B. Datta (Ed.), *And Who Will Make the Chapatis? A Study of All-Women Panchayats in Maharashtra*, pp. 91–109. Calcutta: Stree Publications.

Scacco, A., and S. S. Warren (2018). "Can Social Contact Reduce Prejudice and Discrimination? Evidence from a Field Experiment in Nigeria." *American Political Science Review* 112(3), 654–77.

Schelling, T. (1960). *The Strategy of Conflict.* Cambridge, MA: Harvard University Press.

Schneider, D. M., and K. Gough (1962). *Matrilineal Kinship.* Berkeley: University of California Press.

Scott, J. (1998). *Seeing Like a State: How Certain Schemes to Improve the Human Condition Have Failed.* New Haven, CT: Yale University Press.

(2014). *The Art of Not Being Governed: An Anarchist History of Upland Southeast Asia.* New Haven, CT: Yale University Press.

Seguino, S., A. Sumner, R. van der Hoeven, B. Sen, and M. Ahmed (2013). *Humanity Divided: Confronting Inequality in Developing Countries.* New York: United Nations Development Programme.

Sekher, T. (2012). "Ladlis and Lakshmis: Financial Incentive Schemes for the Girl Child." *Economic and Political Weekly* 47(17), 58–65.

Sekhon, J., and R. Titiunik (2012). "When Natural Experiments Are Neither Natural Nor Experiments." *American Political Science Review* 106(1), 35–57.

Sen, A. (1990). "More Than 100 Million Women Are Missing." *The New York Review of Books*, December 20. www.nybooks.com/articles/1990/12/20/more-than-100-million-women-are-missing/ (accessed June 23, 2017).

(2001a). *Development as Freedom.* Oxford: Oxford University Press.

(2001b, October 27–November 9). "Many Faces of Gender Inequality." *Frontline* *18*(22), https://frontline.thehindu.com/static/html/fl1822/18220040 .htm (accessed December 28, 2019).

Sen, S. (2002). "Towards a Feminist Politics? The Indian Women's Movement in Historical Perspective." In K. Kapadia (Ed.), *The Violence of Development: The Politics of Identity, Gender and Social Inequalities in India*, pp. 459–525. New Delhi: Zed Books.

SERP (2011). "Raising Awareness, Promoting Change: Gender Development in Rural India." NRLM Perspective Plan for the Society for Elimination of Rural Poverty (SERP) Gender Unit.

Shah, N., and N. Gandhi (1991). *The Quota Question: Women and Electoral Seats*. Mumbai: Akshara.

Shami, M. (2019). "Connectivity, Clientelism and Public Provision." *British Journal of Political Science* 49(4), 1227–50.

Shariff, A., and P. Ghosh (2000). "Indian Education Scene and the Public Gap." *Economic and Political Weekly* 35(16), 1396–1406.

Sharma, B. (2012). "Women Fight Back against Witch-Branding in Rajasthan." *The New York Times*, October 26. https://india.blogs.nytimes.com/2012/10/26/women-fight-back-against-witch-branding-in-rajasthan/?_r=0 (accessed June 27, 2017).

Sharma, C. K. (2006). "Decentralization Dilemma: Measuring the Degree and Evaluating the Outcomes." *The Indian Journal of Political Science* 67(1), 49–64.

Sharma, K. (1984). "Women in Struggle: A Case Study of the Chipko Movement." *Samya Shakti: A Journal of Women's Studies* 1(2), 58.

(2004). "From Representation to Presence: The Paradox of Power and Powerlessness." In D. Bandyopadhyay and A. Mukherjee (Eds.), *New Issues in Panchayati Raj*, pp. 48–66. New Delhi: Concept Publishing Company.

Sharma, S. (2018). "Unnao Rape Case: Uttar Pradesh Police and Kuldeep Singh Sengar Conspired to Frame Survivor's Father Says, says CBI." *Firstpost*, May 21. www .firstpost.com/india/unnao-rape-case-uttar-pradesh-police-and-kuldeep-singh-sengar-conspired-to-frame-survivors-father-claims-cbi-4476401.html (accessed March 24, 2019).

Shatrugna, M. (1984). "Emergence of Regional Parties in India: Case of Telugu Desam." In G. Mathew (Ed.), *Shift In Indian Politics: 1983 Elections in Andhra Pradesh and Karnataka*, pp. 95–112. New Delhi: Christian Institute for the Study of Religion and Society.

Shayo, M. (2009). "A Model of Social Identity with an Application to Political Economy: Nation, Class, and Redistribution." *American Political Science Review* 103(2), 147–74.

Shedde, M. (1998). "Nimbut." In B. Datta (Ed.), *And Who Will Make the Chapatis? A Study of All-Women Panchayats in Maharashtra*, pp. 1–6. Calcutta: Stree Publications.

Shiva, V. (1986). "Ecology Movements in India." *Alternatives* 11(2), 255–73.

Shrinivasan, R. (2011). "Fewer Women Having Kids in 30s: Study." *Times of India*, November 28. https://timesofindia.indiatimes.com/india/Fewer-women-having-kids-in-30s-Study/articleshow/10898196.cms (accessed April 19, 2019).

Shugerman, E. (2018). "Incredible Explosion: 40,000 US Women Interested in Running for Office since Trump Election, Report Reveals." *The Independent*, July 3. www.independent.co.uk/news/world/americas/us-politics/midterms-2018-trump-alexandria-ocasio-cortez-election-us-women-candidates-female-a8429031.html (accessed April 23, 2019).

Siim, B. (2000). *Gender and Citizenship: Politics and Agency in France, Britain and Denmark*. Cambridge: Cambridge University Press.

Silaa, T. (2001). "Beyond the Radical Title, a Research on Women's Access to, Ownership and Control of Land in Tanzania." Technical Report, Eastern African Sub-Regional Support Initiative for the Advancement of Women, Kampala. *Documenting Women's Experiences in Access, Ownership and Control over Land in Eastern African Sub-Region; A Draft Study Report for: Ethiopia, Eritrea, Kenya, Tanzania, Uganda*.

Simmons, B. A. (2009). *Mobilizing for Human Rights: International Law in Domestic Politics*. Cambridge: Cambridge University Press.

Simon, H. A. (1982). *Models of Bounded Rationality*. Cambridge, MA: MIT Press.

Simonson, I. (1990). "The Effect of Purchase Quantity and Timing on Variety-Seeking Behavior." *Journal of Marketing Research* 27(2), 150–62.

Singer, W. (2007). *A Constituency Suitable for Ladies: And Other Social Histories of Indian Elections*. London: Oxford University Press.

Singh, P. (1995). *The Naxalite Movement in India*. New Delhi: Rupa.

(2011). "We-ness and Welfare: A Longitudinal Analysis of Social Development in Kerala, India." *World Development* 39(2), 282–93.

(2016). *How Solidarity Works for Welfare: Subnationalism and Social Development in India*. New York: Cambridge University Press.

Singh, S., and R. Samara (1996). "Early Marriage among Women in Developing Countries." *International Family Planning Perspectives Family* 22(4), 148–75.

Singha, R. (1998). *A Despotism of Law: Crime and Justice in Early Colonial India*. Oxford: Oxford University Press.

Sircar, A., and S. Pal (2014). "The Formal and Informal Barriers in the Implementation of the Hindu Succession (Amendment) Act 2005." Landessa Report, Landessa Rural Development Institute.

Skocpol, T. (1992). *Protecting Soldiers and Mothers: The Political Origins of Social Policy in the United States*. Cambridge, MA: The Belknap Press of Harvard University Press.

Special Correspondent (1989). "Fall of Janata Dal Government-Lessons for Democratic Decentralisation." *Economic and Political Weekly* 24(18), 961.

Srinivas, M. N. (1956). "A Note on Sanskritization and Westernization." *The Journal of Asian Studies* 15(4), 481–96.

Srinivasan, S., and A. S. Bedi (2007). "Domestic Violence and Dowry: Evidence from a South Indian village." *World Development* 35(5), 857–80.

Srinivasan, V. (2014). *Delivering Public Services Effectively: Tamil Nadu and Beyond*. New Delhi: Oxford University Press India.

Srivastava, I. (1991). "Woman as Portrayed in Women's Folk Songs of North India." *Asian Folklore Studies* 50, 269–310.

Stasavage, D. (2003). *Public Debt and the Birth of the Democratic State: France and Great Britain 1688–1789*. Cambridge: Cambridge University Press.

(2011). *States of Credit: Size, Power, and the Development of European Polities*. Princeton, NJ: Princeton University Press.

Statistics South Africa (2009–16). "Non-Financial Census of Municipalities." Statistical release, multiple years.

Stein, B. (1985). "State Formation and Economy Reconsidered." *Modern Asian Studies* 19(3), 387–413.

Stone, M. (2018). "A Place of Her Own: Women's Right to Land." *Council on Foreign Relations*, May 21. www.cfr.org/blog/place-her-own-womens-right-land (accessed on January 22, 2019).

Strolovitch, D. Z., J. S. Wong, and A. Proctor (2017). "A Possessive Investment in White Heteropatriachy? The 2016 Election and the Politics of Race, Gender, and Sexuality." *Politics, Groups, and Identities* 5(2), 353–63.

Stuart, H. (1893). *Census of India, 1891*. Superintendent, Government Press.

Sturman, R. (2012). *The Government of Social Life in Colonial India: Liberalism, Religious Law, and Women's Rights*, Volume 21. Cambridge: Cambridge University Press.

Subrahmanyam, S. (1989). "Warfare and State Finance in Wodeyar Mysore, 1724–25: A Missionary Perspective." *The Indian Economic and Social History Review* 26(2), 203–33.

Sudha, S., and S. I. Rajan (1999). "Female Demographic Disadvantage in India 1981–1991: Sex Selective Abortions and Female Infanticide." *Development and Change* 30(3), 585–618.

Sukumar, K. (2017). "Dowries Are Illegal in India: But Families - Including Mine - Still Expect Them." *Vox*, February 6. www.vox.com/first-person/2017/2/6/14403490/dowry-india-bride-groom-dilemma (accessed March 24, 2019).

Sundarayya, P., and H. Chattopadhyaya (1972). *Telangana People's Struggle and Its Lessons*. Delhi: Foundation Books.

Suri, K. (2003). "Andhra Pradesh: From Populism to Pragmatism–1983–2003." *Journal of Indian School of Political Economy* 15(1), 45–78.

Suri, K., and C. Raghavulu (1996). "Agrarian Movements and Land Reforms." In B. Yugandhar (Ed.), *Land Reforms in India: Andhra Pradesh – People's Pressure and Administrative Innovations*, pp. 28–56. New Delhi: Sage Publications.

Suri, K. C. (2002). *Democratic Process and Electoral Politics in Andhra Pradesh, India*. London: Overseas Development Institute.

Swiss, L., K. M. Fallon, and G. Burgos (2012). "Does Critical Mass Matter? Women's Political Representation and Child Health in Developing Countries." *Social Forces* 91(2), 531–58.

Tauchen, H. V., A. D. Witte, and S. K. Long (1991). "Domestic Violence: A Nonrandom Affair." *International Economic Review* 32(2), 491–511.

Teele, D., J. Kalla, and F. Rosenbluth (2018). "The Ties That Double Bind: Social Roles and Women's under Representation in Politics." *American Political Science Review* 112(3), 525–41.

Thaler, R. (1985). "Mental Accounting and Consumer Choice." *Marketing Science* 4(3), 199–214.

     (1999). "Mental Accounting Matters." *Journal of Behavioral Decision Making* 12(3), 183.

Thapar, R. (2002). *History of Early India: From the Origins to AD 1300*. New Delhi: Penguin India.

Thimmaiah, G., and A. Aziz (1983). "The Political Economy of Land Reforms in Karnataka, A South Indian State." *Asian Survey* 23(7), 810–29.

Thomas, D. (1990). "Intra-Household Resource Allocation: An Inferential Approach." *Journal of Human Resources* 25, 635–64.

     (1993). "The Distribution of Income and Expenditure within the Household." *Annales d'Economie et de Statistique* (29), 109–35.

Thomas, S. (2004). "Property Relations and Family Forms in Colonial Keralam." PhD dissertation, Mahatma Gandhi University.

Thompson Reuters Foundation (2018). "The World's Most Dangerous Countries for Women." http://poll2018.trust.org/ (accessed April 23, 2019).

Thucydides (c. 431–428). "History of the Peloponnesian War." http://perseus.uchicago .edu/perseus-cgi/citequery3.pl?dbname=GreekTexts&getid=1&query=Thuc.2.37 (accessed April 19, 2019).

Tilly, C. (1989). "Cities and States in Europe, 1000–1800." *Theory and Society 18*(5), 563–84.

Times of India (2016). "Conflicts over Land in India Stalls Projects Worth Billions of Dollars: Report." *Times of India*, November 15. http://timesofindia.indiatimes.com/ india/Conflicts-over-land-in-India-stall-projects-worth-billions-of-dollars-Report/ articleshow/55449668.cms (accessed March 26, 2017).

Timmons, H. (2014). "Here's How India's Record-Setting Voter Turnout Compares to the Rest of the World." *Quartz*, May 13. http://qz.com/208578/heres-how-indias-record-setting-voter-turnout-compares-to-the-rest-of-the-world/ (accessed June 27, 2017).

Tiwari, N. (2009). "Rethinking the Rotation Term of Reservation in Panchayats." *Economic and Political Weekly 44*(5) 23–5.

Tripp, A. M. (2015). *Women and Power in Post-Conflict Africa*. Cambridge: Cambridge University Press.

Tripp, A. M., and A. Kang (2008). "The Global Impact of Quotas: On the Fast Track to Increased Female Legislative Representation." *Comparative Political Studies 41*(3), 338–61.

Trivedi, A., and H. Timmons (2013). "India's Man Problem." *The New York Times*, January 16, 2013. http://india.blogs.nytimes.com/2013/01/16/indias-man-problem/?_r= 1 (accessed June 27, 2017).

Trotsky, L. (1924). *Problems of Everyday Life: Creating the Foundations of a New Society in Revolutionary Russia*. London: Pathfinder Press.

Tsai, L. (2007). *Accountability without Democracy: Solidary Groups and Public Goods Provision in Rural China*. Cambridge: Cambridge University Press.

Turkmani, S., S. Currie, J. Mungia, N. Assefi, A. J. Rahmanzai, P. Azfar, and L. Bartlett (2013). "Midwives Are the Backbone of Our Health System: Lessons from Afghanistan to Guide Expansion of Midwifery in Challenging Settings." *Midwifery 29*(10), 1166–72.

Uberoi, P. (1994). *Family, Kinship and Marriage in India*. Oxford: Oxford University Press.

Udry, C. (1996). "Gender, Agricultural Production, and the Theory of the Household." *Journal of Political Economy 104*(5), 1010–46.

UN Agencies in Rwanda (2013). "Women Secure 64 Per Cent of Seats in Rwandan Parliamentary Elections." www.rw.one.un.org/press-center/news/women-secure-64-cent-seats-rwandan-parliamentary-elections (accessed February 7, 2019).

UNESCO Institute for Statistics (2019a). "Literacy Rate, Adult Female (% of Females Ages 15 and Above)." https://data.worldbank.org/indicator/SE.ADT.LITR.FE.ZS? view=chart (accessed World Bank Open Data, January 22, 2019).

(2019b). "Literacy Rate, Adult Male (% of Males Ages 15 and Above)." https://data .worldbank.org/indicator/SE.ADT.LITR.MA.ZS?view=chart20& (accessed World Bank Open Data, January 22, 2019).

UNFAO (2010). "Gender and Land Rights Database." United Nations Food and Agriculture Organization. www.fao.org/gender-landrights-database/data-map/statistics/en/ (accessed December 30, 2019).

UNFPA (2015). "Gender Equality: Key Issues." Technical Report, United Nations. www.unfpa.org/gender-equality (accessed December 30, 2019).

United Nations (1995). "Beijing Declaration." www.un.org/womenwatch/daw/beijing/beijingdeclaration.html (accessed December 30, 2019).

(2005). "Progress towards the Millenium Development Goals, 1990–2005: Secretary-General's Millenium Development Goals Report." Report, United Nations, New York.

United Nations Millenium Corporation (2017). "End Poverty 2015 Millenium Campaign." www.endpoverty2015.org/mdg-success-stories/mdg-3-gender-equity/ (accessed June 26, 2017).

Unknown. "The Law of Manu." www.wisdomlib.org/hinduism/book/manusmriti-with-the-commentary-of-medhatithi/d/doc201565.html (accessed June 26, 2017).

UN Women (2019). "Facts and Figures." www.unwomen.org/en/what-we-do/leadership-and-political-participation/facts-and-figures (accessed April 19, 2019).

Uppal, Y. (2009). "The Disadvantaged Incumbents: Estimating Incumbency Effects in Indian State Legislatures." *Public Choice 138*(1–2), 9–27.

Variar, K. S. (1969). *Marumakkathayam and Allied Systems of Law in the Kerala State* Cochin: Author.

Vasavada, S., and M. Rajgor (2015). "Role of PRIs in Asserting Women's Inheritance Rights to Land: Experience and Learning of Working Group of Women and Land Ownership, Gujarat." Research Report, Working Group for Women and Land Ownership, Gujarat, India.

Vasudhevani, R. (2002). "Disintegration of Matrilineal System and Its Impact on Production Relations of Travancore (20th Century)." PhD dissertation, Department of History, University of Calicut.

Verba, S., N. Burns, and K. L. Schlozman (1997). "Knowing and Caring about Politics: Gender and Political Engagement." *The Journal of Politics 59*(4), 1051–72.

Villa, M. (2017). "Women Own Less Than 20% of the World's Land: It's Time to Give Them Equal Property Rights." *World Economic Forum.* www.weforum.org/agenda/2017/01/women-own-less-than-20-of-the-worlds-land-its-time-to-give-them-equal-property-rights/ (accessed March 26, 2018).

Viresalingam, K., and J. R. Hutchinson (2009). *Fortune's Wheel: A Tale of Hindu Domestic Life.* Charleston, SC: BiblioBazaar, LLC.

Wang, V. (2013). "Women Changing Policy Outcomes: Learning from Pro-Women Legislation in the Ugandan Parliament." *Women's Studies International Forum 41*, 113–21.

Washbrook, D. (1973). "Country Politics: Madras 1880 to 1930." *Modern Asian Studies 7*(3), 475–531.

Weber, M., K. E. Maximilian, C. W. Mills, and H. H. Gerth (1958). *From Max Weber: Essays in Sociology.* New York: Oxford University Press.

Weiner, M. (1967). *Party Building in a New Nation: The Indian National Congress.* Chicago: University of Chicago Press.

Wescott, L. (2004). "Hillary Clinton Talks Gender Equality, Not Politics, at Clinton Foundation Event." www.newsweek.com/hillary-clinton-champions-gender-equality-clinton-foundation-event-312433 (accessed December 30, 2019).

Whitney, W. D., and C. R. Lanman (1905). *Atharva-Veda Samhitā*, Volume 8 of Harvard Oriental Series. Cambridge, MA: Harvard University Press.

Williamson, O. E. (1985). *The Economic Institutions of Capitalism: Firms, Markets, Relational Contracting*, Volume 866. New York: Free Press.

Wolbrecht, C., and D. E. Campbell (2007). "Leading by Example: Female Members of Parliament as Political Role Models." *American Journal of Political Science* 51(4), 921–39.

World Bank (2009). "Gender Issues in Land Policy and Administration." Research Report, World Bank, Washington, D.C. Gender in Agriculture Sourcebook.

(2012). "World Development Report 2012: Gender Equality and Development." Research Report, World Bank, Washington, DC. http://documents.worldbank.org/curated/en/492221468136792185/Main-report.

(2015). "2015 World Development Indicators." Technical Report, World Bank, Washington, DC.

(2018). "The State of Social Safety Nets 2018." Washington, DC: World Bank. https://openknowledge.worldbank.org/handle/10986/29115 (accessed December 30, 2019) License: CC BY 3.0 IGO.

(2019a). "Women in Business and Law." https://wbl.worldbank.org/ (accessed April 18, 2019).

(2019b). "World Development Indicators – GDP per Capita (Current USD)." https://data.worldbank.org/indicator/NY.GDP.PCAP.CD (accessed World Bank Data-Bank, January 8, 2019).

World Economic Forum (2018). "The Global Gender Gap Report." Research Report, World Economic Forum, Geneva, Switzerland. www.weforum.org/reports/the-global-gender-gap-report-2018 (accessed December 30, 2019).

Yalman, N. (1963). "On the Purity of Women in the Castes of Ceylon and Malabar." *The Journal of the Royal Anthropological Institute of Great Britain and Ireland* 93(1), 27.

Yoon, M. Y. (2013). "Special Seats for Women in Parliament and Democratization: The Case of Tanzania." *Women's Studies International Forum* 41, 143–9.

Young, I. M., et al. (1985). "Impartiality and the Civic Public: Some Implications of Feminist Critiques of Moral and Political Theory." *Praxis International* 5(4), 381–401.

Yousafzai, M. (2013). "Malala Yousafzai's Speech at the Youth Takeover of the United Nations." https://theirworld.org/explainers/malala-yousafzais-speech-at-the-youth-takeover-of-the-united-nations (accessed May 23, 2017).

Yunus, M. (2007). *Banker to the Poor: Micro-Lending and the Battle against World Poverty*. New York: PublicAffairs.

Index

CPSIA information can be obtained
at www.ICGtesting.com
Printed in the USA
LVHW092046170821
695490LV00001B/137

9 781108 835824